KT-566-987

THE ARDEN SHAKESPEARE
GENERAL EDITOR: W. J. CRAIG
1899-1906: R. H. CASE, 1909

THE TRAGEDY
OF
KING RICHARD THE THIRD

THE WORKS
OF
SHAKESPEARE

THE TRAGEDY OF
KING RICHARD THE THIRD

EDITED BY

A. HAMILTON THOMPSON

METHUEN AND CO. LTD.
36 ESSEX STREET: STRAND
LONDON
Third Edition

First Published . . . August 22nd 1907
Second Edition . . . August 1917
Third Edition . . . 1918

CONTENTS

INTRODUCTION

SIX quarto editions of *The Life and Death of Richard III.* were published before the appearance of the folio of 1623. The title of the first quarto is: THE TRAGEDY OF | King Richard the third. | Containing, | His treacherous Plots against his brother Clarence: | the pittiefull murther of his innocent nephewes: | his tyrannicall vsurpation: with the whole course | of his detested life, and most deserued death. | As it hath beene lately Acted by the | Right honourable the Lord Chamber- | laine his seruants. | AT LONDON | [Pri]nted by Valentine Sims, for Andrew Wise, | dwelling in Paules Chuch-yard [*sic*], at the | Signe of the Angell. | 1597.

In the title of the second quarto (1598), printed for Wise by Thomas Creede, the words "By William Shake-speare" occupy a new line after "seruants." The fourth, fifth, and sixth quartos also spell the author's name with a hyphen. The third quarto (1602), also printed by Creede, gives it as "Shakespeare," and adds, in a line above, the words "Newly augmented" followed by a comma, which appear in the titles of the remaining quartos. The fourth (1605) and the fifth (1612) were printed by Creede for "Mathew Lawe, dwelling in Paules Church-yard, at the Signe of the Foxe, neare S. Austin's Gate." The title of the fifth alters the title of the actors to "the Kings Maiesties seruants." As the licence by virtue of which the Lord Chamberlain's players became the King's bears date 19 May, 1603, this alteration probably should have appeared in the previous quarto. It occurs in the rest. The sixth quarto (1622) was printed for Law by Thomas Purfoot; the seventh (1629) and eighth (1634) by John Norton.

The title of the play in the first folio (1623) is: The

Tragedy of Richard the Third: | with the Landing of Earle Richmond, and the | Battell at Bosworth Field. The pages are headed: *The Life and Death of Richard the Third.* The play is divided into acts and scenes. The fourth scene of Act III. includes scenes iv.-vii. as at present arranged. In Act IV. there are four scenes instead of five, scenes ii. and iii. being treated as one. The second scene of Act V. embraces scenes ii.-v. of the modern editions.

While the quarto editions present many internal variations, they form one text of the play which was derived originally from Q 1, and in the remaining editions underwent steady degeneration. Q 1 is the basis of the text of Q 2; Q 2 supplies a basis for Q 3, and transmits to it, as a general rule, its own characteristic errors and variations. The rest of the quartos, with one possible exception, follow the same plan of reprinting the most recent edition, so that, in each, the accumulation of printer's errors and alterations grows. The Cambridge editors hold that Q 5 was printed, not from Q 4, but from Q 3. For the present edition a minute examination has been made of Qq 1-4 and Q 6; but for Q 5 the editor has relied upon the Cambridge collation. But his impression is that of Mr. P. A. Daniel, who thinks that the Cambridge collation "suggests that Q 5 was printed from a copy made up of Q 3 *and* Q 4." It is sufficient to refer to the first scene of the play, where, at lines 8, 14, 39, 48, 71, the debt of Q 5 to the errors of Q 4 is perfectly manifest. Very probably, as the play advanced, the printer realised that he had been guilty of heinous mistakes in Q 4, and, to avoid them, consulted the copy which in 1602 he had printed for another bookseller. He may have referred, as at I. i. 65, to Q 2, which he also had printed, to correct an error shared by Q 3 and Q 4. But the assumption that Q 5 was not, in the first place, printed from Q 4, involves a number of undesigned coincidences in error between the two editions, which are quite improbable.

A point of greater textual importance is the statement, in Q 3 and its successors, that the play had been "newly augmented." The possible bearing of these words on its authorship will be discussed later. As a matter of fact, the text received no augmentation in the later quartos. Q 3 is indeed responsible for numerous variations from its predecessors: many of these, where they happen to agree with readings in the folios, have taken their place in both the established versions of the text; and it has been a very general opinion that Q 3 was used as one of the authorities for the first folio. But, even if we allow the highest importance to these readings, they cannot be described as "augmentations." It seems unjust to conclude that the printer wished to attract fresh customers by false pretences. Nor have we any evidence that the author, having guaranteed some additions, failed to make good his promise, and that the title-page, printed in anticipation of the fulfilment of that promise, could not be cancelled. The most probable sense which the words can be made to bear is, that the Q text in all its forms is an augmentation of some earlier play, and that these words should have appeared on the title-pages of Q 1 and Q 2, as well as of the later quartos.

The F text, which is common to all the folios, leaves the general form of the play unaltered; but the variations from the Q text which it contains are so many and important, that the question of its derivation and independent value becomes a most intricate problem. The discrepancies between F and Q (as it is convenient, for the sake of brevity, to call the two versions of which F 1 and Q 1 are the original forms) may be summed up under the following general heads:—

(1) Lines or passages peculiar to F;

(2) Lines or passages peculiar to Q;

(3) Variations in lines, phrases, or single words, pointing to a possible revision of one version by the other;

(4) Variations in stage-directions.

The problem which these points raise is concerned with the priority of the texts. Is F a revised and lengthened form of Q; or is Q a revised and shortened form of F? Or, supposing them to be independent revisions of a common original, which should we prefer as the basis for a modern text of the play?

(1) There are in F about 196 lines of ordinary length, 15 short lines, and 17 half-lines or parts of lines, which are additions to the text as represented by Q. In some cases the omission

of these passages from Q can be accounted for quite simply, *e.g.* at I. iv. 36, 37, where the first printer of Q evidently has united the beginning of one line to the end of the next, by a careless, but quite intelligible mistake, which the printer of F has not made. But there are many passages which, if they existed in the original text, cannot have been overlooked accidentally by the original editor or printer of Q. At I. ii. 155-66, II. ii. 89-100, III. vii. 144-53, IV. i. 97-103, IV. iv. 222-35, the F additions are of some length and importance; while at IV. iv. 291-345 the new matter amounts to 55 lines. It is obvious that, at the first appearance of Q in 1597, these passages either did not exist, or were omitted deliberately by the editor. In the first case, they must be later additions, forming part of a revision the result of which was F; in the second case, they must have formed part of the original text, and, as such, establish a claim for F to represent the play as written by the author.

(2) On the other hand, Q contains twenty-three ordinary and nineteen short lines which are not to be found in F. Of these, fourteen ordinary and four short lines occur in a single passage, *viz.* IV. ii. 98-115. When this is deducted from the rest, the matter peculiar to Q is seen to be inconsiderable. Either the editor of F omitted these lines, in some cases wilfully, in others perhaps accidentally; or he had access to a text of the play which supplied the authority for their omission. That text, it is clear, either was revised by Q, or was itself a revision of Q. On the first supposition, these additions are easily explained: on the second, it is hard to see on what principle the reviser, while adding so much, cut out so little, and that little so unimportant; while it is impossible to account for his omission of the one important passage in IV. ii.

(3) The numerous minor differences between Q and F are recorded in the collation which accompanies this text. No attempt at their classification can be wholly satisfactory. In general, they are variations on words and phrases, and indicate that a very minute revision has been exercised, either on Q by the editor of F, or by the editor of Q on the text of which F is representative. Certain systematic differences may be noticed. For "which" in Q, we usually find "that" in F.

Where Q has "betwixt," F has "between." In F we find greater metrical consistency throughout: lines which, in Q, are irregular or hypermetric, become smooth and regular. The passage at I. iv. 84-159, which is printed by Q in a kind of spurious verse, is arranged in F as prose. F also avoids repetitions, which occur in Q, of the same word in a few lines, or transposes words from their arrangement in Q. The student who compares the two texts for himself can hardly fail to recognise that, in point of regularity and order, the balance is in favour of F.

(4) The stage-directions in F are fuller and more perfect than those in Q. Certain minor parts appear in F, which Q either neglects or partly suppresses. The result is a gain in clearness to F, although, in one case, the duplication of the part of Brakenbury in I. iv. by that of the Keeper, the alteration seems unnecessary. It is of course possible that the addition of entrances, exits, and other more minute directions may be entirely due to the editor of F; and the utmost that they can be made to prove is his zeal for accuracy and definiteness.

From the dates of publication, it is obvious that F, as a *printed* text, is later than Q. Probably it was never edited for the press until a little before its appearance in 1623. Appearing at that time, it is probably a revision, to a certain extent, of Q, the hitherto accepted text of the play. There are three main possibilities with regard to the genesis of this revision. It may have been the arbitrary work of the editor. It may have been derived from an original source which was either inaccessible to the editor of Q, or was used by him with arbitrary alterations. Or, thirdly, it may represent a personal revision of the text by the author, after the appearance of the play on the stage and the publication of Q 1.

This third view is substantially the view taken by Pope and Johnson. It involves the existence in 1623 of a MS. of the play, or, at least, an annotated copy of one of the quartos, containing the author's final alterations of his original text, with additions and a few excisions. It seems certain, if this corrected text existed, that the editor of F compared it with Q. The result would be a text which, depending for the most part on this conjectural document, would accept here and there a reading of Q whose origin is probably to be found in the later quartos. Oversights on the part of the editor, and mistakes on the part of the printer, must be allowed for in this as in all other theories.

Many editors, in more recent times, have taken the clearly defined view that Q is a revision, for dramatic purposes, of an original text represented by F. Howard Staunton regarded the long passages peculiar to F as deliberately omitted "to accelerate action," and to "afford space for the more lively and dramatic substitutions which are met with in the quartos alone." For the first of these statements there is much to be said: the omission of such passages as those in IV. iv. for this purpose, is more credible than their subsequent addition for no apparent purpose at all. But the presence of those substitutions which Staunton praised is very questionable. As we have seen, the additions in Q are, with one exception, insignificant and immaterial.

The authority of Q was asserted on other grounds by the Cambridge editors. In their view both Q and F are of Shakespearean origin. Of the author's original MS., which they called A 1, a transcript (B 1) was made for the theatre library; and from this transcript, with its accidental faults and omissions, Q 1 was printed. However, at some unspecified time, the author undertook a complete revision of the play, correcting the original MS. with marginal notes and interlineations, and adding new matter here and there on inserted leaves. At some time, probably after the author's death, this corrected MS. (A 2) was taken in hand by a transcriber, whose copy of it (B 2) was intended probably to take the place of B 1, now worn and tattered, in the theatre library. To judge from the internal evidence of F 1, which was printed from this new transcript, the transcriber "worked in the spirit, though not with the audacity, of Colley Cibber," altering words, even where it was unnecessary, to avoid their recurrence, or to correct a supposed metrical defect; or now and then modifying a word that, in the course of time, was become obsolete. The editor of F 1, therefore, in addition to some unique Shakespearean matter, accepted much that is non-Shakespearean. It follows that the Cambridge editors, while admitting all the additions (two lines excepted) which are peculiar to F, took Q 1 as the basis of their text.

The cardinal point of the Cambridge theory is the existence of the lawless transcriber. In 1872, Delius, writing in the *Jahrbuch* of the German Shakespeare Society, brought forward his theory that Q 1 was nothing more than a pirated edition of the play, in which an unknown editor mangled the original text at his own discretion. Delius' contempt for this "poetaster" surpassed in measure the Cambridge editors' allusions to their "nameless transcriber." For his theory there is one strong argument, to be derived from the preface to F 1. His hypothesis makes good the editors' statement that they were restoring the plays "cur'd, and perfect of their limbes; and . . . absolute in their numbers," to a public that hitherto had been "abus'd with diuerse stolne, and surreptitious copies."

Spedding's exhaustive paper, read before the New Shakspere Society in 1875, maintained the case for F against the Cambridge editors. The most interesting part of his argument is his enumeration of alterations in F which, in his judgment, could not have been made by the author, but were due, for the most part, to editorial and press misunderstandings of marginal corrections, etc., in the MS. from which F 1 was prepared. In a detailed criticism of Spedding's paper, Mr. E. H. Pickersgill supported the main contentions of the Cambridge editors. He definitely regarded the author's final version of his MS. as anterior to the publication of Q 1, which was founded on the actors' copy of the play, omitting the long passages, afterwards inserted in F, for the sake of shortening the dramatic representation. He admitted the presence of a number of blunders in Q, which were afterwards corrected or avoided in F. But the "nameless transcriber" was still made responsible for much tampering with the text. The theory advanced by Koppel, in his *Textkritische Studien über Shakespeare's Richard III.* (1877), is similar in detail to Pickersgill's, but does not adopt the conclusion as to the "nameless transcriber."

The exceptional scholarship and judgment of the Cambridge editors gives much weight to their elaborate theory. But very few students of the two texts, even while admitting the traces of a corrector's hand in F, will agree with their low estimate of his skill. His text is more smooth and regular; but very seldom is it noticeably less vigorous on that account. Where single words differ, there is generally nothing to choose between the texts. No one has put down the additions in F to the credit of a corrector other than the author himself. As to the omissions in F, when we have deducted the long passage in IV. ii., the rest are of so little importance that it is impossible to discover the grounds on which Staunton characterised them as "terse and vigorous bits of dialogue." And, after a careful and prolonged study of the texts, the present editor, while giving full weight to the editor or editors' and printer's responsibility for errors in F, is unable to distinguish its debt to a "nameless transcriber" from that which it may owe to the author's original version of the play. In short, he sees nothing in F which precludes it from consideration as a return, in the main faithful and accurate, to the author's own text, containing passages that had been omitted in Q, and superseding Q as a trustworthy and definite version of the play. On the other hand, the source of Q seems to him to be the stage version of the play, shortened at certain points from the original text, and garnished here and there with a line which breaks up the dialogue or illustrates the action of the play more fully. It is possible, too, that the editor of Q revised his text by comparing it with a performance of the play on the stage, or with his reminiscences of such a performance; for several of his readings are best explained as slips of memory or free interpolations on the part of an actor. When the editors of F 1 charged themselves with curing and perfecting the received text, they doubtless compared one or more editions of Q with a MS.—either the original or a careful transcript—of the play as originally written.

Mr. P. A. Daniel, in his preface to Mr. Griggs' facsimile of Q 1, has given an explanation of this process which sets the whole matter in a very clear light. He believes F to represent the author's text of the play: Q to be a shortened and revised copy of that text. The editor of F carefully revised the text of one of the quartos by the original MS., and sent the corrected volume, with his deletions, interlineations, and marginal additions, to the printer. Comparing F I with the quartos, Mr. Daniel finds that, for two doubtful readings shared by it with Q I, and for one shared with each of the editions Q 3, Q 4, and Q 5, nine, at least, are shared with Q 6. These nine may be increased to twelve, by adding three probable cases. It is thus probable that Q 6 was the copy corrected by the editor of F, who overlooked a few words or wrong letters. The printer took over this copy, and brought F into being, with a certain number of errors and misunderstandings due to the crowded state of the revised page.

To almost every case of difficulty which meets the textual student, Mr. Daniel's hypothesis may be applied with a more than plausible result; and, in the text which the present editor has followed, he has endeavoured to act on the principles laid down by Mr. Daniel as a corollary to his proposition. At the same time, in examining the several variations between the texts, the editor has tested them by the other theories that have been put forward for their solution. While founding his text on F, he has accepted such readings from Q as seem to him to be deliberate improvements; and at II. i. 66-8 and II. iv. I, 2, both highly debateable passages, he has ventured to retain the Q readings which have been rejected, on grounds which appear to him not sufficiently strong, by many editors.

Special instances will be found fully treated in the notes which supplement the text. One point, however, calls for further mention. The collation shows that, for the first 150 lines or so of III. i., and from about V. iii. 80 to the end of the play, the editor of F I found little to alter in his copy of Q. Where he made alterations, it is highly probable that he made them on his own responsibility. Reference to Q I or Q 2 at these passages shows us several times that, where the latter quartos are wrong, the earlier contain a satisfactory reading, which, we cannot doubt, he would have adopted had he possessed authority to guide him. The inference is that his MS. was wanting at these points, and that he had to depend on a later quarto and his own instinct. Again, in I. i., where the variations between the texts are very few, the readings of the earlier quartos in several cases have a weight that cannot be attributed to F. A case in point is I. i. 65, where F reads "That tempts him to this harsh Extremity." This is an obvious correction of a reading common to Qq 2, 5, and 6, "That tempts him to this extreamitie." We might assume, as we can assume in most cases, that the editor of F 1 found the omitted word "harsh" in the original MS., and inserted it accordingly. But, in Q 1, we find a better and more satisfactory reading, "That tempers him to this extremity," which needs no alteration. It seems likely that, in the MS. from which Q 1 was derived, "tempers" was written in its abbreviated form "temps," and that Q 2, not noticing the abbreviation, took the word from the same MS. as "tempts." Q 3 likewise used the MS., and printed it "temps," without regard to sense. In Q 5, this meaningless word was altered to the more obvious "tempts," and so F 1 found it printed in Q 6. Nothing is more likely than that the opening pages of the authentic MS. were torn or illegible from use and the lapse of time. Finding no help here, the editor emended the metre of the line by inserting the word "harsh." To judge from the reading, the early leaves of the MS. were wanting or illegible in part; while the closing leaves, and a leaf or two in the middle, were totally illegible or had perished. There has been a very general opinion that, in passages where original authority was wanting, the editor of F 1 resorted to a copy of Q 3. This may have been the case; but there is no circumstance which tends to show that, to his copy of Q 6, he added in these instances anything more than a talent for cautious emendation.

Richard III., dramatically as well as historically, is a sequel to the three parts of *Henry VI.*, in which Shakespeare's share is generally admitted to have been that of a reviser. The question naturally arises whether Shakespeare was the author of *Richard III.*, or merely the editor and reviser of a sequel to those plays on which he had been engaged previously. Mr. Daniel holds that the play was really the work of the author or authors of the *Henry VI.* plays, and was revised by Shakespeare. Mr. Fleay looks upon it as a Shakespearean recension and completion of an unfinished play by Marlowe, so thorough that any distinction between the original text and the revision is impossible. The only considerations on which an answer can be founded depend upon the style and date of the drama.

(1) The evidence of style places *Richard III.*, beyond all doubt, among Shakespeare's earliest plays. Apart from the ordinary metrical tests, which, applied whether to Q or F, do not differ materially in the result, the verse has everywhere that rhetorical accent with which Marlowe had stamped the language of the stage. The spirit of the verse is in keeping with its accent. No passage can be singled out as an example of that vein of reflective sentiment which, at a not much later date, Shakespeare expressed with so great a command of imagery. The most striking passages, Clarence's account of his dream in I. iv., and Tyrrel's narrative of the murder of the princes in IV. iii., are little more than evenly written pieces of description, with a certain amount of smooth eloquence and picturesque colour. Richard's soliloquies in I. i. and I. ii. are clearly the work of the hand which was responsible for his soliloquies in *3 Henry VI.* III. ii. and V. vi. He declares his aims in the vigorous rhythm which Marlowe makes his heroes use, explicit in sense and full of sound. These speeches, indeed, might have been written by Marlowe in a restrained mood, in which his habitual rhetoric was sobered by a consciousness of his dramatic purpose. If the programme which they reveal is outrageous, their actual words are free from the grotesqueness with which Marlowe's Barabas relates his iniquities, and from the extravagance of the wildly poetic "lunes" of Tamburlaine. On the other hand, they have not that depth of living passion which Marlowe sounds in Tamburlaine's rhapsody on Divine Zenocrate, or in the last soliloquy of Faustus. And, as a matter of fact, where Marlowe worked, as in *Edward II.*, with greater self-restraint, his style has not much in common with that of *Richard III.* The classical allusions, which fill *Edward II.*, and are very noticeable in the *Henry VI.* plays, are nearly absent from *Richard III.* The formal tragic style of such a passage as the lamentation of the women in *Richard III.* IV. iv., has a stateliness which we miss in *Edward II.*

but it has not that lyric fervour which give certain passages of *Edward II.* a pathos that redeems their crudeness. It is conceivable, in short, that Marlowe may have written much of *Richard III.;* but we have nothing from his hand which goes to prove that he must have had a part in it. It may be said that the style of the play is a distinct advance on the style of *Titus Andronicus*, which is closely akin to the style of Marlowe's most literal imitators. The individual quality of its rhetoric has been trained by previous work on the *Henry VI.* plays; while probably the congeniality of a tragic figure like Richard to a taste founded on Marlowe's models has given an opportunity for the independent expression of that quality. Any tendency to exaggeration is softened by an increasing sense of the relation between the dramatist's art and life itself. If we allow Shakespeare to have had any part in the play, then *Richard III.*, whatever may be its debt to older material, shows witness of his hand, at a time when he has reached the stage of untrammelled expression of his meaning, but is still partly dependent on his models for the form that his work takes, and has yet to handle the highest gifts of poetry. The declamatory vigour of *Richard III.* gathers fresh life in the complaints of Constance and the ecstasies of Romeo and Juliet. Its echo is still audible in the balanced melody of the plays of Shakespeare's middle life. And, tame as it is in comparison, it is the first sign of the possibility of that eloquence, compact of fire and air, and pregnant with "immortal longings," which is the case for the huge spirits of his great tragedies.

(2) In date, then, *Richard III.* probably follows immediately upon the third part of *Henry VI.* No allusion exists to settle the year in which the play was first produced. John Weever's epigram to "honie-tong'd Shakespeare," which selects the poems of 1593-4 and the characters of Romeo and Richard for praise, was not published till 1599. It may have been written, as has been conjectured, as early as 1595; but this cannot be proved. All that can be said is that Weever probably chose the names of Romeo and Richard for mention, on account of their popularity on the stage. A book of *Epigrammes and*

Elegies by J. D. and C. M., first published about 1596, contains lines which were probably imitated from Richard's opening soliloquy on his want of polite accomplishments :—

I am not fashion'd for these amorous times,
To court thy beauty with lascivious rhymes ;
I cannot dally, caper, dance, and sing,
Oblige my saint with supple sonnetting.

Collier found, in *The Rising to the Crown of Richard the Third*, appended to Giles Fletcher's *Licia* (1593), evidence that Richard had not yet appeared as a hero on the stage, when the poem was written. Fletcher makes Richard complain of "the Poets of this Age,

Like silly boats in Shallow rivers tost,
Losing their pains, and lacking still their wage,
To write of Women, and of Women's falls."

But the dramatists of 1593 could not be charged with exclusive attention to female misfortune. And if the third part of *Henry VI.* had appeared before September, 1592, as is probable from the famous allusion in Greene's *Groat's-worth of Wit*, *Richard III.*, in which the strong outlines of the character of Gloucester are developed directly from the earlier play, must have followed soon after, probably in the course of 1593. It is the most natural thing to conclude that Shakespeare, having revised the plays which dealt with the tragedy of the house of Lancaster, and having set his own mark on the revision, with increasing certainty of touch as the work proceeded, should continue the series, whether as author or reviser, to the culminating tragedy in which the house of York pays the penalty of its vengeance, and the destroyer of his own family is himself exterminated. And naturally, again, when *Richard III.* had proved a success on the stage, the dramatist would see what could be done with the original events that were the prime cause of all these sorrows, and so undertook the tragedy of *Richard II.* The relative chronology of *Richard III.* and *Richard II.* is an unsettled question, it is true; but it is difficult to disprove the patent fact that *Richard II.* shows just that degree of advance on *Richard III.* in poetic, if not in metrical and dramatic skill, which we might expect. There is nothing in *Richard III.* which can compare, on grounds of poetry, with the dialogue between John of Gaunt and Bolingbroke in *Richard II.* I. iii. 275-303, Gaunt's dying speech (II. i. 31-68), the King's reflections (III. ii. 144-77, III. iii. 143-75), or York's description of Richard's captive entry into London (V. ii. 7-40). In these passages the rhetoric of *Richard III.* has lost self-consciousness and has acquired fresh grace. If the date of *Richard II.* is not later than 1594, as is generally acknowledged, it may be assumed that *Richard III.* was Shakespeare's chief work of 1593.

May it be taken, then, as Shakespeare's own unaided work? His authorship of the play cannot be denied positively. We have no traces of any play on which he could have exercised his revision—not even of any play from which the text that he revised, like that of *Henry VI.*, could have been derived. The comparative evenness of the style shows that the revision, if revision it was, was performed with great skill. There is a concentration and liveliness in the action, which are less noticeable in such hurried chronicles of events as the three parts of *Henry VI.* The occasional humour of the *Henry VI.* plays is certainly almost wanting in *Richard III.*; but they are far surpassed by *Richard III.* in point of dramatic irony. Certain weaknesses which may be detected here and there—for example, Richard's soliloquy on waking from his dreams, in V. iii.—may be explained by the probability that Shakespeare was attempting more than a young dramatist might be expected to achieve on his own account. Such points of style as the abandonment of classical similes favour the supposition that the reviser of the earlier plays was now working as an independent author. The theory that the origin of *Richard III.* was similar to that of the three parts of *Henry VI.* is attractive and not improbable. But, on the other hand, if we recognise that there is such a thing in Shakespeare's work as a current of development and improvement, we cannot surrender whatever seems feeble or commonplace in it to other authors, unless probability is supported by something stronger than itself. *Richard III.*, inferior though it is to Shakespeare's more mature writings, is nevertheless far from being feeble or commonplace. On the contrary, it is conspicuous, among the plays of Marlowe's followers, for its dramatic skill and interest.

There doubtless was an existing play on the same subject, when *Richard III.* appeared on the stage for the first time. *The True Tragedie of Richard III.*, published in 1594, "as it was played by the Queenes Maiesties Players," covers much the same ground as the Shakespearean play; but there is no textual connexion between the two. Possibly the *True Tragedie* was an earlier play, whose publication as the "only original" *Richard III.* was intended to steal a march upon its successful younger rival. But, if Shakespeare simply revised an older drama, the text and original sources of that drama have disappeared altogether. The chief argument in favour of the revised play may be found, perhaps, in the words "newly augmented," which were prefixed to Shakespeare's name for the first time in Q 3. It has been shown already that these words are not true, if applied merely to the editions in which they occur. But it is possible that they supply an omission which had been made in the title-pages of the earlier quartos. Q 1 had been printed without the author's name. In Q 2 Shakespeare had been introduced as the author. Four years later, when Q 3 appeared, his true relation to the play may have been discovered; and it is not unlikely that the words "newly augmented" were inserted to rectify the impression, created by Q 2, that he was the original author. Nothing is more probable than that the publisher of an unauthorised edition of the play should be insufficiently informed as to its true authorship. The word "newly," which was continued on the title-pages of the later quartos, might easily be applied to work which had been done some years before the publication of Q 3. In short, Q, from this point of view, may be regarded as the text of an earlier play augmented by Shakespeare. We might even go further, and surmise that many of the roughnesses of Q were left unsmoothed from the original drama, and that the process of augmentation came before that of revision, which eventually was accomplished in the text represented by F. This view would not diminish, but corroborate the importance of F as the true basis of a text of the play. It is, however, a mere conjecture; and the only conclusions at which we can arrive safely are, that the text as we have it is substantially Shakespeare's, and that either, as in the *Henry VI.* plays, he embroidered skilfully upon an older text, or wrote an entirely new play in a style to which, by practice, his own was become assimilated.

Beside the *True Tragedie of Richard the Third*, there was a Latin play on the same theme by Thomas Legge, Master of Caius, which had been acted at Cambridge in 1579. But the real source of the material used for *Richard III.* was Holinshed's *Chronicles of England*, in which Halle's earlier chronicle and the *History of Richard III.* by Sir Thomas More were embodied almost literally. A reading at V. iii. 325, which is shared by all the printed editions of the play, shows that the second edition of Holinshed (1586-7) must have been used in the preparation of *Richard III.*: the passage at IV. ii. 98-115, peculiar to Q, depends on an insertion added to the same edition. It goes without saying that the treatment of the historical sources in *Richard III.* is free in general, but faithful in minor details. To form a connected action, the events of several years are brought together into a space of time which Mr. Daniel has estimated at eleven days with certain intervals. Thus the imprisonment and death of Clarence (I. i. and iv.) took place in 1478. The events of I. ii., if they were historically possible, would belong to 1471. From II. i. to IV. iv., the events of 1483 follow one another in rapid succession. At the end of IV. iv., the interval between Richmond's separate expeditions of 1483 and 1485 is annihilated, and the drama moves on to its climax at Bosworth. The dramatic convenience of these alterations is obvious: accuracy of date is incompatible, in the space of five acts, with striking presentation of character. The main object of the play is to give bold dramatic relief to the figure of Richard III., whose traits were ready to hand in Holinshed. This is the object of the liberty which is taken with history in the famous scene between Richard and Lady Anne—a scene which has no foundation in fact, but is a most powerful demonstration of the personal influence of the hero on those round him. The interview with the Queen-dowager in IV. iv., where Richard again exercises his faculty of persuasion, is a free deduction from history for the same purpose. Richard's connivance at the death of Clarence, which the historical authorities merely insinuate, becomes in the play a positive fact. The impression of subtlety and wickedness, which is left by the chroniclers, is repeated by Shakespeare in the higher key and more emphatic tone which are required by drama. Now and then, the Shakespearean estimate of a particular character departs slightly from the estimate suggested by Holinshed. The Hastings of the play, vindictive, but gay and imprudent, is a more foolish person than the Hastings of history, who is more closely related to the Shakespearean Buckingham. Even Buckingham is represented as less cautious than he actually was. His bragging, melodramatic words in III. v. 5-11 amount to a confession of imbecility. Hastings and Buckingham, however, are merely dramatic foils to the figure of Richard; and, as such, the depreciation of their characters is unavoidable. Finally, some of the doubtful minor details of history become, where it is necessary in the play, actual facts. This is the case with the confidences of Richard to Buckingham, for which there is only historical probability; while the manner of Clarence's murder is related in accordance with likelihood rather than with ascertained truth.

The treatment of history in *Richard III.* is guided everywhere by loyalty to the traditional principles of tragedy. The irresistible power of Nemesis over-rules the actions of every one of the characters. In the great tragedies of Shakespeare's later life, the misfortunes of the heroes compel our sympathy and regret, while we acknowledge that they are inevitable. But in *Richard III.* the inevitable nature of the tragedy precludes us from sympathy. We are passionless spectators, standing outside the drama. It is true that the *dramatis personæ* interest us more nearly than any persons in the *Henry VI.* plays. Richard himself is a powerful study in sustained villainy: Hastings, his credulous dupe, and Buckingham, his short-sighted fellow-conspirator, although they are merely foils to him, are skilfully drawn as such. There is a pathetic humour in the precocious taunts of young York: the lamentations of the women and children whom Richard has bereaved have real pathos beneath their outward formality. But the abiding power of the tragedy lies in its clear presentation of the moral significance of the events which it relates. *Raro antecedentem scelestum deseruit pede Pœna claudo* are words which would suggest themselves as a fit motto for the play, were it not that here vengeance follows at the very heels of crime. Richard has not had time to enjoy his triumph, when the first blow of vengeance strikes him. Hastings, in the moment of exultation at the death of his enemies, finds himself a partaker in their fate. Buckingham hastens his own downfall by hesitating at the last crime by which he can ensure temporary success. The ruin of Rivers and his friends, the helpless misery of the women, are hurried on by their selfish ambition and intrigue.

It would be inaccurate to say that the author of *Richard III.* was profoundly moved by the spectacle of sin and its punishment in history. The doctrine was the conventional foundation of the tragic art which he practised. Expressed with pious conviction or reluctant acquiescence by the great Athenian dramatists, it had been accepted as an artificial principle by the author of the Senecan tragedies. In the dawn of the Renaissance, the "harm of hem that stode in heigh degree" was a favourite theme of prose and poetry, of which, in England, *The Myrroure for Magistrates* was the crowning example. The frigid atmosphere of that grave poem was the atmosphere of tragedy on the early Elizabethan stage, where Seneca was the formal model of drama. The tragic propriety of *Gorboduc* stirs no emotion of sympathy or horror, beyond the natural repugnance which we feel towards its fatal catastrophes. The crimes and punishment of Queen Eleanor in Peele's *Edward I.* are merely grotesque. In Lodge and Greene's *Looking-Glass for London*, a certain sincerity of feeling underlies the artless machinery of the story. But, in plays like *The Wounds of Civil War*, Greene's *James IV.*, or the three parts of *Henry VI.*, the tragic groundwork is a matter of course; and our estimate of such works depends on the degree of skill with which their leading principle is developed. The same thing, allowing for the exceptional horrors of the action, may be said of *Titus Andronicus*. *Richard III*. is almost the first tragedy of the school of Marlowe, in which the conventional element, used and developed with great clearness, is invested with a real human interest. The characters are something more than mere stage dolls, moved to and fro as the action of the play prescribes. Yet their sin and fate, if they compel our interest, leave our deeper emotions untouched. They are still matters of course. The dramatist has not won as yet that insight into the springs of human sin and folly which gives *Othello* or *King Lear* their eternal pathos. His characters are drawn in simple outline and with uniform colouring. They are good or bad without compensation. They sin without reflection: their punishment is purely mechanical. Richmond, the ultimate avenger, is the most lifeless figure of the play: he is merely the instrument of justice. To the author, in fact, the whole course of such a tragedy was perfectly obvious. It would have been impossible for him, at this date, to make Hastings say, in the hour of his misfortune:—

> As flies to wanton boys, are we to the gods;
> They kill us for their sport.

Margaret or Elizabeth could not yet acknowledge that:—

> The gods are just, and of our pleasant vices
> Make instruments to plague us.

Richmond could not yet confess, over the body of his slain adversary:—

> This shows you are above,
> You justicers, that these our nether crimes
> So speedily can venge.

In *Richard III*., as in *King Lear*, the wheel comes full circle; but the dramatist watches its revolution with imperfect experience, and, as a consequence, with little emotion.

His artistic sympathy is concentrated on the figure of his hero. Every actor in the story receives his degree of life from association with Richard and contact with his malign influence. But, when we speak of the character of the hero and its effect on the play, we recognise in its design the same simplicity which distinguishes the author's perception of the tragic principle. Richard is an ideal conception after the pattern of Marlowe's heroes. Already his audacity, his determination to stick at nothing, have given him heroic prominence in the third part of *Henry VI.*—a prominence which leaves Warwick, the real hero of the piece, in the background. This preliminary revelation of his remorseless nature, devoid of pity, love, and fear, glorying in its powers of dissimulation and treachery, must have whetted the appetite of an Elizabethan audience for a further development of the theme. The key is maintained in *Richard III.* Like Tamburlaine or Barabas, Richard is absolutely consistent to his character and aims. There is no room for any real development of character. No chastening of experience can modify the superhuman passion for self-aggrandisement at any price, the ready-made standard to which Richard's every action must conform. His opening soliloquy lays down his motives and plan of campaign. He follows out all his designs with swiftness and eminent success. Relying on his force of will, he removes his enemies one by one, uses his adherents as his tools, and accomplishes feats like the wooing of Anne and the persuasion of the Queen-dowager to further his plans. It is only when he has done everything that he possibly can do, that Nemesis falls upon him. Even so, he is loyal to his part, and goes to ruin with the callous assurance that has been the keynote of all his actions. No compunction visits him. Once, when he hears of the first serious opposition to his career, the defection of Buckingham and Richmond's invasion, he falters, chides the messengers furiously, and issues contradictory orders to his lieutenants. But, a moment later, he recovers his courage. Once again, after his last night of visions, he wakes with the agonised cry, "Have mercy, Jesu!" and turns to a self-questioning, which, however, compared with his earlier soliloquies, is lifeless and perfunctory. On the field of battle, there is no place for his usual weapons of hypocrisy and treachery. Courage and physical force alone are possible; and in these he is still superhuman, fighting to the end with entire consistency to those early glimpses of his character in the third part of *Henry VI.*, when, after St. Albans, he flung down Somerset's head on the ground with a savage gibe, or when, at Towton, he and his brother Edward, "like a brace of greyhounds, having the fearful flying hare in sight," chased the Lancastrians from the field.

Selfish ambition, physical courage, absolute want of moral scruple and human kindliness, are the fundamental qualities on which the character of Richard is built up. The figure is imposing, because the villainy embodied in its conception is on so large a scale, and is worked out so thoroughly. At the same time, the conception itself is mechanical. The character is made to order, to fulfil an ideal plan. As a study in selfish wickedness, it is far behind such a study as that of Iago. Exceptional though he is, Iago compels our belief by virtue of the complexity of his motives, and of the mind that dwells in him and admits us to its secrets. Richard's motive is simple; he has no individual mind; he is merely an artistic conception of a gigantic villain with no redeeming quality, worked out with great power, and impressive chiefly because of the bulk of the design. Not very long before, Marlowe had made a similar attempt in the Jew of Malta, in whom malevolence and avarice exclude all other qualities. If Barabas supplied some hints for Shylock at a later date, he can hardly have been overlooked in the work of creating or transforming the character of Richard III. Richard is the most striking stage-villain of the type of which Barabas is the most grotesque example. He possesses in an eminent degree those Machiavelian tricks of which Barabas furnishes a shameless demonstration. To "count religion but a childish toy" is one of the fundamental tenets of this statesman who had boasted, in an earlier play, that he was able to "set the murderous Machiavel to school." He steals "odd old ends" from Holy Writ to deceive the ears of those who suspect him. It is by an unblushing parade of piety that he gains his object, in the critical scene where he accepts the crown from the citizens. He is an adept in the art of moralising "two meanings in one word." Examples of the Machiavelian tradition in English drama recur to the mind of every student. Richard, with his ambition, his fearlessness, his unscrupulousness, his calculating hypocrisy, his never-failing irony, his natural defects redeemed by his gifts of insinuation and persuasion, is the *beau idéal* of the Machiavelian, to whom *virtù*, prompt and unscrupulous energy, is indispensable, with whom the semblance of religion must take the place of the reality, in whom the highest perfection of bestial qualities, the cunning of the fox and the courage of the lion, must be combined.

To discuss the relation of this dramatic ideal to its real origin in Machiavelli, or, more properly, in the ideas of the "Englishman Italianate" about Machiavelli, is not to the present purpose. Nor is it necessary to enter into the relationship between the Richard of the drama and the real Richard of history. Something has been said of the minor characters, of the would-be Machiavelian Buckingham, and of the frivolous, sensual Hastings. In the case of Hastings, the dramatic irony of the tragedy, its most distinguishing excellence, is at its best. Richard, and even Buckingham, are too thoroughly alive to their own villainy, and too obviously self-devoted to destruction, to be altogether blind to a possible reversal of their fortunes, or to lend their words that terrible significance with which the thoughtless sinner bears witness on the stage to his real insecurity or prophesies his own downfall. The cynicism with which Richard says of Clarence's murder, "God will revenge it," disarms the situation of half its irony. When Buckingham sets aside Margaret's warning, it is not because he feels himself secure from the necessity to "take heed of yonder dog," but because he thinks himself competent to take care of himself and foresee all means of self-preservation. Hastings, on the other hand, has full confidence in the good faith of the protector. He laughs at Stanley's dreams and caution; he exults in the news of the execution of his enemies; the meeting with the pursuivant, though it recalls an unhappy day in his life, gives him no foreboding qualm. His meeting with the priest fills him with no sense of ill to come: he can laugh over it with Buckingham, and answer his sinister jests with a jeer at the unhappy lords at Pomfret. At the council in the Tower he boasts of his intimate friendship with Gloucester, and praises his friend's simplicity of heart and face, of which he is doubtless ready to take the first advantage. But, in a moment, the fatuous self-complacence that has held us in suspense for two scenes, crumbles to pieces, when the protector, frowning and biting his lip, bursts into the council-chamber, and Hastings, at close quarters with death, realises what the conceit was that had given so cheerful a seeming to his grace's good-morrow, and how ill his face had accorded with the thoughts of his heart.

More pathetic is the irony with which Anne, in her repulsion from the murderer of Henry VI. and of his son, curses the woman who may become Richard's wife, and then, almost in the same breath, yields to his mastery, and consents to be that woman. The scene is a *tour de force;* and the illusion which it produces is rather too violent to be entirely successful. But we are reminded of it at that later date, when Anne, the "woeful welcomer of glory," discloses to the other hapless women who have felt the influence of the "unavoided eye" of the royal basilisk, the fulfilment of her imprecation on herself. Of those women, whose part is almost that of a chorus to the play—a chorus whose personal concerns are most deeply implicated by its events—Anne is the most blameless and the most attractive. The widowed Duchess of York, broken by grief, is surrendered to passionate despair. For Queen Elizabeth in her helplessness we have less sympathy. She has played an ambitious and domineering part in the past: she has been a sharer in that hollow reconciliation by her husband's death-bed, the manifest insincerity of which prejudices us against all concerned in it: her self-interest persuades her to sacrifice her daughter to Richard, at a time when his villainies are no longer any secret. Much praise has been given to the character of Margaret, whose kinship to the models of antique tragedy is become a commonplace of criticism. The sudden appearances of the wrinkled beldame to gloat over the misfortunes of her foes, and the dialogue in which Richard, by his sudden interjection of her own name, diverts the current of her curses, are highly effective from a theatrical point of view. She is little more, however, than a shadowy phantom, the survivor of Richard's early experiments in crime; and her real use, like that of the funeral of her husband in I. ii., is to connect the events of the new play more closely with those of its predecessor, and to add the weight of Richard's past exploits to the load of guilt which he has piled up more recently. When we look forward to Lear, or Coriolanus, or Lady Macbeth, it seems needless to single out Margaret for comparison with the tragic figures of the Athenian stage.

Early records of the stage history of *Richard III.* are connected chiefly with the performance by Burbage of a part which, without involving great intellectual effort in the actor, calls forth his most striking powers of action and declamation. Manningham notes in his diary for 13th March, 1601, a story of a trick played on Burbage by Shakespeare, "vpon a tyme when Burbidge played Richard III." In the same year, the authors of the third part of *The Returne from Parnassus* introduce Burbage catechising Philomusus thus: "I like your face and the proportion of your body for *Richard* the 3. I pray M. *Phil.* let me see you act a little of it." Whereupon Philomusus quotes the opening lines of the play. A third allusion is contained in Bishop Corbet's *Iter Boreale*, written before 1635, in which he describes his visit with a loquacious host to Bosworth Field. The host showed him the position of the armies and the very spot of Richard's death:—

> Besides what of his knowledge he could say,
> He had authenticke notice from the Play;
> Which I might guesse, by 's mustring up the ghosts,
> And policyes, not incident to hosts,
> But cheifly by that one perspicuous thing,
> Where he mistook a player for a king,
> For when he would have sayd, King Richard dyed,
> And call'd—A horse! a horse! he Burbidge cry'de.

It was Burbage, no doubt, who gave the famous line "A horse! a horse! my kingdom for a horse!" its vogue, attested by many allusions in the plays and poems of the earlier part of the seventeenth century. But, although there is ample evidence of the early popularity of *Richard III.*, no allusion to a definite performance is found before 1633, when Sir Henry Herbert notes in the Office-book which he kept as Master of the Revels, that the play was acted at St. James's before Charles I. and Henrietta Maria, soon after the birth of the future James II.

Its popularity seems to have waned after the Restoration. Betterton does not seem to have included Richard in his *répertoire* of Shakespearean characters. Pepys makes no mention of the play; and no dramatist adapted it for the stage until Colley Cibber brought out his famous version early in the eighteenth century. For more than a century and a half this mutilated edition became the playgoer's text of the drama. It was as Cibber's Richard that Garrick made his first appearance at Goodman's Fields, 19th October, 1741: it remained one of his favourite parts until his retirement in June, 1776. In May of that year, Mrs. Siddons, then a member of Garrick's company at Drury Lane, made one of her earliest appearances in London as Lady Anne. Her brothers, John Philip and Charles Kemble, produced a revision of Cibber's version, in which they took the parts of Richard and Richmond, at Covent Garden in 1811. Edmund Kean played Richard with great success at Drury Lane in the seasons of 1813-4 and 1814-5. Macready, who made his fame in the same part about 1819, was the principal actor in the restoration of the Shakespearean text which took place at Covent Garden, 12th and 19th March, 1821. The public, long accustomed to Cibber's adaptation, received this change for the better without enthusiasm. Later actors, like Charles Kean, returned to the mutilated text; and it was not till 29th January, 1877, when Henry Irving produced the play, "arranged for the Stage exclusively from the author's text," at the Lyceum, that Cibber's book was ousted from the boards. Among the famous actors whose *débûts* are connected with the drama, may be mentioned Richard William Elliston, who appeared as a youth at the Bath Theatre in 1791, taking the very minor part of Tressel in the second scene of this play.

From the notes to the present volume it will be seen how much the editor owes to the freely-given help and friendship of the late Mr. Craig. He is also indebted to Mr. P. A. Daniel for advice and suggestions communicated through Mr. Craig. All references to other plays of Shakespeare follow the numbering of lines in the Globe edition of the plays.

THE TRAGEDY

OF

KING RICHARD THE THIRD

DRAMATIS PERSONÆ

KING EDWARD *the Fourth.*

EDWARD, *Prince of Wales, afterwards King Edward V.,* / RICHARD, *Duke of York,* } *sons to the King.*

GEORGE, *Duke of Clarence,* / RICHARD, *Duke of Gloucester, afterwards King Richard III.,* } *brothers to the King.*

A young son of Clarence.

HENRY, *Earl of Richmond, afterwards King Henry VII.*

CARDINAL BOURCHIER, *Archbishop of Canterbury.*

THOMAS ROTHERHAM, *Archbishop of York.*

JOHN MORTON, *Bishop of Ely.*

DUKE OF BUCKINGHAM.

DUKE OF NORFOLK.

EARL OF SURREY, *his son.*

EARL RIVERS, *brother to Elizabeth.*

MARQUESS OF DORSET *and* LORD GREY, *sons to Elizabeth.*

EARL OF OXFORD.

LORD HASTINGS.

LORD STANLEY, *called also* EARL OF DERBY.

LORD LOVEL.

SIR THOMAS VAUGHAN.

SIR RICHARD RATCLIFF.

SIR WILLIAM CATESBY.

SIR JAMES TYRREL.

SIR JAMES BLOUNT.

SIR WALTER HERBERT.

SIR ROBERT BRAKENBURY, *Lieutenant of the Tower.*

CHRISTOPHER URSWICK, *a priest.*

Another Priest.

TRESSEL *and* BERKELEY, *gentlemen attending on the Lady Anne.*

Lord Mayor of London.
Sheriff of Wiltshire.
ELIZABETH, *queen to King Edward IV.*
MARGARET, *widow of King Henry VI.*
DUCHESS OF YORK, *mother to King Edward IV.*
LADY ANNE, *widow of Edward, Prince of Wales, son to King Henry VI.; afterwards married to Richard.*
A young daughter of Clarence.

Ghosts of those murdered by Richard; Lords and other Attendants; a Pursuivant; a Scrivener; Citizens, Murderers, Messengers, Soldiers, etc.

SCENE: *England.*

NOTES ON *DRAMATIS PERSONÆ*

A young son of Clarence] Edward, Earl of Warwick, born 1475: kept in custody at Sheriff Hutton during the reign of Richard III., but knighted during the King's visit to York, 1483. Removed by order of Henry VII. to the Tower of London, 1485, where he was shut up, "out of all companie of men & sight of beasts; insomuch that he could not discerne a goose from a capon" (Holinshed, iii. 787, where five years are added to his age). In IV. ii. 55 below, this simplicity is slightly anticipated. Executed 28th November, 1499, on the charge of conspiracy with Perkin Warbeck and connivance at his escape from the Tower.

CARDINAL BOURCHIER] Thomas, son of William Bourchier, Earl of Eu, by Anne, elder daughter of Thomas, Duke of Gloucester, sixth son of Edward III. His brother Henry, created Earl of Essex, 1461, was an uncle by marriage of Edward IV. and Richard III. By their mother's first marriage, the Bourchiers were half-brothers to the first Duke of Buckingham, grandfather of the Buckingham of the play. The Cardinal was born 1404: he was Chancellor of Oxford and Bishop of Worcester, 1434-5; Bishop of Ely, 1443-4; Archbishop of Canterbury, 1454; Lord Chancellor, 1455-6; Cardinal with title of San Ciriaco in Terme, 1467-8. At first a Lancastrian, he declared for the house of York, 1460. He crowned Edward IV., Queen Elizabeth Woodville, Richard III., and Henry VII., and married Henry VII. to Elizabeth of York. He died at Knole, 30th March, 1486.

THOMAS ROTHERHAM] or Scott, born at Rotherham, 1423. Nominated Bishop of Rochester and Keeper of the Privy Seal, 1467; Chancellor of Cambridge, 1469-71, 1473-8; Bishop of Lincoln, 1472; Archbishop of York, 1480; Lord Chancellor, 1474-83; Master of Pembroke Hall, Cambridge, c. 1480-6. For his part in the play see Appendix II. He was arrested and imprisoned after the council of 13th June, 1483, at which Hastings was entrapped; but seems to have made his peace with Richard, and to have held office as Lord Treasurer for a short time under Henry VII. He died at Cawood in May, 1500. He founded the College of Jesus at Rotherham, and is regarded as the second founder of Lincoln College, Oxford.

JOHN MORTON] Born c. 1420; lawyer and diplomatist; Bishop of Ely, 1479; for his imprisonment and escape see notes on IV. iv. 470-1 and 512-6; rewarded for his services to Richmond with the archbishopric of Canterbury, 1486; Lord Chancellor, 1487; created Cardinal, 1493; Chancellor of Oxford, 1495; died 1500. It is probably from him, through Sir Thomas More, that we derive the traditional account of the character and reign of Richard III.

DUKE OF BUCKINGHAM] Henry Stafford, born c. 1454; succeeded his grandfather as second Duke, 1460; executed at Salisbury, 1483. For his descent see note on III. i. 195. His son, Edward, third Duke, is the Buckingham of *Henry VIII*.

DUKE OF NORFOLK] John Howard, born before 1430; created Duke of Norfolk and Earl Marshal by Richard III., 1483; killed at Bosworth, 1485.

EARL OF SURREY] Thomas Howard, born 1443; fought at Bosworth; imprisoned by Henry VII., but gained distinction afterwards in the service of the Tudors; won battle of Flodden, 1513; created Duke of Norfolk, 1514; died 1524. He is the Norfolk of *Henry VIII*.

EARL RIVERS] Anthony Woodville, born c. 1442; K.G., 1466; executed 1483. His translation, *The Dictes and Sayings of the Philosophers*, was the first book printed by Caxton, 1477. See also Appendix II.

MARQUESS OF DORSET] Thomas Grey, born 1451; succeeded his father as ninth Baron Ferrars of Groby, 1461; Earl of Huntingdon, 1471; Marquess of Dorset, 1475; K.G., 1476; escaped to Brittany, 1483; confirmed in his titles by Henry VII.; died 1501.

LORD GREY] more correctly Lord Richard Grey; executed 1483.

EARL OF OXFORD] John de Vere, born 1443; succeeded his father as thirteenth Earl, 1462; a consistent Lancastrian. His abortive attempt to hold St. Michael's Mount in 1473 led to his attainder and imprisonment at Hammes, 1474-84. He returned with Richmond to England, and died 1513.

LORD HASTINGS] William Hastings, created Baron Hastings of Ashby-de-la-Zouch and Lord Chamberlain, 1461. He was a prominent antagonist of the Woodville faction; but his imprisonment in the Tower, referred to in I. i. and III. ii. is merely an inference drawn by the author of the play from Holinshed, iii. 723, where it is said (following More) that Hastings was "accused vnto King Edward by the Lord Riuers . . . in such wise, as he was for the while (but it lasted not long) farre fallen into the kings indignation, & stood in great feare of himselfe." Executed 1483.

LORD STANLEY] Thomas Stanley, born c. 1435; succeeded his father as second Baron Stanley, 1459; became third husband of Lady Margaret Beaufort, mother of Henry VII.; created Earl of Derby, 1485; died 1504. Strictly speaking, the use of the title "Derby," where it occurs in this play, is wrong, as Stanley was not yet created Earl of Derby at the time of the action. Theobald used "Stanley" throughout, on the ground that the author was not responsible for the inaccuracy. The Cambridge editors retain Derby where both Qq and Ff agree in the reading; and their custom has been followed in the present edition.

LORD LOVEL] more usually Lovell. Francis Lovell, ninth Baron Lovell of Tichmarsh, Northants; created Viscount Lovell and K.G., 1483; Lord Chamberlain to Richard III.; died after fighting for Lambert Simnel at Stoke, 1487.

SIR THOMAS VAUGHAN] Chamberlain to Edward, Prince of Wales (Edward V.), 1471; executed 1483.

SIR RICHARD RATCLIFF] or Radcliffe; knighted at Tewkesbury, 1471; K.G., 1484; killed at Bosworth, 1485; the "Rat" of Colyngborne's couplet.

SIR WILLIAM CATESBY] A lawyer, and *protégé* of Hastings, whose service he forsook for that of Gloucester. Under Richard III. he became Chancellor of the Exchequer, and in 1484 was knight of the shire for Northants and Speaker of the House of Commons. He was taken at Bosworth, and beheaded at Leicester. The "Cat" of Colyngborne's satire. The knighthood given him here is purely a courtesy title.

SIR JAMES TYRREL] more correctly Tyrrell or Tyrell; knighted after Tewkesbury, 1471; Master of the Horse to Richard III.; pardoned and made Lieutenant of Guisnes Castle by Henry VII.; beheaded 1502. See note on IV. ii. 36.

SIR JAMES BLOUNT] son of Sir Walter Blount, Baron Montjoy of Mountjoy; Lieutenant of Hammes Castle, 1476, where he was custodian of the Earl of Oxford; knighted 1485; died 1493.

SIR WALTER HERBERT] See note on IV. v. 10-18.

SIR ROBERT BRAKENBURY] Appointed Constable of the Tower, 1483, so that his connexion with the murder of Clarence (1478) has no warrant in history; killed at Bosworth.

CHRISTOPHER URSWICK] A member of a northern family; confessor to the Countess of Richmond, Henry VII.'s mother; Archdeacon of Richmond; employed in diplomatic missions by Henry VII.; Dean of York, 1488; Dean of Windsor, 1495; died 1522.

TRESSEL and BERKELEY] Names probably chosen by Shakespeare at random.

LORD MAYOR OF LONDON] Sir Edmund Shaw. See note on III. v. 103.

ELIZABETH] Born c. 1437, daughter of Sir Richard Woodville (Baron Rivers, 1448; Earl Rivers, 1466) by Jacquetta of Luxemburg, widow of John, Duke of Bedford; married (1) Sir John Grey, eighth Baron Ferrers of Groby, (2) Edward

IV., 1464-65; died 1492. Her complicity in the designs of Richard III. (see IV. iv.) brought her out of favour with her son-in-law, Henry VII.

MARGARET] See note on IV. iv. 6.

DUCHESS OF YORK] Born 1415; daughter of Sir Ralph Nevill, first Earl of Westmorland, the "cousin Westmoreland" of *Henry V.* IV. iii. 19; married Richard, Duke of York, 1438; died 1495. See notes on III. vii. 179-82; IV. i. 95.

LADY ANNE] Born 1456, younger daughter of Richard Nevill, the great Earl of Warwick; betrothed, but never married, to Edward, son of Henry VI., 1470; married Richard, Duke of Gloucester, 1474; died March, 1485. In *3 Henry VI.* III. iii. 242 she is wrongly called Warwick's "eldest daughter" (see also *ibid.* IV. i. 118). Her elder sister and co-heiress, Isabella, married George, Duke of Clarence; and a dispute over her inheritance was one of the causes of ill-feeling between Clarence and his brothers.

A young daughter of Clarence] Margaret Plantagenet, born 1473; married to Sir Richard Pole; restored to the title and possessions of the earldom of Salisbury by Henry VIII., 1513; attainted for her suspected complicity in the intrigues of her son, Reginald Pole, and others, 1539; executed 27th May, 1541. At IV. iii. 37 she is probably confused with her first cousin, Princess Cicely, whom Richard III. married "to a man found in a cloud, and of an vnknowne linage and familie" (Holinshed, iii. 752), probably a member of the Lincolnshire family of Kyme.

A Pursuivant] See note on III. ii. 94.

THE TRAGEDY OF KING RICHARD THE THIRD

ACT I

SCENE I.—*London. A street.*

Enter RICHARD, *Duke of Gloucester*, *solus.*

Glou. Now is the winter of our discontent
Made glorious summer by this sun of York;
And all the clouds that lour'd upon our house
In the deep bosom of the ocean buried.
Now are our brows bound with victorious wreaths;
Our bruised arms hung up for monuments;

London. A street.] Capell; omitted Qq, Ff. 1. *our*] Qq 1, 2, Ff; omitted Qq 3-8. 2. *sun*] Rowe; *sonne* Qq; *son* Ff.

2. *this sun of York*] Compare *3 Henry VI.* v. iii. 4, 5. Edward IV. assumed a sun for his badge, in consequence of the vision which appeared to him 2nd February, 1461, the day before the battle of Mortimer's Cross. See *3 Henry VI.* II. i. 25-40; Holinshed, *Chronicles*, 2nd ed. 1587, iii. 660. The legend is referred to by Drayton, *Miseries of Queen Margaret*, st. 134, and *Poly-Olbion*, 1622, xxii. 762-84. Aldis Wright quotes from Stow the incident at Barnet, where Warwick's forces, in the mist, took the "starre with streames" on the coats of Lord Oxford's men, their friends, for the sun worn by the supporters of Edward. The readings of Qq and Ff bring out a common play on the words "sun" and "son": compare below, I. iii. 266, 267, and Tourneur, *Revenger's Tragedy*, 1607:—

"The mother's curse is heavy; where that fights,
Sons set in storm, and daughters lose their lights."

In Shakespeare's account of the vision mentioned above, Edward divines the three ominous suns joined in one as an emblem of the three "*sons* of brave Plantagenet."

6. *monuments*] Compare Massinger, *Great Duke of Florence*, 1635, ii. 1:—

"his arms
And his victorious sword and shield hung up
For *monuments*."

A. M. (ap. Hakluyt, *Principal Navigations*, 1599, ii. 135): "They kept there the sword wherewith John Fox had killed the Keeper . . . and hanged it up for a *monument*." The phrase is sometimes taken as referring to the armour hung up over tombs, like those

Our stern alarums chang'd to merry meetings;
Our dreadful marches, to delightful measures.
Grim-visag'd War hath smooth'd his wrinkled front;
And now, instead of mounting barbed steeds,
To fright the souls of fearful adversaries,
He capers nimbly in a lady's chamber,

7. *alarums*] *alarmes* Q 1. 8. *measures*] Qq 1-3, Ff; *pleasures* Qq 4-8.

of the Black Prince or Henry V. Such armour, however, was usually made for the funeral ceremonies, and could not come under the category of "bruised arms"; nor were the members of the house of York at present in need of funeral armour. The allusion, if any is needed, is simply to the custom of ornamenting a hall with the disused armour of the family, like the armour "Hugh's at Agincourt and . . . old Sir Ralph's at Ascalon" in Tennyson's *Princess*, 1847, prol. lines 25, 26, or Mr. Chainmail's "rusty pikes, shields, helmets, swords, and tattered banners" in Peacock's *Crotchet Castle*, 1831, chap. 5.

8. *measures*] slow and solemn dances. Sir John Davies, *Orchestra*, 1596, st. 65, says of Love, who had taught the multitude lighter dances:—

"But after these, as men more civil grew,
He did more grave and solemn *Measures* frame;
With such fair order and proportion true,
And correspondence every way the same,
That no fault-finding eye did ever blame";

and st. 66:—

"Yet all the feet whereon these *measures* go
Are only Spondees, solemn, grave, and slow."

Decker, *Bel-Man of London*, 1608, has "I neither wonder at the stately *measures* of the clouds, the nimble galliards of the water, nor the wanton trippings of the wind" (ed. Smeaton, 1904, p. 71). There is a close parallel between the present passage and Lyly, *Alexander and Campaspe*, 1584, ii. 2 and iv. 3. Shakespeare seems to have had both these passages in mind. In iv. 3 we find "But let us draw in, to see how well it becomes them to tread the *measures* in a dance, that were wont to set the order for a march." Shakespeare's alliteration of "dreadful marches" and "delightful measures" is a trick learned in the school of Lyly.

9. *Grim-visag'd War*] Mr. Craig calls my attention to the recurrence of the same phrase in Drayton, *Poly-Olbion*, 1613, viii. 181: "Yet with *grim-visag'd war* when he her shores did greet," and to the reminiscence in Gray, *Ode on a Distant Prospect of Eton College*, 1797, st. vii.: "*Grim-visaged* comfortless despair."

10. *barbed*] armed for war. So Lyly, *Alexander and Campaspe*, ii. 2: "Is the war-like sound of drum and trump turned to the soft noise of lyre and lute? the neighing of *barbed* steeds . . . converted to delicate tunes and amorous glances?" The word is a corruption of the proper term "barded"; *barde* is a general term for horse-armour in French. Cotgrave, *Dictionarie*, 1611, gives "Bardé: barbed or trapped, as a great horse. Bardes: f. Barbes, or trappings for horses of service, or of shew." "Barbed steeds" occurs again in *Richard II*. III. iii. 117. "Unbarbed," in *Coriolanus*, III. ii. 99, is usually taken to mean "unarmoured." The substantive "barb" is used for horse-armour by Spenser, *Faerie Queene*, 1590, II. ii. 11: "goodly gorgeous *barbes*." For "barded" see Berners' *Froissart*, 1523, i. 41: "It was a great beauty to behold the . . . horses *barded*." "Barded" is sometimes used, *e.g.* by Stow, of men as well as horses. The application of the term "barbed" to the walls of a hall hung with armour (*Ælla*, line 219) was one of the signs that betrayed Chatterton's forgeries.

To the lascivious pleasing of a lute.
But I, that am not shap'd for sportive tricks,
Nor made to court an amorous looking-glass;
I, that am rudely stamp'd, and want love's majesty,
To strut before a wanton ambling nymph;
I, that am curtail'd of this fair proportion,
Cheated of feature by dissembling Nature,
Deform'd, unfinish'd, sent before my time
Into this breathing world, scarce half made up,
And that so lamely and unfashionable,
That dogs bark at me as I halt by them;
Why, I, in this weak piping time of peace,
Have no delight to pass away the time,

13. *lute*] Ff; *loue* Qq. 14. *shap'd for*] Ff; *shapte for* Qq 1-3; *sharpe for* Qq 4, 5; *sharpe of* Qq 6-8. 21. *scarce*] Qq 1, 2; *scarse* Ff; omitted Qq 3-8.

13. *pleasing*] evidently used here for "pleasure." No parallel example is forthcoming.

17. *ambling*] used of leisurely or easy motion, as *Romeo and Juliet*, I. iv. 10; *Hamlet*, III. i. 151. *New Eng. Dict.* quotes an apposite passage from Addison, *The Drummer*, 1716, i. 1: "She has . . . play'd at an assembly, and *ambled* in a ball or two." Mr. Craig suggests that "wanton-ambling" is possibly one of the double epithets so common in this play.

18. *proportion*] regularity of figure. Compare Greene, *Friar Bacon and Friar Bungay*, 1594 (ed. Dyce, p. 158):—

"*Proportion'd* as was Paris, when, in grey,
He courted Œnon in the vale by Troy";

Decker, *Guls Horn-Booke*, 1609 (ed. Smeaton, 1904, p. 30): "a head al hid in haire gives even to a most wicked face a sweet *proportion*."

19. *feature*] outward appearance (Lat. *factura*, Fr. *faiture*), as Kyd, *Spanish Tragedy*, c. 1588, act ii.: "My *feature* is not to content her sight"; Spenser, *Faerie Queene*, I. viii. 49; *Two Gentlemen of Verona*, II. iv. 73. "Feature" and "proportion" occur together again in Fletcher, *False One*, 1647, i. 2:—

"Cæsar is amorous,
And taken more with the title of a queen, . . .
Than *feature* or proportion."

Shakespeare does not here imply beauty of appearance: it is the shape of his body of which Richard has been cheated. Its "feature" is imperfect: as he explains lower down, he is "scarce half made up."

dissembling Nature] The idea of cheating is probably emphasised in "dissembling." Warburton explained the phrase as meaning "Nature that puts together things of a dissimilar kind, as a brave soul and a deformed body," *i.e.* dis-assembling Nature. But this idea seems rather far-fetched.

21. *this breathing world*] Compare Sonnet lxxxi. 12. See also *2 Henry VI*. I. ii. 21 (Craig).

22. *lamely and unfashionable*] For this double adverb with a single termination compare Ben Jonson, *Poetaster*, 1601, i. 1: "What, hast thou buskins on, Luscus, that thou swearest so tragically and high." Sometimes the adverbial termination is given to the second of the two words, as Fletcher, *False One*, iv. 2:—

"we make louder prayers to die nobly,
Than to live high and wantonly."

24. *piping*] The pipe was an instrument proper to times of peace, as the fife to times of war. Compare *Much Ado About Nothing*, II. iii. 13-15.

Unless to spy my shadow in the sun,
And descant on mine own deformity.
And therefore, since I cannot prove a lover,
To entertain these fair well-spoken days,
I am determined to prove a villain,
And hate the idle pleasures of these days.
Plots have I laid, inductions dangerous,
By drunken prophecies, libels, and dreams,
To set my brother Clarence and the king
In deadly hate the one against the other:
And if King Edward be as true and just,
As I am subtle, false, and treacherous,
This day should Clarence closely be mew'd up,
About a prophecy, which says that G

26. *spy*] *spie* Qq; *see* Ff. 39. *a prophecy*] *adrohesie* Qq 4, 5.

27. *descant*] The usual meaning of "descant" in music was the art of constructing variations on a simple melody called the "ground" or "plain-song." Richard's deformity is the plain-song of his descant. *New Eng. Dict.* quotes Cotgrave, *s.v. Contre*, "To sing . . . the Plainesong whereon another *descants*." Compare below, III. vii. 49; Edwards, *Damon and Pithias*, 1571, refers to the jests passed on ladies by Aristippus: "They are your playne song to singe *descant* upon"; Lyly, *Euphues*, 1579 (ed. Arber, p. 137): "He that alwayes singeth one note without *deskant* breedeth no delight." In *Eastward Ho*, 1605, Wolf the prison-keeper answers to Touchstone's puns, "Sir, your worship may *descant* as you please o' my name."

29. *entertain . . . days*] Compare *Measure for Measure*, III. i. 75; Sonnet xxxix. 11. Shakespeare uses the word in this act with three different senses, (1) as here; (2) as in I. ii. 257, with which compare *King Lear*, III. vi. 83; (3) as in I. iii. 4, where it corresponds to our phrase "to entertain a hope."

30. Gloucester has expressed this intention previously, *3 Henry VI.* v. vi. 78-9. The soliloquy of the Duke of Epire in Machin and Markham, *Dumb Knight*, 1608, act i., is a recollection of this passage:—

"I am resolv'd, since virtue hath disdain'd
To clothe me in her riches, henceforth to prove
A villain fatal, black and ominous."

32. *inductions*] beginnings, preparations; as below, IV. iv. 5. Compare *1 Henry IV.* III. i. 2; Cook, *Green's Tu Quoque*, c. 1599: "False dice say amen: for that's my *induction*." In drama, the "induction" is the scene or scenes preparatory to a play, like the inductions to *Taming of the Shrew*, or Jonson's *Cynthia's Revels*, or Webster's induction to Marston's *Malcontent*.

38. *mew'd up*] confined, properly of a hawk while mewing (*muer*) or moulting its feathers. It is used again below, line 132 and I. iii. 139. Compare Spenser, *Faerie Queene*, II. iii. 34; *Midsummer-Night's Dream*, I. i. 71; Beaumont and Fletcher, *Woman-Hater*, 1607, iii. 1: "Is this your *mewing-up*, your strict retirement?" The cage was called a "mew": see Chaucer, *Canterbury Tales*, A. 349; *Troilus and Criseyde*, iii. 602. In London, the fact that the royal stables originally were built on the site of the king's mews for hawks, gave rise to the name commonly applied to stables of town houses.

39. *a prophecy*] Compare Halle (ap. Holinshed, iii. 703), "a foolish prophesie,

Of Edward's heirs the murderer shall be.
Dive, thoughts, down to my soul! here Clarence comes.

Enter CLARENCE, *guarded, and* BRAKENBURY.

Brother, good day: what means this armed guard
That waits upon your grace?
Clar. His majesty,
Tendering my person's safety, hath appointed
This conduct, to convey me to the Tower.
Glou. Upon what cause?
Clar. Because my name is George.
Glou. Alack, my lord, that fault is none of yours;
He should for that commit your godfathers.
O, belike his majesty hath some intent
That you shall be new-christ'ned in the Tower.
But what's the matter, Clarence? may I know?
Clar. Yea, Richard, when I know; for I protest
As yet I do not: but, as I can learn,
He hearkens after prophecies and dreams,
And from the cross-row plucks the letter G,

40. *murderer*] *murtherer* Qq 3-8, Ff; *murtherers* Qq 1, 2. 41. *Dive . . . comes*] one line as Ff; two lines Qq, divided after *soule*. *Enter . . . Brakenbury.*] Rowe; *Enter Clarence with a guard of men.* Qq; *Enter Clarence and Brakenbury, guarded.* Ff. 42. *day*] Ff; *dayes* or *daies* Qq. 43-45. *That waits . . . the Tower.*] arranged as Pope; *That waits . . . Grace? His . . . appointed This . . . the Tower* (3 lines) Qq; *That waits . . . Grace? His . . . safety, Hath . . . th' Tower.* Ff. 48. *godfathers*] Qq 1-3, F 1; *good fathers* Qq 4-6; *grandfathers* Ff 2-4. 50. *shall be*] Qq 2-8; *shalbe* Q 1; *should be* Ff. 51. *what 's*] Ff; *whats* Qq 1, 2; *what is* Qq 3-8. 52. *know*] *doe know* Q 6. *for*] Qq; *but* Ff.

which was, that, after K. Edward, one should reigne, whose first letter of his name should be a G." Q 5 follows Q 4 in the extraordinary misprint "adrohesie."

44. *tendering*] having regard to. The word is used about twenty times by Shakespeare, *e.g.* II. iv. 72 below; *Richard II.* I. i. 32; *Hamlet*, I. iii. 107; *Tempest*, II. i. 270: compare *1 Henry IV.* V. iv. 49. See also Lyly, *Euphues* (Arber, 147): "When as I see many fathers more cruell to their children then carefull of them, which thinke it not necessarye to haue those about them, that most *tender* them"; Lodge and Greene, *Looking-Glass for London and England*, 1594 (Dyce, 124): "the duty of lawyers in *tendering* the right cause of their clients."

54. *hearkens after*] Compare *Much Ado About Nothing*, V. i. 216. *New Eng. Dict.* quotes Berners' *Froissart*, i. 303: "There abode styll the Englysshmen to *hearken after* other newes."

prophecies] Malone notes the statements of Philippe de Commines "that the English at that time were never unfurnished with some prophecy or other, by which they accounted for every event."

55. *cross-row*] the alphabet or Christcross-row, so called from the cross which was placed before the alphabet

And says, a wizard told him that by G
His issue disinherited should be:
And, for my name of George begins with G,
It follows in his thought that I am he.
These, as I learn, and such like toys as these,
Have mov'd his highness to commit me now.

Glou. Why, this it is, when men are rul'd by women:
'Tis not the king that sends you to the Tower;
My Lady Grey his wife, Clarence, 'tis she
That tempers him to this extremity.
Was it not she, and that good man of worship,
Anthony Woodville, her brother there,
That made him send Lord Hastings to the Tower,
From whence this present day he is delivered?
We are not safe, Clarence, we are not safe.

Clar. By heaven, I think there is no man secure
But the queen's kindred and night-walking heralds

61. *Have*] Qq, F 4; *Hath* Ff 1-3. 65. *tempers*] Q 1; *tempts* Qq 2, 5-8, Ff; *temps* Qq 3, 4. *this*] Qq; *this harsh* Ff. 71. *secure*] Ff; *is securde* Qq 1-3; *securde* Q 4; *sceurde* Q 5; *secur'd* Q 6.

in horn-books. Cotgrave gives "*La croix de par Dieu:* The Christ's cross row, hornebooke wherein a child learns it." The sixteenth century screen in the tower-arch of Probus Church, Cornwall, is ornamented with a series of small shields in its lower panels, the first of which bears a cross, and the rest the opening letters of the alphabet cut in relief. *New Eng. Dict.* quotes a formula repeated before the alphabet from Morley, *Plaine and Easie Introduction to Practicall Musicke*, 1597: "Christ's crosse be my speede, in all vertue to proceede, A, b, c," etc. Halliwell, *s.v. Christ-Cross*, notes a variant beginning "Christe cross me spede in all my worke." Skelton refers to one or other of these formulas, *Against Venemous Tongues*, ant. 1529 (Chalmers, *English Poets*, ii. 235): "In your *crosse rowe*, nor Christ crosse you spede."

60. *toys*] trifles, idle fancies; very common in all writers of this age. Compare Lyly, *Euphues* (Arber, 208): "They that inuented this *toie* were unwise, and they that reported it vnkinde."

65. *tempers*] Reasons for adopting this reading, peculiar to Q 1, have been given in the Introduction. The queen tempers Edward's will as one tempers or moulds wax: compare for the metaphor *2 Henry IV.* IV. iii. 140: "I have him already *tempering* between my finger and thumb, and shortly will I seal with him." For "temper" in the sense of "govern, control," see Greene, *Friar Bacon* (Dyce, 178):—

"mine art,
Which once I *temper'd* in my secret cell."

67. *Woodville*] pronounced as a trisyllable. The name originally was spelt Wydeville, and a full syllabic value given to the middle *e*. Steevens mentions that, in his day, one of the bearers of the name Woodville pronounced it in this way. "England" and "Henry," among other words, are often found in places where it is necessary to pronounce them as trisyllables, as in Qq readings of IV. iv. 264, IV. ii. 94 below. Compare Chaucer, *Canterbury Tales*, A. 16 "Engelond," A. 389 "Dertemouthe."

That trudge betwixt the king and Mistress Shore.
Heard you not what an humble suppliant
Lord Hastings was to her for his delivery?

Glou. Humbly complaining to her deity
Got my lord chamberlain his liberty.
I 'll tell you what; I think it is our way,
If we will keep in favour with the king,
To be her men and wear her livery.
The jealous o'er-worn widow and herself,
Since that our brother dubb'd them gentlewomen,
Are mighty gossips in this monarchy.

Brak I beseech your graces both to pardon me;
His majesty hath straitly given in charge,
That no man shall have private conference,
Of what degree soever, with his brother.

Glou. Even so; an 't please your worship, Brakenbury,
You may partake of any thing we say.

74. *you*] Ff, Qq 7, 8; *ye* Qq 1-6. 75. *was to her for his*] Qq; *was, for her* F 1; *was, for his* Ff 2, 3; *was for his* F 4. 83. *this*] Qq; *our* Ff. 87. *his*] Qq; *your* Ff. 88. *an 't*] Pope; *and* Qq 1, 2, Ff; *&* Qq 3-6. *Brakenbury*] Ff; *Brokenbury* Qq.

73. *Mistress Shore*] Jane Shore was daughter of a Cheapside mercer and wife of a goldsmith in Lombard Street. More says that she used her influence with the king "to manie a mans comfort and releefe. Where the king tooke displeasure, shee would mitigate and appease his mind: where men were out of fauour, she would bring them in his grace." In 1483 Gloucester, as Protector (see below, III. iv.) accused her of sorcery against his person. No proof being found against her, she was condemned to do penance in St. Paul's for incontinency. She died in poverty c. 1527.

75. *to her for his*] Qq, although adding an extra foot to the line, have the better reading. "For *her* delivery" in Ff can mean only "for delivery at *her* hands," which is strained and awkward.

81. *o'erworn*] Compare Chapman (?), *Alphonsus Emperor of Germany*, 1654, i. 2: "Joachim Carolus, Marquess of Brandenburg, *o'erworn* with age."

82. *gentlewomen*] There was no question of Elizabeth's gentry. Richard brackets her name with that of Mistress Shore in a spirit of malicious insinuation. That erroneous accounts of her origin were current appears from a phrase in the translation of Polydore Vergil (ed. Ellis, 1844, p. 117), where the king is said to have kept his marriage secret "because the woman was of meane caulyng."

83. *gossips*] familiar acquaintances. So *Gammer Gurton's Needle*, 1575, "mother Chat, my *gossip*"; *Midsummer-Night's Dream*, II. i. 47; *Merchant of Venice*, III. i. 9; Jonson, *Bartholomew Fair*, 1614, i. 1: "All the poets and poet-suckers in town . . . are the players' *gossips*." Nares quotes Verstegen for the origin of the word, "Such as undertooke for the child at baptisme, called each other by the name of *Godsib*, that is, of kin together through God." The sense of vulgar familiarity implied by Richard is found in *Piers the Plowman*, B-text, v. 310 (A-text, 152), and Chaucer, *Canterbury Tales*, D. 548. Compare Fr. *compère*, *commère*.

We speak no treason, man; we say the king
Is wise and virtuous, and his noble queen
Well struck in years, fair, and not jealous;
We say that Shore's wife hath a pretty foot,
A cherry lip, a bonny eye, a passing pleasing tongue;
And that the queen's kindred are made gentle-folks:
How say you, sir? can you deny all this?

Brak. With this, my lord, myself have nought to do.

Glou. Naught to do with Mistress Shore? I tell thee, fellow,
He that doth naught with her, excepting one,
Were best to do it secretly alone.

Brak. What one, my lord?

Glou. Her husband, knave: wouldst thou betray me?

Brak. I beseech your grace to pardon me, and withal
Forbear your conference with the noble duke.

92. *jealous*] Qq; *iealious* Ff. 97. *nought*] Qq 1, 6, Ff; *naught* Qq 2-5. 98-100. *Naught . . . alone*] arranged as Qq 1-7; Ff, Q 8 divide thus, *Naught . . . Shore? I tell . . . with her* (*Excepting one*) *. . . alone.* 100. *to do*] Ff, Q 8; *he do* Qq 1-7. 101, 102. *What one . . . betray me?*] omitted Q 1. 103. *beseech*] Qq; *do beseech* Ff. 103, 104. *I beseech . . . noble duke*] arranged as Capell; Qq divide thus, *I beseech . . . forbeare Your . . . Duke;* Ff thus, *I do beseech your Grace To pardon . . . forbeare Your . . . Duke* (3 lines).

92. *struck in years*] Aldis Wright points out that this phrase means "well gone" or "far run" in years. "Struck" is from A.S. *strican* = to go, run: compare Ger. *streichen.* "Strike" is used with this meaning in a lyric poem on *Springtime*, c. 1300 (Morris and Skeat, *Specimens*, new ed. 1879, ii. 48): "Asse streme þat strikeþ stille." Halliwell, *sub* Strike (2) and Streke, gives thirteenth and fourteenth century examples. See *George a Greene*, 1599: "Three men come *striking* through the corn, my love," and *Eastward Ho*, i. 1:—

"prouder hopes, which daringly *o'erstrike*
Their place and means."

Elizabeth could not be said to be "struck in years" or "o'erworn" (line 81). She was about thirty-seven when Edward IV. died. All Richard's remarks are coloured by insinuation.

jealous] a trisyllable. Ff print "iealious." Compare Drayton, *Eng. Her. Epp.* 1597, Mary of France to Charles Brandon, 72: "That we by nature all are *jealous*," where the same pronunciation is necessary.

94. Steevens emended the metre by giving a whole line to "A cherry lip." Pope omitted "a bonny eye." Is it not possible that the line is a snatch from some old song in "fourteen" metre?

94. *bonny*] Compare *2 Henry VI.* v. ii. 12; *Much Ado About Nothing*, II. iii. 69; Greene, *Friar Bacon* (Dyce, 174):—

"May it please your highness give me leave to post
To Fresingfield, I'll fetch the *bonny* girl."

100. *Were best to do it*] The ordinary phrase would be "he . . . were best do it." Compare *Taming of the Shrew*, v. i. 15; Lyly, *Alexander and Campaspe*, iv. 1: "You *were* as good eat my master." The earliest example cited in *New Eng. Dict.* belongs to 1483. Before that time the pronoun was in the dative, "him were best." The reading in Qq is confused and ungrammatical, and I have found no parallel for it.

Clar. We know thy charge, Brakenbury, and will obey.
Glou. We are the queen's abjects, and must obey.
Brother, farewell: I will unto the king,
And, whatsoe'er you will employ me in,
Were it to call King Edward's widow sister,
I will perform it to enfranchise you.
Meantime, this deep disgrace in brotherhood
Touches me deeper than you can imagine.
Clar. I know it pleaseth neither of us well.
Glou. Well, your imprisonment shall not be long;
I will deliver you, or else lie for you:
Meantime, have patience.
Clar. I must perforce: farewell.
[*Exeunt Clarence, Brakenbury, and guard.*
Glou. Go, tread the path that thou shalt ne'er return,
Simple, plain Clarence!—I do love thee so,
That I will shortly send thy soul to heaven,
If heaven will take the present at our hands.
But who comes here? the new-delivered Hastings?

Enter LORD HASTINGS.

Hast. Good time of day unto my gracious lord!
Glou. As much unto my good lord chamberlain!
Well are you welcome to this open air:
How hath your lordship brook'd imprisonment?
Hast. With patience, noble lord, as prisoners must;
But I shall live, my lord, to give them thanks
That were the cause of my imprisonment.

108. *whatsoe'er*] *whatsoe're* Ff; *whatsoeuer* Qq. 115. *or else*] Ff; *or* Qq. *Exeunt . . . guard.*] Capell; *Exit Clar.* (or *Cla.*) Qq, Ff. 124. *this*] Qq 3-8, Ff; *the* Qq 1, 2.

106. *abjects*] used in an exaggerated sense for "subjects." Monck Mason and others explain, "the most servile of her subjects." So Lyly, *Alexander and Campaspe*, i. 1: "You shall not be as *abjects* of war, but as subjects to Alexander." There is a similar play between "abject" and "object" in *Henry VIII*. I. i. 127.

109. *King Edward's widow*] *i.e.* the widow whom King Edward has made his wife.

115. *lie for you*] On their face, the words mean, "lie in prison instead of you." But Gloucester, no doubt, uses "lie" in a double sense. He really means "I will deliver you, or else will tell falsehoods about you." See below, lines 147, 148.

116. *patience . . . perforce*] Steevens sees an allusion to the proverb "*Patience perforce* is a medicine for a mad dog."

Glou. No doubt, no doubt; and so shall Clarence too;
For they that were your enemies are his,
And have prevail'd as much on him as you.
Hast. More pity that the eagle should be mew'd,
While kites and buzzards prey at liberty.
Glou. What news abroad?
Hast. No news so bad abroad as this at home:
The king is sickly, weak, and melancholy;
And his physicians fear him mightily.
Glou. Now, by Saint Paul, that news is bad indeed!
O, he hath kept an evil diet long,
And overmuch consum'd his royal person:
'Tis very grievous to be thought upon.
What, is he in his bed?
Hast. He is.
Glou. Go you before, and I will follow you. [*Exit Hastings.*
He cannot live, I hope, and must not die
Till George be pack'd with post-horse up to heaven.
I'll in, to urge his hatred more to Clarence,
With lies well steel'd with weighty arguments;
And if I fail not in my deep intent,
Clarence hath not another day to live;
Which done, God take King Edward to his mercy,
And leave the world for me to bustle in!

132. *eagle*] Qq; *Eagles* Ff. 133. *While*] Qq; *Whiles* Ff. *prey*] Qq; *play* Ff. 138. *Saint Paul*] Qq; *S. John* Ff. *that*] Ff; *this* Qq. 142. *What, is he*] Qq; *Where is he,* Ff.

136. *sickly*] See below, II. iii. 30, "this *sickly* land," and compare Lyly, *Euphues* (Arber, 227): "Cassander . . . being both aged and *sickly*, found such weaknesse in himselfe, that he thought nature would yeeld to death."

137. *fear*] fear for. *New Eng. Dict.* suggests that the pronoun may originally have been in the dative, like Lat. *timere alicui*, and quotes Berners, *Hystorye of the moost noble and valiaunt Knyght Arthur of lytell Brytayne*, c. 1530 (ed. 1814, p. 213): "Arthur fered his horse, lest that the lyon sholde haue slayne him." See also *Merchant of Venice*, III. v. 3, 33; *1 Henry IV.* IV. i. 24.

139. *evil diet*] So More (ap. Holinshed, iii. 712): "The king his brother (whose life he looked that *euill diet* should shorten)."

148. *steel'd*] pointed with steel, like a lance; and so, armed, fortified. Compare *2 Henry VI.* III. i. 331: "Now, York, or never, *steel* thy fearful thoughts," where, however, "steel" approximates more nearly to the sense of "harden," as "the steeled gaoler" in *Measure for Measure*, IV. ii. 90.

152. *bustle*] busy myself energetically. Compare Lyly, *Alexander and Campaspe*, iv. 1: "See, they begin to flock, and behold my master *bustles* himself to fly"; *Merry Devil of Ed-*

For then I 'll marry Warwick's youngest daughter.
What though I killed her husband and her father?
The readiest way to make the wench amends
Is to become her husband and her father:
The which will I, not all so much for love
As for another secret close intent,
By marrying her which I must reach unto.
But yet I run before my horse to market:
Clarence still breathes; Edward still lives and reigns;
When they are gone, then must I count my gains. [*Exit.*

SCENE II.—*The same. Another street.*

Enter the corpse of KING HENRY VI., *Gentlemen with halberds to guard it;* LADY ANNE *being the mourner.*

Anne. Set down, set down your honourable load—
If honour may be shrouded in a hearse—
Whilst I awhile obsequiously lament
The untimely fall of virtuous Lancaster.
Poor key-cold figure of a holy king!

SCENE II. The same. Another street.] Capell. *Enter . . . mourner*] *Enter the Coarse of Henrie the sixt with Halberds to guard it . . . Mourner.* Ff.; *Enter Lady Anne, with the hearse of Harry the 6.* Qq. 1. *load*] Ff; *l* [rest imperfect] Q 1; *lord* Qq 2-8.

monton, 1617: "Let us alone to *bustle* for the set." In the same play, the keeper Brian uses the word thus:—

"Let me alone to *bustle* with your fathers;
I warrant you that I will keep them play
Till you have quit the Chase."

154. *her husband and her father*] For the traditinal part taken by Richard in the slaying of Prince Edward after Tewkesbury, see below, I. ii. 242, and *3 Henry VI.* v. v. 39: "Her father" cannot mean Warwick. Gloucester commanded the vanguard at Barnet, where Warwick fell; but only in this general sense could he be called Warwick's murderer. On the other hand, he was credited with the murder of Henry VI., Anne's father-in-law. The later Qq use "father" for "father-in-law" below, I. ii. 231; and compare *Romeo and Juliet*, IV. i. 2, etc.

158. *secret close*] The second adjective intensifies the first: compare "secretly alone" above, line 100 For "close" compare below, IV. ii. 35.

Scene II.

3. *obsequiously*] as befits a funeral, mournfully. Compare *3 Henry VI.* II. v. 118. For the more usual and modern sense, see *Merry Wives of Windsor*, IV. ii. 2, and *Othello*, I. i. 46.

5. *key-cold*] as cold as a key, *i.e.* very cold. Aldis Wright quotes Gower, *Confessio Amantis*, vi. 244-7:—

"For certes there was never *keie*
Ne frosen is vpon the walle
More inly *cold*, than I am alle."

Compare *Lucrece*, 1774; Decker, *Seuen Deadly Sinnes of London*, 1606 (Arber, p. 19): "Such fellowes [the porters at the city-gates] are *key-cold* in their comming downe to Strangers, except

Pale ashes of the house of Lancaster!
Thou bloodless remnant of that royal blood!
Be it lawful that I invocate thy ghost,
To hear the lamentations of poor Anne,
Wife to thy Edward, to thy slaught'red son,
Stabb'd by the selfsame hand that made these wounds!
Lo, in these windows that let forth thy life
I pour the helpless balm of my poor eyes.
O cursed be the hand that made these holes!
Cursed the heart that had the heart to do it!
Cursed the blood that let this blood from hence!
More direful hap betide that hated wretch,
That makes us wretched by the death of thee,
Than I can wish to adders, spiders, toads,
Or any creeping venom'd thing that lives!

11. *hand*] Ff; *hands* Qq. *wounds*] Ff; *holes* Qq. 12. *these*] Ff; *those* Qq. 14. *O cursed*] Ff; *Curst* Qq. *these*] Ff; *these fatall* Qq 1, 2; *the fatall* Qq 3-8. 15. *Cursed*] Ff; *Curst be* Qq. 16. *Cursed . . . hence!*] Ff; omitted Qq. 19. *adders*] Qq; *Wolues, to* Ff.

they be brybed." The earliest example in *New Eng. Dict.* is of 1529. Mr. Craig furnishes several examples, *e.g.* John Heywood, *Proverbes*, 1546 (ed. Sharman, 1876, p. 121): "Hot as a toste, it grew cold as a *kay*"; Fletcher, *Wild-Goose Chase*, 1652, iv. 3: "till they be *key-cold* dead, there 's no trusting of 'em."

8. *invocate*] invoke, as *1 Henry VI.* I. i. 52. *New Eng. Dict.* quotes *Institution of a Christian Man*, 1537: "Whensoever I do *invocate* and call upon him in right faith and hope." Compare Milton, *Samson Agonistes*, 1671, 1146:—

"Go to his Temple, *invocate* his aid
With solemnest devotion."

11. *hand*] In line 92 below, Ff apparently fall into the error of printing "hands" for "hand," which in this line they correct.

19. *adders*] In favour of Ff it may be conceded that "any creeping venom'd thing" in the next line does not necessarily refer to the creatures mentioned in this. At the same time, "wolves" is incongruous with "spiders, toads." The alteration in Ff could hardly be a mere editorial conjecture, for which no reason could be alleged but the recurrence of the same syllable in "adders" and "spiders." If, as is likely, the editor of F 1 was conservative in his emendations, the probability is that some intended alteration, begun, but not extended to the whole line, had found its way into the margin of the corrected Q which he used, and was embodied by him in his new text without question. Spedding's view was that Shakespeare had begun such an alteration, intending to change "creeping venom'd things," significant of treacherous and underhand dealing, into words compatible with acts of open violence. This theory is somewhat discounted by the fact that "open violence" is hardly characteristic of a wolf's behaviour. Pickersgill thought that Ff represented Shakespeare's original text, and thus expressed the "blood-thirsty ferocity" of Gloucester by "wolves," and by the rest the loathing which Anne felt for him. For Richard's biting, wolfish nature is insisted upon in these plays. But Qq give us a more consistent reading, whether it be due to Shakespeare or not, which is also more in keeping with the general sense of the passage.

If ever he have child, abortive be it,
Prodigious, and untimely brought to light,
Whose ugly and unnatural aspect
May fright the hopeful mother at the view,
And that be heir to his unhappiness!
If ever he have wife, let her be made
More miserable by the death of him
Than I am made by my young lord and thee!
Come now towards Chertsey with your holy load,
Taken from Paul's to be interred there;
And still, as you are weary of this weight,
Rest you, whiles I lament King Henry's corse.

Enter GLOUCESTER.

Glou. Stay, you that bear the corse, and set it down!
Anne. What black magician conjures up this fiend,
To stop devoted charitable deeds?
Glou. Villains, set down the corse! or, by Saint Paul,
I'll make a corse of him that disobeys!
Gent. My lord, stand back, and let the coffin pass.

25. *And that . . . unhappiness!*] Ff; omitted Qq. 26. *made*] *mad:* Q 6. 27. *More*] Ff; *As* Qq. 28. *Than*] *Then* Ff; *As* Qq. *young*] Ff; *poore* Qq. 31. *weary*] Qq 1, 2, Ff; *a wearie* Qq 3-6. *this*] Ff; *the* Qq. 36. *Villains*] *Villaines* F 1; *Villaine* Qq. 38. *My Lord*] omitted Q 6.

22. *prodigious*] monstrous, unnatural. Compare *King John*, III. I. 46.

25. *unhappiness*] capacity for working mischief. "Unhappy" is mischievous: see *All's Well that Ends Well*, IV. v. 66; and compare Skelton, *Against Venemous Tongues:* "Such tongues *unhappy* hath made great division." Compare Lyly, *Alexander and Campaspe*, v. 4: "I am no thought-catcher, but I guess *unhappily*"; Fletcher and Massinger, *Elder Brother*, 1637, iii. 5: "He speaks *unhappily*"; Wilkins, *Miseries of Inforst Marriage*, 1607, act v.: "I am sure they are greater sinners that made this match, and were *unhappy* men"; Psalm xiv. 7 (Prayer-Book version): "Destruction and *unhappiness* is in their ways."

29, 30. See Holinshed, iii. 690, 691. The body of Henry VI. was "conueied with billes and glaues pompouslie (if you will call that a funerall pompe)" from the Tower to St. Paul's on Ascension Eve, 22nd May, 1471. It remained in St. Paul's during Ascension Day "on a beire or coffen bare faced," where it was reported to have bled in the presence of spectators. It was then taken to the Blackfriars, "and bled there likewise." Next day, it was taken by boat to Chertsey "without priest or clerke, torch or taper, singing or saieng," and was buried in the abbey. Richard III., in August, 1484, removed the body to St. George's Chapel at Windsor. Henry VII. strove to obtain leave from Pope Julius II. for the removal of the body from Windsor to Westminster.

36. *by Saint Paul*] Richard's favourite oath, as above, I. i. 138; below, line 41; III. iv. 78, etc.

Glou. Unmanner'd dog, stand thou when I command!
Advance thy halberd higher than my breast,
Or, by Saint Paul, I 'll strike thee to my foot,
And spurn upon thee, beggar, for thy boldness!
Anne. What, do you tremble? are you all afraid?
Alas, I blame you not; for you are mortal,
And mortal eyes cannot endure the devil.
Avaunt, thou dreadful minister of hell!
Thou hadst but power over his mortal body,
His soul thou canst not have; therefore be gone.
Glou. Sweet saint, for charity, be not so curst.
Anne. Foul devil, for God's sake, hence, and trouble us not!
For thou hast made the happy earth thy hell,
Fill'd it with cursing cries and deep exclaims.
If thou delight to view thy heinous deeds,
Behold this pattern of thy butcheries.
O gentlemen, see, see! dead Henry's wounds

39. *Unmanner'd . . . command*] one line as Qq; two lines Ff, divided after *dog*. *stand*] Qq 1-7, Ff 2-4; *stand'st* F 1, Q 8. 50. *Foul devil . . . us not*] one line as Qq; two lines Ff, divided after *devil*.

39. *Unmanner'd*] unmannerly. So Beaumont and Fletcher, *Faithful Shepherdess*, c. 1609, ii. 4: "I fear I am too much *unmanner'd*, far too rude." Forms of this kind are common in Shakespeare. Compare above, line 20, "venom'd" for "venomous"; *Measure for Measure*, III. i. 121, "delighted" for "delightful"; *ibid.* III. ii. 62, "unshunned" for "unavoidable"; *ibid.* IV. ii. 13, "unpitied" for "pitiless."

49. *curst*] spiteful, cantankerous. *New Eng. Dict.* quotes Coverdale, *Spirit. Perle*, 1550, who calls Xanthippe Socrates' "*curst* and shrewd wife," a phrase repeated by Shakespeare, *Taming of the Shrew*, I. ii. 70. Compare Lodge, *Wounds of Civil War*, 1594, act ii.:—

"No, Sylla, my discourse is resolute,
Not coin'd to please thy fond and *cursed* thoughts";

Marlowe, *Edward II.*, 1594, v. 2: "Speak *curstly* to him." The proverb "God sends a *curst* cow short horns" is quoted in *Much Ado About Nothing*, II. i. 25. Mr. Craig furnishes several instances of references to this proverbial use, *e.g.* North's Plutarch, 1579, *Life of Crassus* (ed. Rouse, 1899, vi. 13): "The manner was then at Rome, if any man had a *curst* bullock that would strike with his horn, to wind hay about his head."

50. *exclaims*] Compare *Richard II.* I. ii. 2; *Troilus and Cressida*, v. iii. 91; Kyd, *Spanish Tragedy*, act iii.:—

"Mine *exclaims*, that have surcharg'd the air
With ceaseless plaints."

54. *pattern*] Compare *Othello*, v. ii. 11; Haughton, *Grim the Collier of Croydon*, c. 1599, act i.: "Stand forth, thou ghastly *pattern* of despair." The use may be illustrated by Machin and Markham, *Dumb Knight*, act iii.: "Ascend, poor model [of] calamity."

55. The current legend was (see note on lines 29, 30) that Henry VI.'s corpse bled in the presence of eye-witnesses. Shakespeare, for dramatic purposes, combines this legend with the common superstition that dead bodies bled in the presence of their murderers. Instances are given by Brand, *Pop.*

Open their congeal'd mouths and bleed afresh.
Blush, blush, thou lump of foul deformity!
For 'tis thy presence that exhales this blood
From cold and empty veins where no blood dwells.
Thy deed, inhuman and unnatural,
Provokes this deluge most unnatural.
O God, which this blood mad'st, revenge his death!
O earth, which this blood drink'st, revenge his death!
Either heav'n with lightning strike the murderer dead,
Or earth, gape open wide and eat him quick,
As thou dost swallow up this good king's blood,
Which his hell-govern'd arm hath butchered!

Glou. Lady, you know no rules of charity,
Which renders good for bad, blessings for curses.

Anne. Villain, thou know'st no law of God nor man:
No beast so fierce but knows some touch of pity.

Glou. But I know none, and therefore am no beast.

Anne. O wonderful, when devils tell the truth!

Glou. More wonderful, when angels are so angry.
Vouchsafe, divine perfection of a woman,

60. *deed*] Qq; *deeds* Ff. 70. *no*] Qq; *nor* Ff. 73. *truth*] *troth* Q 1.

Antiquities, ed. Ellis, new ed. 1901, iii. 229-32. Steevens quotes *Arden of Feversham*, 1592:—

"The more I sound his name, the more he bleeds:
This blood condemns me, and in gushing forth
Speaks as it falls, and asks me why I did it."

Aldis Wright notices Scott's use of the tradition in *Fair Maid of Perth*, 1828, ch. xxiii. See Scott's note on his employment of the legend.

58. *exhales*] draws out. Compare line 165 below. For the simplest sense of the word see Jonson, *Poetaster*, iii. 1: "Nay, I beseech you, gentlemen, do not *exhale* me thus"; and Pistol, *more suo*, in *Henry V.* II. i. 66. The true sense of the Latin derivation, "to breathe out," is overlooked by Shakespeare and his contemporaries: Shakespeare usually applies the word to a meteor or "bright exhalation" *drawn out* of matter by the sun, not *breathed out* in vapour. Compare Lodge and Greene, *Looking-Glass for London* (Dyce, 123):—

"These are but common *exhalations*,
Drawn from the earth";

Decker, *Bel-Man of London*, pref. (Smeaton, 68): "But of such rare temper are your eies, that (as if they had sunne-beames in them) they are able to *exhale* up all these contagious breathes which poison a kingdome."

75-80. Qq seem preferable to Ff. The parallelism of lines 75-77 and 78-80 requires "evils" in line 76, and "a man" in line 78, to give the passage its full weight and balance. On the other hand, Ff, by substituting "Of" instead of "For" in line 79, preserve the balance at the expense of grammar. Either the editor of F 1 was misled by his MS., or attempted in lines 76, 78 metrical emendations on his own account. "Evils," in the first case, has a monosyllabic value: in the second, there was no necessity for giving "infection" its full value of four syllables by cutting the indefinite article out of

Of these supposed evils, to give me leave,
By circumstance but to acquit myself.
Anne. Vouchsafe, defus'd infection of a man,
For these known evils, but to give me leave,
By circumstance to curse thy cursed self.
Glou. Fairer than tongue can name thee, let me have
Some patient leisure to excuse myself.
Anne. Fouler than heart can think thee, thou canst make
No excuse current, but to hang thyself.
Glou. By such despair, I should accuse myself.
Anne. And, by despairing, shouldst thou stand excus'd
For doing worthy vengeance on thyself,
That didst unworthy slaughter upon others.
Glou. Say that I slew them not?
Anne. Why, then they are not dead:
But dead they are, and, devilish slave, by thee.
Glou. I did not kill your husband.
Anne. Why, then he is alive.
Glou. Nay, he is dead, and slain by Edward's hand.

76. *evils*] Qq; *crimes* Ff. 78. *a man*] Qq; *man* Ff. 79. *For*] Qq; *Of* Ff. 83, 84. *Fouler . . . hang thyself*] two lines as Qq; three lines Ff, divided after *thee*, *current*. 86. *shouldst*] Qq; *shalt* Ff. 88. *That*] Ff; *Which* Qq. 89. *Why, then they are not dead*] Qq; *Then say they were not slaine* Ff. 92. *hand*] Qq; *hands* Ff.

the line. In line 79 the MS. is probably entirely to blame; but the editor, if this is the case, ought to have detected its error. Spedding suggested that "curse" in line 80 was to have been altered into "accuse," thus explaining the variation in line 79; but this conjecture applies merely to his own general theory.

77. *By circumstance*] by detailed argument, circumstantially. Compare *Two Gentlemen of Verona*, I. i. 36, 37; *Troilus and Cressida*, III. iii. 114; *Cymbeline*, II. iv. 61.

78. *defus'd*] diffused: *i.e.* spread abroad (compare Milton, *Samson Agonistes*, 118), and so, shapeless. See Mr. Craig's note on *King Lear*, I. iv. 2, and Mr. Hart on *Merry Wives of Windsor*, IV. iv. 55 [54].

78. *infection*] a retort to "perfection" in line 75. The original sense of the word is a "corrupted or diseased condition." *New Eng. Dict.* quotes Burton, *Anatomy of Melancholy*, 1621, I. § i. 3. 1 (ed. Shilleto, 1896, i. 193) [Melancholy is, according to Galen] "a privation or *infection* of the middle cell of the head."

82. *patient*] tranquil. Compare the verbal use of "patient" in *Titus Andronicus*, I. i. 121.

89. *dead*] Qq add to the force of "dead they are" in the next line, and so to that of the whole passage.

92. Holinshed's account (taken from Halle) of Prince Edward's murder (iii. 688) is that Edward IV. "thrust him from him, or (as some saie) stroke him with his gantlet; whom, incontinentlie, George duke of Clarence, Richard duke of Glocester, Thomas Greie marquesse Dorcet, and William lord Hastings, that stood by, suddenlie murthered." See below, lines 241, 242; I. iii. 210-12; I. iv. 52-57. Also compare the scene of

Anne. In thy foul throat thou liest: Queen Margaret saw
Thy murderous falchion smoking in his blood;
The which thou once didst bend against her breast,
But that thy brothers beat aside the point.
Glou. I was provoked by her slanderous tongue,
That laid their guilt upon my guiltless shoulders.
Anne. Thou wast provoked by thy bloody mind,
That never dreamt on ought but butcheries:
Didst thou not kill this king?
Glou. I grant ye.
Anne. Dost grant me, hedge-hog? Then God grant me too
Thou may'st be damned for that wicked deed!
O, he was gentle, mild, and virtuous!
Glou. The better for the King of heaven, that hath him.
Anne. He is in heaven, where thou shalt never come.
Glou. Let him thank me, that holp to send him thither;
For he was fitter for that place than earth.
Anne. And thou unfit for any place but hell.
Glou. Yes, one place else, if you will hear me name it.
Anne. Some dungeon.
Glou. Your bed-chamber.

93. *In thy . . . saw*] one line as Qq; two lines Ff, divided after *ly'st*. 94. *murderous*] *murd'rous* Ff; *bloudy* Qq 1, 2; *bloodly* Qq 3-6. 98, 100. *That*] Ff; *Which* Qq. 100. *dreamt*] Qq; *dream'st* Ff. 101. *ye*] Ff; *yee* Qq 3-8; *yea* Qq 1, 2. 102. *Dost . . . grant me too*] one line as Qq; two lines Ff, divided after *hedge-hog*. 103. *may'st be damned*] Ff; *maiest be damnd* Qq 1, 2; *maiest be damned* Qq 3-6. 105. *better*] Ff; *fitter* Qq. 110. *you*] Qq 1, 2, 6-8, Ff; *ye* Qq 3-5.

the murder, *3 Henry VI*. v. v. 38-40. In *The True Tragedie of Richard Duke of Yorke*, sc. xxi., Edward is the murderer. From the same source, and from no historical authority, comes the story, repeated in *3 Henry VI*., and below, line 95, that Gloucester threatened Queen Margaret's life on the same occasion.

101. Gloucester's admission is in entire keeping with the audacity of his character as Shakespeare designed it. It need hardly be said that it rests on no historical basis. The only authority for Richard's guilt in the case of Henry VI. was "constant fame" (Holinshed, iii. 690).

107. *holp*] For the strong preterite, compare *King John*, I. i. 240; *King Lear*, III. vii. 62. Pope altered it here to "help'd". Kyd, *Spanish Tragedy*, act iii., uses "holp" as past participle, "He runs to kill, whom I have *holp* to catch." Tennyson is fond of this form of the preterite, *e.g. Princess*, i. 198, "and himself . . . *holp* to lace us up."

111. The broken metre emphasises the brevity of Anne's taunt and Gloucester's retort. There is room for a pause between the two, to allow him to recover from the stinging severity of her answer. The proposed emendations—*e.g.* Steevens, "Some dungeon perhaps. *Glou*. Your bed-chamber," in which "dungeon" is a trisyllable—seem to be unnecessary.

Anne. Ill rest betide the chamber where thou liest!
Glou. So will it, madam, till I lie with you.
Anne. I hope so.
Glou. I know so. But, gentle Lady Anne,
To leave this keen encounter of our wits
And fall something into a slower method,
Is not the causer of the timeless deaths
Of these Plantagenets, Henry and Edward,
As blameful as the executioner?
Anne. Thou wast the cause and most accurs'd effect.
Glou. Your beauty was the cause of that effect;
Your beauty, that did haunt me in my sleep
To undertake the death of all the world,
So I might live one hour in your sweet bosom.
Anne. If I thought that, I tell thee, homicide,
These nails should rend that beauty from my cheeks.
Glou. These eyes could not endure that beauty's wrack;
You should not blemish it, if I stood by:
As all the world is cheered by the sun,
So I by that; it is my day, my life.

115. *keen*] Q 1, Ff; *kind* Qq 2-8. 116. *something*] Ff; *somewhat* Qq. 120. *wast*] Ff; *art* Qq. 122. *that*] Ff; *which* Qq. 124. *live*] Ff; *rest* Qq. 126. *rend*] Qq; *rent* Ff. 127. *not*] Ff; *neuer* Qq. *that*] Ff; *sweet* Qq. 128. *it*] Ff; *them* Qq.

116. *slower method*] Steevens explains as "more serious," *i.e.* slow as opposed to "quick" in the sense of "lively." Perhaps "more deliberate" is a better interpretation.

117. *timeless*] untimely. Aldis Wright notices Shakespeare's use of the word in his earliest plays and poems: *e.g. Richard II.* IV. i. 5; *Romeo and Juliet*, V. iii. 162; *Lucrece*, 44. Compare Marlowe, *2 Tamburlaine*, 1590, V. 3: "Let Earth and Heaven his *timeless* death deplore." R. C. Browne, on Milton, *Death of Fair Infant*, line 2 (Clar. Press ed. i. 250), refers to Spenser, *Faerie Queene*, VI. 2. 14, where "knightlesse" = unknightly.

120. *effect*] efficient power, agent. Richard is at once the causer and the executioner of the deaths of Henry and Edward. Malone understood the passage thus. "Effect," meaning "agency, operative influence," is used by Marlowe, *Doctor Faustus*, c. 1588, sc. x.: "none . . . can compare with thee for the rare *effects* of magic"; and *New Eng. Dict.* gives a more recent instance from Sir David Brewster's *Natural Magic*, 1833: "It will act like a concave when the cooling *effect* has reached the axis." In the present line both "cause" and "effect" are used in a concrete sense, to be retorted in the next with their ordinary abstract meaning. Warburton explained "effect" as "executioner," which amounts to the same as Malone's reading; Steevens and Johnson took the word in its usual sense. Hanmer proposed: "Thou wast the cause and most accurs'd th' *effect*."

128. *blemish it*] *i.e.* your beauty, referring to line 126. Qq "them" refers, of course, to "cheeks" in line 126; but Gloucester's mention of his eyes in the previous line makes such a reference ambiguous.

Anne. Black night o'ershade thy day, and death thy life!
Glou. Curse not thyself, fair creature; thou art both.
Anne. I would I were, to be reveng'd on thee.
Glou. It is a quarrel most unnatural,
To be reveng'd on him that loveth thee.
Anne. It is a quarrel just and reasonable,
To be reveng'd on him that kill'd my husband.
Glou. He that bereft thee, lady, of thy husband,
Did it to help thee to a better husband.
Anne. His better doth not breathe upon the earth.
Glou. He lives that loves thee better than he could.
Anne. Name him.
Glou. Plantagenet.
Anne. Why, that was he.
Glou. The self-same name, but one of better nature.
Anne. Where is he?
Glou. Here. [*She spitteth at him.*
Why dost thou spit at me?
Anne. Would it were mortal poison, for thy sake!
Glou. Never came poison from so sweet a place.
Anne. Never hung poison on a fouler toad.
Out of my sight! thou dost infect mine eyes.
Glou. Thine eyes, sweet lady, have infected mine.
Anne. Would they were basilisks, to strike thee dead!

131. *o'ershade*] *ore-shade* Ff; *ouershade* or *ouershad* Qq. 132. *Curse not . . . both*] one line as Qq; two lines Ff, divided after *creature*. 135. *thee*] Ff; *you* Qq. 137. *kill'd*] Ff; *slew* Qq. 141. *He*] Ff; *Go to, he* Qq. *thee* Ff; *you* Qq. 142. *that*] Qq 1, 2, Ff; *what* Qq 3-8. 148. *mine*] Ff; *my* Qq,

141. *He lives*] Qq "go to" at the beginning of the line may have been an ejaculation added on the stage, which found its way into theatrical MSS. and so into the text. In Qq, the murderers' conversation in I. iv. is full of such expletives and interjections. See also line 187 below.

150. *basilisks*] In popular superstition, the basilisk was a creature "with legs, wings, a serpentine and winding tail, and a crest or comb somewhat like a cock." It was the offspring of a cock's egg, hatched under a toad or serpent, and had the power of killing at a distance with the poison of its eye. See Sir T. Browne, *Pseud. Epid.*, 1646. iii. 7, where also the real basilisk is described, a small serpent distinguished by its habit of "advancing his head," and by "some white marks or coronary spots on the crown," which gave it its name of *basiliscus* (Vulgate, Ps. xci. 13) or *regulus* (Prov. xxiii. 32). Gloucester (*3 Henry VI.* III. ii. 187) says he will "slay more gazers than the *basilisk*." See also *2 Henry VI.* III. ii. 52, 324; *Cymbeline*, II. iv. 107; *Winter's Tale*, I. ii. 388. Compare Jonson, pref. speech to *Poetaster*:—

"Are there no players here? no
poet-apes,

Glou. I would they were, that I might die at once;
For now they kill me with a living death.
Those eyes of thine from mine have drawn salt tears,
Sham'd their aspects with store of childish drops—
These eyes, which never shed remorseful tear,
No, when my father York and Edward wept
To hear the piteous moan that Rutland made
When black-fac'd Clifford shook his sword at him;
Nor when thy warlike father like a child
Told the sad story of my father's death,
And twenty times made pause to sob and weep,
That all the standers-by had wet their cheeks,
Like trees bedash'd with rain—in that sad time
My manly eyes did scorn an humble tear;
And what these sorrows could not thence exhale
Thy beauty hath, and made them blind with weeping.
I never sued to friend nor enemy;
My tongue could never learn sweet smoothing word:
But, now thy beauty is propos'd my fee,
My proud heart sues, and prompts my tongue to
speak. [*She looks scornfully at him.*
Teach not thy lip such scorn, for it was made
For kissing, lady, not for such contempt.

154. *aspects*] Ff; *aspect* Qq. 155-166. *These eyes . . . weeping*] Ff; omitted Qq. 168. *smoothing*] Ff, Qq 7, 8; *soothing* Qq 1-6. *word*] Ff; *words* Qq. 170. *She looks . . .*] Ff; omitted Qq. 171. *lip*] Ff; *lips* Qq. *it was*] Ff; *they were* Qq.

That come with *basilisk's* eyes, whose forked tongues
Are steep'd in venom, as their hearts in gall";

Fletcher, *False One*, iv. 2:—

"I will . . . put a look on, arm'd with all my cunning,
Shall meet him like a *basilisk*, and strike him."

Lodge, *Wounds of Civil War*, act ii., speaking of the kind of cannon called, for obvious reasons, a basilisk, carries out the metaphor in detail:—

". . . these Roman *basilisks*,
That seek to quell us with their currish looks."

157. *Rutland*] second son of Richard, Duke of York. For his supposed murder by John, Lord Clifford, after the battle of Wakefield, see *3 Henry VI.* I. iii. York's tears at the news (line 156) are recorded *ibid.* I. iv. 147. The tidings were brought to Edward and Gloucester on the field of Mortimer's Cross (*ibid.* II. i.). Warwick (line 159) does not bring them in Shakespeare, but enters after they have been told. Gloucester's indignation at the news forbade him to weep. Once, however, in *3 Henry VI.* (II. iii. 46) he is allowed to "shed remorseful tear," when the prospect at Towton is unpromising for the Yorkist party.

168. *smoothing*] flattering. See below, I. iii. 48, and *2 Henry VI.* I. i. 156.

If thy revengeful heart cannot forgive,
Lo, here I lend thee this sharp-pointed sword,
Which if thou please to hide in this true breast,
And let the soul forth that adoreth thee,
I lay it naked to the deadly stroke,
And humbly beg the death upon my knee.
[*He lays his breast open: she offers at it with his sword.*
Nay, do not pause: for I did kill King Henry;
But 'twas thy beauty that provoked me.
Nay, now dispatch: 'twas I that stabb'd young Edward;
But 'twas thy heavenly face that set me on.
[*Here she lets fall the sword.*
Take up the sword again, or take up me.

Anne. Arise, dissembler: though I wish thy death,
I will not be thy executioner.

Glou. Then bid me kill myself, and I will do it.

Anne. I have already.

Glou. That was in thy rage.
Speak it again; and, even with the word,
This hand, which, for thy love, did kill thy love,
Shall, for thy love, kill a far truer love:
To both their deaths shalt thou be accessary.

Anne. I would I knew thy heart.

Glou. 'Tis figur'd in my tongue.

Anne. I fear me, both are false.

175. *breast*] Ff; *bosom* Qq. 177. *the*] *thy* Qq 6-8, F 3. aft. 178. *He lays . . . at it . . . sword.*] F (*at* F 1); omitted Qq. 179. *for I . . . Henry*] Ff; *twas I that kild your husband* Qq. 181. *stabb'd young Edward*] Ff; *kild King Henry* Qq. aft. 182. *lets fall*] Qq; *fals* Ff. 185. *thy*] Ff; *the* Qq. 187. *That*] Ff; *Tush, that* Qq. *thy*] *the* Qq 3-7. 189. *This*] Ff; *That* Qq. 191. *shalt thou*] Q 1, Ff; *thou shalt* Qq 2-8.

178. *the death*] death after judicial sentence, as St. Mark vii. 10: "He that curseth father or mother, let him die *the death*." See *Henry V.* IV. i. 181; *Measure for Measure*, II. iv. 165; Chapman (?), *Alphonsus*, v. 2: "Thou shalt obtain thy boon and die *the death*."

183. The line recalls the first part of *Jeronimo*, c. 1587 (Dodsley, 1825, iii. 68): "Take up thy pen, or I 'll take up thee."

192-201. Steevens arranged these lines in more or less regular blank verse; his lines end "figur'd in . . . man . . . sword . . . know . . . men . . . ring" (Camb.). His divisions are out of keeping with those characteristic of this period of Shakespeare's work; and their metrical accuracy is open to criticism.

Glou. Then never man was true.
Anne. Well, well, put up your sword.
Glou. Say then my peace is made.
Anne. That shalt thou know hereafter.
Glou. But shall I live in hope?
Anne. All men, I hope, live so.
Glou. Vouchsafe to wear this ring.
Anne. To take is not to give.
Glou. Look, how my ring encompasseth thy finger:
Even so thy breast encloseth my poor heart;
Wear both of them, for both of them are thine.
And if thy poor devoted servant may
But beg one favour at thy gracious hand,
Thou dost confirm his happiness for ever.
Anne. What is it?
Glou. That it may please you leave these sad designs
To him that hath most cause to be a mourner,
And presently repair to Crosby Place;
Where, after I have solemnly interr'd
At Chertsey monast'ry this noble king,

195. *man was*] Qq 3-8, Ff; *was man* Qq 1, 2. 198. *shalt thou*] Ff; *shall you* Qq. 199. *shall I*] Q 1, Ff; *I shall* Qq 2-8. 201. *Glou.*] Qq; omitted Ff. 202. *Anne. To . . . give*] La. *To . . . give* Qq; omitted Ff. 203. *my*] F 1; *this* Qq; *thy* Ff 2-4. *thy finger*] Qq, F 1; *my finger* Ff 2-4. 206. *devoted*] Q 1, Ff; omitted Qq 2-8. *servant*] Ff; *suppliant* Qq. 210. *may*] Ff; *would* Qq. *you*] Ff; *thee* Qq. 211. *most*] Ff; *more* Qq. 212. *Place*] Qq; *House* Ff.

201. Ff continue this line from Anne's speech in the line before, and omit line 202 altogether. This omission may be attributed to a quite comprehensible printer's error. The passage, as printed, would have read thus:—

> *An.* All men, I hope, live so.
> *Rich.* Vouchsafe to wear this ring.
> *Rich.* Look, how my ring, etc.

In the final revision of F 1, it seems probable that the error was altered summarily: the first *Rich.* was struck out, and the line was set back so that the V of "Vouchsafe" ranged immediately below the A of "*An.*" The sense was confused by this hasty emendation.

212. *presently*] immediately, as III. i. 34 below; *Julius Cæsar*, III. i. 28; Philippians ii. 23: "Him therefore I hope to send *presently*."

212. *Crosby Place*] See Stow, *Survey*, ed. Strype, 1720, I. pt. ii. p. 106. The site of Crosby Place or House (now called Crosby Hall) was leased in 1466 to Sir John Crosby by the prioress and convent of St. Helen's. The house, fronting on Bishopsgate Street Within, was built by Sir John, "of stone and timber, very large and beautiful, and the highest at that time in London." Sir John was alive at the time of the burial of Henry VI. Later, "Richard, Duke of Gloucester, and lord protector, was lodged in this house," which, in Shakespeare, is the centre from which he works his plots. See below, I. iii. 345, etc.

And wet his grave with my repentant tears,
I will with all expedient duty see you.
For divers unknown reasons, I beseech you,
Grant me this boon.

Anne. With all my heart; and much it joys me too
To see you are become so penitent.
Tressel and Berkeley, go along with me.

Glou. Bid me farewell.

Anne. 'Tis more than you deserve;
But, since you teach me how to flatter you,
Imagine I have said farewell already.
[*Exeunt Lady Anne, Tressel, and Berkeley*

Glou. Sirs, take up the corse.

Gent. Towards Chertsey, noble lord?

Glou. No, to White-Friars; there attend my coming.
[*Exeunt all but Gloucester*
Was ever woman in this humour woo'd?
Was ever woman in this humour won?
I'll have her, but I will not keep her long.
What! I, that kill'd her husband and his father,
To take her in her heart's extremest hate,
With curses in her mouth, tears in her eyes,
The bleeding witness of her hatred by,

aft. 224. *Exeunt . . .*] *Exit two with Anne.* Ff; *Exit.* Qq. 225. *Glou. Sirs . . . corse*] Qq; omitted Ff. aft. 227. *Exeunt . . .*] *Exit Coarse.* Ff; *Exeunt. Manet Glo.* Qq (aft. 228). 231. *What! I*] *What? I* Ff; *What I* Qq 1, 2, 5, 6; *What I?* Qq 3, 4. *his*] Qq 1, 2, Ff; *her* Qq 3-8. 232. *hate*] Q 1, Ff; *heate* Qq 2-8. 234. *her*] Qq; *my* Ff.

224. *farewell already*] After these words, Cibber, regarding the whole scene as in need of some safeguard against criticism, added a remark by Tressel:—

"When future chronicles shall speak of this,
This will be thought romance, not history."

227. *White-Friars*] The chroniclers give *Black*friars as the intermediate stage of Henry's obsequies.

228, 229. Kindred passages are found in *Titus Andronicus*, II. i. 82, 83, and *1 Henry VI.* v. iii. 77, 78. The origin of this effective dramatic tag may spring from the earlier of these passages, or from some previous play. See also the quotation from Greene in Mr. Baildon's edition of *Titus Andronicus*, 1904, p. 32.

234. *her hatred*] Qq reading is preferable. Henry's bleeding wounds bore witness to the justice of Anne's hatred. Spedding defends Ff by saying that Henry's corpse was the "*motive* or *ground* of Anne's hatred of Richard, whereas it was really the *witness* of Richard's hatred of her father-in-law." The difference between the readings lies in the sense which "witness" is made to bear.

Having God, her conscience, and these bars against
me,
And I no friends to back my suit withal
But the plain devil and dissembling looks—
And yet, to win her, all the world to nothing!
Ha!
Hath she forgot already that brave prince,
Edward her lord, whom I, some three months since,
Stabb'd in my angry mood at Tewkesbury?
A sweeter and a lovelier gentleman,
Fram'd in the prodigality of nature,
Young, valiant, wise, and, no doubt, right royal,
The spacious world cannot again afford:
And will she yet abase her eyes on me,
That cropp'd the golden prime of this sweet prince,
And made her widow to a woful bed—
On me, whose all not equals Edward's moiety—
On me, that halt and am unshapen thus?
My dukedom to a beggarly denier,
I do mistake my person all this while!
Upon my life, she finds, although I cannot,
Myself to be a marvellous proper man.

236. *no friends*] Ff; *nothing* Qq. *withal*] Qq 3-8, Ff; *at all* Qq 1, 2. 247. *abase*] Ff; *debase* Qq. 251. *halt*] Qq; *halts* Ff. 252. *to*] *to be* Qq 5-8.

241. *three months since*] In reality, Tewkesbury was fought on 4th May; Henry was buried on 23rd May, 1471.

244. *the prodigality of nature*] nature's most prodigal mood. Holinshed (iii. 688) speaks of Prince Edward as "a faire and well proportioned yoong gentleman."

245. *valiant*] must be read as a full trisyllable for the sake of metre. For alterations like Pope's "wise and valiant" there is no need.

245. *royal*] "It is hard to believe that this is what Shakespeare wrote" (Aldis Wright). But why? Gloucester means that Edward no doubt was royal by nature, and not merely by birth—handsome, young, brave, wise, in every respect fit to be a king. Steevens' suggestion that the word contains a sneer at Edward's legitimacy is possible, but is not needed to make sense; while Johnson's emendation "loyal" (*i.e.* to his wife) does not improve matters.

252. *denier*] A small copper coin, equivalent to the twelfth part of a *sou* or the "tenth part of an English pennie" (Cotgrave); Lat. *denarius*. Compare *Taming of the Shrew*, Ind. i. 9; Fletcher, *Monsieur Thomas*, 1639, i. 2:—

"No money, no more money,
Monsieur Launcelot,
Not a *denier*, sweet signior."

The first quotation in *New Eng. Dict.* is c. 1425. "Denier" is also equivalent to a pennyweight in Troy weight.

255. *proper*] handsome, well-liking: compare *Taming of the Shrew*, I. ii. 144; *As You Like It*, I. ii. 129.

I'll be at charges for a looking-glass,
And entertain a score or two of tailors
To study fashions to adorn my body:
Since I am crept in favour with myself,
I will maintain it with some little cost.
But first I'll turn yon fellow in his grave,
And then return lamenting to my love.
Shine out, fair sun, till I have bought a glass,
That I may see my shadow as I pass. [*Exit.*

SCENE. III.—*The Palace.*

Enter QUEEN ELIZABETH, LORD RIVERS, *and* LORD GREY.

Riv. Have patience, madam: there's no doubt his majesty
Will soon recover his accustom'd health.
Grey. In that you brook it ill, it makes him worse:
Therefore, for God's sake, entertain good comfort,
And cheer his grace with quick and merry words.
Q. Eliz. If he were dead, what would betide on me?
Riv. No other harm but loss of such a lord.
Q. Eliz. The loss of such a lord includes all harms.
Grey. The heavens have bless'd you with a goodly son,
To be your comforter when he is gone.
Q. Eliz. Ah! he is young; and his minority

257. *a*] Ff; *some* Qq. 258. *adorn*] *adore* Qq 3-6. 260. *some*] *a* Qq 3-8.

Scene III.

SCENE *III.* *The Palace.*] Theobald. *Queen Elizabeth*] *Queene* Qq; *Queene Mother* Ff. 5. *words*] Qq; *eyes* Ff. 6. *on*] Ff; *of* Qq. 8. *harms* Ff; *harme* Qq. 11. *Ah*] Ff; *Oh* Qq.

256. *at charges*] at the expense. Compare Chapman, *An Humorous Day's Mirth*, 1599 (ed. Shepherd, 1874, p. 42): "Here's the poor man hath been *at great charges* for the preparation of a lottery." For the use of "charge, charges," in the sense of "expense, cost," see Jonson, *Cynthia's Revels*, 1600, i. 1: "*Amo.* . . . your travel is your only thing that rectifies . . . *Aso.* I think it be great *charge* though, sir"; Marston, *Malcontent*, 1604, act iii.: "Madam, I am going embassador for Florence; 'twill be great *charges* to me"; 1 Maccabees iii. 30: "He feared that he should not be able to bear the *charges* any longer."

Scene III.

5. *quick*] lively: compare *Love's Labour's Lost*, v. ii. 283; *Antony and Cleopatra*, v. ii. 216; Jonson, *Cynthia's Revels*, iv. 1: "This tire, methinks, makes me look very ingeniously, *quick*, and spirited." See also line 196 below.

Is put unto the trust of Richard Gloucester,
A man that loves not me, nor none of you.
Riv. Is it concluded he shall be protector?
Q. Eliz. It is determin'd, not concluded yet;
But so it must be, if the king miscarry.

Enter BUCKINGHAM *and* DERBY.

Grey. Here come the lords of Buckingham and Derby.
Buck. Good time of day unto your royal grace!
Der. God make your majesty joyful as you have been!
Q. Eliz. The Countess Richmond, good my lord of Derby,
To your good prayer will scarcely say amen.
Yet, Derby, notwithstanding she's your wife
And loves not me, be you, good lord, assur'd
I hate not you for her proud arrogance.
Der. I do beseech you, either not believe
The envious slanders of her false accusers;

14. *Is it*] *It is* Q 6. aft. 16. *Derby*] *Stanley* Theobald (*passim*). 17. *come the lords*] Qq 1, 2; *comes the Lords* Qq 3-8; *comes the Lord* Ff. 21. *prayer*] Ff; *prayers* Qq. 24. *arrogance*] Qq 1, 2, Ff; *arrogancie* Qq 3-8. 25. *do*] Qq 1, 2, Ff; omitted Qq 3-8. 26. *false*] Qq 1, 2, Ff; omitted Qq 3-8.

15. *determin'd, not concluded*] The matter is settled, but the official formalities are not completed. Aldis Wright notes that at Trinity College, Cambridge, the official entries of decisions arrived at by the Master and Seniors are entered in a book called the Conclusion Book. A treaty is determined before it is officially concluded. So *Merry Devil of Edmonton*:—

"... After we'll *conclude*
The cause of this our coming,"

i.e. the betrothal.

16. *miscarry*] Compare *Measure for Measure*, III. i. 218; Chapman, *All Fools*, 1605, i. 1:—

"How would his father grieve, should he be maim'd,
Or quite *miscarry* in the ruthless war."

17. *come the lords*] The Ff reading is either due to the printer, or, which is hardly credible, reintroduces an error of the MS. which the editor employed. It seems likely that the original reading had the old plural "comes the lords," like the quartos from Q 3 onwards; that the editor of F 1 found this both in his Q and the MS. by which he checked it; and that the printer eventually altered "lords" into "lord," perhaps assuming that Buckingham and Derby were two titles of the same person, and certainly anxious to get rid of the plural meaning of "comes."

20. *Countess Richmond*] Margaret Beaufort (1443-1509), daughter and heiress of John Beaufort, first Duke of Somerset, and great-grand-daughter of John of Gaunt. She married in 1455 Edmund Tudor (d. 1456), Earl of Richmond, son of Owen Tudor and Katharine, widow of Henry V. By him she had Henry Tudor, afterwards Henry VII. She married secondly, Lord Henry Stafford, a son of the first Duke of Buckingham, and uncle of the Buckingham of this play. Her third husband was Thomas, Lord Stanley.

25. *not believe*] Compare "not equals" above, I. ii. 250.

26. *atonement*] reconciliation, setting at one (at-one-ment). Compare *2 Henry IV.* IV. i. 221; More (ap. Holinshed, iii. 714): "hauing more regard to their old variance, than their new

Or, if she be accus'd on true report,
Bear with her weakness, which, I think, proceeds
From wayward sickness, and no grounded malice.

Riv. Saw you the king to-day, my lord of Derby?

Der. But now the Duke of Buckingham and I
Are come from visiting his majesty.

Q. Eliz. What likelihood of his amendment, lords?

Buck. Madam, good hope; his grace speaks cheerfully.

Q. Eliz. God grant him health! Did you confer with him?

Buck. Ay, madam: he desires to make atonement
Between the Duke of Gloucester and your brothers,
And between them and my lord chamberlain,
And sent to warn them to his royal presence.

Q. Eliz. Would all were well!—but that will never be.
I fear our happiness is at the height.

Enter GLOUCESTER, HASTINGS, *and* DORSET.

Glou. They do me wrong, and I will not endure it.
Who are they that complain unto the king,
That I, forsooth, am stern and love them not?
By holy Paul, they love his grace but lightly,
That fill his ears with such dissentious rumours!
Because I cannot flatter and look fair,
Smile in men's faces, smooth, deceive, and cog,

27. *on*] Ff; *in* Qq. 32. *Are come*] Ff; *Came* Qq. 33. *What*] Qq 3-8, Ff; *With* Qq 1, 2. 36. *Ay, Madam*] *I Madam* Ff; *Madam we did* Qq. 37. *Between*] Ff; *Betwixt* Qq. 38. *between*] Ff; *betwixt* Qq. 39. *to his*] *of his* Q 6. 41. *height*] Ff; *highest* Qq. 43. *are they*] Qq; *is it* Ff. *complain*] Q 8; *complaines* Qq 1-7, Ff. 47. *look*] Ff; *speak* Qq.

attonement." See also *Antony and Cleopatra*, II. ii. 102; Fletcher and Massinger, *Spanish Curate*, 1622, iii. 4: "I have been *atoning* two most wrangling neighbours." For an intransitive use see *Coriolanus*, IV. vi. 72:—

"He and Aufidius can no more *atone*
Than violentest contrariety."

39. *warn*] summon, as *King John*, II. i. 201.

43. "Complaines" in Qq 1-7 is not a singular, but the old plural form. Ff seem to attempt to modernise the grammar. This might be taken as a return to an original MS. reading; but the tell-tale "them," which has been overlooked in the next line, is against this theory.

48. *Smooth*] See note on I. ii. 168 above. Theobald suggested "sooth."

cog] used originally of cheating at dice. A common word. *New Eng. Dict.* quotes *Dice Play*, 1532: "There be divers kinds of cogging, but of all other the Spanish *cogg* bears the bell, and seldom raises any smoke." Compare *Love's Labour's Lost*, V. ii. 235: "Since you can *cog*, I'll play no more with you." Mr. Craig notes that, in Ireland, "to cog" is used by schoolboys

Duck with French nods and apish courtesy,
I must be held a rancorous enemy.
Cannot a plain man live and think no harm,
But thus his simple truth must be abus'd
With silken, sly, insinuating Jacks?

Grey. To whom in all this presence speaks your grace?

Glou. To thee, that hast nor honesty nor grace:
When have I injur'd thee? when done thee wrong?
Or thee? or thee? or any of your faction?
A plague upon you all! His royal person—
Whom God preserve better than you would wish!—
Cannot be quiet scarce a breathing-while,
But you must trouble him with lewd complaints.

Q. Eliz. Brother of Gloucester, you mistake the matter.
The king, on his own royal disposition,

52. *his*] *in* Qq 5-8. 53. *With*] Ff; *By* Qq. 54. *Grey*] Ff (*Gray* Ff 3, 4); *Ri.* or *Ry.* Qq. *whom*] *who* F 1; *home* Q 6. *all*] omitted Qq 6-8. 58. *person*] Qq; *grace* Ff. 63. *on*] Ff; *of* Qq.

in the sense of "to copy work from another" at an examination, and that a "cog" is used of a translation from a classical author, like the English "crib."

49. *French nods and apish courtesy*] In Decker, *Seuen Deadly Sinnes of London* (Arber, 35), the fifth sin is "Apishnesse," the sin of "counterfetting or imitation." "Much about the year when *Monsieur* came in, was hee begotten, betweene a French Tayler, and an English Court-Seamster." François, Duke of Alençon, and, after 1574, Duke of Anjou and, by courtesy, Monsieur de France, the youngest son of Henry II. and Caterina de' Medici, visited England in 1579 and 1581 as a suitor to Elizabeth, and was regarded for a time as her prospective husband. The popular attitude to the foreign marriage is gauged by such allusions as these, which, written several years after the event, retain the deep impression which it created. Compare *Eastward Ho*: "dost thou think our Englishmen are so Frenchified, that a man knows not whether he be in France or in England, when he sees 'hem?"; Fletcher, *Monsieur Thomas*, i. 2: "Sirrah, no more of your French shrugs, I advise you."

53. *Jacks*] Used contemptuously: low-bred fellows. Compare *1 Henry IV.* II. iv. 12; *Romeo and Juliet*, II. iv. 160; Wilkins, *Miseries of Inforst Marriage*, act i.: "Now death of me, shall I be crossed by such a *jack?*"; act v.: "Peace, saucy *Jack*." See also the conversation in Martin Marprelate, *Epistle*, 1588 (Arber, 20), between John Aylmer, Bishop of London, and one Madox: "That is my meaning, ka dumb Iohn, and I tell thee Madox that thou art but a *Iacke* to use me so: Master Madox replying sayd that in deed his name was Iohn, and if euery Iohn were a Iacke, he was content to bee a Iacke (there he hit my L[ord] ouer the thumbs)."

63-69. *The king . . . remove it*] The meaning of the sentence is obvious; but the grammar is hopelessly confused. The words "royal disposition" have deposed "the king" from its place as the true nominative. The words "Aiming . . . hatred" are intended to qualify "royal disposition"; the "interior hatred" of Gloucester being the antithesis to the royal nature of the king. Elizabeth goes on to explain how this hatred shows itself. But she loses the thread of her sentence; and, when she comes to her verb, the "royal disposition" is

And not provok'd by any suitor else—
Aiming, belike, at your interior hatred,
That in your outward action shows itself
Against my children, brothers, and myself,
Makes him to send, that thereby he may gather
The ground of your ill-will, and so remove it.

Glou. I cannot tell: the world is grown so bad,
That wrens make prey where eagles dare not perch.
Since every Jack became a gentleman,
There's many a gentle person made a Jack.

Q. Eliz. Come, come, we know your meaning, brother Gloucester;
You envy my advancement and my friends'.
God grant we never may have need of you!

Glou. Meantime, God grants that we have need of you!
Our brother is imprison'd by your means,
Myself disgrac'd, and the nobility
Held in contempt, while great promotions
Are daily given to ennoble those
That scarce, some two days since, were worth a noble.

66. *That*] Ff; *Which* Qq. *action*] Ff; *actions* Qq. 67. *children*] Ff; *kindred* Qq. *brothers*] Ff; *brother* Qq. 68, 69. *that thereby . . . The ground . . . so remove it*] Steevens; *that thereby . . . The ground . . . to remove it* Qq 1-5; *that thereby . . . The grounds . . . to remove it* Q 6; *that he may learne the ground* Ff; *whereby . . . The ground . . . to remove it* Qq 7, 8. 71. *make*] Qq 1, 2, Ff; *may* Qq 3-6. 75. *my*] Q 1, Ff; *mine* Qq 2-8. 77. *grants*] Qq 1, 2, Ff; *grant* Qq 3-8. *we*] Qq; *I* Ff. 80. *while*] Ff; *whilst* Qq. *great*] Ff; *many faire* Qq.

uppermost in her mind, and becomes the subject of the sentence. Abbott, *Shakespearian Grammar*, § 413, quotes *Cymbeline*, v. v. 344, 345:—

"Beaten for loyalty
Excited me to treason";

but the case does not seem exactly parallel. In behalf of Qq, Aldis Wright quotes the Prayer-Book version of Ps. lxxxviii. 81: "That they might put their trust in God, and not to forget," etc. Ff seem to adopt a summary method of emendation by removing the main difficulty. If, on Mr. Daniel's theory, the editor of F 1 used a copy of Q 6, the plural "grounds" in line 69 would have complicated the problem which he thus solved. Even if the involved construction of the speech is due to hasty writing, it is exactly the agitated and incoherent defence which a woman would make, face to face with a dangerous enemy, and powerless against his insinuations.

72. *every Jack*] "Jack" (see note on line 53 above) is here used in the original sense of peasant: compare John Heywood, *Proverbes* (Sharman, 61): "*Jacke* would be a gentleman, if he could speake French" (Craig).

77. *need of you*] Gloucester plays on the double meaning of "need." Elizabeth has prayed that she and her family may never be under the necessity of asking his help. He rejoins that he and his friends are in necessity owing to her intrigues.

Q. Eliz. By Him that rais'd me to this careful height
From that contented hap which I enjoy'd,
I never did incense his majesty
Against the Duke of Clarence, but have been
An earnest advocate to plead for him!
My lord, you do me shameful injury,
Falsely to draw me in these vile suspects.
Glou. You may deny that you were not the mean
Of my Lord Hastings' late imprisonment.
Riv. She may, my lord, for——
Glou. She may, Lord Rivers! why, who knows not so?
She may do more, sir, than denying that:
She may help you to many fair preferments,
And then deny her aiding hand therein,
And lay those honours on your high desert.
What may she not? she may, ay, marry, may she,—
Riv. What, marry, may she?
Glou. What, marry, may she! marry with a king,
A bachelor and a handsome stripling too:
I wis your grandam had a worser match.
Q. Eliz. My Lord of Gloucester, I have too long borne
Your blunt upbraidings and your bitter scoffs:
By heaven, I will acquaint his majesty
Of those gross taunts that oft I have endur'd!
I had rather be a country servant-maid

90. *mean*] Ff; *cause* Qq. 92. *lord, for*—] Ff; *Lord* Qq. 97. *desert*] Ff; *deserts* Qq. 98. *ay*] *I* Ff; *yea* Qq. 101. *and*] Ff; omitted Qq. 106. *Of*] Ff; *With* Qq. *that oft I*] Ff; *I often* Qq.

83. *careful*] full of trouble. Compare Lyly, *Euphues* (Arber, 65): "Thou hast hetherto founde me a cheerefull companion in thy myrth, and nowe shalt thou finde me as *carefull* with thee in thy moane"; Lodge, *Wounds of Civil War*, act v.: "the coverts of my *carefull* eyes."

89. *draw me in*] Compare Wilkins, *Miseries of Inforst Marriage*, act ii.: "Draw all her soul in th' compass of an oath."

suspects] suspicions, as *2 Henry VI.* III. ii. 139; Marlowe, *Edward II.* 1594, act iv.: "Free from *suspect*, and fell invasion."

90. *deny that you were not*] For the intensified negative, *New Eng. Dict.* quotes Captain Smith, *Virginia*, 1624, iv. 157: "Taxing the poore king of treason, who denied to the death not to know of any such matter."

102. *I wis*] certainly. See Mr. Pooler's note on *Merchant of Venice*, ii. ix., 68. The O.E. form "iwis" (= A.S. *gewis*: compare German *gewiss*) is found as early as the twelfth century; see Morris, *Specimens of E. Eng.* i. 2nd ed. 1898, p. 32: "Mi fleis is *wis* mete, and mi blod *iwis* drinke."

102. *worser*] So *Hamlet*, III. iv. 157, etc.

Riv. My Lord of Gloucester, in those busy days,
Which here you urge to prove us enemies,
We follow'd then our lord, our sovereign king:
So should we you, if you should be our king.
Glou. If I should be! I had rather be a pedlar:
Far be it from my heart, the thought thereof!
Q. Eliz. As little joy, my lord, as you suppose
You should enjoy, were you this country's king,
As little joy you may suppose in me
That I enjoy, being the queen thereof.
Q. Mar. A little joy enjoys the queen thereof;
For I am she, and altogether joyless.
I can no longer hold me patient. [*Advancing.*
Hear me, you wrangling pirates, that fall out
In sharing that which you have pill'd from me!
Which of you trembles not that looks on me—
If not that, I being queen, you bow like subjects,
Yet that, by you depos'd, you quake like rebels?
Ah, gentle villain, do not turn away!
Glou. Foul wrinkled witch, what mak'st thou in my sight?
Q. Mar. But repetition of what thou hast marr'd;
That will I make before I let thee go.
Glou. Wert thou not banished on pain of death?
Q. Mar. I was; but I do find more pain in banishment

147. *sovereign*] *soueraigne* Ff; *lawfull* Qq. 148. *we you*] *we now* Q 6. 150. *thereof*] Ff; *of it* Qq. 151. *Q. Eliz.*] *Qu.* Qq 1, 2, Ff; *Q. M.* Qq 3, 4; *Q. Nar.* Q 5; *Qu. Mar.* Q 6. 153. *you may*] Ff; *may you* Qq. aft. 157. *Advancing*] Capell. 159. *sharing*] Q 1, Ff; *sharing out* Qq 2-6. 161. *being*] Qq; *am* Ff. 163. *Ah*] Ff; *O* Qq. 167-69. *Glou. Wert thou . . . my abode*] Ff; omitted Qq.

logical scheme of the heavens is called the "cacodemon," as being significant of misfortune to the native.

153. *in me*] as regards me, in my case.

158. *you wrangling pirates*] Mr. Craig notes a parallel from *2 Henry VI.* I. i. 222.

159. *pill'd*] robbed, pillaged. Compare *Richard II.* II. i. 246. Halliwell and Aldis Wright quote examples of "to rob and pill" from Halle's chronicle. "To pill" is the same word as "to peel," *i.e.* to strip clean. Mr. Craig supplies an instance from Caxton, *Historye of Reynart the Foxe*, 1481 (Arber, 114): "thyse false beestis . . . whan they be myghty and doubted then ben they extorcionners and scatte and *pylle* the peple."

160-62. The construction is somewhat involved and confusing. "You all tremble as you look on me, if not because, as subjects, you bow in awe of me, your queen, at any rate because, as rebels, you quake before me, the sovereign whom you have deposed." The sense is easy to see, and hard to express.

Than death can yield me here by my abode.
A husband and a son thou ow'st to me;
And thou a kingdom; all of you allegiance:
This sorrow that I have by right is yours,
And all the pleasures you usurp are mine.

Glou. The curse my noble father laid on thee,
When thou didst crown his warlike brows with paper,
And with thy scorns drew'st rivers from his eyes,
And then, to dry them, gav'st the duke a clout
Steep'd in the faultless blood of pretty Rutland—
His curses, then from bitterness of soul
Denounc'd against thee, are all fall'n upon thee;
And God, not we, hath plagu'd thy bloody deed.

Q. Eliz. So just is God to right the innocent.

Hast. O, 'twas the foulest deed to slay that babe,
And the most merciless that e'er was heard of.

Riv. Tyrants themselves wept when it was reported.

Dor. No man but prophesied revenge for it.

Buck. Northumberland, then present, wept to see it.

Q. Mar. What! were you snarling all before I came,
Ready to catch each other by the throat,
And turn you all your hatred now on me?
Did York's dread curse prevail so much with heaven,
That Henry's death, my lovely Edward's death,
Their kingdom's loss, my woful banishment,
Should all but answer for that peevish brat?
Can curses pierce the clouds and enter heaven?
Why then, give way, dull clouds, to my quick curses!

170. *ow'st to*] Ff; *owest to* Qq 1-5; *owest unto* Qq 6-8. 172. *This*] Ff; *The* Qq. 173. *are*] Qq 1, 2, Ff; *is* Qq 3-8. 176. *scorns*] Ff; *scorne* Qq. 178. *faultless*] omitted Qq 3-8. 180. *all*] omitted Qq 3-8. 184. *e'er*] *ere* Ff; *euer* Qq. 190. *all . . . now*] Qq 1, 2, Ff; *now . . . all* Qq 2-6. 194. *Should*] Ff; *Could* Qq.

174. For York's curse see *3 Henry VI.* I. iv. 164-66.

187. *Northumberland*] See *3 Henry VI.* I. iv. 150-51, 169-74. Sir Henry Percy, third Earl of Northumberland, grandson of Hotspur. He was killed at Towton, 29th March, 1461.

194. *peevish*] childish, fretful. Compare below, IV. iv. 420. See *3 Henry VI.* v. vi. 18; Lodge, *Wounds of Civil War*, act ii.: "*peevish* eld discoursing by a fire." Below, III. i. 31, is an example more nearly approximating to our own use, as meaning "wayward and querulous." "Peevish" is constantly applied to a boy, as a conventional epithet.

Though not by war, by surfeit die your king'
As ours by murder, to make him a king!
Edward thy son, that now is Prince of Wales,
For Edward my son, that was Prince of Wales,
Die in his youth by like untimely violence!
Thyself a queen, for me that was a queen,
Outlive thy glory, like my wretched self!
Long may'st thou live to wail thy children's loss,
And see another, as I see thee now,
Deck'd in thy rights, as thou art stall'd in mine!
Long die thy happy days before thy death;
And, after many lengthen'd hours of grief,
Die neither mother, wife, nor England's queen!
Rivers and Dorset, you were standers-by,
And so wast thou, Lord Hastings, when my son
Was stabb'd with bloody daggers—God I pray Him,
That none of you may live his natural age,
But by some unlook'd accident cut off!

Glou. Have done thy charm, thou hateful wither'd hag!

Q. Mar. And leave out thee? stay, dog, for thou shalt hear me!
If heaven hath any grievous plague in store,
Exceeding those that I can wish upon thee,
O, let them keep it till thy sins be ripe,
And then hurl down their indignation

197. *Though*] Ff; *If* Qq. 198. *ours*] *our* Qq 3, 5, 6; *out* Q 4. 199. *that*] Ff; *which* Qq. 200. *my*] Qq; *our* Ff. *that*] Ff; *which* Qq. 204. *loss*] Qq; *death* Ff. 206. *rights*] Q 1, Ff; *glorie* Qq 2-8. 211. *wast*] Qq 1, 2, Ff, Q 8; *was* Qq 2-7. 213. *his*] Ff; *your* Qq.

206. *stall'd*] installed. Aldis Wright quotes Greene, *Friar Bacon* (Dyce, 155): "A friar newly *stall'd* in Brazen-nose." Compare *id.*, *Orlando Furioso*, 1594 (Dyce, 95):—

"Nor can there sit within the sacred shrine
Of Venus more than one *installed* heart."

In Decker, *Bel-Man of London*, 1608 (Smeaton, 83), a candidate for initiation in the ragged regiment of beggars is asked "if hee were *stalled* to the Rogue or no? the poore Hungarian answered, yes, *He was*: then was he asked by Whom he was *Stalled*, and where, and in what manner of complement it was done."

214. The sense is obvious, but the syntax is elliptic. The construction of "cut off" is either (1) co-ordinate with the wish in the previous line, "But [that you may be] cut off," or (2) proleptic, "But [that you may live until you are] cut off." This latter is the more probable.

219. *them*] Notice the plural pronoun after "heaven," as though Margaret had said "the gods."

220. *elvish-mark'd*] Compare *King John*, III. i. 47, and the lines immediately preceding. For this malig-

On thee, the troubler of the poor world's peace!
The worm of conscience still begnaw thy soul!
Thy friends suspect for traitors while thou livest,
And take deep traitors for thy dearest friends!
No sleep close up that deadly eye of thine,
Unless it be while some tormenting dream
Affrights thee with a hell of ugly devils!
Thou elvish-mark'd, abortive, rooting hog!
Thou that wast seal'd in thy nativity
The slave of nature and the son of hell!
Thou slander of thy heavy mother's womb!
Thou loathed issue of thy father's loins!
Thou rag of honour! thou detested——

Glou. Margaret!

Q. Mar. Richard!

Glou. Ha!

223. *while*] *whilst* Q 6. 226. *while*] Ff; *whilest* or *whilst* Qq. 231. *heavy mother's*] Ff; *mothers heauy* Qq. 233. *detested*—] Ff 1, 3, 4; *detested* F 2; *detested, &c.* Qq.

nant sense of "elvish" compare *1 Jeronimo*, c. 1587:—

"Oh fate thou *elf!*
To kill Andrea, which here kill'd himself."

See also Chaucer, *Canterbury Tales*, G. 751 [of alchemy]: "our *elvish* craft."

228. *rooting hog*] Richard's badge was a white boar, as below, III. ii. 11, etc. Steevens cites the "Complaint of Collingbourne" in *Myroure for Magistrates*, "For where I meant the king by name of *hog*, I only alluded to his badge the bore." In 1484, William Colyngborne, a Wiltshire gentleman, was executed for publishing the doggrel lines, "The Cat, the Rat, and Louell our dog, Rule all England vnder an *hog*"—"meaning," adds Halle (ap. Holinshed, iii. 746), "by the *hog*, the dreadfull wild boare, which was the kings cognisance." Fuller, *Worthies of England*, 1662, p. 214, refers to a boar, one of the supporters of a rose in the gateway to the Schools quadrangle at Cambridge, built while Archbishop Rotherham was chancellor of the university: "The truth is that *Rotheram* having felt the Sharp Tuskes of that *Boar* . . . advanced his Armes thereon, meerly to engratiate himself."

230. *slave of nature*] Conjectural emendations, such as "shame of nature," quoted by Theobald, seem unnecessary. Aldis Wright explains it as a term of contempt. In Fletcher, *False One*, iv. 2, Cleopatra refers contemptuously to "hated lucre," on which Cæsar has cast his eyes covetously, as "the slave of nature." Warburton and Malone both took the phrase here as referring "to the ancient custom of masters branding their profligate slaves"; and Malone notes the coupling of a "slavish wipe" and "birth-hour's blot" in *Lucrece*, 537. We may compare the application of "stigmatic" to Richard in *2 Henry VI.* v. i. 215, and *3 Henry VI.* II. ii. 136. Nature, in this sense, has sealed him her slave in his nativity by branding him with deformity.

233. *rag*] Compare *Taming of the Shrew*, IV. iii. 112, and Mr. Bond's note on the passage. See also below, v. iii. 329; Jonson, *Cynthia's Revels*, v. 2: "Heart! who let in that *rag* there amongst us?" Warburton proposed to read "wrack."

Q. Mar. I call thee not.
Glou. I cry thee mercy then, for I did think
That thou hadst call'd me all these bitter names.
Q. Mar. Why, so I did, but look'd for no reply.
O, let me make the period to my curse!
Glou. 'Tis done by me, and ends in "Margaret."
Q. Eliz. Thus have you breath'd your curse against yourself.
Q. Mar. Poor painted queen, vain flourish of my fortune!
Why strew'st thou sugar on that bottled spider,
Whose deadly web ensnareth thee about?
Fool, fool! thou whet'st a knife to kill thyself.
The day will come that thou shalt wish for me
To help thee curse that poisonous bunch-back'd toad.
Hast. False-boding woman, end thy frantic curse,
Lest to thy harm thou move our patience.

235. *I cry . . . then*] Ff; *Then I crie thee mercy* Qq. *did think*] Ff; *had thought* Qq. 236. *That thou*] Q 1, Ff; *Thou* Qq 2-6. 237. *look'd*] *looke* Q 6. 239. *in*] *by* Q 6. 245 *day*] Ff; *time* Qq. *that*] Q 1, Ff; *when* Qq 2-8. 246. *poisonous*] Q 1, Ff; *poisoned* Qq 2-8.

238. *period*] the conclusion, which rounds off my curse. See below, II. i. 44; *Antony and Cleopatra*, IV. xiv. 107; and compare Fletcher and Massinger, *Spanish Curate*, i. 3: "The *period* of human happiness"; *Elder Brother*, i. 2:—

"I might well conclude
My name were at a *period*."

241. *painted*] counterfeit. So *Hamlet*, III. i. 53, refers to fair-seeming speeches which are really hollow and empty. Compare *Eastward Ho*, act ii.: "marriage is but a form in the school of policy, to which scholars sit fastened only with *painted* chains."

241. *vain flourish*] empty decoration of a fortune which is mine by right. We still speak of "flourishes" in connection with ornamental handwriting or a highly decorated speech. Compare *Hamlet*, v. ii. 187. Steevens quotes Massinger, *Great Duke of Florence*, iii. 1:—

"I allow these
As *flourishes* of fortune, with which princes
Are often sooth'd."

See also Wilkins, *Miseries of Inforst Marriage*, act iii.: "How ill it will stand with the *flourish* of your reputations," and act v.: "Who bear a *flourish* in the outward show"; Fletcher, *False One*, i. 1:—

"To be honest,
Religious and thankful, in themselves
Are forcible motives, and can need no *flourish*
Or gloss in the persuader."

There is a good parallel to the present line in *Love's Labour's Lost*, IV. iii. 238-39. For the verbal use of "flourish" see *Measure for Measure*, IV. i. 75.

242. *bottled*] bottle-shaped, swollen: applied again to Richard, IV. iv. 81 below. Steevens quotes the absurd opinion of Robert Heron, that "a *bottled* spider is evidently a spider kept in a bottle long fasting, and of consequence the more spiteful and venomous." Mr. Craig ("Little Quarto," *Richard III.* 1904, p. 58) notes that the bluebottle fly in North Lincolnshire is called the "bottle fly."

Q. Mar. Foul shame upon you! you have all mov'd mine.
Riv. Were you well serv'd, you would be taught your duty.
Q. Mar. To serve me well, you all should do me duty,
Teach me to be your queen, and you my subjects:
O, serve me well, and teach yourselves that duty!
Dor. Dispute not with her; she is lunatic.
Q. Mar. Peace, master marquess, you are malapert:
Your fire-new stamp of honour is scarce current.
O, that your young nobility could judge
What 'twere to lose it, and be miserable!
They that stand high have many blasts to shake them,
And, if they fall, they dash themselves to pieces.
Glou. Good counsel, marry: learn it, learn it, marquess.
Dor. It touches you, my lord, as much as me.
Glou. Ay, and much more; but I was born so high,
Our aery buildeth in the cedar's top,
And dallies with the wind and scorns the sun.
Q. Mar. And turns the sun to shade, alas, alas!
Witness my son, now in the shade of death,
Whose bright out-shining beams thy cloudy wrath
Hath in eternal darkness folded up.
Your aery buildeth in our aery's nest.
O God, that seest it, do not suffer it!
As it was won with blood, lost be it so!
Buck. Peace, peace, for shame, if not for charity!

259. *blasts*] *blast* Q 1. 262. *touches*] Ff; *toucheth* Qq. 263. *Ay*] *I* Ff; *Yea* Qq. 267. *son*] *sunne* Qq 5-8. 272. *was*] Qq; *is* Ff. 273. *Peace, peace*] Ff; *Haue done* Qq.

255. *malapert*] impudent. An emphatic form of "apert," *i.e.* free-spoken, our modern "pert." Compare Chaucer, *Troilus and Criseyde*, iii. 87: "Al nere he *malapert*, or made it tough"; Chapman (?), *Alphonsus*, act i.: "What, boy, so *malapert?*"; *Twelfth Night*, IV. i. 47.

256. *fire-new*] newly-coined, fresh from assay. Dorset's title had been granted 18th April, 1475. Compare *Twelfth Night*, III. ii. 23, 24, and see Mr. Craig on *King Lear*, V. iii. 133 [132]. *New Eng. Dict.* quotes Sylvester, *Hymn of Almes*, 1611, line 197: "Or *Fire-new* Fashion in a sleeve or slop" (Works, 1641, p. 516).

264. *aery*] the brood of an eagle. Compare *King John*, V. ii. 149, where *New Eng. Dict.* is surely wrong in taking "aery" to mean simply the nest. For this latter sense compare Massinger, *Maid of Honour*, 1632, i. 2:—

"One *aery* with proportion ne'er discloses
The eagle and the wren."

Q. Mar. Urge neither charity nor shame to me:
Uncharitably with me have you dealt,
And shamefully my hopes by you are butcher'd.
My charity is outrage, life my shame,
And in that shame still live my sorrow's rage!
Buck. Have done, have done!
Q. Mar. O princely Buckingham, I 'll kiss thy hand,
In sign of league and amity with thee:
Now fair befall thee and thy noble house!
Thy garments are not spotted with our blood,
Nor thou within the compass of my curse.
Buck. Nor no one here; for curses never pass
The lips of those that breathe them in the air.
Q. Mar. I will not think but they ascend the sky,
And there awake God's gentle-sleeping peace.
O Buckingham, take heed of yonder dog!
Look, when he fawns, he bites; and, when he bites,
His venom tooth will rankle to the death.
Have not to do with him, beware of him!
Sin, death, and hell have set their marks on him,
And all their ministers attend on him.
Glou. What doth she say, my Lord of Buckingham?
Buck. Nothing that I respect, my gracious lord.
Q. Mar. What, dost thou scorn me for my gentle counsel,
And soothe the devil that I warn thee from?
O, but remember this another day
When he shall split thy very heart with sorrow,
And say poor Margaret was a prophetess.

276. *my hopes by you*] Ff; *by you my hopes* Qq. 278. *that shame*] Ff; *my shame* Qq. *still*] *shall* Qq 6-8. 279. *Have done, have done*] Ff; *Haue done* Qq. 280. *I'll*] *Ile* Ff; *I will* Qq. 282. *noble*] Ff; *princely* Qq. 287. *I will not think*] Ff; *Ile not beleeue* Qq. 289. *take heed*] Ff; *beware* Qq. 291. *rankle*] *rackle* Q 1. *to the*] Ff; *thee to* Qq. 297. *What . . . counsel*] one line as Qq; two lines Ff, divided after *scorne me.*

291. *venom tooth*) "Venom" for "venomed" occurs also *3 Henry VI.* II. ii. 138; *Lucrece*, 850. Compare the use of "honey" in Lodge, *Wounds of Civil War*, act v.: "honey words make foolish minds," and at IV. i. 79 below.

298. *soothe*] flatter, as *Coriolanus*, II. ii. 77. "Soothing" for "flattery" occurs *ibid.* I. ix. 44. See also Jonson, *Poetaster*, iv. 3:—

"thy violent wrong
In *soothing* the declin'd affections
Of our base daughter."

Live each of you the subjects to his hate,
And he to yours, and all of you to God's! [*Exit.*

Hast. My hair doth stand an end to hear her curses.

Riv. And so doth mine: I muse why she 's at liberty.

Glou. I cannot blame her: by God's holy mother,
She hath had too much wrong; and I repent
My part thereof that I have done to her.

Q. Eliz. I never did her any, to my knowledge.

Glou. Yet you have all the vantage of her wrong.
I was too hot to do somebody good,
That is too cold in thinking of it now.
Marry, as for Clarence, he is well repaid;
He is frank'd up to fatting for his pains—
God pardon them that are the cause thereof!

Riv. A virtuous and a Christian-like conclusion,
To pray for them that have done scathe to us.

Glou. So do I ever—[*Aside*] being well advis'd;
For, had I curs'd now, I had curs'd myself.

302. *subjects to*] Ff; *subiects of* Qq 1-6. 303. *yours*] Ff; *your* Qq 1, 2; *you* Qq 3-8. 304. *Hast.*] Qq; *Buc.* Ff. *an*] Ff; *on* Qq. 305. *muse why*] Ff; *wonder* Qq. 308. *to her*] Ff; omitted Qq. 309. *Q. Eliz.*] Camb.; *Qu.* Qq 1-5; *Hast.* Qq 6-8; *Mar.* Ff 1, 2; *Der.* Ff 3, 4; *Dors.* Rowe. 310. *Yet*] Ff; *But* Qq. *her*] Ff; *this* Qq. 315. *thereof*] Ff; *of it* Qq. 318. *Aside*] Camb.; omitted Qq; *Speakes to himselfe* Ff (after *advis'd*); Rowe marks both lines *Aside.* 319. *curs'd now, I*] *curst now, I* Q 4, Ff; *curst, now I* Qq 1-3, 5-8.

305. *I muse*] I wonder. Compare *George a Greene* (Dodsley, 1825, iii. 23):—

"*I muse*, if thou be Henry Momford, Kendall's earl,
That thou wilt do poor George a Greene this wrong."

Milton, *Of Reformation in England*, 1641, book ii.: "How then this third and last sort that hinder reformation will justify that it stands not with reason of state, *I much muse*."

314. *frank'd up*] See also below, IV. v. 3. Nares, after Cotgrave, gives "*Frank.* A place to fatten a boar in; a sty," as *2 Henry IV.* II. ii. 160. *New Eng. Dict.* quotes Holland's *Livy*, 1600: "The Commons doe feed and *franke vp*, even for the shambles and butchers knife the fautors and maintainers of their weale and libertie." Malone quotes Harrison, *Description of Britaine*, 1577: "The husbandmen and farmers never *fraunke* them above three or four months, in which time he is dyeted with otes and peason, and lodged on the bare planches of an uneasy cote."

317. *scathe*] injury. The 13th century version of Genesis, printed in Morris, *Specimens of Early English*, part i. (2nd ed. p. 164), has (line 2298) "Iosep ne ðoht ðor-of no scaðe," *i.e.* no harm. See also Chaucer, *Canterbury Tales*, A. 446: "But she was som-del deef, and that was *scathe*," *i.e.* a misfortune. See *Romeo and Juliet*, I. v. 86, for "scathe" used as a verb.

Enter CATESBY.

Cates. Madam, his majesty doth call for you,
And for your grace, and you, my noble lords.
Q. Eliz. Catesby, we come. Lords, will you go with us?
Riv. We wait upon your grace. [*Exeunt all but Gloucester.*
Glou. I do the wrong, and first begin to brawl:
The secret mischiefs that I set abroach
I lay unto the grievous charge of others.
Clarence, whom I indeed have cast in darkness,
I do beweep to many simple gulls,
Namely to Derby, Hastings, Buckingham,
And tell them 'tis the queen and her allies
That stir the king against the duke my brother.
Now they believe it, and withal whet me
To be reveng'd on Rivers, Vaughan, Grey:
But then I sigh, and, with a piece of Scripture,
Tell them that God bids us do good for evil;
And thus I clothe my naked villainy
With odd old ends stolen forth of Holy Writ,
And seem a saint, when most I play the devil.

Enter Catesby.] Ff; omitted Qq. 321. *your grace*] Qq 1, 2, Ff; *your noble grace,* Qq 3-8. *you . . . lords.*] Capell; *you my noble Lo:* Qq 1, 2; *you my noble Lord* Qq 3-6; *yours my gracious Lord* Ff. 322. *we . . . us*] Qq; *I . . . mee* Ff. 323. *We*] Ff; *Madam we* Qq. *wait upon*] Ff; *will attend* Qq. 324. *begin*] Ff; *began* Qq. 325. *mischiefs*] *mischiefe* Qq 3-8. 327. *whom*] *who* F 1. *cast*] Ff; *laid* Qq. 329. *Derby, Hastings*] Ff; *Hastings, Darby* Qq. 330. *tell them 'tis*] Ff; *say it is* Qq 1-7. 332. *it*] Ff; *me* Qq. 333. *Vaughan*] Qq; *Dorset* Ff. 334. *I*] omitted Qq 3, 5-8. 337. *odd old*] *odde old* Ff; *old odde* (or *od*) Qq. *forth*] Ff; *out* Qq.

325. *set abroach*] a common metaphor. See *Romeo and Juliet*, I. i. 111; Lodge, *Wounds of Civil War*, act i.: "this discord, newly *set abroach*"; Chapman, *All Fools*, act ii.:—

"shall I be made
A foolish novice, my purse *set abroach*
By every cheating come-you-seven."

337. *odd old ends*] For "odd old," compare Marston, *Malcontent*, act v.: "fables feign'd, *odd old* fools' chat"; Beaumont and Fletcher, *Woman-Hater*, ii. 1: "Any *odd old* gentlewoman, that mourns for the death of her husband." "Old ends" occurs *Much Ado About Nothing*, I. i. 290, and Jonson, *Volpone*, 1607, pro. 23: "Nor hales he in a gull *old ends* reciting." Milton has "odd ends," *Apology for Smectymnuus*, 1642 (Prose Works, ed. St. John, iii. 110): "His *odd ends*, which from some penurious book of characters he had been culling out and would fain apply." "Ends" are tags, commonplace quotations, as in *Eastward Ho*, ii. 1, where Touchstone rebukes his dissolute apprentice, "Well said, change your gold-ends for play-ends."

Enter two Murderers.

But soft! here come my executioners.
How now, my hardy, stout, resolved mates!
Are you now going to despatch this thing?

First Murd. We are, my lord; and come to have the warrant,
That we may be admitted where he is.

Glou. Well thought upon! I have it here about me.
[*Gives the warrant.*
When you have done, repair to Crosby Place.
But, sirs, be sudden in the execution,
Withal obdurate: do not hear him plead;
For Clarence is well-spoken, and perhaps
May move your hearts to pity, if you mark him.

First Murd. Tut, tut, my lord, we will not stand to prate.
Talkers are no good doers: be assur'd
We go to use our hands, and not our tongues.

Glou. Your eyes drop mill-stones, when fools' eyes fall tears;
I like you, lads: about your business straight!
Go, go, dispatch!

First Murd. We will, my noble lord. [*Exeunt.*

Enter two Murderers] Ff (*murtherers*); *Enter Executioners.* Qq (aft. 339). 339. *come*] Q 1, Ff; *comes* Qq 2-8. 341. *you now*] Qq 1, 2, Ff; *ye now* Qq 3-5; *ye not* Q 6; *you not* Qq 7, 8. *thing*] Ff; *deed* Qq. 342, 350. *First Murd.*] 1. *M.* Capell; *Execu.* Qq [var.]; *Vil.* Ff (and 355). 344. *Well*] Ff; *It was well* Qq. *Gives the warrant.*] Capell. 350. *Tut, tut*] Ff; *Tush feare not* Qq; *Fear not* Pope. 352. *go*] Ff; *come* Qq. 353. *fall*] Ff; *drop* Qq. 354. *straight*] Ff; omitted Qq. 355. *Go, go . . . lord.*] Ff; omitted Qq. *Exeunt*] Qq [aft. 354]; omitted Ff.

346. *sudden*] hasty, immediate. Chapman (?), *Alphonsus*, act v., has "Be therefore *sudden* lest we die ourselves"; and, almost a repetition of the present line, "I will be *sudden* in the execution." Compare below, IV. ii. 19.

348. *well-spoken*] Compare Chapman, *All Fools*, act i.:—

"I know he is *well-spoken*, and may much prevail
In satisfying my father."

In Beaumont and Fletcher, *Woman-Hater*, v. 1, one of the intelligencers says of Lucio: "He's excellently spoken."

351. *Talkers are no good doers*] Probably proverbial. Mr. Craig found "Talking pays no toll" in Grose's collection of proverbs.

353. *mill-stones*] The expression was proverbial: see *Troilus and Cressida*, I. ii. 158. Steevens quotes *Cæsar and Pompey*, 1607: "Men's eyes must *mill-stones* drop, when fools shed tears"; and (on I. iv. 239 below) Massinger, *City Madam*, 1632, iv. 3:—

"He, good gentleman,
Will weep when he hears how we are used.
1 *Serj.* Yes, *mill-stones*."

fall tears] let tears fall. Compare stage-direction in Ff, I. ii. 182 above: "She *fals* the Sword"; *Measure for Measure*, II. i. 6.

SCENE IV.—*London. The Tower.*

Enter CLARENCE *and* BRAKENBURY.

Brak. Why looks your grace so heavily to-day?
Clar. O, I have pass'd a miserable night,
So full of fearful dreams, of ugly sights,
That, as I am a Christian faithful man,
I would not spend another such a night,
Though 'twere to buy a world of happy days,
So full of dismal terror was the time!
Brak. What was your dream, my lord? I pray you tell me.
Clar. Methoughts that I had broken from the Tower,
And was embark'd to cross to Burgundy,
And, in my company, my brother Gloucester,

Scene iv.] *Scene v.* Pope. *Brakenbury*] *Brokenbury*. Qq; *Keeper*. Ff. 1. *Brak.*] *Brok.* Qq; *Keep.* Ff. (and 34, 42, 64, 75). 3. *fearful . . . sights*] Ff; *vgly sights, of gastly dreames* Qq. 8. *my lord . . . tell me*] Ff; *I long to heare you tell it* Qq. 9. *Methoughts*] *Me thought* Qq 4-8. 9, 10. *that I . . . Burgundy*] Ff; *I was imbarkt for Burgundy* Qq.

Brakenbury] In Ff Brakenbury does not enter till after line 75, and his part in the dialogue is assigned to a keeper. Possibly, in the original draft of the play, Brakenbury and the keeper were distinct persons, but were united for acting purposes, and so appeared in Qq as one. The editor of F 1 perhaps restored the double part from his MS. Spedding explained the absence of "Exit Keeper" at line 75 in Ff as an "error of press or pen, the context showing conclusively that the 'keeper' is supposed to retire on the entrance of his chief." The part of the keeper, however, is not necessary. Clarence is more likely to have told his story to Brakenbury than to a casual warder; and he might apply the term "keeper," as altered by Ff in lines 66, 73, to the Lieutenant of the Tower, in whose custody he was.

9. *Methoughts*] A corrupt form, evidently "on the false analogy of 'methinks'" (Aldis Wright). In line 18 below, all the printed copies read "me thought." In line 58, Q 1 alone reads "me thoughts," which the present editor has adopted in harmony with this passage. The form occurs in *Winter's Tale*, I. ii. 154, and *Merchant of Venice*, I. iii. 70 (Q 2 and Ff, not Q 1).

10. *Burgundy*] *i.e.* the Netherlands, part of the domains of the Valois Dukes of Burgundy. The princes of the house of York found a natural shelter in these provinces. After Wakefield, Clarence, then a child, resided under Burgundian protection in the episcopal city of Utrecht. In 1468, his sister Margaret became the second wife of Charles the Bold, last duke of his line. Edward IV., in 1470, took refuge in Holland from the coalition of Warwick and Clarence with Queen Margaret. Clarence had been a suitor for the hand of Mary, daughter of Charles the Bold by his first wife, and heiress of his duchy. Edward IV. put his veto on Clarence's suit; this being one of the causes of discontent that led to the imprisonment of Clarence. The year before Clarence was murdered, Burgundy proper was seized by Louis XI. of France, after the death of Charles the Bold; and the dominions of the Duchess were restricted to the Netherlands and the County of Burgundy (Franche Comté).

Who from my cabin tempted me to walk
Upon the hatches: thence we look'd toward England,
And cited up a thousand heavy times,
During the wars of York and Lancaster
That had befall'n us. As we pac'd along
Upon the giddy footing of the hatches,
Methought that Gloucester stumbled, and, in falling,
Struck me, that thought to stay him, overboard,
Into the tumbling billows of the main.
Lord, Lord! methought what pain it was to drown!
What dreadful noise of waters in mine ears!
What ugly sights of death within mine eyes!
Methoughts I saw a thousand fearful wracks,
A thousand men that fishes gnaw'd upon,
Wedges of gold, great anchors, heaps of pearl,
Inestimable stones, unvalu'd jewels,
All scatter'd in the bottom of the sea.
Some lay in dead men's skulls; and, in the holes
Where eyes did once inhabit, there were crept,
As 'twere in scorn of eyes, reflecting gems,
That woo'd the slimy bottom of the deep,
And mock'd the dead bones that lay scatter'd by.

Brak. Had you such leisure in the time of death
To gaze upon these secrets of the deep?

Clar. Methought I had: and often did I strive

13. *thence*] Qq 1-5; *there* Qq 6-8, Ff. 14. *heavy*] Ff; *fearefull* Qq. 16. *pac'd*] Ff; *pact* Q 1; *past* Qq 2-8. 18. *falling*] Ff; *stumbling* Qq. 21. *Lord, Lord*] Qq; *O Lord* Ff. 22. *waters*] Qq 1-5; *water* Qq 6-8, Ff. 22, 23. *mine . . . mine*] *my . . . my* Q 1. 23. *ugly sights of*] Qq; *sights of ugly* Ff. 24. *Methoughts*] Ff; *Methought* Qq. 25. *A thousand*] Ff; *Ten thousand* Qq. 28. *All . . . sea*] Ff; omitted Qq. 29. *the holes*] Ff; *those holes* Qq. 32. *That*] Ff; *Which* Qq. 35. *these*] Ff; *the* Qq. 36, 37. *and often . . . ghost*] Ff; omitted Qq.

13. *thence*] Ff have "there" in common with Q 6. See also line 22 below, where both have "water" for "waters." Such errors may be mere coincidences due to printers; but they may point equally to the use of Q 6 as the printed foundation of the text of Ff.

21. *Lord, Lord*] Qq may give the result of a stage alteration; but they have the advantage of emphasis over Ff, which may show an attempt to soften the phrase in accordance with the act of 3 James I. c. 21, "To restraine the abuses of Players."

26. *anchors*] Aldis Wright mentions a conjectural emendation to "ingots."

27. *unvalu'd*] invaluable, as Marlowe, *1 Tamburlaine*, c. 1587, I. 2, "this success and loss *unvaluèd*." "Unparagon'd" is used for "incomparable" in *Cymbeline*, I. iv. 87; II. ii. 17. See note on I. ii. 39 above.

To yield the ghost; but still the envious flood
Stopt in my soul, and would not let it forth
To find the empty, vast, and wandering air,
But smother'd it within my panting bulk,
Which almost burst to belch it in the sea.

Brak. Awak'd you not in this sore agony?

Clar. No, no, my dream was lengthen'd after life:
O, then began the tempest to my soul,
Who pass'd, methought, the melancholy flood,
With that sour ferryman which poets write of,
Unto the kingdom of perpetual night.
The first that there did greet my stranger-soul
Was my great father-in-law, renowned Warwick,
Who spake aloud, "What scourge for perjury
Can this dark monarchy afford false Clarence?"
And so he vanish'd: then came wandering by
A shadow like an angel, with bright hair
Dabbled in blood; and he squeak'd out aloud,

37. *but*] Ff; *for* Qq. 38. *Stopt*] *Stop'd* Ff; *Kept* Qq. 39. *find*] Ff; *seeke* Qq 1, 2; *keepe* Qq 3-8. *empty, vast, and*] Qq 2, 6-8, Ff; *emptie vast and* Qq 1, 3-5; *empty vast, and* Malone. 41. *Which*] Qq; *Who* Ff. 42. *in*] Ff; *with* Qq. 43. *No, no*] Ff; *O no* Qq. 45. *Who*] Qq; *I* Ff. 46. *sour*] Ff; *grim* Qq. 49. *renowned*] *renowmed* Qq 1-5. 50. *spake*] Ff; *cried* Qq. 53. *with*] Ff; *in* Qq. 54. *squeak'd*] *squeakt* Qq 2-8; *squakt* Q 1; *shriek'd* Ff.

37. *envious*] malicious. Compare *3 Henry VI.* III. ii. 157, where the envy or malice of Nature is transferred to the defect which it causes.

39. *empty, vast*] Malone suggested that "empty vast" means "immense vacuity," like Tennyson's "illimitable inane" in *Lucretius*, line 40. Shakespeare uses "vast" as a substantive in the plays of his later and middle life, see *Hamlet*, I. ii. 198; *Winter's Tale*, I. i. 33; *Tempest*, I. ii. 327. In his earlier plays it is an adjective, as *King John*, IV. iii. 152. However, Lodge, *Wounds of Civil War*, printed 1594, but probably written some years earlier, has (act i.): "Whose vows have pierc'd and search'd the deepest *vast*," and (act ii.):—

"Those fatal fears
That dwell below amidst the dreadful *vast*."

Compare Tennyson, *In Memoriam*, 1850, epilogue, st. 31:—

"A soul shall draw from out the *vast*
And strike his being into bounds."

40. *bulk*] the frame of the body, as *Hamlet*, II. i. 95. Compare first part of *Jeronimo* (Dodsley, 1825, iii. 60):—

"I have a mischief
Within my breast, more than my *bulk* can hold."

Chapman (?), *Alphonsus*, act iv.: "Still looking when his poison'd *bulk* would break."

45. *Who pass'd*] Ff break up the sentence too much; and Qq have the better reading. In line 41 above there is nothing to choose between the readings.

45, 46. Compare the speech of Andrea's ghost at the beginning of Kyd, *Spanish Tragedy*, act i.:—

"When I was slain, my soul descended straight
To pass the flowing stream of Acheron," etc.

54. *squeak'd*] "Squeak," applied to

"Clarence is come, false, fleeting, perjur'd Clarence,
That stabb'd me in the field by Tewkesbury:
Seize on him, Furies, take him unto torment!"
With that, methoughts, a legion of foul fiends
Environ'd me, and howled in mine ears
Such hideous cries, that with the very noise
I trembling wak'd, and for a season after
Could not believe but that I was in hell,
Such terrible impression made my dream.

Brak. No marvel, my lord, though it affrighted you;
I am afraid, methinks, to hear you tell it.

Clar. Ah, keeper, keeper! I have done those things,
That now give evidence against my soul,
For Edward's sake; and see how he requites me!
O God! if my deep prayers cannot appease Thee,
But Thou wilt be aveng'd on my misdeeds,
Yet execute Thy wrath in me alone;
O, spare my guiltless wife and my poor children!—

57. *unto torment*] Ff; *to your torments* Qq. 58. *methoughts*] *me thoughts* Q 1; *me thought* Qq 2-8, Ff 1-3. 59. *me, and*] Ff; *me about, and* Qq. 63. *my*] Ff; *the* Qq. 64. *my lord*] Qq; *Lord* Ff. 65. *I am afraid, methinks*] Ff; *I promise you, I am afraid* Qq. 66. *Ah keeper, keeper,*] Ff; *O Brokenbury* Qq. *those*] Qq; *these* Ff. 67. *That*] Ff; *Which* Qq. *give*] Ff; *beare* Qq. 69-72. *O God . . . children*] Ff; omitted Qq. 71. *in me*] *on me* Rowe.

a voice "thin as voices from the grave," is found in *Hamlet*, I. i. 116 [not in Ff]. Compare "squeal" in *Julius Cæsar*, II. ii. 24, and Mr. Macmillan's note in Arden ed. In *Antony and Cleopatra*, v. ii. 220, "squeaking" is used of a boy-actor's voice. Perhaps, in 1623, the word was losing its application to supernatural sounds; and the editor of F 1 altered it on his own account.

55. *fleeting*] fickle, deceitful. Steevens refers to *Antony and Cleopatra*, v. ii. 240, "the *fleeting* moon," which is the same thing as "the inconstant moon" of *Romeo and Juliet*, II. ii. 109. There are two examples in Lyly, *Euphues* (Arber, 48): "Whom thou maist make . . . partaker of all thy misfortune without mistrust of *fleeting*"; and (p. 106): "If Lucilla reade this trifle, shee will . . . condemne me of mischiefe in arming young men against *fleeting* minions." The earliest example in *New Eng. Dict.* is from *Ancren Riwle*, c. 1225: "Mid te fleotinde word, to fleoteð þe heorte."

64. *marvel*] pronounced as a monosyllable, and often so spelt. Compare J. Cook, *Green's Tu Quoque* (Dodsley, 1825, vii. 94): "I *marl'd* indeed that all things were so quiet." The alteration in Ff points to a growth of dissyllabic pronunciation. For "no marvel . . . though" compare *Gammer Gurton's Needle*, 1575, act v.: "Was it any *marvaile*, though the poor woman arose."

71. *in me*] either "on me," or "in respect of me" (as I. iii. 153 above). Compare Ezekiel v. 10: "I will execute judgments in thee," where, however, the meaning may be "in the midst of thee" (LXX, ἐν σοί).

72. *my guiltless wife*] Clarence's wife, Isabella Neville, died before his imprisonment took place. By that time he had attempted to win Mary of Burgundy for his second wife.

Keeper, I prithee sit by me awhile;
My soul is heavy, and I fain would sleep.

Brak. I will, my lord: God give your grace good rest!
[*Clarence sleeps.*
Sorrow breaks seasons and reposing hours,
Makes the night morning, and the noon-tide night.
Princes have but their titles for their glories,
An outward honour for an inward toil;
And, for unfelt imaginations,
They often feel a world of restless cares:
So that, between their titles and low name,
There's nothing differs but the outward fame.

Enter the two Murderers.

First Murd. Ho! who's here?

Brak. What wouldst thou, fellow, and how cam'st thou hither?

First Murd. I would speak with Clarence, and I came hither on my legs.

Brak. What, so brief?

73. *Keeper . . . awhile*] Ff; *I pray thee gentle keeper stay by me* Qq; *I pray thee, Brakenbury, stay by me* Pope. Capell adds *Retiring to a chair.* aft.; 75. *Clarence sleeps.*] Johnson; *Enter Brakenbury the Lieutenant.* Ff. 76. *Bra.* Ff. 80. *imaginations*] Ff; *imagination* Qq. 82. *between*] Ff; *betwixt* Qq. *their*] *your* Qq 3-8. *name*] Ff; *names* Qq. 84, 85. *First Murd. Ho! . . . Brak.*] Ff; omitted Qq. 85. *What wouldst . . . hither?*] Ff; *In God's name what are you and how came you hither?* Qq; *In God's name, what art thou? how cam'st thou hither?* Pope. 86. *First Murd.*] *Execu.* Qq; *2. Mur.* Ff. 88. *What, so brief*] Ff; *Yea, are you so briefe* Qq 1, 2, 8; *Yea, are ye so briefe* Qq 3-7.

78. *glories*] Johnson thought that "troubles" "would more impress the purpose of the speaker, and correspond better with the following lines."

80. *for unfelt imaginations*] instead of imaginations which cannot be gratified. "Unfelt" is on a par with "unvalu'd," line 27 above.

85. From this point to line 158, the discrepancies between Qq and Ff are more than usually numerous. The bulk of the dialogue originally must have been written as prose. The only lines that scan, with the exception of line 89 (Ff), belong to Brakenbury. Qq arrange the whole passage roughly in lines, without any attempt at scansion. Ff print mainly as prose, with one or two exceptions. The chief difference between the two versions is that the style of Ff is more set and literary; while Qq abound in ejaculations and colloquial forms which may have entered the text from the stage. On the other hand, Ff have forms like "there 's," "hee 'l," "'tis," where Qq print "there is," "he will," "it is." See collation.

Sec. Murd. 'Tis better, sir, than to be tedious.
Let him see our commission, and talk no more.
[*Brakenbury reads it.*

Brak. I am in this commanded to deliver
The noble Duke of Clarence to your hands.
I will not reason what is meant hereby,
Because I will be guiltless from the meaning.
There lies the duke asleep, and there the keys.
I 'll to the king, and signify to him
That thus I have resign'd to you my charge.

First Murd. You may, sir, 'tis a point of wisdom: fare you well.
[*Exit Brakenbury.*

Sec. Murd. What, shall we stab him as he sleeps?

First Murd. No; he 'll say 'twas done cowardly, when he wakes.

Sec. Murd. Why, he shall never wake until the great judgment-day.

First Murd. Why, then he 'll say we stabb'd him sleeping.

Sec. Murd. The urging of that word "judgment" hath bred a kind of remorse in me.

89. *Sec. Murd.*] 2. *Exe.* Qq; 1. Ff. *'Tis . . . tedious*] Ff; *O sir, it is better to be briefe then tedious* Qq 1, 2, 7, 8; *O sir, it is better be briefe then tedious* Qq 3-6. 90. *Let him see*] Ff; *Shew him* Qq. 93. *hereby*] *thereby* Qq 3-8. 94. *from*] Ff; *of* Qq. 95. *There . . . keys*] Ff; *Here are the keies there sits the Duke asleepe* Qq. 96. *I 'll . . . him*] Ff; *Ile to his Maiesty, and certifie his Grace* Qq. 97. *to you my charge*] Ff; *my charge to you* Qq 1, 2; *my place to you* Qq 3-8. 99. *You may, sir, 'tis*] Ff; *Doe so, it is* Qq. *fare you well*] Ff; omitted Qq. 100. *we*] *I* Qq 1, 2. 101. *he 'll*] *hee 'l* Ff; *then he will* Qq. 103. *Why*] Ff; *When he wakes, Why foole* Qq. 103. *until the great*] Ff; *till the* Qq. 105. *he 'll*] *hee 'l* Ff; *he will* Qq.

89. "It is better to be brief than tedious" is possibly proverbial. Mr. Craig calls attention to *All's Well that Ends Well*, II. iii. 33, 34: "that is the brief and the tedious of it."

96. It may be noted, in connection with Qq reading here, that Shakespeare, if he was responsible for it, used the terms "majesty" and "grace" with little discrimination. The title of "majesty" was first used by Charles V. as King of Spain, after his election as Emperor, 1519; and was borrowed in imitation by Henry VIII. and other princes. What Brakenbury really would have said in 1478 would have been: "I 'll to the king, and certify his grace"; and therefore it would be an improvement to read it here. But for an editor to do so would be to commit himself to a principle of arbitrary selection between Qq and Ff. The whole line in Ff, as it stands, is better than the line in Qq.

101. *cowardly*] For adverbs of a similar kind, compare Marston, *Malcontent*, act V.: "she most *courtly* finds fault with them one after another"; Fletcher, *False One*, iii. 1.: "Let us consider *timely* what we must do"; Suckling, *Upon . . . the Lord Leppington*, c. 1637:—

"Describes each thing so *lively* that we are
Concern'd ourselves before we are aware."

First Murd. What, art thou afraid?

Sec. Murd. Not to kill him, having a warrant; but to be damn'd for killing him, from the which no warrant can defend me.

First Murd. I thought thou hadst been resolute.

Sec. Murd. So I am, to let him live.

First Murd. I'll back to the Duke of Gloucester, and tell him so.

Sec. Murd. Nay, I prithee stay a little: I hope this passionate humour of mine will change; it was wont to hold me but while one tells twenty.

First Murd. How dost thou feel thyself now?

Sec. Murd. Some certain dregs of conscience are yet within me.

First Murd. Remember our reward, when the deed's done.

Sec. Murd. 'Zounds! he dies! I had forgot the reward.

First Murd. Where's thy conscience now?

Sec. Murd. O, in the Duke of Gloucester's purse.

First Murd. When he opens his purse to give us our reward, thy conscience flies out.

109. *warrant*] Ff; *warrant for it* Qq. 110. *the which*] Ff; *which* Qq. 111. *me*] Ff; *vs* Qq. 112, 113. *First Murd. I . . . live*] Ff; omitted Qq. 114. *I'll back*] *Ile backe* Ff; *Backe* Qq. *and tell*] Ff; *tell* Qq. 116. *Nay, I prithee*] Ff; *I pray thee* Qq. *a little*] Ff; *a while* Qq. 116, 117. *this passionate . . . mine*] Ff; *my holy humor* Qq; *this compassionate humour of mine* Capell. 117. *it was*] Ff; *twas* Qq. 118. *tells*] Ff; *would tel* Qq. 120. *Some*] Ff; *Faith, some* Qq. 122. *deed 's*] Ff; *deede is* Qq. 124. *Zounds*] Qq; *Come* Ff. 125. *Where's*] Ff; *Where is* Qq. 126. *O, in*] Ff; *In* Qq. 127. *When*] Ff; *So when* Qq.

117. *passionate*] Malone thought that the editor of F 1 altered Qq on account of the statute of 1605-6, which was passed "for the preventing and avoiding the great abuse of the holy name of God in stage-plays, interludes, may-games, shewes and such like." See note on line 21 above. The alteration at line 85 above may be due to this reason, to which may be ascribed the omission of "Zounds" at lines 124, 143, and the radical change in lines 188, 189 below. The omission of "Faith" in line 120 is another probable instance. No change was made in Qq after the passing of the act. Collier, *Annals of the Stage*, 1831, ii. 56, 57, quotes a note from Sir Henry Herbert's Office-Book, relating to D'Avenant's *Wits*, 1636. Charles I., on the author's petition, restored several exclamations, which the Master of the Revels had crossed out from the play. Sir Henry noted: "The King is pleased to take *faith*, *death*, *slight*, for asseverations and no oaths, to which I do humbly submit as my master's judgment; but under favour conceive them to be oaths, and enter them here to declare my opinion and submission." In the present case, an alteration could hardly have been deemed necessary within the terms of the statute, even by the most puritanical critic.

Sec. Murd. 'Tis no matter, let it go: there's few or none will entertain it.

First Murd. What if it come to thee again?

Sec. Murd. I'll not meddle with it: it makes a man a coward: a man cannot steal, but it accuseth him; a man cannot swear, but it checks him; a man cannot lie with his neighbour's wife, but it detects him. 'Tis a blushing shamefast spirit, that mutinies in a man's bosom; it fills a man full of obstacles: it made me once restore a purse of gold that by chance I found; it beggars any man that keeps it; it is turn'd out of towns and cities for a dangerous thing; and every man that means to live well endeavours to trust to himself and to live without it.

First Murd. 'Zounds, 'tis even now at my elbow, persuading me not to kill the duke!

Sec. Murd. Take the devil in thy mind, and believe him not: he would insinuate with thee but to make thee sigh.

First Murd. I am strong-fram'd: he cannot prevail with me.

129. *'Tis no matter*] Ff; omitted Qq. 131. *What*] Ff; *How* Qq. 132. *it: it makes*] Ff; *it, it is a dangerous thing, It makes* Qq. 134. *a man . . . a man*] Ff; *he . . . He* Qq. *swear*] *steale* Qq 3-8. 136. *'Tis*] Ff; *It is* Qq. 136. *shamefast*] Qq 1, 3, 6; *shamfast* Q 2; *shamfact* Qq 4, 5; *shamefac'd* Ff. 137. *a man*] Ff; *one* Qq. 138. *purse*] *piece* Qq 3-8. *by chance*] Ff; omitted Qq. 140. *towns*] Ff; *all Townes* Qq. 141. *to live*] Qq 1-6; *liue* Ff. 143. *Zounds*] Qq; omitted Ff. *'tis*] Ff; *it is* Qq. 146. *but*] Ff; omitted Qq. 148. *I am strong-fram'd*] Ff; *Tut, I am strong in fraud* Qq. 149. *me.*] *me, I warrant thee.* Qq.

136. *shamefast*] the correct form of the word. Compare "steadfast." The variations of spelling in successive editions show a transformation in orthography. "Shame-faced" suggests a wrong etymology. Aldis Wright notes a like discrepancy between Qq and Ff in *3 Henry VI.* IV. viii. 52; Lyly, *Euphues*, 1579 (Arber, 69), has "shamefastnes."

145. There are two possible meanings to this line: (1) Take the devil into thy mind, and believe not conscience—the blushing shamefast spirit, for which the devil will be more than a match. This is substantially Warburton's explanation. It involves the use of "in" = "into." Compare above, I. iii. 89. "Him" also must in this case refer to "conscience," hitherto alluded to as "it." (2) Take hold of, *i.e.* grapple with conscience, which is the devil in thy mind, and believe him not. This is adopted by Aldis Wright, and is more simple. Capell avoided the difficulty by reading "Shake the devil out of thy mind."

Sec. Murd. Spoke like a tall man that respects thy reputation. Come, shall we fall to work?

First Murd. Take him on the costard with the hilts of thy sword, and then throw him into the malmsey-butt in the next room.

Sec. Murd. O excellent device! and make a sop of him.

150. *Spoke*] *Soode* Q 4; *Stood* Qq 5-8. *man*] Ff; *fellow* Qq. *thy*] Ff; *his* Qq. 151. *fall to work*] Ff; *to this geere* Qq. 152. *on*] Ff; *ouer* Qq. 152, 153. *thy sword*] *my sword* Qq 3-8. 153. *throw him into*] Ff; *we wil chop him in* Qq. 155. *and*] Ff; omitted Qq. *sop*] *scoope* Q 3.

150. *a tall man*] "Tall" is fine, brave; usually in the sense of "swaggering," as we speak of "tall talk." Mercutio in *Romeo and Juliet*, II. iv. 31, ridicules the fashionable employment of the word. Chapman, *Blind Beggar of Alexandria*, 1598 (Shepherd, 7), has "I do hold thee for the most *tall*, resolute, and accomplished gentleman on the face of the earth." Qq "tall fellow" is common, *e.g.* Decker, *Seuen Deadly Sinnes of London* (Arber, 21): "Though a *Lye* haue but short legs (like a Dwarfes) yet it goes farre in a little time, *Et crescit eundo*, and at last prooues a *tall* fellow"; Wilkins, *Miseries of Inforst Marriage*, 1607, act iv.: "had you kept half a dozen *tall* fellows." "Tall man" occurs in Lodge and Greene, *Looking-Glass for London* (Dyce, 138): "Then may I count myself, I think, *a tall man*, that am able to kill a devil."

thy] The mixture of persons involved in this sentence is natural in the mouth of a rough and ill-educated man. There is no necessity to keep Qq "his."

152. *Take him*] strike him. Mr. Craig gives illustrations in the note to his "Little Quarto" edition of the play, p. 80, and refers further to *Taming of the Shrew*, III. ii. 165.

costard] A costard is a kind of large apple; hence the word was applied vulgarly to the head. Compare *King Lear*, IV. vi. 247, and Moth's jest on Costard in *Love's Labour's Lost*, III. i. 71. See *Gammer Gurton's Needle*, act v.: "Well, knave, and I had the alone, I wold surely rap thy *costard*." The word is common.

hilts] Compare *1 Henry IV*. II. iv. 229; Cook, *Green's Tu Quoque*, "All the while his money is losing, he swears by the cross of this silver; and, when it is gone, he changeth it to the *hilts* of his sword." Qq 7, 8 "hilt" may point to a transition from the plural to the singular use.

153. *throw*] This is weaker than the colloquial "chop" of Qq. So also the reading "fall to work" in line 151 is weaker than Qq "to this gear." See note on line 85 above. In *The True Tragedie of Richard the Third*, quoted by Aldis Wright, we find "He spares none whom he but mistrusteth to be a hinderer to his proceedings, he is straight chopped up in prison." Quotations for this use of "chop" in *New Eng. Dict.* range from 1560 to 1708.

malmsey] Boswell Stone, *Shakspere's Holinshed*, 1896, p. 348, notes that the execution of Clarence in the butt of malmsey is the only detail of this scene which Shakespeare did not invent. Malmsey or Malvoisie was a Greek wine from Napoli di Malvasia (Monemvasia) on the south-east coast of Laconia. According to Howell, *Epp. Ho.-El.*, ii. 54, "some few Muscadells or *Malmsies* . . . brought over in small Casks" were the only wines suitable for transportation from Greece. Compare Burton, *Anatomy of Melancholy* (Shilleto, i. 255): "All black wines overhot, compound, strong thick drinks, as Muscadine, *Malmsey*, Alicant, Rumney, Brown Bastard, Metheglin, and the like." In Jonson, *Bartholomew Fair*, i. 1, Littlewit says of Busy, "Some time the spirit is so strong with him, it gets quite out of him, and then my mother, or Win, are fain to fetch it again with *malmsey* or aqua cælestis." See Mr. Hart's note on *Measure for Measure*, III. ii. 3, 4.

155. *make a sop*] Mr. Craig illustrates from *King Lear*, II. ii. 35, and *Troilus and Cressida*, I. iii. 113.

First Murd. Soft, he wakes!
Sec. Murd. Strike!
First Murd. No, we 'll reason with him.
Clar. [*awaking*]. Where art thou, keeper? give me a cup of wine.
First Murd. You shall have wine enough, my lord, anon.
Clar. In God's name, what art thou?
First Murd. A man, as you are.
Clar. But not, as I am, royal.
First Murd. Nor you, as we are, loyal.
Clar. Thy voice is thunder, but thy looks are humble.
First Murd. My voice is now the king's, my looks mine own.
Clar. How darkly and how deadly dost thou speak!
Your eyes do menace me: why look you pale?
Who sent you hither? wherefore do you come?
Both. To, to, to——
Clar. To murder me?
Both. Ay, ay.
Clar. You scarcely have the hearts to tell me so,
And therefore cannot have the hearts to do it.
Wherein, my friends, have I offended you?
First Murd. Offended us you have not, but the king.
Clar. I shall be reconciled to him again.
Sec. Murd. Never, my lord: therefore prepare to die.
Clar. Are you drawn forth, among a world of men,
To slay the innocent? What is my offence?

156. *Soft, he wakes*] Ff; *Harke he stirs, shall I strike* Qq. 157. *Sec. Murd. Strike*] Ff; omitted Qq. 158. *First Murd.*] 1 Ff; 2 Qq (and 163, 167). *we 'll*] *wee 'l* Ff; *first lets* Qq. 159. *awaking*] *Cla. awaketh* Qq 3-8. 165. *First Murd.*] 1 Qq 5-8, Ff; 2 Qq 1-4. 169. *Your . . . pale*] Ff; omitted Qq. 170. *Who . . . come*] Ff; *Tell me who are you, wherefore come you hither* Qq. 171. *Both*] *Am.* Qq; 2 Ff. 173. *Both. Ay, ay*] *Both. I, I* Ff; *Am. I* Qq. 174. *hearts*] *heart* Qq 6-8. 180. *drawn forth, among*] *drawne forth among* Ff; *cald foorth from out* Qq.

158. *reason*] talk, as below, II. iii. 39, and constantly in the Authorised Version of the Bible.

180. *drawn*] In support of Qq, Steevens quotes *Nobody and Somebody*, 1598:—

"Art thou call'd forth amongst a thousand men
To minister this soveraigne antidote?"

Johnson read "culled"—an unnecessary emendation. "Among a world of men" is put here within commas, in order to emphasise the stress evidently laid by Clarence on "you."

Where is the evidence that doth accuse me?
What lawful quest have given their verdict up
Unto the frowning judge? or who pronounc'd
The bitter sentence of poor Clarence' death?
Before I be convict by course of law,
To threaten me with death is most unlawful.
I charge you, as you hope to have redemption
By Christ's dear blood shed for our grievous sins,
That you depart and lay no hands on me!
The deed you undertake is damnable.

First Murd. What we will do we do upon command.

Sec. Murd. And he that hath commanded is our king.

Clar. Erroneous vassals! the great King of kings
Hath in the table of His law commanded
That thou shalt do no murder. Will you then
Spurn at His edict, and fulfil a man's?
Take heed; for He holds vengeance in His hand,
To hurl upon their heads that break His law.

Sec. Murd. And that same vengeance doth He hurl on thee,
For false forswearing, and for murder too.
Thou didst receive the holy Sacrament,
To fight in quarrel of the house of Lancaster.

182. *is*] Ff; *are* Qq. *that doth*] Ff; *that doe* Qq 1, 2; *to* Qq 3-8. 187. *threaten*] *thteaten* Q 3; *thereaten* Qq 4-6. 188, 189. *to have . . . sins*] Qq; *for any goodnesse* Ff. 193. *our*] Ff; *the* Qq. 194. *vassals*] Ff; *vassaile* Qq. 195. *the table*] Ff; *the tables* Qq 1, 2; *his tables* Qq 3-6. 196. *Will you*] Ff; *and wilt thou* Qq. 198. *hand*] Ff; *hands* Qq. 200. *hurl*] Ff; *throw* Qq. 202, 203. *holy . . . To . . . Lancaster*] Qq; *Sacrament to fight In . . . Lancaster* Ff.

183. Clarence's imprisonment and execution, if hasty, were carried out after trial and condemnation. Gairdner, *Richard the Third*, new ed. p. 32, comments on the one-sided character of the trial.

188, 189. *to have . . . sins*] See note on line 117 above; Qq would be subject to the fine of £10 inflicted by the statute there mentioned.

194. *Erroneous*] Compare Fletcher, *Monsieur Thomas*, i. 2: "Your worship is *erroneous*."

202, 203. F 1 appears to have altered the passage either in order to smooth out the Alexandrine in line 202, or to omit "holy" before "Sacrament." This use of "holy" would be far more likely to fall under the statute already referred to than the use in line 117 (Qq). There is no reason why "holy," if not in the original MS., should have been added in Qq; and, consequently, why it should be omitted in Ff.

203. *in quarrel*] Compare Fletcher, *False One*, i. 1:—

"He pities them whose fortunes are embark'd
In his unlucky *quarrel*."

First Murd. And, like a traitor to the name of God,
Didst break that vow, and with thy treacherous blade
Unrip'dst the bowels of thy sovereign's son.
Sec. Murd. Whom thou wast sworn to cherish and defend.
First Murd. How canst thou urge God's dreadful law to us,
When thou hast broke it in such dear degree?
Clar. Alas! for whose sake did I that ill deed?
For Edward, for my brother, for his sake:
He sends you not to murder me for this,
For in that sin he is as deep as I.
If God will be avenged for the deed,
O, know you yet, He doth it publicly.
Take not the quarrel from His powerful arm;
He needs no indirect or lawless course
To cut off those that have offended Him.
First Murd. Who made thee then a bloody minister,
When gallant-springing brave Plantagenet,
That princely novice, was struck dead by thee?
Clar. My brother's love, the devil, and my rage.

207. *wast*] *was't* Ff; *wert* Qq. 209. *such*] Ff; *so* Qq. 212. *He*] Ff; *Why sirs, he* Qq. *you*] Ff; *ye* Qq. 213. *that*] Ff; *this* Qq. 214. *avenged*] Ff; *reuenged* Qq. *the deed*] Ff; *this deed* Qq. 215. *O . . . publicly*] Ff; omitted Qq. *you yet*] *you, that* Steevens (Farmer conj.). 217. *or*] Ff; *nor* Qq. *lawless*] Q 1, Ff; *lawfull* Qq 2-8. 220. *gallant-springing*] Q 1, Ff (hyphened Pope); *gallant spring* Qq 2-8; *gallant springall* Capell (conj.). 221. *That*] *The* Qq 6-8.

209. *dear*] "A word of mere enforcement" (Steevens). Compare *King Lear*, IV. iii. 53; *Troilus and Cressida*, V. iii. 9. There is an ironical use in Jonson, *Cynthia's Revels*, i. 1, where Crites says to Asotus: "Leave it to me, I'll forget none of your *dear* graces, I warrant you."

212. The "Why, sirs" preceding this line in Qq, is printed by Cambridge editors as a line by itself. It is probably an ejaculation introduced from the colloquial stage-alterations of this dialogue.

220. *gallant-springing*] For "springing" compare Spenser, *Shepherd's Calendar*, 1579, February, 52:—

"I scorn thy skill,
That wouldest me my *springing* youngth to spill."

The double adjective, of which the first part qualifies the second and takes the place of an adverb, is common in this play, and in Elizabethan literature generally. Compare Greene, *Orlando Furioso* (Dyce, 91): "fortune, or some deep-inspiring fate"; Fletcher and Massinger, *Spanish Curate*, iii. 3: "an easy-yielding wanton." There are three good examples in Tourneur, *Revenger's Tragedy*, act i.: "And thou his son, as impious-steep'd as he"; "Be not so cruel-wise"; and

"All which and more
She, foolish chaste, sent back."

Compare "childish-foolish" above, I. iii. 142; "wrong-incensed" below, II. i. 51; "high-swoll'n," II. ii. 117.

First Murd. Thy brother's love, our duty, and thy faults,
Provoke us hither now to slaughter thee.
Clar. If you do love my brother, hate not me:
I am his brother, and I love him well.
If you are hir'd for meed, go back again,
And I will send you to my brother Gloucester,
Who shall reward you better for my life
Than Edward will for tidings of my death.
Sec. Murd. You are deceiv'd, your brother Gloucester hates you.
Clar. O, no, he loves me, and he holds me dear:
Go you to him from me.
Both. Ay, so we will.
Clar. Tell him, when that our princely father York
Bless'd his three sons with his victorious arm,
And charg'd us from his soul to love each other,
He little thought of this divided friendship:
Bid Gloucester think of this, and he will weep.
First Murd. Ay, millstones; as he lesson'd us to weep.
Clar. O, do not slander him, for he is kind.
First Murd. Right,
As snow in harvest. Come, you deceive yourself:
'Tis he that sends us to destroy you here.
Clar. It cannot be; for he bewept my fortune,
And hugg'd me in his arms, and swore with sobs
That he would labour my delivery.

223. *our duty*] Ff; *the diuell* Qq. *faults*] Ff; *fault* Qq. 224. *Provoke*] Ff; *Haue brought* Qq. *slaughter*] Ff; *murder* Qq. 225. *If you do*] Ff; *Oh if you* Qq. *my brother*] *brother* Qq 4-6. 227. *are*] Ff; *be* Qq. *meed*] Q 1, Ff; *neede* Qq 2-8. 229. *shall*] Ff; *will* Qq. 231. *You . . . hates you*] one line Qq; *You are deceiu'd, Your . . . hates you* (two lines) Ff. 233. *Both*] *Am.* Qq; 1 Ff. 236. *And . . . each other*] Qq; omitted Ff. 238. *of this*] *on this* Qq 6-8, Ff. 239. *First Murd.*] 1 Ff; *Am.* Qq. 241, 242. *Right, As*] Camb.; *Right as* Qq 1, 2; *Right, as* Qq 3-8, Ff; *As* Pope. 242. *Come . . . yourself*] Ff; *thou deceiu'st thy selfe* Qq. 243. *that sends . . . here*] Ff; *hath sent us hither now to slaughter thee* Q 1; *that sent us hither now to murder thee* Qq 2-8. 244, 245. *he . . . fortune, And*] Ff; *when I parted with him, He* Qq.

239. *lesson'd*] The murderer refers to I. iii. 353 above. Compare *Coriolanus*, II. iii. 185; Spenser, *Faerie Queene*, III. vi. 51.

240. *kind*] naturally affectionate, as *Hamlet*, I. ii. 65. The murderer, in answer, plays on the more ordinary meaning, "natural."

246. *labour my delivery*] busy him-

First Murd. Why, so he doth, when he delivers you
From this earth's thraldom to the joys of heaven.
Sec. Murd. Make peace with God; for you must die, my lord.
Clar. Have you that holy feeling in your souls,
To counsel me to make my peace with God,
And are you yet to your own souls so blind
That you will war with God by murdering me?
O sirs, consider, they that set you on
To do this deed, will hate you for the deed.
Sec. Murd. What shall we do?
Clar. Relent, and save your souls.
First Murd. Relent! no, 'tis cowardly and womanish.
Clar. Not to relent is beastly, savage, devilish.
Which of you, if you were a prince's son,
Being pent from liberty, as I am now,
If two such murderers as yourselves came to you,
Would not entreat for life?
My friend, I spy some pity in thy looks;
O, if thine eye be not a flatterer,
Come thou on my side, and entreat for me,
As you would beg, were you in my distress!
A begging prince what beggar pities not?

247. *First Murd.*] 1 Ff; 2 Qq. *when*] Ff; *now* Qq. *you*] Ff; *thee* Qq. 248. *earth's*] Ff; *worlds* Qq. 250. *Have you . . . your souls*] Ff; *Hast thou . . . thy soule* Qq. 252. *are you . . . your own souls*] Ff; *art thou . . . thy own soule* Qq. 253. *you will*] Ff; *thou wilt* Qq. *by*] *for* Qq 3-8. 254. *O*] Ff; *Ah* Qq. *they*] Ff; *he* Qq. 255. *for the deed*] Ff; *for this deede* Qq. 257-68. *First Murd. Relent! no . . . my lord!*] arranged as Steevens (Tyrwhitt conj.), Camb.; Ff. arrange thus, 259, 260, 261, 262, 266, 257, 258, 263, 264, 265, 267, 268; Qq. thus, 257, 258, 263, 264, 265, 267 [omitting 259-62, 266, 268]; Pope as Qq, but omitting 267. 257. *no*] Ff; omitted Qq. 258. *devilish*] Q 1, Ff; *and diuelish* Qq 2-8. 262. *Would . . . life*] *Would . . . life, as you would begge, Were you in my distresse* F; *Would . . . life? Ah! you would beg, Were . . . distress* Theobald. 263. *thy*] *your* Qq 6, 8. 264. *thine*] Ff; *thy* Qq. 266. *As . . . distress*] see line 262 above.

self to procure my delivery. So Kyd, *Spanish Tragedy*, act iii. :—

"My lord, I write as my extremes require,
That you would *labour my delivery*";

and Marlowe, *Jew of Malta*, c. 1589-90, act iii. :—

"It is not yet long since
That I did *labour thy delivery*."

Compare *Eastward Ho*, act v.: "I do wonder . . . that you, being the keeper of a prison, should *labour* the release of your prisoners."

257-68. See Appendix I.

267. There is perhaps a reminiscence of this line in Chapman (?), *Alphonsus*, v. 2 (Shepherd, 413), where the Emperor says to his murderer, "Think what I am that beg my life of thee."

Sec. Murd. Look behind you, my lord!

First Murd. Take that, and that! [*Stabs him*] if all this will not do,
I 'll drown you in the malmsey-butt within.
[*Exit, with the body.*

Sec. Murd. A bloody deed, and desperately dispatch'd!
How fain, like Pilate, would I wash my hands
Of this most grievous murder—

Re-enter First Murderer.

First Murd. How now! what mean'st thou that thou help'st me not?
By heaven, the duke shall know how slack you have been!

Sec. Murd. I would he knew that I had sav'd his brother!
Take thou the fee, and tell him what I say;
For I repent me that the duke is slain. [*Exit.*

First Murd. So do not I: go, coward as thou art!
Well, I 'll go hide the body in some hole,
Till that the duke give order for his burial:
And, when I have my meed, I will away;
For this will out, and then I must not stay. [*Exit.*

269. *Take that, and that*] Ff; *I thus, and thus* Qq. *if all . . . do*] Ff; *if this will not serue* Qq; *and, if this will not serve* Capell. 270. *drown you*] Ff; *chop thee* Qq. *within*] Ff; *in the next roome* Qq. *Exit, with the body*] Steevens; *Exit.* Ff; omitted Qq. 271. *dispatch'd*] Ff; *perform'd* Qq. 272. *hands*] Ff; *hand* Qq 1-7. 273. *grievous murder*] Ff; *grievous guilty murder done* Qq. *Re-enter . . .*] Camb.; *Enter . . .* Ff; omitted Qq. 274. *How now . . . not*] Ff (as prose); *Why doest thou not helpe me* Qq. 275. *heaven*] Qq 6-8, Ff; *heavens* Qq 1-5. *you have been*] Ff (as prose); *thou art* Qq. 280. *Well, I'll go*] Ff; *Now must I* Qq. *the body*] Ff; *his body* Qq. 281. *Till that*] Ff; *Vntill* Qq. *give*] Ff; *take* Qq. 282. *will*] Ff; *must* Qq. 283. *then*] Ff; *here* Qq. *Exit.*] Ff; *Exeunt.* Qq.

272. Compare *Richard II.* IV. i. 239.

ACT II

SCENE I.—*London. The Palace.*

Flourish. Enter KING EDWARD *sick*, QUEEN ELIZABETH, DORSET, RIVERS, HASTINGS, BUCKINGHAM, GREY, *and others.*

K. Edw. Why, so: now have I done a good day's work.
You peers, continue this united league:
I every day expect an embassage
From my Redeemer, to redeem me hence;
And now in peace my soul shall part to heaven,
Since I have made my friends at peace on earth.
Rivers and Hastings, take each other's hand;
Dissemble not your hatred, swear your love.

Riv. By heaven, my soul is purg'd from grudging hate;
And with my hand I seal my true heart's love!

Hast. So thrive I, as I truly swear the like!

K. Edw. Take heed you dally not before your king;

ACT II. SCENE I. *Flourish.*] Ff; omitted Qq. *Enter King Edward . . . others.*] *Enter the King sicke, the Queene, Lord Marquesse Dorset, Riuers, Hastings, Catesby, Buckingham, Wooduill,* Ff; *Enter King, Queene, Hastings, Ryuers, Dorcet, &c.* Qq (Qq 3-8 omit *Dorcet*). 1. *Why, so*] *Why so* Ff; *So* Qq. *have I*] Ff; *I have* Qq. 5. *now in peace*] Qq; *more to peace* Ff. *part to*] Qq 3-8, Ff; *part from* Qq 1, 2. 6. *made*] Ff; *set* Qq. 7. *Rivers and Hastings*] Qq; *Dorset and Riuers* Ff. 9. *soul*] Ff; *heart* Qq. 11. *truly*] omitted Qq 3-8.

5. *now in peace*] Ff have evidently a printer's error for "more in peace," which is Steevens' reading.

7. *Rivers and Hastings*] Ff here are clearly wrong. The editor was probably misled by some marginal correction in his MS. Rivers and Hastings had been on bad terms. Rivers and Dorset, on the contrary, were uncle and nephew, and the leaders of the Woodville party. It is curious that the editor, who added line 25 below, did not see that the present alteration was inappropriate.

8. *Dissemble not your hatred*] The meaning is obvious; but the phrase is capable of another interpretation. Malone's explanation is needlessly elaborate. The line may be paraphrased thus: Do not hide your hatred beneath a mere show of friendship; but swear truly to be friends.

Lest He that is the supreme King of kings
Confound your hidden falsehood, and award
Either of you to be the other's end.
Hast. So prosper I, as I swear perfect love!
Riv. And I, as I love Hastings with my heart!
K. Edw. Madam, yourself is not exempt from this,
Nor you, son Dorset; Buckingham, nor you:
You have been factious one against the other.
Wife, love Lord Hastings, let him kiss your hand;
And what you do, do it unfeignedly.
Q. Eliz. There, Hastings; I will never more remember
Our former hatred, so thrive I and mine!
K. Edw. Dorset, embrace him; Hastings, love lord marquess.
Dor. This interchange of love, I here protest
Upon my part, shall be inviolable.
Hast. And so swear I. [*They embrace.*
K. Edw. Now, princely Buckingham, seal thou this league
With thy embracements to my wife's allies,
And make me happy in your unity.
Buck. [*To the Queen.*] Whenever Buckingham doth turn his hate
Upon your grace, but with all duteous love
Doth cherish you and yours, God punish me
With hate in those where I expect most love!

18. *is*] Ff; *are* Qq. *from this*] Ff; *in this* Qq. 19. *you,*] Ff; *your* Qq. 23. *There*] Ff; *Here* Qq. 25. *K. Edw. Dorset . . . marquess*] *King. Dorset . . . him: Hastings . . . Marquesse* (two lines) Ff; omitted Qq. 26. *This*] Q 1, Ff; *Thus* Qq 2-8. 27. *inviolable*] Ff; *unuiolable* Qq. 28. *swear I.*] Ff; *sweare I my Lord.* Qq. *They embrace*] Capell. 32. *To the Queen.*] Rowe. 33. *Upon your grace*] Ff; *On you or yours* Qq. *but with all*] *and not with* Pope.

20. *factious*] Johnson explains as "active" or "urgent." Mr. Craig suggests that the meaning here is "in active opposition." Probably the derived meaning "guilty of faction" is really implied.

30. *embracements*] Used again, *Comedy of Errors*, I. i. 44; *Troilus and Cressida*, IV. v. 148; *Henry VIII*. I. i. 10. Decker, *Bel-Man of London*, speaks of branches of trees that "in their *embracements* held so fast together, that their boughs made a goodlie greene roofe."

32-34. Pope's emendation of 34, mentioned above, avoids the difficulty of the passage, which seems to arise from the attempt to combine two strong asseverations, whose meaning is opposed, in one connected sentence. The doubtful passage in *Winter's Tale*, I. ii. 459, 460, may be explained by a similar attempt to combine two opposite thoughts together.

When I have most need to employ a friend,
And most assured that he is a friend,
Deep, hollow, treacherous, and full of guile,
Be he unto me! This do I beg of God,
When I am cold in love to you or yours.
[*They embrace.*

K. Edw. A pleasing cordial, princely Buckingham,
Is this thy vow unto my sickly heart.
There wanteth now our brother Gloucester here,
To make the blessed period of this peace.

Buck. And, in good time, here comes the noble duke.

Enter GLOUCESTER.

Glou. Good morrow to my sovereign king and queen;
And, princely peers, a happy time of day!

K. Edw. Happy indeed, as we have spent the day.
Gloucester, we have done deeds of charity,
Made peace of enmity, fair love of hate,
Between these swelling wrong-incensed peers.

Glou. A blessed labour, my most sovereign lord.
Among this princely heap, if any here,
By false intelligence, or wrong surmise,

39. *God*] Qq; *heauen* Ff. 40. *love*] Ff; *zeale* Qq. 44. *blessed*] Ff; *perfect* Qq. 45. *And . . . duke*] Qq; *And in good time, Heere comes Sir Richard Ratcliffe, and the Duke* (two lines) Ff. *Enter Gloucester.*] Qq (before 45); *Enter Ratcliffe, and Gloster.* Ff. 49. *Gloucester*] *Gloster* Ff; *Brother* Qq. 52. *my*] omitted Qq 3-8. *lord*] Ff; *liege* Qq. 53. *Among*] Ff; *Amongst* Qq.

37. *most assured*] *i.e.* I am most assured. The construction is elliptical.

45. The alteration in Ff of this line and the stage-direction following seems unnecessary. Ratcliff says and does nothing in what follows; nor is it likely that his name would be mentioned before Gloucester's, unless the metre made it unavoidable. But, since a whole line which was metrically perfect had to be altered into a line and a half, in order to introduce Ratcliff's name, the editor of F 1 must have had some ground to go upon. Probably his MS. contained the name of Ratcliff. But Ratcliff's silent part may have been omitted in the stage performance, when there were not too many actors to spare; and so the passage passed into Qq, metrically emended, and in a more satisfactory form.

51. *swelling*] Compare *Othello*, II. iii. 57. But the metaphor in the present case is "swelling with wrath" rather than "swelling with ambition." See below, II. ii. 117.

53. *heap*] assembly (O.E. *heáp*, a multitude). Compare *Julius Cæsar*, I. iii. 23; Chaucer, *Canterbury Tales*, A. 575: "The wisdom of an *heep* of lerned men." *New Eng. Dict.* quotes Earl Rivers, *Dictes and notable Wise Sayings of the Philosophers*, 1477, p. 105: "A great *heep* of sheep."

Hold me a foe;
If I unwittingly, or in my rage,
Have ought committed that is hardly borne
By any in this presence, I desire
To reconcile me to his friendly peace:
'Tis death to me to be at enmity;
I hate it, and desire all good men's love.
First, madam, I entreat true peace of you,
Which I will purchase with my duteous service;
Of you, my noble cousin Buckingham,
If ever any grudge were lodg'd between us;
Of you, Lord Rivers, and Lord Grey, of you,
That all without desert have frown'd on me,
Dukes, earls, lords, gentlemen, indeed of all:
I do not know that Englishman alive,
With whom my soul is any jot at odds,
More than the infant that is born to-night:
I thank my God for my humility.

Q. Eliz. A holy day shall this be kept hereafter:

55, 56. *Hold . . . rage*] arranged as Malone (sugg. Capell); one line Qq, Ff. 56. *unwittingly*] Qq; *vnwillingly* Ff. *or in my rage*] omitted Pope. 58. *By*] Qq; *To* Ff. 62. *true*] omitted Qq 3-8. 66. *Of you, Lord . . . of you*] Qq 1-4; *Of you my Lord . . . of you* Qq 5-8; *Of you and you, Lord Riuers and of Dorset* Ff. aft. 67. Ff adds *Of you Lord Wooduill, and Lord Scales of you.*

56. *in my rage*] in unthinking passion. Compare Greene, *Orlando Furioso* (Dyce, 99):—

"Theseus *in his rage*
Did never more revenge his wrong'd Hippolytus
Than I will on the false Angelica";

ibid. (108):—

"as cruel death
As fell to Nero's mother *in his rage*."

See *King Lear*, IV. vii. 78; *Coriolanus*, V. vi. 148; and line 106 below.

57. *hardly borne*] "To bear hard" is to bear a grudge. Compare the Latin *ægre ferre.* See *Julius Cæsar*, II. i. 215. Two further instances occur *ibid.* I. ii. 317; III. i. 157. *New Eng. Dict.* quotes *Life of Thomas Cromwell*, 1602, IV. ii. 112: "You bear me hard about the abbey lands."

6668. See Appendix II.

67. *without desert*] *i.e.* without desert on my part.

69-72. Milton, *Eikonoklastes*, 1649, chap. i., in support of the thesis that "the deepest policy of a tyrant hath been ever to counterfeit religious," says that the poets "have been in this point so mindful of decorum, as to put never more pious words in the mouth of any person, than of a tyrant. I shall not instance an abstruse author, wherein the king [Charles I.] might be less conversant, but one whom we well know was the closest companion of these his solitudes, William Shakespeare; who introduces the person of Richard the Third, speaking in as high a strain of piety and mortification as is uttered in any passage of this book [*Eikon Basilike*], and sometimes to the same sense and purpose with some words in this place: 'I intended,' saith he, 'not only to oblige my friends, but my enemies.'"

I would to God all strifes were well compounded.
My sovereign lord, I do beseech your highness
To take our brother Clarence to your grace.

Glou. Why, madam, have I offer'd love for this,
To be so flouted in this royal presence?
Who knows not that the gentle duke is dead?
[*They all start.*
You do him injury to scorn his corse.

K. Edw. Who knows not he is dead! who knows he is?

Q. Eliz. All-seeing heaven, what a world is this!

Buck. Look I so pale, Lord Dorset, as the rest?

Dor. Ay, my good lord; and no man in the presence,
But his red colour hath forsook his cheeks.

K. Edw. Is Clarence dead? the order was revers'd.

Glou. But he, poor soul, by your first order died,
And that a winged Mercury did bear;
Some tardy cripple bare the countermand,
That came too lag to see him buried.
God grant that some, less noble and less loyal,
Nearer in bloody thoughts, and not in blood,
Deserve not worse than wretched Clarence did,
And yet go current from suspicion!

75. *lord*] Ff; *liege* Qq. *highness*] Ff; *maiestie* Qq. 78. *so flouted*] Ff; *thus scorned* Qq (*scornde* Q 6). 79. *gentle*] Ff; *noble* Qq. *They all start.*] Ff; omitted Qq. 81. *K. Edw.*] *King.* Ff; *Riu.* Qq. *Who . . . he is*] one line as Qq; two lines (*Who . . . dead? Who . . . is?*) Ff. 84. *no man*] Ff; *no one* Qq. *the presence*] Ff; *this presence* Qq. 87. *soul*] Qq; *man* Ff. 89. *bare*] Ff; *bore* Qq. 92. *and not*] Ff; *but not* Qq.

83. See below, line 136. Buckingham's remark on the sudden pallor of Dorset himself and his relations is malicious. They are Buckingham's enemies; and he wishes to fasten the stigma of guilt upon them.

84. *in the presence*] "Presence" is used in the sense of "noble company," *Midsummer-Night's Dream*, I. i. 61. In *Richard II.* I. iii. 289 it means "presence-chamber."

89. *Some tardy cripple*] Steevens mentions a proverbial expression found in Drayton, *Barons' Wars*, 1603, ii. st. 28:—

"Ill news hath wings, and with the winde doth goe;
Comfort's a *cripple*, and comes ever slow."

90. *lag*] late. Compare *King Lear*, I. ii. 6, and see Mr. Craig's note.

92. Steevens cites *Macbeth*, II. iii. 146, 147.

94. *go current*] Compare Decker, *Guls Horn-Booke*, chap. iii.: "Certaine I am, that when none but the golden age went *currant* upon earth, it was higher treason to clip haire, then to clip money." See also Machin and Markham, *Dumb Knight*, act iii.: "My plot is *current* and it cannot miss."

Enter DERBY.

Der. A boon, my sovereign, for my service done!
K. Edw. I prithee, peace: my soul is full of sorrow.
Der. I will not rise, unless your highness hear me.
K. Edw. Then say at once, what is it thou demand'st.
Der. The forfeit, sovereign, of my servant's life,
Who slew to-day a riotous gentleman,
Lately attendant on the Duke of Norfolk.
K. Edw. Have I a tongue to doom my brother's death,
And shall that tongue give pardon to a slave?
My brother kill'd no man: his fault was thought;
And yet his punishment was bitter death.
Who sued to me for him? who, in my rage,
Kneel'd at my feet, and bade me be advis'd?
Who spoke of brotherhood? who spoke of love?
Who told me how the poor soul did forsake
The mighty Warwick, and did fight for me?
Who told me, in the field by Tewkesbury,
When Oxford had me down, he rescued me,
And said "Dear brother, live, and be a king"?
Who told me, when we both lay in the field,
Frozen almost to death, how he did lap me
Even in his garments, and did give himself,
All thin and naked, to the numb cold night?
All this from my remembrance brutish wrath

96. *prithee*] F 4; *prethee* Ff 1-3; *pray thee* Qq. 97. *hear me*] Ff; *grant* Qq. 98. *say*] Ff; *speake* Qq. *demand'st*] Qq (*demaundest* Q 6); *requests* Ff. 103. *that tongue*] Ff; *the same* Qq. 104. *kill'd*] Ff; *slew* Qq. 105. *bitter*] Ff; *cruell* Qq. 106. *rage*] Qq; *wrath* Ff. 107. *at my feet*] Qq; *and my feet* Ff. 108. *Who spoke*] Ff; *Who spake* Qq. *spoke of love*] F 1; *spoke in love* Ff 2-4; *of love* Qq. 111. *by*] Qq; *at* Ff. 116. *his garments*] Ff; *his owne garments* Qq 1-5; *his owne armes* Qq 6-8. *did give*] Ff; *gaue* Qq.

99. *The forfeit*] Johnson explains, "the remission of *the forfeit*."

107. *be advis'd*] be cautious, as *2 Henry VI.* II. iv. 36; *Merchant of Venice*, II. i. 42. See also *Measure for Measure*, V. i. 469.

112. *Oxford*] John de Vere, thirteenth Earl of Oxford (1443-1513), could not have been present at Tewkesbury, for he escaped to France immediately after the battle of Barnet, where he fought on the side of Warwick.

115. *lap*] cover, enfold, as *Macbeth*, I. ii. 54; *Cymbeline*, V. v. 360. See also song in *Gammer Gurton's Needle*, act ii.:—

"I am so wrapt, and throwly *lapt*,
Of jolly good ale and old";

Decker, *Seuen Deadly Sinnes of London* (Arber, 27): "his legges, that are *lapt* rounde about with peeces of Rugge."

Sinfully pluck'd, and not a man of you
Had so much grace to put it in my mind.
But when your carters or your waiting-vassals
Have done a drunken slaughter, and defac'd
The precious image of our dear Redeemer,
You straight are on your knees for pardon, pardon;
And I, unjustly too, must grant it you:
But for my brother not a man would speak,
Nor I, ungracious, speak unto myself
For him, poor soul! The proudest of you all
Have been beholding to him in his life;
Yet none of you would once beg for his life.
O God, I fear Thy justice will take hold
On me, and you, and mine, and yours for this!
Come, Hastings, help me to my closet. Ah, poor Clarence!
[*Exeunt some with King and Queen.*

Glou. This is the fruit of rashness. Mark'd you not
How that the guilty kindred of the queen
Look'd pale when they did hear of Clarence' death?
O! they did urge it still unto the king:
God will revenge it. Come, lords, will you go
To comfort Edward with our company?

Buck. We wait upon your grace. [*Exeunt.*

122. *defac'd*] *defaste* Qq 1-3. 126. *not a man*] *not a mast* Qq 3-5. 127. *speak*] *spake* Rowe. 129. *beholding*] *beholden* Qq 5, 6. 130. *beg*] Ff; *pleade* Qq. 133. *Come . . . Clarence*] one line as Qq; two lines (*Come . . . Closset, Ah . . . Clarence*) Ff; *Come* [*to Hastings*], *help me . . . Clarence* Capell. *Ah*] Ff; *Oh* Qq. *Exeunt . . . Queen.*] Ff; *Exit* Qq. 134. *fruit*] Qq; *fruits* Ff. *rashness*] *rawnes* Qq 3-5; *rawnesse* Qq 6-8. 138. *Come . . . go*] Ff; *But come lets in* Qq. 140. *Buck. We . . . grace*] Ff; omitted Qq.

126. Holinshed, iii. 703, following Halle, describes Edward's grief for Clarence's "sudden execution." "When anie person sued to him for the pardon of malefactors condemned to death, he would accustomablie saie, & openlie speake: 'Oh infortunate brother, for whose life not one would make sute!'"

137. *still*] continually; a very general usage. Mr. Craig notes that it is common in Ulster.

SCENE II.—*The Palace.*

Enter the DUCHESS OF YORK, *with the two children of* CLARENCE.

Boy. Good grandam, tell us, is our father dead?
Duch. No, boy.
Girl. Why do you weep so oft, and beat your breast,
And cry "O Clarence, my unhappy son"?
Boy. Why do you look on us, and shake your head,
And call us orphans, wretches, castaways,
If that our noble father were alive?
Duch. My pretty cousins, you mistake me both.
I do lament the sickness of the king.
As loath to lose him, not your father's death:
It were lost sorrow to wail one that 's lost.
Boy. Then you conclude, my grandam, he is dead.
The king mine uncle is to blame for it:
God will revenge it, whom I will importune
With earnest prayers, all to that effect.
Girl. And so will I.
Duch. Peace, children, peace! the king doth love you well.
Incapable and shallow innocents,
You cannot guess who caus'd your father's death.
Boy. Grandam, we can; for my good uncle Gloucester

Enter the Duchess . . . Clarence.] *Enter the old Dutchesse . . . Clarence.* Ff; *Enter Dutches of Yorke with Clarence Children.* Qq. 1. *Boy.*] Qq; *Edw.* Ff. *Good grandam, tell us*] Ff; *Tell me good Granam* Qq. 3. *Girl*] *Daugh.* Ff; *Boy.* Qq. *do you*] do Ff. *weep so oft*] Ff; *wring your hands* Qq. 5. *Boy.*] Ff; *Gerl.* Qq. 6. *orphans, wretches*] Ff; *wretches, orphans* Qq. 8. *both*] Ff; *much* Qq. 10. *not your father's death*] *now your fathers dead* Qq 6-8. 11. *sorrow to wail*] Ff; *labour to weepe for* Qq. 12. *you . . . grandam*] Ff; *Granam you conclude that* Qq. 13. *for it*] Ff; *for this* Qq. 15. *earnest*] Ff; *daily* Qq. 16. *Girl. And . . . I*] *Daugh. And . . . I* Ff; omitted Qq.

8. *cousins*] relations. The usage is not altogether obsolete in our own day. Compare *Much Ado About Nothing*, I. ii. 2. In Wilkins, *Miseries of Inforst Marriage*, act i., an uncle says to his nephew: "Thanks, my good *coz*." Richard speaks below of Edward V. and the Duke of York as his cousins.

15, 16. Pope combined the two lines thus:—

"With daily earnest prayers.
Girl. And so will I."

18. *Incapable*] destitute of capacity, without power of understanding. So *Hamlet*, IV. vii. 179, and see Prof. Dowden's note in Arden ed. Compare Greene, *Friar Bacon* (Dyce, 164): "Doctors, whose doting night-caps are not *capable* of my ingenious dignity."

Told me, the king, provok'd to it by the queen,
Devis'd impeachments to imprison him;
And when my uncle told me so, he wept,
And pitied me, and kindly kiss'd my cheek;
Bade me rely on him, as on my father,
And he would love me dearly as a child.

Duch. Ah! that deceit should steal such gentle shape,
And with a virtuous vizard hide deep vice!
He is my son, ay, and therein my shame;
Yet from my dugs he drew not this deceit.

Boy. Think you my uncle did dissemble, grandam?

Duch. Ay, boy.

Boy. I cannot think it. Hark! what noise is this?

Enter QUEEN ELIZABETH, *with her hair about her ears;* RIVERS *and* DORSET *after her.*

Q. Eliz. Ah! who shall hinder me to wail and weep,
To chide my fortune, and torment myself?
I'll join with black despair against my soul,
And to myself become an enemy.

Duch. What means this scene of rude impatience?

Q. Eliz. To make an act of tragic violence.
Edward, my lord, thy son, our king, is dead.
Why grow the branches when the root is gone?
Why wither not the leaves that want their sap?
If you will live, lament: if die, be brief,

21. *provok'd to it*] Ff; *prouoked* Qq. 23. *my uncle*] Ff; *hee* Qq. 24. *pitied me*] Ff; *hugd me in his arme* Qq. *cheek*] *cheekes* Qq 6-8. 25. *Bade*] *Bad* Ff; *And bad* Qq. *on my*] *in my* Q 1. 26. *a child*] Ff; *his child* Qq. 27. *Ah*] Ff; *Oh* Qq. *shape*] Ff; *shapes* Qq. 28. *deep vice*] Ff; *foule guile* Qq. 29. *ay*] *I* Ff; *yea* Qq 1-3, 5-8; omitted Q 4. aft. 33. *Enter Queen Elizabeth . . . after her.*] *Enter the Queene . . . after her.* Ff; *Enter the Queene.* Qq. 34. *Ah*] Ff; *Oh* Qq 1, 2, 4; *Wh* Q 3; omitted Qq 5-8. 36. *soul*] *selfe* Qq 5-8. 40. *thy*] Ff; *your* Qq. 41. *when . . . is gone*] Ff; *now . . . is witherd* Qq. 42. *that want their sap*] Ff; *the sap being gone* Qq.

23, 24. Qq are here stronger and more lively than Ff. But the words "And hugg'd me in his arm," which spoil the metre of line 24, might very well be the result of a happy impromptu on the stage, preserved in an acting copy of the play. Cambridge editors suggest the omission of "kindly" in line 24.

34. *hinder me to wail*] For "hinder . . . to" compare Acts viii. 36. For a parallel construction, see Chapman, *An Humorous Day's Mirth* (Shepherd, 30): "The sight thereof doth half *dismay me to make proof.*"

39. *make*] make up, complete. Compare *Cymbeline*, I. iv. 9.

That our swift-winged souls may catch the king's,
Or, like obedient subjects, follow him
To his new kingdom of ne'er-changing night.

Duch. Ah! so much interest have I in thy sorrow,
As I had title in thy noble husband.
I have bewept a worthy husband's death,
And liv'd with looking on his images:
But now two mirrors of his princely semblance
Are crack'd in pieces by malignant death;
And I for comfort have but one false glass,
That grieves me when I see my shame in him.
Thou art a widow; yet thou art a mother,
And hast the comfort of thy children left;
But death hath snatch'd my husband from mine arms,
And pluck'd two crutches from my feeble hands,
Clarence and Edward. O! what cause have I,
Thine being but an moiety of my moan,
To overgo thy woes and drown thy cries!

46. *ne'er-changing night*] Ff; *perpetuall rest* Qq. 47. *have I*] Qq; *haue* Ff. 50. *with*] Ff; *by* Qq. 54. *That*] Ff; *Which* Qq. 56. *left*] Ff; *left thee* Qq. 57. *husband*] Ff; *children* Qq. 58. *hands*] Ff; *limmes* Qq. 59. *Clarence and Edward*] Ff; *Edward and Clarence* Qq. 60. *Thine . . . an moiety*] *Thine . . . a moity* Ff; *Then, . . . moity* Qq 1, 2; *Then, . . . moitie* Qq 3-5; *Then, . . . motitie* Q 6. *moan*] Ff; *griefe* Qq 1-5; *selfe* Qq 6-8. 61. *woes*] Ff; *plaints* Qq (*plants* Q 2). *thy cries*] *the cries* Qq 5, 6.

46. *ne'er-changing night*] This is without doubt the better, and probably the original, reading. This gloomy and spacious idea of the life after death is in keeping with the spirit of the tragic writers of Shakespeare's youth. Pickersgill argued for Qq, on the ground that Elizabeth is not oppressed by the terrors of death, but that life has lost its value to her; and that "perpetual rest" is the form in which the idea of death would most naturally occur to one in her frame of mind. Ff seemed to him to contain "a sort of stock phrase," lofty, but not appropriate. That it is, in a certain sense, a stock phrase, is corroborated by I. iv. 47 above. That it represents a very general and appropriate notion in contemporary tragedy, is seen by such passages as Marlowe, *1 Tamburlaine*, iv. 4, where Theridamas speaks of Olympia's soul as wandering, brighter than the sun, "about the black circumference" of hell. Compare also the prologue to *Spanish Tragedy*, c. 1588, where the ghost of Andrea, on his way to Pluto's court, passes "thro' dreadful shades of ever glooming night." Qq probably perpetuate a stage-corruption, the result of an attempt to remedy a possible confusion with I. iv. 47.

50-54. These metaphors are used by old Lucretius in *Lucrece*, 1758-64.

60. *moiety*] In Shakespeare, "moiety" does not necessarily bear its strict meaning of "half." Compare *All's Well that Ends Well*, III. ii. 69, where it means, as here, a portion. On the other hand, see Fletcher and Massinger, *Spanish Curate*, 1622, v. 3:—

"Your brother hath deserved well.
Hen. And shall share
The *moiety* of my state."

Boy. Ah, aunt! you wept not for our father's death:
How can we aid you with our kindred tears?
Girl. Our fatherless distress was left unmoan'd;
Your widow-dolour likewise be unwept!
Q. Eliz. Give me no help in lamentation;
I am not barren to bring forth complaints:
All springs reduce their currents to mine eyes,
That I, being govern'd by the watery moon,
May send forth plenteous tears to drown the world.
Ah! for my husband, for my dear lord Edward!
Chil. Ah! for our father, for our dear lord Clarence!
Duch. Alas! for both, both mine, Edward and Clarence!
Q. Eliz. What stay had I but Edward? and he 's gone.
Chil. What stay had we but Clarence? and he 's gone.
Duch. What stays had I but they? and they are gone.
Q. Eliz. Was never widow had so dear a loss!
Chil. Were never orphans had so dear a loss!
Duch. Was never mother had so dear a loss!
Alas! I am the mother of these griefs:
Their woes are parcell'd, mine is general.
She for an Edward weeps, and so do I;
I for a Clarence weep, so doth not she:

62. *Ah*] Ff; *Good* Qq. 63. *kindred*] Ff; *kindreds* Qq. 64. *Girl.*] *Gerl.* Qq; *Daugh.* Ff. 65. *widow-dolour*] Ff; *widdowes dolours* Qq; *widow dolours* Pope. 67. *complaints*] Ff; *laments* Qq. 68-70. Put in margin by Pope. 69. *moon*] Ff, Qq 7, 8; *moane* Qq 1-6. 71. *Ah*] Ff; *Oh* Qq. (and below, 72). *dear*] Ff; *eire* Q 1; *eyre* Q 2; *heire* Qq 3-8. 72. *Chil.*] Ff; *Ambo.* Qq. (and below, 78). 74. *he 's*] Ff; *he is* Qq 1-5; *is he* Q 6 (and below, 75). 76. *stays*] *stay* Qq 6-8. 78. *Were*] Ff; *Was* Qq. *never*] Q 1, Ff; *euer* Qq 2-8 (and below, 79). *so dear a*] Ff, Qq 7, 8; *a dearer* Qq 1-6. 79. *so dear a*] Ff; *a dearer* Qq. 80. *griefs*] Ff; *mones* Qq. 81. *mine is*] Ff; *mine are* Qq. 82. *an Edward*] Ff; *Edward* Qq. 83. *weep*] *weepes* F 1.

65. *widow-dolour*] The hyphen is inserted in Ff, and should be kept as in "widow-comfort" (*King John*, III. iv. 105). An instance of arbitrary hyphening in Ff is found below, line 112, "You clowdy-Princes, & hart-sorowing-Peeres."

68. *reduce*] in the literal sense of "bring back," as below, v. v. 36. Compare D'Avenant's prologue to *The Woman Hater*, 1649: "'Twas he *reduced* Evadne from her scorn."

69, 70. Elizabeth compares her eyes to the sea, receiving back from the rivers the moisture which it gives forth, and governed by the influence of the moon. When we have accepted the first part of the comparison, it is difficult to agree with Johnson that "the introduction of the moon is not very natural."

81. *parcell'd*] Compare *Antony and Cleopatra*, v. ii. 163.

These babes for Clarence weep, and so do I;
I for an Edward weep, so do not they.
Alas! you three on me, threefold distress'd,
Pour all your tears. I am your sorrow's nurse,
And I will pamper it with lamentation.

Dor. Comfort, dear mother: God is much displeas'd
That you take with unthankfulness His doing.
In common worldly things, 'tis call'd ungrateful,
With dull unwillingness to repay a debt
Which with a bounteous hand was kindly lent;
Much more to be thus opposite with heaven,
For it requires the royal debt it lent you.

Riv. Madam, bethink you, like a careful mother,
Of the young prince your son: send straight for him;
Let him be crown'd; in him your comfort lives.
Drown desperate sorrow in dead Edward's grave,
And plant your joys in living Edward's throne.

Enter GLOUCESTER, BUCKINGHAM, DERBY, HASTINGS, *and* RATCLIFF.

Glou. Sister, have comfort: all of us have cause
To wail the dimming of our shining star;
But none can help our harms by wailing them.
Madam, my mother, I do cry you mercy;

84, 85. *These babes . . . so do not they*] Q 1; *These babes . . . and so do they* Qq 2-8; *These babes for Clarence weepe, so do not they* (one line) Ff. 87. *Pour*] *Proue* Q 2. 88. *lamentation*] Ff; *lamentations* Qq. 89-100. *Dor. Comfort . . . throne*] Ff; omitted Qq. aft. 100. *SCENE III.* Pope. *Enter Gloucester . . . Ratcliff*] *Enter Richard . . . Ratcliffe.* Ff; *Enter Glocest. with others* Qq. 101. *Sister*] Ff; *Madame* Qq. 103. *help our*] Ff; *cure their* Qq.

84, 85. Q 1, being the only form in which these lines make sense, may be taken as the original form of the passage. In later editions of Qq, line 85 was altered, with more regard to sound than sense. F 1 probably restored the true reading from the MS. source; but the printer, working with the interlined Q, could easily have overlooked the end of line 84 and the beginning of line 85, and so produced a nonsense line.

89. *dear mother*] Dorset addresses Queen Elizabeth. The transition is abrupt, and should be noted in the text.

92. *repay*] Pope emended the metre by reading "pay." The first syllable of "repay" is not strong enough to make the verse noticeably discordant.

94. *opposite with heaven*] Compare *Twelfth Night*, II. v. 162; Lyly, *Alexander and Campaspe*, act i.: "Thou thinkest it a grace to be opposite with Alexander." See also *Timon of Athens*, I. i. 284.

I did not see your grace: humbly on my knee
I crave your blessing.

Duch. God bless thee, and put meekness in thy breast,
Love, charity, obedience, and true duty!

Glou. Amen: [*Aside*] and make me die a good old man!
That is the butt-end of a mother's blessing;
I marvel that her grace did leave it out.

Buck. You cloudy princes and heart-sorrowing peers,
That bear this heavy mutual load of moan,
Now cheer each other in each other's love:
Though we have spent our harvest of this king,
We are to reap the harvest of his son.
The broken rancour of your high-swoll'n hates,
But lately splinter'd, knit and join'd together,
Must gently be preserv'd, cherish'd, and kept:
Me seemeth good, that, with some little train,
Forthwith from Ludlow the young prince be fet
Hither to London, to be crown'd our king.

Riv. Why with some little train, my Lord of Buckingham?

Buck. Marry, my lord, lest, by a multitude,

105. *your grace*] *you* Pope. 109. *Aside.*] Hanmer (before *Amen*). *and make me*] *make me* Q 6; *make me to* Qq 7, 8. 110. *That is*] Ff; *That,* Qq. *a mother's*] Q 1, Ff; *my mothers* Qq 2-8. 111. *that*] Ff; *why* Qq. 113. *heavy mutual*] Ff; *mutuall heauy* Qq. 115. *of this*] Q 1, Ff; *for this* Qq 2-8. 117. *hates*] Ff; *hearts* Qq. 118. *splinter'd*] *splinted* Qq 2-8. 119. *gently*] Q 1, Ff; *greatly* Qq 2-8. 121. *fet*] Ff; *fetcht* Qq. 123-40. *Riv. Why . . . say I.*] Ff; omitted Qq.

112. *cloudy*] melancholy, as *Lucrece*, 1084; *Macbeth*, III. vi. 41; *The Tempest*, II. i. 142.

113. *load of moan*] Compare *Troilus and Cressida*, II. ii. 107.

117-19. *broken rancour . . . kept*] Some doubt has been cast upon the text of this difficult passage; and it has been suggested that "rancour" should be altered to some other word, such as "concord." But there can be very little doubt that the subject of the verbs in line 119 is, not any special word in the preceding lines, but the general idea contained in them. Paraphrased, the sense is as follows: Now that your dissensions, which, having swollen high, had broken out in rancour, have been healed, and the wound has been splinted and sewn up, the healthy condition, which is the result of that healing, must be preserved. The quotation from *Cymbeline*, V. v. 344, 345, given by Abbott to illustrate I. iii. 63-69 above (see note), is more applicable here.

118. *splinter'd*] *i.e.* splinted, bound up with splints. Compare *Othello*, II. iii. 329.

121. *Ludlow*] See More (ap. Holinshed, iii. 714). At the time of his father's death, Edward V. "kept his household at Ludlow in Wales [*sic*], which countrie being farre off from the law and recourse to justice, . . . the prince was in the life of his father sent thither, to the end that the authoritie of his presence should refraine euill disposed persons from the boldnesse of their former outrages."

124. More (*u.s.*) gives the reasons,

The new-heal'd wound of malice should break out;
Which would be so much the more dangerous,
By how much the estate is green and yet ungovern'd.
Where every horse bears his commanding rein,
And may direct his course as please himself,
As well the fear of harm, as harm apparent,
In my opinion, ought to be prevented.

Glou. I hope the king made peace with all of us;
And the compact is firm and true in me.

Riv. And so in me; and so, I think, in all:
Yet, since it is but green, it should be put
To no apparent likelihood of breach,
Which haply by much company might be urg'd:
Therefore I say with noble Buckingham,
That it is meet so few should fetch the prince.

Hast. And so say I.

Glou. Then be it so; and go we to determine
Who they shall be that straight shall post to Ludlow.

134-40. *Riv. And . . . prince. Hast. And . . . I.*] *Hast. And . . . prince. Stan. And . . . I.* Capell. 139. *so few*] *but few* Hanmer. 142. *Ludlow*] Qq; *London* Ff (and 154 below).

which Shakespeare attributes to Buckingham, as Richard's personal conclusions, derived from consultation with Buckingham and Hastings. "Should all the realme fall on a rore," the guilt of breach of truce would fall upon the queen and her kindred.

127. *estate*] The risk is the more imminent, in proportion to the novelty of the change in the state, and the absence of any supreme controlling hand. Buckingham emphasises the need of control, and so points obliquely to Gloucester as the man who is fit to exercise it. In line 135 below, Rivers calls the newly-made compact "green."

134. Malone followed Capell in assigning this speech to Hastings, and line 140 to Stanley. This would only make Gloucester's party acquiesce in an arrangement favourable to themselves; and for this Hastings' brief assent in line 140 is sufficient. Shakespeare's object surely was to bring out the ready agreement of the queen's partisans, intimidated by their fear of Gloucester, yet willing, against hope, to show their adhesion to the new-made peace, on whose maintenance he and his friends were laying such stress.

139. *so few*] a certain limited number.

142. *Ludlow*] Ff reading is indefensible. Spedding attributed the error to the printer; but it occurs twice in thirteen lines. The editor of F 1 seems to have had little knowledge of history (compare II. i. 66-68 above; II. iv. 1, 2 below). Probably in the MS. he found "London" written here by mistake for "Ludlow"—a very comprehensible error. He would have altered his Q in consequence, and "Ludlow" again in line 154 to match. Richard was at York about this time, and actually met the king on his way from York to London. The editor of F 1 is hardly likely to have known this. If he did, he was guilty of a misplaced accuracy, for which there was no warrant in the text.

Madam, and you, my mother, will you go
To give your censures in this business?

Q. Eliz.
Duch. } With all our hearts.

[*Exeunt all but Buckingham and Gloucester.*

Buck. My lord, whoever journeys to the prince,
For God's sake, let not us two stay at home:
For, by the way, I'll sort occasion,
As index to the story we late talk'd of,
To part the queen's proud kindred from the prince.

Glou. My other self, my counsel's consistory,
My oracle, my prophet!—My dear cousin,
I, as a child, will go by thy direction.
Toward Ludlow then, for we'll not stay behind.

[*Exeunt.*

143. *mother*] Qq; *Sister* Ff. 144. *business*] Ff; *waighty busines* Qq. 145. *Q. Eliz. Duch. With . . . hearts.*] *Ans. With . . . hearts* Qq; omitted Ff. *Exeunt . . . Gloucester.*] *Exeunt manet Glo. Buck.* Qq; *Manet Buckingham and Richard.* Ff. 147. *stay*] Q 1, Ff; *be* Qq 2-8. *at home*] Ff; *behinde* Qq. 149. *late*] Q 1; Ff 1-3; *lately* Qq 2-8, F 4. 150. *prince*] Ff; *King* Qq. 152. *prophet!—My*] Theobald (sugg. Warburton); *prophet, my* Qq, Ff. 153. *as*] Ff; *like* Qq. 154. *Toward*] Ff; *Towards* Qq. *we'll*] Ff; *we will* Qq. *Exeunt.*] Ff; *Exit.* Qq 3-8; omitted Qq 1, 2.

143. *mother*] Gloucester would naturally address the queen-dowager before his mother, of whom she took precedence. Qq therefore have the better reading.

144. *censures*] judgments. So *1 Henry VI.* II. iii. 10; *Winter's Tale*, II. i. 37; Fletcher, *False One*, i. 1:—

"my opinion
Is, still committing it to graver *censure*,
You pay the debt you owe him."

Compare Chapman (?), *Alphonsus*, i. 1: "as for Mentz, I need not *censure* him," *i.e.* give my opinion of him.

148. *sort occasion*] choose, contrive an opportunity. For "sort" compare *1 Henry VI.* II. iii. 27; *3 Henry VI.* V. v. 87; *1 Henry IV.* II. iii. 13: "The purpose you undertake is dangerous . . . the time itself *unsorted*."

149. *index*] prelude, preface. "Index" was the name given to the finger printed in the margin of a book, and pointing to its main arguments or other important contents, as they might occur. An abstract or list of these, prefixed to the book, became known in course of time as the index. See Mr. Hart on *Othello*, II. i. 263. Compare *Troilus and Cressida*, I. iii. 343; and IV. iv. 85 below.

SCENE III.—*London. A street.*

Enter two Citizens, meeting.

First Cit. Good morrow, neighbour: whither away so fast?
Sec. Cit. I promise you, I scarcely know myself:
Hear you the news abroad?
First Cit. Yes, that the king is dead.
Sec. Cit. Ill news, by 'r lady, seldom comes the better:
I fear, I fear, 'twill prove a giddy world.

Enter another Citizen.

Third Cit. Neighbours, God speed!
First Cit. Give you good morrow, sir.
Third Cit. Doth the news hold of good king Edward's death?
Sec. Cit. Ay, sir, it is too true, God help the while!
Third Cit. Then, masters, look to see a troublous world.
First Cit. No, no; by God's good grace, his son shall reign.
Third Cit. Woe to that land that 's govern'd by a child!
Sec. Cit. In him there is a hope of government,

SCENE III.] *SCENE IV.* Pope. *Enter . . . meeting.*] Capell; *Enter two Cittizens.* Qq; *Enter one Citizen at one doore, and another at the other.* Ff. 1. *Good morrow, neighbour*] Ff; *Neighbour well met* Qq. 3. *Hear*] Ff; 1. *Heare* Qq. 3. *First Cit. Yes*] 1. *Yes* Ff; 2. *I* Qq. *that*] omitted Ff 2-4. 4. *Sec. Cit. Ill*] 2. *Ill* Ff; 1. *Bad* Qq. 5. *giddy*] Ff; *troublous* Q 1; *troublesome* Qq 2-8. 6. *Third Cit. Neighbours . . . morrow, sir.*] Ff; 3. *Cit. Good morrow neighbours* Qq. 7. *the news*] Ff; *this newes* Qq. 8. *Sec. Cit. Ay . . . while*] Ff; 1. *It doth* Qq. 10. *good*] Q 1, Ff; omitted Qq 2-8.

4. *seldom comes the better*] Reed quotes *The English Courtier and Country Gentleman*, 1586, sig. B: "As the proverb sayth, *seldome come the better.*" Pope's alteration, "a better," is discountenanced, as Malone remarks, by Reed's parallel.

7. *hold*] continue unchanged, hold good, as *King Lear*, v. i. 1; Beaumont and Fletcher, *Faithful Shepherdess*, i. 3: "Speak, shall our meeting *hold?*"

11. Ecclesiastes x. 16. The same text is used by Langland with reference to the minority of *Richard II.*: see *Piers the Plowman*, prologue 192: "þere þe catte is a kitoun, þe courte is full elyng; þat witnesseth holiwrite who-so wil it rede, *Ve terre ubi puer rex est, &c.*"

12-15. These lines suffer from the connexion by one verb of two ideas, one present, the other future. A somewhat similar difficulty of construction has been noted above, II. i. 32-34. The pessimist of the party has quoted Scripture to vouch for the dangers of a minority. His more hopeful friend rebukes his forebodings: "We may hope for good government in the case of this king, who, while he is still under age, shall govern well through his council, and shall govern us well in his own person, when he is come to his majority." The meaning is more easy to see than to paraphrase; and the expression of the thought is more than a little redundant. Qq "that" may be a conjunction, introducing a sentence explanatory of "hope." This makes as good sense as Ff.

Which, in his nonage, council under him,
And, in his full and ripened years, himself,
No doubt, shall, then and till then, govern well.

First Cit. So stood the state, when Henry the sixth
Was crown'd in Paris but at nine months old.

Third Cit. Stood the state so? No, no, good friends, God wot!
For then this land was famously enrich'd
With politick grave counsel; then the king
Had virtuous uncles to protect his grace.

First Cit. Why, so hath this, both by his father and mother.

Third Cit. Better it were they all came by his father,
Or by his father there were none at all;
For emulation, who shall now be nearest,
Will touch us all too near, if God prevent not.
O! full of danger is the Duke of Gloucester,
And the queen's sons and brothers haught and proud;

13. *Which*] Ff; *That* Qq. 16. *Henry*] Ff, Q 8; *Harry* Qq 1-7. 17. *in Paris*] Ff; *at Paris* Qq. 18. *No, no . . . God wot*] Ff; *no good my friend not so* Qq. 22. *First Cit. Why, so*] Ff; 2. *So* Qq. 22. *his father*] Ff; *the father* Qq (and below, 23, 24). 25. *who shall now be*] Ff; *now, who shall be* Qq. 26. *Will*] Q 1, Ff; *Which* Qq 2-8. 28. *sons and brothers haught*] Ff; *kindred hauty* Qq; *kindred haughty are* Capell. *haught and proud*] *haughty, proud* Pope.

16. *Henry*] probably a trisyllable. Compare *1 Henry VI.* III. i. 76, and see note on I. i. 67 above.

17. *crown'd*] Henry VI. was proclaimed king of France in Paris, after the death of his grandfather, Charles VI., October, 1422. He was then about a year old. He was not crowned in Paris till December, 1430, when he was nine *years*, not nine *months*, old.

19. *famously*] excellently. Compare *Coriolanus*, I. i. 37. Miss Austen, *The Watsons*, p. 326, makes a young man of fashion say: "I shall retreat in as much secrecy as possible to the most remote corner of the house, where I shall order a barrel of oysters, and be *famously* snug."

27. The popular apprehension of Gloucester is illustrated by an anecdote, told on good authority by More (ap. Holinshed, iii. 712), which Shakespeare must have remarked. "The selfe night, in which king Edward died, one Mistlebrooke, long yer morning, came in great haste to the house of one Pottier dwelling in Redcrosse-strete without Creplegate: and when he was with hastie rapping quickelie letten in, he shewed unto Pottier, that king Edward was departed. 'By my truth man,' quoth Pottier, 'then will my maister the Duke of Glocester be king.'"

28. *haught*] Compare *3 Henry VI.* II. i. 169: "the *haught* Northumberland"; Greene, *Orlando Furioso* (Dyce, 106): "the pride of *haught* Latona's son." One of the 1608 Qq of *Richard II.* reads "haught" in IV. i. 254. In *2 Henry VI.* I. iii. 71, where F 1 reads "haughtie," Ff 2-4 read "haught." Dyce reads for "haughtie" in Lodge and Greene, *Looking-Glass* (p. 117): "If doughty deeds more *haught* than any done." In the present case, Qq perhaps represent the corruption of the line on the stage.

And, were they to be rul'd, and not to rule,
This sickly land might solace as before.
First Cit. Come, come, we fear the worst; all will be well.
Third Cit. When clouds are seen, wise men put on their cloaks;
When great leaves fall, then winter is at hand;
When the sun sets, who doth not look for night?
Untimely storms make men expect a dearth.
All may be well; but, if God sort it so,
'Tis more than we deserve, or I expect.
Sec. Cit. Truly, the hearts of men are full of fear:
You cannot reason almost with a man,
That looks not heavily and full of dread.
Third Cit. Before the days of change, still is it so:
By a divine instinct, men's minds mistrust
Pursuing danger; as, by proof, we see
The water swell before a boist'rous storm.
But leave it all to God. Whither away?
Sec. Cit. Marry, we were sent for to the justices.
Third Cit. And so was I: I'll bear you company. [*Exeunt.*

29. *to rule*] *rule* Qq 6-8. 31. *First Cit.*] Ff; 2. Qq. *will*] Ff; *shall* Qq. 32. *are seen*] Ff; *appeare* Qq. 33. *then*] Ff; *the* Qq. 35. *make*] Qq; *makes* Ff. 38. *Sec. Cit.*] Ff; 1. Qq. *hearts*] Ff; *soules* Qq. *fear*] Ff; *bread* Qq 1, 2; *dread* Qq 3-8. 39. *You*] Ff; *Yee* Qq. *reason almost*] *reason* (*almost*) Ff; *almost reason* Qq. 40. *dread*] Ff; *feare* Qq. 41. *days*] Ff; *times* Qq. 43. *Pursuing danger*] Ff; *Ensuing dangers* Qq. 44. *water*] Ff; *waters* Qq. 46. *Marry, we were*] Ff; *We are* Qq. *justices*] Ff; *Iustice* Qq; *justice's* Anon conj. ap. Camb.

30. *solace*] Compare *Cymbeline*, I. vi. 86.

32. Compare Sonnet xxxiv. 1-4.

36. *sort*] appoint, dispose, as *Merchant of Venice*, V. i. 132. Compare "sort occasion," above, II. ii. 148.

41-44. The sentiment is More's (ap. Holinshed, iii. 721): "Before such great things, mens hearts of a secret instinct of nature misgiue them; as the sea without wind swelleth of himselfe sometime before a tempest."

SCENE IV.—*London. The Palace.*

Enter the ARCHBISHOP OF YORK, *the young* DUKE OF YORK, QUEEN ELIZABETH, *and the* DUCHESS OF YORK.

Arch. Last night, I hear, they lay at Northampton;
At Stony-Stratford will they be to-night:
To-morrow, or next day, they will be here.
Duch. I long with all my heart to see the prince:
I hope he is much grown since last I saw him.
Q. Eliz. But I hear no; they say my son of York
Has almost overta'en him in his growth.
York. Ay, mother; but I would not have it so.
Duch. Why, my young cousin, it is good to grow.
York. Grandam, one night, as we did sit at supper,
My uncle Rivers talk'd how I did grow
More than my brother: "Ay," quoth my uncle Gloucester,
"Small herbs have grace, great weeds do grow apace:"
And since, methinks, I would not grow so fast,
Because sweet flowers are slow, and weeds make haste.
Duch. Good faith, good faith, the saying did not hold
In him that did object the same to thee.
He was the wretched'st thing when he was young,

Enter the Archbishop . . .] *Enter Arch-bishop, yong Yorke, the Queene, and the Dutchesse.* Ff; *Enter Cardinall, Dutches of Yorke, Quee.* [or *Qu.*], *young Yorke.* Qq. 1. *Arch.*] Ff; *Car.* Qq (and so in line 36, etc.). *hear*] Qq; *heard* Ff. *Northampton*] Qq; *Stony Stratford* Ff. 2. *At Stony-Stratford will they be*] Qq; *And at Northampton they do rest*, Ff. 6. *no*] *not* Pope. 7. *Has*] Ff; *Hath* Qq. *almost*] omitted Qq 6-8. 9. *young*] Qq; *good* Ff. 13. *do grow*] Ff.; *grow* Qq.

Archbishop of York] For this stage-direction and the reading in lines 1, 2, see Appendix III.

6. *my son of York*] According to Holinshed, iii. 719, York was at this time anything but the healthy, active boy whom Shakespeare pictures. Elizabeth pleads with the Cardinal that, "beside his infancie, that also needeth good looking to," he "hath a while beene so sore diseased, vexed with sicknesse, and is so newlie rather a little amended, than well recouered, that I dare put no person earthlie in trust with his keeping, but my selfe onelie."

13. *great weeds do grow apace*] Aldis Wright quotes Heywood's *Proverbes*:—

"Ill weede growth fast, that is showyng
In the show of thy fast growyng."

Compare Chapman, *An Humorous Day's Mirth* (Shepherd, 36): "Whatsoever I say to Monsieur Rowl, he shall say, 'Oh, sir, you may see an ill weed grows apace.'"

So long a-growing, and so leisurely,
That, if his rule were true, he should be gracious.
Arch. And so no doubt he is, my gracious madam.
Duch. I hope he is; but yet let mothers doubt.
York. Now, by my troth, if I had been remembred,
I could have given my uncle's grace a flout,
To touch his growth nearer than he touch'd mine.
Duch. How, my young York? I prithee, let me hear it.
York. Marry, they say my uncle grew so fast,
That he could gnaw a crust at two hours old:
'Twas full two years ere I could get a tooth.
Grandam, this would have been a biting jest.
Duch. I prithee, pretty York, who told thee this?
York. Grandam, his nurse.
Duch. His nurse! why, she was dead ere thou wast born.
York. If 'twere not she, I cannot tell who told me.
Q. Eliz. A parlous boy! go to, you are too shrewd.
Arch. Good madam, be not angry with the child.
Q. Eliz. Pitchers have ears.

20. *his rule were true*] Ff; *this were a true rule* Qq 1, 2; *this were a rule* Qq 3-8; *this rule were true* Camb. 21. *Arch.*] *Car.* Qq; *Yor.* Ff. *And so . . . Madam*] Ff; *Why Madame, so no doubt he is* Qq. 22. *he is*] Ff; *so too* Qq. 25. *To touch . . . mine*] Ff; *That should haue neerer toucht his growth then he did mine* Qq. 26. *How . . . hear it*] one line as Qq; *How . . . Yorke, I . . . heare it* (two lines) Ff. *young*] Ff; *prety* Qq. 27. *say my uncle*] Q 1, Ff; *say, that my Vnckle* Qq 2-8. 30. *biting*] Q 1, Ff; *pretie* Qq 2-8. 31. *prithee*] Ff; *pray thee* Qq. *this*] Ff; *so* Qq. 33. *His nurse!*] Q 1, Ff; omitted Qq 2-8. *wast*] Ff; *wert* Qq. 35. *parlous*] Ff; *perilous* Qq.

20 *gracious*] Compare *Julius Cæsar*, III. ii. 198; *Hamlet*, I. i. 164.

23. *had been remembr'ed*] Compare *Measure for Measure*, II. i. 109, 110.

27, 28. The legend is mentioned by More (ap. Holinshed, iii. 712). Shakespeare alludes to it and its significance, *3 Henry VI.* v. vi. 53, 54, 74-77, and IV. iv. 49 below. Compare Margaret's warning above, I. iii. 289-291.

35. *parlous*] a popular corruption of "perilous." Shakespeare uses it as an emphatic epithet, *Midsummer-Night's Dream*, III. i. 14; *As You Like It*, III. ii. 45. Compare Tourneur, *Rev. Trag.* act iv.: "A *parlous* melancholy"; Beaumont and Fletcher, *Elder Brother*, II. ii.: "You are so *parlously* in love with learning." Here and below, III. i. 154, the sense is much that in which we speak of a precocious boy or girl as a "terrible child"; but a sarcastic intention in the child's precocity is also implied. Compare *Measure for Measure*, II. iv. 172. Milton, *Animadversions upon Remonstrant's Defence*, 1641, has: "sure some pedagogue stood at your elbow, and made it itch with their *parlous* criticism." Decker and Middleton, *Roaring Girl*, 1611, ii. 1, refer to "*Parlous* pond," which Reed conjectured to be Peerless (*i.e.* Perilous) Pool in Clerkenwell (see Hone, *Every-Day Book*, i. 485-9), so called from the number of people who lost their lives there.

shrewd] malicious, as *Much Ado About Nothing*, II. i. 20-22, where "curst" (see I. ii. 49 above) is used as a synonym in the same passage.

37. *Pitchers have ears*] See *Taming*

Enter a Messenger.

Arch. Here comes a messenger. What news?
Mess. Such news, my lord, as grieves me to report.
Q. Eliz. How doth the prince?
Mess. Well, madam, and in health.
Duch. What is thy news?
Mess. Lord Rivers and Lord Grey are sent to Pomfret,
With them Sir Thomas Vaughan, prisoners.
Duch. Who hath committed them?
Mess. The mighty dukes,
Gloucester and Buckingham.
Arch. For what offence?
Mess. The sum of all I can, I have disclos'd:
Why or for what the nobles were committed
Is all unknown to me, my gracious lord.
Q. Eliz. Ay me! I see the ruin of my house!
The tiger now hath seiz'd the gentle hind;
Insulting tyranny begins to jet

aft. 37. *Enter a Messenger.*] Ff; *Enter Dorset.* Qq. 38. *Here comes . . . news*] Ff; *Here comes your sonne, Lo: M. Dorset. What newes Lord Marques* (two lines) Qq. 39. *Mess.*] Ff; *Dor.* Qq (and so line 42, etc.). *report*] Ff; *vnfold* Qq. 40. *doth*] Ff; *fares* Qq. 41. *thy*] Q 1, Ff; *the* Qq 2-8. *news*] Ff; *newes then* Qq. 42, 43. *Lord Rivers . . . prisoners*] arranged as Qq; *Lo: Riuers . . . Grey Are sent . . . and with them Sir Thomas . . . prisoners* (3 lines) Ff; *Lord Rivers and Lord Grey Are sent to Pomfret prisoners; and with them Sir Thomas Vaughan* Capell. 44, 45. *Who hath . . . offence*] arranged as Pope, Camb.; 3 lines, one to each speech, Qq, Ff. 45. *Arch.*] Ff; *Car.* Qq; *Queen.* Johnson; *Q. Eliz.* Camb. 47. *the nobles*] Ff; *these nobles* Qq. 48. *lord*] Ff; *lady* Qq. 49. *Ay*] *Ah* Rowe. *ruin*] Ff; *downfall* Qq. *my house*] Ff; *our house* Qq. 51. *jet*] Qq; *Iutte* Ff.

of the Shrew, IV. iv. 52, and Mr. Bond's note. Malone quotes William Bulleyn, *A Dialogue both pleasaunt and pietifull*, 1564, "Small *pitchers have great ears.*"

Enter a Messenger] The speeches which follow seem to suit an ordinary messenger better than Dorset, who appears here in Qq. In More's account, it is by a messenger from Hastings that Rotherham learns the fatal news.

42. More (ap. Holinshed, iii. 715) says that "the lord Riuers, and the lord Richard, with Sir Thomas Vaughan" were sent from Northampton "into the north countrie, into diverse places to prison; and afterward all to Pomfret, where they were in conclusion beheaded." Rivers was at Sheriff Hutton in the interval; Lord Richard Grey was at Gloucester's other Yorkshire castle of Middleham.

50. The image is used also in *Lucrece*, 543. It is reversed in *Midsummer-Night's Dream*, II. i. 232, 233.

51, 52. *jet Upon*] encroach upon. Compare *Titus Andronicus*, II. i. 64, where Ff and later editors adopt the form "jut." "To jet," used absolutely, means "to strut, swagger," as *Twelfth Night*, II. v. 36; Decker, *Seuen Deadly Sinnes* (Arber, 15): "he *iets vp* and downe in silks wouen out of other mens stocks." Mr. Craig ("Little Quarto" Shakespeare) remarks upon the un-

Upon the innocent and aweless throne:
Welcome, destruction, blood, and massacre!
I see, as in a map, the end of all.

Duch. Accursed and unquiet wrangling days,
How many of you have mine eyes beheld!
My husband lost his life to get the crown;
And often up and down my sons were toss'd,
For me to joy and weep their gain and loss:
And being seated, and domestic broils
Clean over-blown, themselves, the conquerors,
Make war upon themselves, brother to brother,
Blood to blood, self against self: O, preposterous
And frantic outrage, end thy damned spleen;
Or let me die, to look on death no more!

Q. Eliz. Come, come, my boy; we will to sanctuary.
Madam, farewell.

Duch. Stay, I will go with you.

Q. Eliz. You have no cause.

Arch. My gracious lady, go;

52. *aweless*] Ff; *lawlesse* Qq. 53. *blood*] Ff; *death* Qq. 60. *seated, and domestic broils*] *seated and domestike broiles*, Q 1. 61. *over-blown, themselves*] *ouerblowne themselues*, Q 1. 62, 63. *brother to brother, Blood to blood*] Ff; *blood against blood* Qq. 65. *death*] Qq; *earth* Ff. 67. *Madam, farewell*] Ff; omitted Qq. *Stay, I will go with you*] Ff; *Ile goe along with you* Qq. 68. *Arch.* [*To the Queen.*] Malone.

commonness of the present usage, of which *New Eng. Dict.* contains only two instances. He suggests in an unpublished note that IV. iii. 42 below may throw some light on its meaning.

52. *aweless*] which does not inspire awe. *New Eng. Dict.* quotes T. Adams, *Practical Works*, 1614, "It is a lawless school where there is an *awless* monitor." Qq "lawlesse" makes doubtful sense, unless it can bear the meaning of "without the power of administering law." But this is a strained interpretation.

63. Spedding thought that F 1 intended to read "Blood to blood, self 'gainst self: preposterous." Pope emended Qq "most preposterous."

65. *death*] Spedding attributed Ff reading to a printer's error. It possibly was in the original text, in which case Qq make a distinct emendation. Or, again, it may have been a MS. error peculiar to the copy which F 1 appears to have followed with such fidelity.

66. *sanctuary*] More (ap. Holinshed, iii. 715) says that Elizabeth, on hearing of Gloucester's *coup d'état*, "gat hir selfe in all the hast possible with hir yoonger sonne and hir daughters out of the palace of Westminster (in which she then laie) into the *sanctuarie;* lodging hir selfe and hir companie there in the abbats place." Halle adds, "and she and all her chyldren and compaignie were regestred for *sanctuarye* persons." The abbot of Westminster at this period was John Esteney. In 1470, Elizabeth had taken refuge with his predecessor, William Millyng. The "abbats place" stood south of the abbey church: its remains form part of the present Deanery and College Hall.

And thither bear your treasure and your goods.
For my part, I 'll resign unto your grace
The seal I keep: and so betide to me
As well I tender you and all of yours!
Come, I 'll conduct you to the sanctuary.

[*Exeunt.*

71. *to me*] *it me* Ff 2-4. 73. *Come*] Ff; *Go* Qq.

70. Rotherham's words are thus reported by More (*u.s.*): "Madame . . . be yee of good cheere, for I assure you, if they crowne anie other king than your sonne, whome they now haue with them, we shall on the morow crowne his brother, whome you haue here with you. And here is the great seale, which in likewise as that noble prince your husband deliuered it vnto me; so here I deliuer it vnto you, to the vse and behoofe of your sonne."

ACT III

SCENE I.—*London. A street.*

The trumpets sound. Enter the young PRINCE, *the Dukes of* GLOUCESTER *and* BUCKINGHAM, CARDINAL BOURCHIER, CATESBY, *and others.*

Buck. Welcome, sweet prince, to London, to your chamber!
Glou. Welcome, dear cousin, my thoughts' sovereign!
The weary way hath made you melancholy.
Prince. No, uncle; but our crosses on the way
Have made it tedious, wearisome, and heavy:
I want more uncles here to welcome me.
Glou. Sweet prince, the untainted virtue of your years
Hath not yet div'd into the world's deceit:
No more can you distinguish of a man
Than of his outward show; which, God He knows,

London.] Pope. *A street.*] Capell. *Cardinal Bourchier*] *Cardinall* Qq; *Lord Cardinall* Ff. *Catesby.*] Capell; omitted Qq, Ff. 1. *Welcome . . . chamber*] one line as Qq; *Welcome . . . London, To your Chamber* (two lines) Ff. 8. *Hath*] *Haue* Qq 6-8. 9. *No*] Ff, Q 8; *Nor* Qq 1-7.

Cardinal Bourchier] See Appendix III. and notes on *dramatis personæ.*

1. *chamber*] Camden, *Britannia*, tr. Holland, 1610, p. 427 B, says that, after the Norman Conquest, London, "through the speciall fauour and indulgence of Princes . . . beganne to bee called *The King's Chamber*." Compare *ibid.* p. 421 D: "London, the Epitome or Breviary of all Britain, the seat of the British Empire, and the *Kings of Englands Chamber.*" So Heywood, *If you know not Me, you know Nobody*, 1633, part 2 (quoted by Steevens): "This city, our great *chamber.*" *New Eng. Dict.* quotes Weever, *Ancient Funerall Monuments*, 1631: "This his Citie of Maldon, then the *chamber* of his kingdome." In the pageant devised by Jonson for the coronation procession of King James, an erection in Fenchurch Street, symbolical of London, bore the title "Londinium," and below, in smaller characters, "Camera Regis" (Jonson, ed. Gifford, 1 vol. ed. p. 527). Giovanni Villani, *Cronica*, i. 41, says of Florence: "La città di Firenze in quello tempo era camera d' imperio."

9, 10. *No more . . . show*] You can distinguish nothing more in a man than that which you can distinguish in his outward behaviour. The second "of" confuses the meaning a little, but is not superfluous.

Seldom or never jumpeth with the heart.
Those uncles which you want were dangerous:
Your grace attended to their sug'red words,
But look'd not on the poison of their hearts:
God keep you from them, and from such false friends!

Prince. God keep me from false friends! but they were none.

Glou. My lord, the mayor of London comes to greet you.

Enter the Lord Mayor, and his train.

May. God bless your grace with health and happy days!

Prince. I thank you, good my lord, and thank you all.
I thought my mother and my brother York
Would long ere this have met us on the way:
Fie! what a slug is Hastings, that he comes not
To tell us whether they will come or no!

Enter LORD HASTINGS.

Buck. And, in good time, here comes the sweating lord.

Prince. Welcome, my lord! what, will our mother come?

Hast. On what occasion God He knows, not I,
The queen your mother and your brother York
Have taken sanctuary: the tender prince
Would fain have come with me to meet your grace,
But by his mother was perforce withheld.

Buck. Fie! what an indirect and peevish course
Is this of hers! Lord cardinal, will your grace
Persuade the queen to send the Duke of York
Unto his princely brother presently?

16. aft. *Prince.* [*Aside.*] Camb. conj. *God . . . none*] one line as Qq; *God . . . Friends, But . . . none* (two lines) Ff. aft. 17. *and his train.*] Capell; omitted Qq, Ff. 29. *have come*] *come* Qq 3, 5-8. 33. *to send*] *the send* Q 3; *they send* Q 5.

11. *jumpeth with*] agrees with, as *Merchant of Venice*, II. ix. 32; *1 Henry IV.* I. ii. 78. *New Eng. Dict.* quotes R. D., *Hypnerotomachia*, 1592: "The corners of which triangle did *iumpe* with the sides and lymbus of the subjacent plynth." Compare Lyly, *Alexander and Campaspe*, i. 3:—

"*Crates.* Thou thinkest it a grace to be opposite with Alexander.
Diogenes. And thou to be *jump* with Alexander."

31. *peevish*] See note on I. iii. 194 above, and compare *Hamlet*, I. ii. 100' *Othello*, IV. iii. 90.

If she deny, Lord Hastings, go with him,
And from her jealous arms pluck him perforce.

Card. My Lord of Buckingham, if my weak oratory
Can from his mother win the Duke of York,
Anon expect him here; but, if she be obdurate
To mild entreaties, God in heaven forbid
We should infringe the holy privilege
Of blessed sanctuary! not for all this land
Would I be guilty of so deep a sin.

Buck. You are too senseless-obstinate, my lord,
Too ceremonious and traditional.
Weigh it but with the grossness of this age,
You break not sanctuary in seizing him.

35. *him*] *them* Qq 5-8. 39. *Anon*] omitted, Steevens conj. 39, 40. *Anon . . . forbid*] *Anon . . . she be Obdurate to entreaties, God forbid* Pope. 40. *in heaven*] omitted Qq 3-8, Ff. 42. *blessed*] omitted Pope. 43. *deep*] *great* Qq 3-8, Ff. 44. *senseless-obstinate*] hyphened Theobald. 46. *grossness of this*] *greatnesse of this* Q 6; *greatnesse of his* Qq 7, 8; *greenness of his* Hanmer (from Warburton).

40-43. More (ap. Holinshed, iii. 717) quotes the Cardinal's words as Archbishop Rotherham's. "And therefore (quoth the archbishop of Yorke) God forbid that anie man should, for aniething earthlie, enterprise to breake the immunitie & libertie of the sacred sanctuarie, that hath beene the safegard of so manie a good mans life. And I trust (quoth he) with God's grace, we shall not need it. But for anie maner need, I would not we should doo it." In view of the confusion, due to More, between Bourchier and Rotherham, it should be noted that, both in More and Shakespeare, the Cardinal already has consented to attempt *persuasion*, but objects to *force*. It is very unlikely that Rotherham would have undertaken persuasion so readily, and very improbable that the opportunity should have been offered to him. See Appendix III. and the appendix to Canon Leigh-Bennett's *Archbishop Rotherham*, 1901, p. 178.

44. *senseless-obstinate*] Of the alternative conjectures which the vehemence of the expression has provoked, Staunton's "needless-obstinate" comes nearest within the bounds of reason.

46. *grossness*] Literally "coarseness, want of refinement" (*New Eng. Dict.*; Schmidt). The implied meaning seems to be: Judge the matter by the vulgar, practical standard of the present age. "Gross" is applied by Shakespeare to denote things plain and obvious: compare *Othello*, I. ii. 72; and so it is used of unconcealed coarseness of language, as in *Measure for Measure*, II. iv. 82. Buckingham speaks as a man of the world, to assuage the scruples of the cardinal. Warburton argues for "greenness of his age" on the ground that "grossness" means superstition; in which case, Buckingham's appeal, if obeyed, would have a precisely opposite effect to its intention. Johnson takes "grossness" as equivalent to "licentious practices." See note on IV. i. 79 below.

47. More gives Buckingham a long speech of which this sentiment is the hypothesis. While there are many who deserve the right of sanctuary, there are thriftless debtors, thieves, bankrupts, etc., who take advantage of it. The evil might be amended without prejudice to innocent refugees in *lawful* peril of their body. But the Duke of York is not one of these. He is innocent before all the world; "and so sanctuary, neither none he needeth, nor also none can have." Again, a

The benefit thereof is always granted
To those whose dealings have deserv'd the place,
And those who have the wit to claim the place:
The prince hath neither claimed it nor deserv'd it,
And therefore, in mine opinion, cannot have it;
Then, taking him from thence that is not there,
You break no privilege nor charter there.
Oft have I heard of sanctuary men,
But sanctuary children ne'er till now.

Card. My lord, you shall o'er-rule my mind for once.
Come on, Lord Hastings, will you go with me?

Hast. I go, my lord.

Prince. Good lords, make all the speedy haste you may.

[*Exeunt Cardinal and Hastings.*

Say, uncle Gloucester, if our brother come,
Where shall we sojourn till our coronation?

Glou. Where it seems best unto your royal self.
If I may counsel you, some day or two
Your highness shall repose you at the Tower;
Then where you please, and shall be thought most fit
For your best health and recreation.

Prince. I do not like the Tower, of any place.
Did Julius Cæsar build that place, my lord?

52. *And*] omitted Ff 2-4. 53. *taking*] *take* Qq 6-8. 56. *ne'er*] Ff; *neuer* Qq. 57. *o'er-rule*] Ff; *ouerrule* Qq. 60. *Exeunt . . .*] Camb.; *Exit . . .* Qq 3-8, Ff (after 59); omitted Qq 1, 2. 63. *seems*] *think'st* Qq 3-8, Ff.

sanctuary man must not claim the right by proxy. The Duke is kept in sanctuary by his mother, perhaps against his will. What scruple of conscience, what breach of privilege, can be urged here? If any be allowed, it follows that no one may be taken out of sanctuary who says he will stay there. A child will be able to claim the right for fear of his schoolmaster. In this case there is not even the excuse of fear. "And verelie," adds Buckingham in parenthesis, "I have often heard of sanctuarie men, but I neuer heard earst of sanctuarie children" (see lines 55, 56). A terse summing-up of his argument concludes a speech with successful effect. For the history of sanctuary privileges and illustrations of the above arguments, see Raine's *Sanctuarium Dunelmense et Sanctuarium Beverlacense* (Surtees Society publications, vol. 5), and *Rites of Durham*, ed. J. T. Fowler, 1903, pp. 41, 42, 226, etc. (*ibid.* vol. 107).

58. *Lord Hastings*] According to More, the Cardinal went to the sanctuary "with diuers other lords with him." Halle names "the lord Haward" as using words to persuade the queen against any idea of danger. This was John, Lord Howard, afterwards Duke of Norfolk. Hastings is not mentioned.

69. *Julius Cæsar*] "It hath been the common opinion, and some have written—but of none assured ground—that Julius Cæsar . . . was the original author and founder as well" of the

Buck. He did, my gracious lord, begin that place;
Which, since, succeeding ages have re-edified.
Prince. Is it upon record, or else reported
Successively from age to age, he built it?
Buck. Upon record, my gracious lord.
Prince. But say, my lord, it were not regist'red,
Methinks the truth should live from age to age,
As 'twere retail'd to all posterity,
Even to the general all-ending day.
Glou. [*Aside.*] So wise, so young, they say, do never live long.
Prince. What say you, uncle?
Glou. I say, without characters, fame lives long.
[*Aside.*] Thus, like the formal vice, Iniquity,

70. *Buck.*] *Glo.* Steevens. 70, 71. *He did . . . re-edified*] *He did, my lord . . . since Succeeding . . . re-edified* Steevens conj. 71. *re-edified*] *rebuilt* Hanmer. 74. *Upon*] *It is upon* Capell. 78. *general all-ending*] Q 1; *generall ending*] Qq 2-8, Ff. 79. [*Aside.*] Johnson (and so 94). *never*] *ne'er* Pope. 82. [*Aside.*] Ff 2-4. *Thus*] *That* Qq 6-8.

Tower of London, "as also of many other towers, castles, and great buildings within this realm" (Stow, *Survey*, ed. Morley, p. 73).

73. *Successively*] Mr. Craig sends a parallel from Holland, *Pliny*, vii. 11 (1634, pt. i. p. 160): "In the race and family of the Lepidi it is said there were three of them (not *successively* one after another, but out of order after some intermission) who had . . . at their birth a little pannicle of thin skin growing over their eyes." Compare III. vii. 135 below.

77. *retail'd*] reported. Compare IV. iv. 338 below, where the meaning is probably the same. Malone quotes Minsheu, *Ductor in Linguas*, 1617: "to retail or retell, G. renombrer, à Lat. renumerare." Warburton explains that the story, being thus retailed, "like most other *retailed* things, became adulterated." He proposed "intail'd" instead, "which is finely and sensibly expressed, as though truth were the natural inheritance of our children; which it is impiety to deprive them of." Johnson supposed that "retail'd" might mean "diffus'd, dispersed."

78. *general all-ending*] The reading of all the printed copies save Q 1 may be due to the printer of Q 2, who confounded "all," on this supposition, with the last syllable of "general." The occurrence of the error in Ff may point, however, to its source in some early MS. of the play. For "all-ending" compare "all-shaking" in *King Lear*, III. ii. 6.

79. Steevens quotes "Is cadit ante senem, qui sapit ante diem." Reed gives an English form from Timothy Bright, *A Treatise of Melancholie*, 1586: "They be of short life who are of wit so pregnant." Aldis Wright refers to Holland's translation of *Pliny*, 1601, vii. 51, where the proverb is attributed to Cato the Censor.

81. *characters*] written records. Compare *Winter's Tale*, III. iii. 47. The word is usually accented on the first syllable; but, in *Hamlet*, I. iii. 59, the verb "character" has the penultimate accent. Compare "charáctery" in *Merry Wives of Windsor*, V. v. 77; *Julius Cæsar*, II. i. 308.

82. *the formal vice, Iniquity*] The nearest parallel in Shakespeare to this much-disputed passage is *1 Henry IV.* II. iv. 499, 500. References to the Vice of the Morality-plays are also found, *e.g.*, *Twelfth Night*, IV. ii. 134; *1 Henry IV.* II. iv. 151; *Henry V.* IV. iv. 75-77. In Jonson, *The Devil is an Ass*, 1616, i. 1, Pug asks Satan to let

I moralise two meanings in one word.
Prince. That Julius Cæsar was a famous man;
With what his valour did enrich his wit,
His wit set down to make his valour live:
Death makes no conquest of this conqueror,

83. *moralise*] *moralize:* Warburton; *moralize,—* Capell. 87. *this*] Q 1; *his* Qq 2-8, Ff.

him wander about the world for a fortnight, and take a Vice with him. When asked what kind of Vice he wishes, he answers "Why any: Fraud, Or Covetousness, or Lady Vanity, or old Iniquity." Iniquity then introduces himself. This shows (1) that the Vice often represented one special sin, but (2) that he frequently appeared under the general name of Iniquity. This is further indicated by Jonson, *Staple of News*, 1625, interact ii.: "the old way, when *Iniquity* came in like Hokos Pokos, in a juggler's jerkin, with false skirts, like the knave of clubs." "Formal" unquestionably means "according to form, usual, regular," as in *Antony and Cleopatra*, II. v. 41; compare *Merry Devil of Edmonton*, sc. i.: "The *formal* deed 'twixt me and thee." Thus it seems that Iniquity was the customary name under which the Vice appeared. Warburton wished to read "formal-wise antiquity," arguing (1) that the Vice was anything but formal (*i.e.* sober) in demeanour; (2) that Shakespeare would not allow an exact speaker, discoursing on antiquity, to wander off to a simile which had so little to do with his theme. He concludes complacently: "Formal-wise is a compound epithet, an extreme fine one, and admirably fitted to the character of the speaker, who thought all *wisdom* but *formality*. It must therefore be read for the future with a hyphen." Of course, Warburton takes "formality" in its derived sense: Polonius would be an excellent example of a "formal-wise" statesman. So Lucio, in Beaumont and Fletcher, *Woman-Hater*, is described as "a weak, formal statesman," *i.e.* devoted to the formalities of his office. Malone thought that "formal" might mean "shrewd, sensible"; but in his parallels (*Comedy of Errors*, v. i. 105; *Twelfth Night*, II. v. 128) the word simply means "normal."

83. The sense is "I imply a double meaning in one phrase." (1) We may assume that *double entendre* was part of the Vice's business during his career on the stage. It is the most effective weapon of Mathew Merygreeke, his direct descendant, in *Ralph Roister-Doister*. (2) For "moralise" in this sense see *As You Like It*, II. i. 44; *Lucrece*, 103; and compare "moral" in the sense of "hidden meaning," *Much Ado About Nothing*, III. iv. 78-80. (3) The "one word" which Richard moralises, as Monck Mason and others explain, is the phrase "lives long," repeating the "live long" of line 79. The Prince has caught the last words of his uncle's aside; and Richard repeats them for his benefit, altering the beginning and meaning of his sentence. For "word" in the sense of a collection of words, like Fr. *mot*, It. *motto*, compare *Richard II.* I. iii. 152. (4) Warburton explains his colon after "moralise" thus: "I moralise as the ancients [see previous note] did. And how was that? the having two meanings to one word." Capell understands "two meanings in one word" as a gloss which Richard adds to "moralise." The sentence as it stands, without alteration, would have been perfectly clear to an audience of Shakespeare's day.

85. *With what*] *i.e.* that with which his valour, etc.

87. *of this*] Later Qq and Ff readings may be defended on the ground that Cæsar, by perpetuating his fame in written history, has conquered the oblivion which Death brings. He is thus Death's conqueror, not Death his. On the other hand, it is equally probable that the printer of Q 2 dropped the "t" of "this," and that his error,

For now he lives in fame, though not in life.
I 'll tell you what, my cousin Buckingham,—
Buck. What, my gracious lord?
Prince. An if I live until I be a man,
I 'll win our ancient right in France again,
Or die a soldier, as I liv'd a king.
Glou. [*Aside.*] Short summers lightly have a forward spring.

Enter young YORK, HASTINGS, *and the* CARDINAL.

Buck. Now, in good time, here comes the Duke of York.
Prince. Richard of York! how fares our loving brother?
York. Well, my dread lord—so must I call you now.
Prince. Ay, brother, to our grief, as it is yours:
Too late he died that might have kept that title,
Which by his death hath lost much majesty.
Glou. How fares our cousin, noble Lord of York?
York. I thank you, gentle uncle. O, my lord,
You said that idle weeds are fast in growth:
The prince my brother hath out-grown me far.
Glou. He hath, my lord.
York. And therefore is he idle?
Glou. O, my fair cousin, I must not say so.
York. Then he is more beholding to you than I.
Glou. He may command me as my sovereign;
But you have power in me as in a kinsman.
York. I pray you, uncle, give me this dagger.
Glou. My dagger, little cousin? with all my heart.
Prince. A beggar, brother?

91. *An*] Theobald; *And* Qq, Ff. (and so 148). 94. *summers . . . have*] *summers . . . has* Pope (ed. 1); *summer . . . has* Pope (ed. 2); *summer . . . hath* Capell (conj.). 96. *loving*] *noble* Qq 3-8, Ff. 97. *dread*] *deare* Qq 3-8, Ff. 107. *beholding*] *beholden* Pope. 110. *uncle*] *uncle then* Hanmer. *this*] *this your* Warburton.

having some warrant in sense, was adopted by subsequent editions.

94. *lightly*] usually. Steevens quotes the proverb: "There 's lightning *lightly* before thunder," and Jonson, *Cynthia's Revels*, ii. 1: "He is not *lightly* within to his mercer." So Berners' *Froissart*, i. 38: "Sir John of Hainault and the lord of Fauquemont ever rode *lightly* together." Perhaps this whole line is proverbial.

99. *late*] lately. Hanmer altered to "soon," apparently failing to grasp this not uncommon use of the word.

109. *in me*] with me, as regards me. Collier's MS. contained the suggestion "o'er me."

York. Of my kind uncle, that I know will give;
And being but a toy, which is no grief to give.
Glou. A greater gift than that I 'll give my cousin.
York. A greater gift? O, that's the sword to it.
Glou. Ay, gentle cousin, were it light enough.
York. O, then, I see, you will part but with light gifts;
In weightier things you 'll say a beggar nay.
Glou. It is too heavy for your grace to wear.
York. I weigh it lightly, were it heavier.
Glou. What, would you have my weapon, little lord?
York. I would that I might thank you as you call me.
Glou. How?
York. Little.
Prince. My Lord of York will still be cross in talk:
Uncle, your grace knows how to bear with him.
York. You mean to bear me, not to bear with me:
Uncle, my brother mocks both you and me;
Because that I am little, like an ape,
He thinks that you should bear me on your shoulders.
Buck. With what a sharp-provided wit he reasons!
To mitigate the scorn he gives his uncle,

114. *but*] omitted Ff 2-4. *which is*] *it is* Ff 2-4; omitted, Steevens conj. *grief*] *gift* Qq 6-8. 120. *heavy*] Q 1; *waightie* Qq 2-8, Ff. 121. *I*] *I'd* Hanmer. 123. *as*] *as as* Q 3; *as, as,* F 1. 132. *sharp-provided*] hyphened Theobald. 133. *gives*] *giue* Qq 3-7.

114. *being but a toy*] since what I ask is but a trifle, it is no grief to give it. The construction is elliptic. F 2 emends both construction and metre, but apparently without authority. York's meaning is perfectly clear.

130, 131. The point of the jest lies, of course, in the relation between the words "bear" and "ape." (1) Johnson refers to the custom, at country shows, of taking a monkey and bear about together, and setting the monkey on the bear's back. Compare Beatrice's jest in *Much Ado About Nothing*, II. i. 43. York likens himself to an ape, and his uncle to a bear; while the grotesqueness of the jest is heightened by the "envious mountain" which Nature has heaped on Gloucester's back. (2) Steevens, disregarding the probable *double entendre* in "bear," understands the allusion as referring to the custom by which the fool in large households carried an ape perched on his back, and quotes Ulpian Fulwel, *Ars Adulandi*, etc. 1596: "Thou hast an excellent back to carry my lord's ape," and Jonson, *Masque of the Gipsies Metamorphosed*, 1621: "The fellow with the ape, Or the ape on his shoulder." *New Eng. Dict.* quotes Overbury, *Characters*, 1614 [A Rhymer]: "There is nothing in the earth so pitiful—no, not an ape-carrier." Shakespeare alludes to the custom, *Winter's Tale*, IV. iii. 101.

132. *sharp-provided*] Compare "senseless-obstinate" above, line 44.

133. *the scorn*] the taunt. Compare *1 Henry IV*. III. ii. 64; *Othello*, IV. i. 83.

He prettily and aptly taunts himself:
So cunning and so young is wonderful.

Glou. My lord, will 't please you pass along?
Myself and my good cousin Buckingham
Will to your mother, to entreat of her
To meet you at the Tower and welcome you.

York. What, will you go unto the Tower, my lord?

Prince. My lord protector needs will have it so.

York. I shall not sleep in quiet at the Tower.

Glou. Why, what should you fear?

York. Marry, my uncle Clarence' angry ghost:
My grandam told me he was murder'd there.

Prince. I fear no uncles dead.

Glou. Nor none that live, I hope.

Prince. An if they live, I hope I need not fear.
But come, my lord; and with a heavy heart,
Thinking on them, go I unto the Tower.

[*A Sennet. Exeunt all but Gloucester, Buckingham and Catesby.*

Buck. Think you, my lord, this little prating York
Was not incensed by his subtle mother
To taunt and scorn you thus opprobriously?

Glou. No doubt, no doubt: O, 'tis a perilous boy,
Bold, quick, ingenious, forward, capable:
He is all the mother's, from the top to toe.

136. *lord*] *gracious lord* Hanmer. *you*] *your highness* Capell. 141. *needs*] Q 1; omitted Qq 2-8, Ff. 149. *and*] Ff; omitted Qq. 150. *A Sennet.*] F 1. *Exeunt . . . Catesby.*] *Exeunt Prin. Yor. Hast. Dors. manet Rich.* [*Bich.* Q 5; *Bish.* Qq 6-8] *Buc.* Qq; *Exeunt Prince, Yorke, Hastings, and Dorset. Manet* [*Manent* F 2] *Richard, Buckingham, and Catesby.* Ff. aft. 150. SCENE II. Pope. 154. *perilous*] *perlous* Qq 7, 8; *parlous* Camb.

141. *needs*] Q 1 supplies the syllable missing from the rest of the printed copies. Hanmer conjectured the omitted monosyllable to be "here"; Collier MS. suggested "e'en."

148. *fear*] The prince has used "fear" in its ordinary sense (line 146). Now his thoughts revert to the uncles whom he has left in such jeopardy, and he uses it as above, I. i. 137.

150. *A Sennet*] A set flourish of trumpets, used to mark such occasions as the royal progress in this scene. See Mr. Craig on *King Lear*, I. i. 34.

152. *incensed*] instigated, as *Much Ado About Nothing*, V. i. 242. In *Henry VIII.* V. i. 43 "incens'd" is not merely equivalent, as *New Eng. Dict.* takes it, to "insens'd," *i.e.* informed, but implies that, by his information, Gardiner has instigated the suspicion of the council against Cranmer.

154. *perilous*] The full form of the word is found in all copies of Qq and Ff except the latest Qq.

155. *capable*] intelligent. See II. ii. 18 above, and note. Compare *Hamlet*, III. iv. 127; *Troilus and Cressida*, III. iii. 310.

Buck. Well, let them rest. Come hither, Catesby.
Thou art sworn as deeply to effect what we intend,
As closely to conceal what we impart:
Thou know'st our reasons urg'd upon the way;
What think'st thou? is it not an easy matter
To make William Lord Hastings of our mind,
For the instalment of this noble duke
In the seat royal of this famous isle?
Cates. He for his father's sake so loves the prince
That he will not be won to ought against him.
Buck. What think'st thou then of Stanley? will not he?
Cates. He will do all in all as Hastings doth.
Buck. Well, then, no more but this: go, gentle Catesby,
And, as it were far off, sound thou Lord Hastings,
How he doth stand affected to our purpose;
And summon him to-morrow to the Tower,
To sit about the coronation.
If thou dost find him tractable to us,

157-59. *Come hither . . . impart*] *Come, Catesby, thou art sworn As deeply . . . impart* Pope; *Come hither, gentle Catesby, thou art sworn As deeply . . . impart* Capell (*Well . . . rest* separate line); Camb. edd. conj. *Thou art sworn* as separate line. 160. *know'st*] Ff; *knowest* Qq. 161. *think'st*] Ff; *thinkest* Qq. 162. *William Lord*] *lord William* Pope. 167. *will not*] Ff; *what will* Qq. 169-71. *Well . . . purpose*] arranged as Pope; *Well . . . this: Goe . . . farre off, Sound . . . Hastings, How . . . purpose* Ff; *Well . . . this: Go . . . a farre off, Sound . . . how he stands affected Vnto our purpose* Qq. 170. *sound thou*] *Sound* Qq 3-8. 172, 173. *And summon . . . coronation*] Ff; omitted Qq. 174. *If thou . . . us*] Ff; *if he be willing* Qq.

160. *upon the way*] Two councils at least had been held upon the journey, the night-council at Northampton before the arrest of Rivers, and another the next day, after the return from Stony Stratford. Shakespeare, condensing history, makes the Protector's designs known to his private friends at a moment when, according to the historians, they were matured only in his own mind.

165. Holinshed and More bear frequent testimony to the friendship between Hastings and Edward IV. When Edward fled to Lynn in 1470, Hastings and Gloucester were his companions. Queen Elizabeth disliked Hastings "for the great fauour the king bare him; and also for that she thought him secretlie familiar with the king in wanton companie" (Holinshed, iii. 713). Although "sore inamoured upon" Jane Shore during the lifetime of Edward, "yet he forbore hir; ether for reuerence, or for a certeine friendlie faithfulnesse" (*ibid.* 724). Gloucester seems to have liked him: his only reason for sacrificing him without hesitation was "feare least his life should haue quailed their purpose" (*ibid.* 722.)

169-75. Possibly Qq here, as in other cases, represent the passage as it was corrupted, when spoken hastily on the stage.

170. *far off*] "For which cause he mooued Catesbie to prooue with some words cast out *a farre off*, whether he could thinke it possible to win the lord Hastings unto their part" (More, ap. Holinshed, iii. 722). Compare below, III. v. 93 and note.

Encourage him, and tell him all our reasons:
If he be leaden, icy-cold, unwilling,
Be thou so too, and so break off the talk,
And give us notice of his inclination;
For we to-morrow hold divided councils,
Wherein thyself shalt highly be employ'd.

Glou. Commend me to Lord William: tell him, Catesby,
His ancient knot of dangerous adversaries
To-morrow are let blood at Pomfret castle;
And bid my lord, for joy of this good news,
Give Mistress Shore one gentle kiss the more.

Buck. Good Catesby, go, effect this business soundly.

Cates. My good lords both, with all the heed I can.

Glou. Shall we hear from you, Catesby, ere we sleep?

Cates. You shall, my lord.

Glou. At Crosby Place, there shall you find us both.

[*Exit Catesby.*

Buck. Now, my lord, what shall we do, if we perceive

175. *tell*] Ff; *show* Qq. 176. *icy-cold*] Camb. (from Ingleby's conj.); *icie, cold* Qq; *ycie, cold* Ff. 177. *the talk*] Ff; *your talke* Qq. 184. *lord*] Ff; *friend* Qq 1-5; *friends* Qq 6-8. 185. *Mistress*] *gentle Mistresse* Qq 3-8. 186. *go, effect*] Ff; *effect* Qq. 187. *can*] Ff; *may* Qq. 190. *Place*] Qq; *House* Ff. *Exit Catesby.*] Ff; after 189 Qq 3-8; omitted Qq 1, 2. 191. *Now . . . perceive*] one line as Qq; *Now, my Lord, What . . . perceiue* (two lines) Ff. *Now*] omitted Pope.

179. *divided councils*] "But the protector and the duke, after that they had sent the lord cardinall, the archbishop of Yorke, . . . the bishop of Elie, the lord Stanleie, and the lord Hastings . . . with manie other noble men, to common & deuise about the coronation in one place, as fast were they in an other place, contriuing the contrarie, and to make the protector king" (More, ap. Holinshed, iii. 721). Gairdner (pp. 62, 63) shows that Gloucester allowed every facility to the council which sat at the Tower, to mature their plans, with the king's privity, undisturbed.

182. *knot*] company, confederacy, as *Merry Wives of Windsor*, III. ii. 52, IV. ii. 123; *Julius Cæsar*, III. i. 117. Among the plays presented by the King's Players at the wedding festivities of Princess Elizabeth, 1613, was one called *A Knot of Fools*. So Pepys, *Diary*, 16th Dec. 1662: ". . . the world says of me; that all do conclude Mr. Coventry, and Pett, and me, to be of a *knot;* and that we do now carry all things before us."

185. *Mistress Shore*] She had become Hastings' mistress after the death of Edward IV. When Hastings was executed, she was deprived of her goods and sent to prison. Gloucester failed to convict her of conspiracy with Hastings, and fell back on the charge of her known incontinence. "And for this cause (as a goodlie continent prince, cleane and faultlesse of himself, sent out of heauen into this vicious world for the amendment of mens maners) he caused the bishop of London to put hir to open penance, going before the crosse in procession vpon a sundaie with a taper in hir hand" (More, ap. Holinshed, iii. 724).

Lord Hastings will not yield to our complots?
Glou. Chop off his head: something we will determine:
And look, when I am king, claim thou of me
The earldom of Hereford, and all the moveables
Whereof the king my brother was possess'd.
Buck. I'll claim that promise at your grace's hand.
Glou. And look to have it yielded with all kindness.
Come, let us sup betimes, that afterwards
We may digest our complots in some form.
[*Exeunt.*

192. *Lord*] Ff; *William Lord* Qq. 193. *Chop . . . determine*] *Chop . . . Head: Something . . . determine* (two lines) Ff. *head*] Ff; *head, man* Qq. *something*] Ff; *somewhat* Qq. *determine*] Ff; *do* Qq. 195. *Hereford*] *Herford* Qq 3-5; *Hertford* Q 6. *all*] Ff; omitted Qq. 196. *was*] Ff; *stood* Qq. 197. *hand*] Ff; *hands* Qq. 198. *all kindness*] Ff; *all willingnesse* Q 1; *willingnesse* Qq 2-8.

192. *complots*] Below, line 200, the same word is used with the accent changed to the penultimate, which is the customary usage. Compare *Titus Andronicus*, II. iii. 265, V. i. 65, V. ii. 147; *2 Henry VI.* III. i. 147. So the verb is accented in *Richard II.* I. iii. 189.

195. Humphrey de Bohun, Earl of Hereford, Essex, and Northampton, left two daughters. (1) The elder, Eleanor, married the youngest son of Edward III., Thomas, Duke of Gloucester and Earl of Buckingham, who was styled Earl of Essex in right of his wife. They had a daughter Anne, who married Edmund, Earl of Stafford: her son Humphrey was created Duke of Buckingham by Henry VI.; and his grandson, the second Duke of Buckingham, is the Buckingham of this play. (2) The lands of Hereford were conveyed by the younger co-heiress, Mary, to her husband Henry, Earl of Derby, son of John of Gaunt, afterwards Henry IV. In 1397, three years after his wife's death, he was created Duke of Hereford. The fief continued in his line, and passed, with the other possessions of the crown, to the House of York: at this time it was in the hands of the King. Buckingham's claim to the Earldom of Hereford was thus a claim to the moiety of the Bohun possessions which, by the marriage of a younger co-heiress, had passed to an elder branch of the royal family. The third Duke of Buckingham, who occurs in *Henry VIII.*, was actually styled Earl of Hereford.

200. *digest*] arrange, give shape to, as Tourneur, *Revenger's Tragedy*, act iii.: "most dreadfully *digested!*"

SCENE II.—*Before Lord Hastings' house.*

Enter a Messenger.

Mess. My lord, my lord!
Hast. [*Within.*] Who knocks?
Mess. One from the Lord Stanley.

Enter LORD HASTINGS.

Hast. What is 't o'clock?
Mess. Upon the stroke of four.
Hast. Cannot thy master sleep these tedious nights?
Mess. So it appears by that I have to say.
First, he commends him to your noble self.
Hast. What then?
Mess. Then certifies your lordship that this night
He dreamt the boar had razed off his helm.
Besides, he says there are two councils kept;
And that may be determin'd at the one

SCENE II.] *SCENE III.* Pope. *Before . . . house*] Theobald. *Enter a Messenger.*] *Enter a messenger to Lord Hastings.* Qq; *Enter a Messenger to the doore of Hastings.* Ff. 1. *My lord, my lord*] Ff; *What ho my Lord* Qq. 2. *Who knocks*] Ff; *Who knockes at the dore* Qq. 3. *One*] Ff; *A messenger* Qq. *Enter Lord Hastings.*] Qq; after 5 Ff. 4. *What is 't o'clock*] Ff; *Whats a clocke* Qq. 6. *thy master*] Qq; *my Lord Stanley* Ff. *these*] Q 1, Ff; *the* Qq 2-6. 7. *appears*] Ff; *should seeme* Qq. 8. *self*] Ff; *Lordship* Qq. 9, 10. *What . . . night*] Ff; *And then. Mes. And then he sends you word* (one line) Qq. 11. *He dreamt*] Ff; *He dreamt to night* Qq. *boar*] Qq 6-8, Ff; *beare* Qq 1-5. *razed off*] Ff; *raste* Qq 1-4; *caste* Q 5; *cast* Qq 6-8. 12. *kept*] Ff; *held* Qq.

5. *Upon the stroke of four*] More (ap. Holinshed, iii. 723) says that Stanley sent his messenger at midnight.

6. *thy master*] Ff, contrary to the usual custom, derange the metre. The probability, as Spedding suggests, is that the editor of F 1 meant to alter "thy master" to "Lord Stanley," but forgot to strike out "thy"; that the printer noticed the weakness of the phrase "thy Lord Stanley," and changed "thy" to "my."

11. *razed off*] More (*u.s.*) uses the word: "him thought that a boare with his tuskes so *rased* them both by the heads, that the bloud ran about both their shoulders." Steevens says that the term "*rased* or *rashed* is always given to describe the violence inflicted by a boar." Compare *Sir Lancelot du Lake* (ap. Percy, *Reliques*, i. bk. 2, no. 10):—

"They buckled them together so,
Like unto wild boares *rashing*";

Qq reading of *King Lear*, III. vii. 58; Spenser, *Faerie Queene*, V. iii. 8, uses it with the simile of a lion: "*Rashing off* helms, and riving plates asonder." For the word applied in a general sense, see Berners' *Froissart*, i. 147: "Then the new town and bastide . . . was pulled down, and the castle that stood on the haven *rashed* down," *i.e.* razed. In *Hamlet*, III. ii. 288, "*razed* shoes" are shoes slashed or cut in patterns.

Which may make you and him to rue at the other.
Therefore he sends to know your lordship's pleasure,
If you will presently take horse with him,
And with all speed post with him toward the north,
To shun the danger that his soul divines.

Hast. Go, fellow, go, return unto thy lord:
Bid him not fear the separated councils;
His honour and myself are at the one,
And at the other is my good friend Catesby,
Where nothing can proceed that toucheth us
Whereof I shall not have intelligence.
Tell him his fears are shallow, wanting instance;
And, for his dreams, I wonder he's so simple
To trust the mockery of unquiet slumbers.
To fly the boar before the boar pursues,
Were to incense the boar to follow us
And make pursuit, where he did mean no chase.
Go, bid thy master rise and come to me;
And we will both together to the Tower,
Where, he shall see, the boar will use us kindly.

Mess. I'll go, my lord, and tell him what you say. [*Exit.*

16. *you will presently*] Ff; *presently you will* Qq. 17. *with him toward*] Ff; *into* Qq; *hence into* Capell. 19. *Go, fellow*] *Good fellow* Qq 3-8. 20. *councils*] Qq; *Councell* Ff. 22. *good friend*] Ff; *seruant* Qq. 25. *wanting*] Qq; *without* Ff. *instance*] Q 1, Ff; *instancie* Qq 2-8. 26. *he's so simple*] Ff; *he is so fond* Qq 1-3, 5-8; *he is fond* Q 4. 28. *pursues*] Ff; *pursues us* Qq 1, 2; *pursue us* Qq 3-6. 30. *no chase*] *to chase* Q 4. 34. *I'll go . . . and*] Ff; *My gratious Lord Ile* Qq. *Exit.*] omitted Qq 1, 2.

21. *His honour*] Stanley. Malone says that this was the usual title by which noblemen were addressed in Shakespeare's day. It was used indiscriminately with "his lordship." See Richard Field's dedication of Puttenham's (?) *Arte of English Poesie*, 1589, to Lord Burghley, or Bishop Hall's dedications of *Contemplations*, books 1 and 14, to the Earls of Exeter and Montgomery. The use of "his honour" was not confined to noblemen: for instance, book 13 of *Contemplations* is dedicated to Sir Thomas Edmonds, a knight and member of the Privy Council, whom Hall addresses as "your Honour."

25. *instance*] cause, motive, as *Henry V.* II. ii. 119; *Merry Wives of Windsor*, II. ii. 256; *Hamlet*, III. ii. 192.

26, 27. *so simple To*] For the omission of "as," compare Tourneur, *Revenger's Tragedy*, act i.:—

"But I had so much wit to keep my thoughts
Up in their built houses."

33. *kindly*] Hastings means that Richard will use them kindly, *i.e.* gently, courteously. But the audience know that he will use them kindly in another sense, *i.e.* after his boarish nature or kind.

Enter CATESBY.

Cates. Many good morrows to my noble lord!
Hast. Good morrow, Catesby; you are early stirring:
What news, what news, in this our tottering state?
Cates. It is a reeling world indeed, my lord;
And I believe 'twill never stand upright
Till Richard wear the garland of the realm.
Hast. How! wear the garland! dost thou mean the crown?
Cates. Ay, my good lord.
Hast. I'll have this crown of mine cut from my shoulders,
Before I'll see the crown so foul misplac'd!
But canst thou guess that he doth aim at it?
Cates. Ay, on my life, and hopes to find you forward
Upon his party for the gain thereof;
And thereupon he sends you this good news,
That this same very day your enemies,
The kindred of the queen, must die at Pomfret.
Hast. Indeed, I am no mourner for that news,
Because they have been still my adversaries;
But, that I'll give my voice on Richard's side,
To bar my master's heirs in true descent,
God knows I will not do it, to the death.
Cates. God keep your lordship in that gracious mind!
Hast. But I shall laugh at this a twelve-month hence,
That they which brought me in my master's hate,
I live to look upon their tragedy.

aft. 34. *Enter Catesby.*] *Enter Catesby to L. Hastings.* Qq 3-8. 39. *'twill* Qq 3-8; *it will* Qq 1, 2; *will* Ff. 41. *How . . . crown*] one line as Qq; *How . . . Garland? Doest . . . Crowne?* (two lines) Ff. 44. *Before I'll*] Ff; *Ere I will* Qq. 51. *that news*] *this newes* Qq 4, 6-8. 52. *my adversaries*] Ff; *mine enemies* Qq. 58. *which*] Ff; *who* Qq.

40. *garland*] Compare *2 Henry IV.* IV. v. 202. *New Eng. Dict.* quotes Grafton's continuation of Harding's *Chronicles*, 1543: "What about ye getting of the *garland*, keping it, lesing and winning again, it hath coste more English blood then hath the twise winning of France."

43. *crown*] Compare *1 Henry IV.* II. iv. 420.

49. Shakespeare derived this statement from More. Hastings' arrest and execution took place on 13th June; the lords were not beheaded apparently till 25th June.

55. *to the death*] *i.e.* even if my refusal cost me my life.

Well, Catesby, ere a fortnight make me older,
I 'll send some packing that yet think not on 't.

Cates. 'Tis a vile thing to die, my gracious lord,
When men are unprepar'd and look not for it.

Hast. O monstrous, monstrous! and so falls it out
With Rivers, Vaughan, Grey; and so 'twill do
With some men else, that think themselves as safe
As thou and I, who, as thou know'st, are dear
To princely Richard and to Buckingham.

Cates. The princes both make high account of you:
[*Aside.*] For they account his head upon the bridge.

Hast. I know they do; and I have well deserv'd it.

Enter LORD STANLEY.

Come on, come on; where is your boar-spear, man?
Fear you the boar, and go so unprovided?

Stan. My lord, good morrow; good morrow, Catesby:
You may jest on; but, by the holy rood,
I do not like these several councils, I.

Hast. My lord,
I hold my life as dear as you do yours;

60. *Well . . . older*] Ff; *I tell thee Catesby. Cat. What my Lord? Hast. Ere a fortnight make me elder* Qq. 61. *on 't*] Ff; *on it* Qq. 66. *that*] Ff; *who* Qq. 70. *Aside*] Rowe. 72. *Come on, come on*] Ff; *What my Lord* Qq. 74. *morrow; good*] *morrow, and good* Pope. 77, 78. *My lord, I . . . yours*] two lines as Johnson; one line Qq; *My Lord, I hold my life as deare as yours* Ff.

61. *packing*] Compare above, I. i. 146; Tourneur, *Revenger's Tragedy*, act iii.:—

"He being *pack'd* we 'll have some trick and wile,
To wind our younger brother out of prison."

"To send *packing*," *i.e.* to send away, dismiss summarily (*New Eng. Dict.*), is still used colloquially, though perhaps more rarely now than formerly. The intransitive "to pack," *i.e.* to go away, bag and baggage, is used by Shakespeare, *e.g. The Taming of the Shrew*, II. i. 178. Compare Lodge and Greene, *Looking-Glasse* (Dyce, 131): "Old dotard, *pack*, move not my patience." Mr. Craig calls attention to the Scottish use of "pack," in which, according to Jamieson's *Dictionary*, haste is not implied, as in English. He also notes "Let the canting liar *pack*" in Tennyson, *Vision of Sin*, iv. st. 12.

70. In their account, his head is as good as exposed already on London Bridge, with those of other traitors. Compare Wilkins, *Miseries of Inforst Marriage*: "A knave's head, shook seven years in the weather upon London Bridge."

76. *I do not . . . I*] For the emphatic repetition of "I," compare *Two Gentlemen of Verona*, v. iv. 132, and Marlowe, *Jew of Malta*, prol. line 28: "I come not, I, to read a lecture here in Britain."

78. *as you do yours*] Qq, in spite of Steevens' expressed contempt, introduce a great improvement on Ff. Ff reading

And never in my days, I do protest,
Was it so precious to me as 'tis now:
Think you, but that I know our state secure,
I would be so triumphant as I am?

Stan. The lords at Pomfret, when they rode from London,
Were jocund and suppos'd their states were sure,
And they indeed had no cause to mistrust;
But yet, you see, how soon the day o'ercast.
This sudden stab of rancour I misdoubt:
Pray God, I say, I prove a needless coward!
What, shall we toward the Tower? the day is spent.

Hast. Come, come, have with you! Wot you what, my lord?
To-day the lords you talk of are beheaded.

Stan. They, for their truth, might better wear their heads,
Than some that have accus'd them wear their hats.
But come, my lord, let us away.

79. *days*] Ff; *life* Qq. 80. *so . . . as*] Ff; *more . . . then* Qq. *'tis*] Ff; *it is* Qq. 81. *our state*] *the state* Ff 3, 4. 84. *states were*] Ff; *states was* Qq; *state was* Camb. 85. *they*] omitted Qq 3-8. 86. *o'ercast*] *ouercast* Qq 1, 2. 87. *stab*] Ff; *scab* Qq. 89. *What . . . spent*] Ff; *But come my Lo: shall we to the tower* Qq. 90. *Come, come . . . my lord*] *Come. . . you: Wot . . . Lord* (two lines) Ff; *I go: but stay, heare you not the newes* Qq. 91. *the lords you talk of*] Ff; *those men you talkt of* Qq 1, 2; *those men you talke of* Qq 3-8. 93. *hats*] *hat* Qq 2-5. 94. *But come, my lord, let us away*] Qq; *But come, my Lord, lets away* Ff; *But come, my lord, away* Pope; *Come, let us away* Capell.

may be an example of Shakespeare's "elliptical mode of expressing himself"; but, if so, it is an example which involves a misunderstanding. Its only obvious meaning is that Hastings sets an equal value on his own life and Stanley's; and this would be a remark without point. Qq give us what we naturally should expect him to say.

83. *London*] The reading of all the printed editions. Shakespeare must have meant to write "Ludlow." The lords in question were at Ludlow with the prince, when Edward IV. died; and it was on the ride from Ludlow to London that the sudden overcasting of their happiness took place. Compare Ff at II. ii. 142, 154, where the error is more conspicuous.

87. *misdoubt*] Compare *Love's Labour's Lost*, IV. iii. 194.

89. *the day is spent*] Ff, here and in line 90, have a great metrical advantage over Qq. It is a little difficult, however, to reconcile these words with the time of the scene as already indicated in line 5 above, or to explain them as meaning "the day is wearing itself away." Shakespeare already had pushed on an hour which the historians gave as midnight to four in the morning, and was condensing the several interviews recorded in the chronicles into one scene, the prelude to the forenoon council at the Tower and the discomfiture of Hastings. The phrase is either unusual or due to a lapse of memory.

90. *have with you*] This and kindred phrases, *e.g.* have at, after, or among you, are frequently found as announcing the arrival or departure of characters on the stage. For "have with you," compare the title of Nash's pamphlet, *Haue with you to Saffron Walden*, 1596.

Enter a Pursuivant.

Hast. Go on before; I'll talk with this good fellow.
[*Exeunt Lord Stanley and Catesby.*
How now, sirrah! how goes the world with thee?
Purs. The better that your lordship please to ask.
Hast. I tell thee, man, 'tis better with me now
Than when thou met'st me last where now we meet:
Then was I going prisoner to the Tower,
By the suggestion of the queen's allies;
But now, I tell thee—keep it to thyself—
This day those enemies are put to death,
And I in better state than e'er I was.
Purs. God hold it, to your honour's good content!
Hast. Gramercy, fellow: there, drink that for me.
[*Throws him his purse.*
Purs. I thank your honour! [*Exit.*

aft. 94. *Enter a Pursuivant.*] Ff; *Enter Hast. a Pursiuant* Qq 1, 2; *Enter Hastings a Pursiuant* Qq 3-8 (after 95). 95. *Go on . . . fellow*] Ff; *Go you before, Ile follow presently* Qq. *Exeunt . . .*] *Exit . . .* Ff; *Exit . . .* Qq 3-8 (after 94); omitted Qq 1, 2. 96. *How now, sirrah*] Ff; *Well met Hastings* Qq; *Sirrah, how now* Pope. 97. *your lordship please*] Ff; *it please your Lo:* Qq 1, 2; *it please your good Lordship* Qq 3-8. 98. *man*] Ff; *fellow* Qq. 99. *thou met'st me*] Ff; *I met thee* Qq. 104. *e'er*] Ff; *euer* Qq. 106. *fellow . . . me*] Ff; *Hastings, hold spend thou that* Qq. *Throws*] Ff; *He gives* Qq. 107. *I thank your honour*] Ff; *God saue your lordship* Qq. *Exit.*] *Exit Pur.* Qq 3-8, Ff; omitted Qq 1, 2.

aft. 94. *Enter a Pursuivant*] The stage-directions of Qq are in accordance with the historians, as are also the readings at lines 96, 106. The name of the pursuivant was Hastings. Compare More (ap. Holinshed, iii. 723): "Upon the verie Tower wharfe, so neare the place where his head was off [so] soone after there met he with one Hastings, a *purseuant* of his own name." This detail, in drama, becomes confusing; and Ff reading has rightly been adopted by all editors. A pursuivant is, strictly speaking, an attendant upon a herald. Chaucer, *Hous of Fame*, line 1321, speaks of "*purseuauntes* and heraudes, That cryen riche folkes laudes." The rest of the present passage in Shakespeare is in substantial agreement with More.

100, 101. Hastings' imprisonment has been mentioned above, I. i. 68, etc. Rivers, according to More, was the chief mover of his disgrace with the king. Shakespeare, I. i. 67, follows this statement.

101. *By the suggestion*] by the crafty instigation. Compare *1 Henry IV.* IV. iii. 51; *Henry VIII.* IV. ii. 35.

105. *God hold it*] God continue it. Compare *Much Ado About Nothing*, I. i. 91.

106. *Gramercy*] We sometimes find the form "gramercies," *e.g. Taming of the Shrew*, I. i. 41. A somewhat parallel case is the alternative use of "methought" and "methoughts": see note on I. iv. 9 above.

Enter a Priest.

Priest. Well met, my lord; I am glad to see your honour.
Hast. I thank thee, good sir John, with all my heart.
I am in your debt for your last exercise;
Come the next Sabbath, and I will content you.
[*He whispers in his ear.*
Priest. I 'll wait upon your lordship.

Enter BUCKINGHAM.

Buck. What, talking with a priest, lord chamberlain?
Your friends at Pomfret, they do need the priest;
Your honour hath no shriving work in hand.

108, 109. *Priest. Well met . . . my heart.*] Ff; *What sir John you are well met* Qq. 110. *I am . . . exercise*] Ff; *I am beholding to you for your last daies exercise* Qq. 111. *Sabbath*] *sabaoth* Qq 1, 2; *Sabboth* Qq 3-7, Ff 1, 2. *He whispers . . .*] Qq; omitted Ff. 112. *Priest. I 'll . . . lordship*] Ff; omitted Qq. 113. *What . . . chamberlain*] Ff; *How now Lo: Chamberlaine, what talking with a priest* Qq.

109. *Sir John*] The title "sir" was habitually applied to a priest in England, even after the Reformation. The parson in the *Merry Devil of Edmonton* is Sir John; there is Sir Hugh Evans in *Merry Wives of Windsor;* and, in this play, IV. v., Sir Christopher Urswick was a priest, not a knight. "Sir John" was a common nickname for a priest: compare Chaucer, *Canterbury Tales*, B. 4010: "This swete preest, this goodly man, *sir John.*"

110. *exercise*] sermon, exposition of Scripture. *New Eng. Dict.* quotes *Constitutions and Canons Ecclesiastical*, 1604: "Sermons, commonly tearmed by some Prophesies or *Exercises* in market-towns, or other places." Compare J. Udall, *Diotrephes*, 1588 (ed. Arber, p. 29): "Take heed aboue al things, that the *exercises* . . . of prophesie come not vp again . . . and you must beware of the *exercises* that ministers haue at their meetings"; Bishop Hall, *Letter sent from the Tower*, 1641 (*Works*, ed. Pratt, 1808, vol. i. p. xlix.): "Can they say . . . that I barred the free course of religious *exercises*, by the suppression of painful and peaceable preachers." Malone took "exercise" in the present case to mean "confession." Buckingham speaks of "shriving work" below; and, in III. vii. 64, Richard's exercise with the bishops appears to be meditation, prayer, and confession combined. In *Othello*, III. iv. 41, private meditation and prayer are implied.

111. *Sabbath*] Qq 1, 2 are paralleled by *Merchant of Venice*, IV. i. 36 (Q 2), on which see Mr. C. K. Pooler's note.

aft. 112. *Enter Buckingham*] In the historians, a knight, sent by Richard, fetches Hastings to the Tower, "as it were of courtesie." According to Halle, he was Sir Thomas Howard, a son of John, Lord Howard (see note on III. i. 58 above). They met the priest in Tower Street. The knight "brake his [Hastings'] tale, and said merilie to him: 'What, my lord, I pray you come on, whereto talke you so long with that priest? you haue no need of a priest yet': and therwith he laughed vpon him, as though he would say, 'Ye shall haue soone.' But so little wist the tother what he ment, and so little mistrusted, that he was neuer merier, nor neuer so full of good hope in his life; which selfe thing is oft seene a signe of change" (More, ap. Holinshed, iii. 723).

115. *shriving work*] confession and absolution. Compare "shriving-time," *Hamlet*, v. ii. 47.

Hast. Good faith, and, when I met this holy man,
The men you talk of came into my mind.
What, go you toward the Tower?

Buck. I do, my lord; but long I cannot stay there:
I shall return before your lordship thence.

Hast. Nay, like enough, for I stay dinner there.

Buck. [*Aside.*] And supper too, although thou know'st it not.
Come, will you go?

Hast. I'll wait upon your lordship.

[*Exeunt.*

SCENE III.—*Pomfret Castle.*

Enter SIR RICHARD RATCLIFF, *with halberds, carrying* RIVERS, GREY, *and* VAUGHAN *to death.*

Rat. Come, bring forth the prisoners.

Riv. Sir Richard Ratcliff, let me tell thee this:
To-day shalt thou behold a subject die
For truth, for duty, and for loyalty.

Grey. God bless the prince from all the pack of you!
A knot you are of damned blood-suckers.

Vaug. You live that shall cry woe for this hereafter.

Rat. Dispatch; the limit of your lives is out.

117. *The men*] Ff; *Those men* Qq. 118. *toward the Tower*] Ff; *to the tower my Lord* Qq. 119. *my lord*] omitted Qq. *cannot stay there*] Ff; *shall not stay* Qq. 121. *Nay*] Ff; *'Tis* Qq. 122. *Aside.*] Rowe. 123. *Come . . . lordship*] Ff; *Come shall we go along* Qq.

Scene III.

SCENE III.] *SCENE IV.* Pope. *Pomfret Castle.*] Theobald. *Enter . . .*] Camb.; *Enter . . . carrying the Nobles to death at Pomfret.* Ff; *Enter Sir Richard Ratliffe, with the Lo: Riuers, Gray and Vaughan, prisoners.* Qq. 1. *Rat. Come . . . prisoners*] Qq; omitted Ff. 5. *bless*] Ff; *keep* Qq. 7, 8. *Vaug. You live . . . is out*] Ff; omitted Qq.

5, 6. *pack . . . knot*] See note on III. i. 182 above, and the passage quoted there from *Merry Wives of Windsor.*

6. *blood-suckers*] So Warwick, *2 Henry VI.* III. ii. 226, calls Suffolk: "Pernicious *blood-sucker* of sleeping men." *New Eng. Dict.* explains "blood-sucker" as "a blood-thirsty or blood-guilty person." Mr. Craig illustrates from Middleton and Rowley, *A Fair Quarrel*, 1617, i. 1: "If it be so, you're a *blood-sucking* churl."

7. Without this line, Vaughan would be merely a walking figure in the play. It is not clear why it and line 8 should have been left out in Qq, which, in the stage-directions, expressly mention Vaughan. That the alteration must have been deliberate is shown by the virtual transference, in Qq, of line 8 to line 24.

Riv. O Pomfret, Pomfret! O thou bloody place,
Fatal and ominous to noble peers!
Within the guilty closure of thy walls
Richard the second here was hack'd to death;
And, for more slander to thy dismal seat,
We give to thee our guiltless blood to drink.

Grey. Now Margaret's curse is fall'n upon our heads,
When she exclaim'd on Hastings, you, and I,
For standing by when Richard stabb'd her son.

Riv. Then curs'd she Hastings, then curs'd she Buckingham,
Then curs'd she Richard. O, remember, God,
To hear her prayer for them, as now for us!
And for my sister and her princely sons,
Be satisfied, dear God, with our true blood,
Which, as thou know'st, unjustly must be spilt.

Rat. Make haste; the hour of death is expiate.

Riv. Come, Grey, come, Vaughan, let us here embrace.
Farewell, until we meet again in heaven. [*Exeunt.*

10. *ominous*] *dominious* Qq 2, 3; *ominious* Qq 4, 5. 13. *seat*] Ff; *soule* Qq; *soile* Capell conj. 14. *to thee*] Ff; *thee vp* Qq. *blood*] *blouds* Qq 1-6. 16. *When . . . and I*] Ff; omitted Qq, Camb. 18, 19. *Then . . . Hastings, then . . . Buckingham, Then . . . Richard*] Qq; *Then . . . Richard, Then . . . Buckingham, Then . . . Hastings* (3 lines) Ff. 18. *then*] omitted Pope. 20. *prayer*] Ff; *prayers* Qq. 21. *sons*] Ff; *sonne* Qq. 24. *Make . . . expiate*] Ff; *Come come dispatch, the limit of your liues is out* Qq. *expiate*] F 1; *expir'd* Ff 2-4; *expirate* Singer (from Steevens); *expedite* Collier conj. 26. *Farewell . . . again*] Ff; *And take our leaue vntill we meete* Qq.

10. Pontefract Castle had been the scene (19th June, 1322) of the execution of Thomas, Earl of Lancaster, for rebellion against his cousin Edward II. Richard II. died there, probably by murder, 14th Feb., 1400. In 1405, Archbishop Scrope was imprisoned there before his execution; and in 1461, after Wakefield, Richard Nevill, Earl of Salisbury, father of the "King-maker," was murdered there by order of Margaret of Anjou.

13. *seat*] Capell's conjecture "soil" probably explains Qq. For "seat" = site, compare *Macbeth*, I. vi. 1.

16. The grammar of this line, in which "I" is used for "me," is the only valid reason for rejecting it. But, in *Othello*, IV. ii. 3, Shakespeare has "Yes, you have seen Cassio and she together."

18, 19. The more effective arrangement in Qq leads up to the name of the chief criminal. On the other hand, Ff call our attention to the fact that Hastings is fulfilling the curse at the very moment at which these words are spoken.

24. *expiate*] terminated. The hour of death is come to an end. "Expiate" here is, of course, a past participle. Malone refers to Sonnet xxii. 4. *New Eng. Dict.* quotes Marlowe and Nash, *Dido*, 1594, act v.:—

"Cursed Iarbas, die to *expiate*
The grief that tires upon thine inward soul";

and Tofte, *Honours Academie*, 1610: "Nothing could appease and *expiat* his cankered rage." Monck Mason supports F 2. Steevens' "expirate" means, of course, "breathed out"; but the word is seldom used.

SCENE IV.—*The Tower of London.*

Enter BUCKINGHAM, DERBY, HASTINGS, *the* BISHOP OF ELY, RATCLIFF, LOVEL, *with others, and take their seats at a table.*

Hast. Now, noble peers, the cause why we are met
Is to determine of the coronation.
In God's name, speak! when is the royal day?
Buck. Is all things ready for the royal time?
Der. It is, and wants but nomination.
Ely. To-morrow, then, I judge a happy day.
Buck. Who knows the lord protector's mind herein?
Who is most inward with the noble duke?
Ely. Your grace, we think, should soonest know his mind.
Buck. Who? I, my lord!
We know each other's faces: for our hearts,
He knows no more of mine than I of yours,
Or I of his, my lord, than you of mine.
Lord Hastings, you and he are near in love.

SCENE IV.] *SCENE V.* Pope. *Enter* . . .] Camb.; *Enter Buckingham, Darby, Hastings, Bishop of Ely, Norfolke, Ratcliffe, Louell, with others, at a Table.* Ff; *Enter the Lords to Councell* Qq. 1. *Now, noble peers*] Ff (*Peere* F 2); *My Lords at once* Qq. 3. *speak*] Ff; *say* Qq. *the royal*] Ff; *this royall* Qq (*rayall* Q 6). 4. *Is*] Ff; *Are* Qq. *ready*] Ff; *fitting* Qq. *the royal*] Ff; *that royall* Qq. 5. *It is*] *They are* Rowe, Capell. *wants but*] Qq 1, 2, Ff, Capell; *let but* Qq 3, 5-7; *lack but* Q 4; *yet in* Q 8; *want but* Rowe. 6. *Ely*] Ff; *Ryu.* Qq 1, 2; *Bish.* Qq 3-8. *judge*] Ff; *guesse* Qq. *day*] Ff; *time* Qq. 9. *Your grace . . . should*] Ff; *Why you my Lo: me thinks you should* Qq. 10. *Who . . . lord*] Qq; omitted Ff. 11. *for*] Ff; *but for* Qq. 13. *Or . . . lord*] Ff; *nor I no more of his* Qq.

5. *It is*] This reading may have arisen from the use of "is" as a plural verb in the preceding line, which Ff retain. It is curious that it should have been kept by Qq when line 4 was altered. Perhaps what Shakespeare wrote in line 4 was: "Is all thing ready for the royal time?" which Qq altered to "Are all things fitting." Thus, when the editor of F 1 altered his copy of Q, he restored "Is" and "ready," but by an oversight left "things" unchanged. The meaning of line 5 thus would be "All thing (*i.e.* everything) is ready, and all that is wanting is the nomination of the date." "All thing" occurs often for "everything" in early English literature. Compare *Romaunt of Rose*, Frag. A, 53; and the metrical prayer ascribed to Henry VIII.: "O God, the maker of all thing." It is found in *Macbeth*, III. i. 13, where the later Ff have "all things"; there, however, Aldis Wright takes it to be an adverb.

8. *inward*] intimate. Compare Tourneur, *Revenger's Tragedy*, act ii.:—

"one
That is most *inward* with the duke's son's lust";

Measure for Measure, III. ii. 138. See also *Much Ado About Nothing*, IV. i. 247.

Hast. I thank his grace, I know he loves me well;
But, for his purpose in the coronation,
I have not sounded him, nor he deliver'd
His gracious pleasure any way therein.
But you, my noble lords, may name the time;
And in the duke's behalf I 'll give my voice,
Which, I presume, he 'll take in gentle part.

Enter GLOUCESTER.

Ely. In happy time here comes the duke himself.
Glou. My noble lords and cousins all, good morrow.
I have been long a sleeper; but, I trust,
My absence doth neglect no great design,
Which by my presence might have been concluded.
Buck. Had you not come upon your cue, my lord,
William Lord Hastings had pronounc'd your part,—
I mean, your voice,—for crowning of the king.
Glou. Than my Lord Hastings no man might be bolder;
His lordship knows me well, and loves me well.
Hast. I thank your grace.
Glou. My Lord of Ely, when I was last in Holborn,

18. *gracious*] Ff; *Graces* Qq. 19. *my noble lords*] Singer, Camb.; *my noble Lo:* Qq 1, 2; *my L.* Qq 3-7; *my Honorable Lords* Ff 1, 4; *my Honorable Lord* Ff 2, 3; *my Lord* Q 8; *my noble lord* Pope. 21. *he 'll*] Ff; *he will* Qq. *gentle*] *good* Q 6. aft. 21. *Enter Gloucester*] Ff; after 22 Qq. 22. *In happy time*] Ff; *Now in good time* Qq. 24. *a sleeper*] *a sleepe* Q 6. *but*] Q 1, Ff; *but now* Qq 2-8. *trust*] Ff; *hope* Qq. 25. *design*] Ff; *designes* Qq. 27. *you not*] Ff; *not you* Qq. *cue*] *kew* Qq; *Q* Ff. 28. *had*] Ff; *had now* Qq. 28, 29. *part,— . . . voice,—*] Capell, Camb.; *part: . . . voice* Qq; *part; . . . Voice*, Ff. 32. *Hast. I . . . grace*] Qq; omitted Ff. 33. *Glou. My . . . Holborn*] Ff; *Glo. My Lo: of Elie, Bish. My Lo. Glo. When . . . Holborne* Qq.

17. *deliver'd*] expressed, made public. Compare *Twelfth Night*, I. ii. 42; Fletcher and Massinger, *Elder Brother*, i. 2:—

"For what concerns tillage
Who better can *deliver* it than Virgil
In his Georgicks?"

24. "The lords so sitting togither communing of this matter, the protector came in amongst them, first about nine of the clocke, saluting them courteouslie, and excusing himselfe that he had beene from them so long; saieng merilie that he had beene a sleeper that daie" (More, ap. Holinshed, iii. 722).

27. *upon your cue*] Compare *Henry V.* III. vi. 130. The theatrical phrase "was derived, doubtless, from the French, *queue;* being literally the tail of a speech." (Nares, *s.v.* Cue.) Buckingham continues this actor's metaphor in the next line.

29. *voice*] vote. So *Coriolanus*, II. ii. 144, III. i. 34, etc.

33. The Qq addition here is one of those that may have arisen in the

I saw good strawberries in your garden there:
I do beseech you send for some of them.

Ely. Marry, and will, my lord, with all my heart. [*Exit.*

Glou. Cousin of Buckingham, a word with you.
[*Drawing him aside.*
Catesby hath sounded Hastings in our business,
And finds the testy gentleman so hot,
That he will lose his head, ere give consent
His master's child, as worshipfully he terms it,
Shall lose the royalty of England's throne.

Buck. Withdraw yourself awhile; I'll go with you.
[*Exit Gloucester, Buckingham following.*

Der. We have not yet set down this day of triumph.
To-morrow, in my judgment, is too sudden;
For I myself am not so well provided
As else I would be, were the day prolong'd.

35. *I do*] *I now* Q 4. 36. *Marry . . . heart*] Ff; *I go my Lord* Qq. *Exit.*] *Exit Bishop* Ff; omitted Qq. 37. *of*] Ff; omitted Qq. *Drawing him aside*] Capell, Camb. 40. *That*] Ff; *As* Qq. 41. *child*] Ff; *sonne* Qq. *worshipfully*] Ff; *worshipful* Qq. 43. *yourself . . . go with*] Ff; *you hence, my Lo. Ile follow* Qq. *Exit . . .*] Camb.; *Ex. Gl.* Qq; *Exeunt.* Ff. 45. *my judgment*] Ff; *mine opinion* Qq. *sudden*] *soone* Qq 2-8.

custom of the stage, and so have been transferred to print. More has "After a little talking with them, he said vnto the Bishop of Elie: My lord, you haue very good strawberies at your garden in Holborn, I require you let vs haue a messe of them. Gladlie, my lord (quoth he), would God I had some better thing as readie to your pleasure as that! And therewithall in all the hast he sent his seruant for a messe of strawberies." Gloucester's irrelevant request to the Bishop was obviously intended to throw dust in the eyes of the lords who might suspect him.

33. *Holborn*] The chapel of Ely House, with its undercroft, remains in Ely Place, on the north side of Holborn. The site of the house was given to his successors by Bishop John of Kirkby (d. 1290). Further additions to the gift were made by Bishop Hotham (d. 1336). At the end of the fourteenth century, Bishop Arundell repaired the house. Some years before this play was produced, the fee-simple had been alienated, under pressure from the Crown, to Sir Christopher Hatton, the memory of whose tenure survives in the name of Hatton Garden. Stow mentions that Ely House, in his time, "for the large and commodious rooms thereof," was used for "divers great and solemn feasts . . . especially by the sergeants-at-the-law." The chapel was founded by Bishop William of Louth (d. 1298), and is a beautiful example of the latest type of thirteenth-century architecture. In Sir Christopher Hatton's time, half the undercroft was used as a wine-shop; the chapel, in the next reign, was appropriated to the services of the Spanish embassy. Ely House was pulled down in 1772: for many years the chapel was used for Welsh services, but is now occupied by a community of Romanist clergy.

47. *prolong'd*] postponed, as *Much Ado About Nothing*, IV. i. 256.

Re-enter the BISHOP OF ELY.

Ely. Where is my lord the Duke of Gloucester?
I have sent for these strawberries.
Hast. His grace looks cheerfully and smooth this morning;
There's some conceit or other likes him well,
When that he bids good-morrow with such spirit.
I think there's never a man in Christendom
Can lesser hide his love or hate than he;
For by his face straight shall you know his heart.
Der. What of his heart perceive you in his face
By any livelihood he show'd to-day?
Hast. Marry, that with no man here he is offended;
For, were he, he had shown it in his looks.
Der. I pray God he be not, I say!

Re-enter GLOUCESTER *and* BUCKINGHAM.

Glou. I pray you all, tell me, what they deserve
That do conspire my death with devilish plots
Of damned witchcraft, and that have prevail'd
Upon my body with their hellish charms?
Hast. The tender love I bear your grace, my lord,
Makes me most forward in this princely presence

aft. 47. *Re-enter*] *Enter* Qq, Ff. 48, 49. *Where . . . strawberries*] arranged as Ff; one line Qq; as prose Camb. 48. *the Duke of Gloucester*] Ff; *protector* Qq. 49. *sent*] *sent straitway* Hanmer. *these*] *these same* Capell. 50. *this morning*] Ff; *to day* Qq. 52. *that he bids*] Ff; *he doth bid* Qq. *such*] Ff; *such a* Qq. 53. *there's never*] Ff; *there is neuer* Qq; *there's ne'er* Pope. 54. *Can lesser*] Ff; *That can lesser* Qq 1-7; *That can less* Q 8, Camb. 57. *livelihood*] Ff; *likelihood* Qq. 58. *he is*] *he's* Pope. 59. *were he . . . shown*] Ff; *if he were, he would haue shewen* Qq. *looks*] Q 1, Ff; *face* Qq 2-8. 60. *Der. I . . . say*] Qq; omitted Ff. aft. 60. *Re-enter . . .*] *Enter Richard, and Buckingham.* Ff; *Enter Glo.* Qq. 61. *tell me, what they*] Ff; *what do they* Qq. 66. *princely*] Ff; *noble* Qq.

51. *conceit*] ingenious notion. Compare *Taming of the Shrew*, IV. iii. 162, 163. "Conceit," used absolutely by Shakespeare, means "fancy," as *Romeo and Juliet*, II. vi. 30.

likes him well] So *Hamlet*, II. ii. 80, and numerous other passages in Shakespeare.

57. *livelihood*] *All's Well that Ends Well*, I. i. 58, supplies a parallel for Ff. Qq, however, have "likelihood" (*i.e.* apparent sign), for which there is something to be said. Aldis Wright refers to *All's Well that Ends Well*, I. iii. 128.

61-81. The whole of this passage is closely condensed from More. More's account of the arrest, the entry of the men-at-arms, and the turmoil in which Stanley was wounded, are omitted by Shakespeare, doubtless to concentrate our attention on the real victim of the scene. In lines 78, 79 he reproduces More almost literally: "by St. Paul (quoth he) I will not to dinner till I see thy head off.'

To doom the offenders, whosoe'er they be:
I say, my lord, they have deserved death.
Glou. Then be your eyes the witness of their evil!
Look, how I am bewitch'd! behold! mine arm
Is like a blasted sapling wither'd up:
And this is Edward's wife, that monstrous witch,
Consorted with that harlot, strumpet Shore,
That by their witchcraft thus have marked me.
Hast. If they have done this deed, my noble lord,—
Glou. If! thou protector of this damned strumpet,
Talk'st thou to me of "ifs"? Thou art a traitor.
Off with his head! now by Saint Paul I swear,
I will not dine until I see the same!
Lovel and Ratcliff, look that it be done:
The rest that love me, rise and follow me.
[*Exeunt all but Hastings, Ratcliff, and Lovel.*
Hast. Woe, woe for England! not a whit for me;
For I, too fond, might have prevented this.
Stanley did dream the boar did raze his helm;
And I did scorn it, and disdain to fly:
Three times to-day my foot-cloth horse did stumble,

67. *whosoe'er*] Ff; *whatsoeuer* Qq. 69. *their evil*] Ff; *this ill* Qq. 70. *Look*] Ff; *See* Qq. 72. *And this is*] Ff; *This is that* Qq. 74. *witchcraft*] Q 1, Ff; *witchcrafts* Qq 2-6. 75. *deed*] Ff; *thing* Qq. *noble*] Ff; *gratious* Qq. *lord,—*] Rowe, Camb. 77. *Talk'st thou to me*] *Telst thou me* Qq; *Tellest thou me* Camb. 78-80. *Off . . . done*] Ff; *Off with his head. Now by Saint Paule, I will not dine to day I sweare, Vntill I see the same, some see it done* Qq. 81. *rise*] Ff; *come* Qq. *Exeunt . . .*] Camb.; *Exeunt. Manet Louell and Ratcliffe, with the Lord Hastings.* Ff (*Manent* Ff 2, 4); *Exeunt. manet Cat. with Ha.* Qq; *Exeunt. Manent Lovel and Catesby, with the Lord Hastings.* Theobald. 84. *raze his helm*] *race his helme* Qq; *rowse our Helmes* Ff; *rase our helms* Rowe. 85. *And I . . . disdain*] Ff; *But I disdain'd it, and did scorne* Qq.

71. *blasted sapling*] Compare *3 Henry VI.* III. ii. 156.

84. *raze his helm*] See note on III. ii. 11 above. Ff "our Helmes" is in keeping with Stanley's dream as recorded by the chroniclers. But "rowse" must be a printer's error.

86. *foot-cloth horse*] More says that, as Hastings went to the Tower, his "horsse twise or thrise stumbled with him, almost to the falling." A "foot-cloth horse" is a horse equipped with foot-cloths, *i.e.* trappings hanging over the horse's sides and covering the rider's feet. In *2 Henry VI.* IV. vii. 51, Cade asks Lord Say: "Thou dost ride in a *foot-cloth*, dost thou not?" and rebukes him for letting his "horse wear a cloak, when honester men . . . go in their hose and doublets." In the same play, IV. i. 54, Suffolk reminds his murderer that in times past he has "bare-headed plodded by my *foot-cloth* mule." The social importance of the "foot-cloth riders," classed among the "valiant stomachs of the court," by Fletcher,

And started, when he look'd upon the Tower,
As loath to bear me to the slaughter-house.
O, now I need the priest that spake to me:
I now repent I told the pursuivant,
As too triumphing, how mine enemies
To-day at Pomfret bloodily were butcher'd,
And I myself secure in grace and favour.
O Margaret, Margaret! now thy heavy curse
Is lighted on poor Hastings' wretched head.

Rat. Come, come, dispatch; the duke would be at dinner:
Make a short shrift; he longs to see your head.

Hast. O momentary grace of mortal men,
Which we more hunt for than the grace of God!
Who builds his hope in air of your good looks,
Lives like a drunken sailor on a mast,
Ready with every nod to tumble down
Into the fatal bowels of the deep.

Lov. Come, come, dispatch; 'tis bootless to exclaim.

Hast. O, bloody Richard! miserable England!

87. *started*] Ff; Qq 7-8; *startled* Qq 1-6. 89. *need*] Ff; *want* Qq 1-6. 91. *too triumphing, how*] Ff; *twere triumphing at* Qq. 92. *To-day*] Ff; *How they* Qq. 95. *lighted*] *lightened* Qq 6, 7. 96. *Rat.*] *Ra.* Ff; *Cat.* Qq. *Come, come, dispatch*] Ff; *Dispatch, my lord* Qq. 98. *grace of mortal*] Qq; *state of worldly* Ff. 99. *than*] *then for* Qq 3-8. *God*] Ff; *heauen* Qq. 100. *hope*] Ff; *hopes* Qq. *good*] Ff; *faire* Qq. 101. *a drunken sailor*] *drunken Saylers* Q 4. 104-107. *Lov. Come . . . upon*] Ff; omitted Qq.

Woman-Hater, i. 2, is alluded to by Machin and Markham, *Dumb Knight*, act iii., in reference to a pleader who has made his fortune:—

> "his father was
> An honest proiner of our country vines;
> Yet he 's shot to his *foot-cloth*."

Steevens made the mistake of supposing "foot-cloth" in such passages to be a mere synonym for the horse. Mr. Craig supplies a reference from Shirley, *The Brothers*, c. 1626, i. 1:—

> "I am a gentleman
> With as much sense of honour as the proudest,
> One that doth ride on's *foot-cloth*."

87. *started*] Aldis Wright quotes *As You Like It*, IV. iii. 13, in support of Qq.

97. *short shrift*] More says of Hastings: "heauilie he tooke a priest at aduenture, and made a *short shrift*."

101. The figure of the sailor on the mast is used again in *2 Henry IV*. III. i. 18-25.

rotten armour] rusty armour. Halliwell, *s.v.* Rotten, cites Richard of Hampole: "When I am *rotyn*, rub of the rust." More says that Gloucester "with the Duke of Buckingham stood harnessed in old ill faring briganders." The brigander or brigandine was a jacket, composed of small plates of metal between leather or quilted canvas coverings, over which on the outside velvet, silk, or satin was laid, the rivets being visible on the outer covering. See Fairholt, *Costume in England* (4th ed. 1896), ii. 91, 92.

I prophesy the fearfull'st time to thee
That ever wretched age hath look'd upon.
Come, lead me to the block; bear him my head:
They smile at me who shortly shall be dead.

[*Exeunt.*

SCENE V.—*The Tower-walls.*

Enter GLOUCESTER *and* BUCKINGHAM *in rotten armour, marvellous ill-favoured.*

Glou. Come, cousin, canst thou quake and change thy colour,
Murder thy breath in middle of a word,
And then again begin, and stop again,
As if thou were distraught and mad with terror?
Buck. Tut! I can counterfeit the deep tragedian,
Speak and look back, and pry on every side,
Tremble and start at wagging of a straw,
Intending deep suspicion: ghastly looks
Are at my service, like enforced smiles;
And both are ready in their offices,

109. *who*] Ff; *that* Qq.

Scene V.

SCENE V.] SCENE VI. Pope; omitted Ff. *The Tower-walls.*] Theobald. *Enter Gloucester . . .*] *Enter Richard . . .* Ff; *Enter Duke of Glocester and Buckingham in armour.* Qq. *rotten*] *rusty* Rowe. 1. *Come . . . colour*] one line as Qq; *Come Cousin, Canst . . . colour* (two lines) Ff. 3. *again begin*] Ff; *beginne againe* Qq. 4. *were*] Ff; *wert* Qq. 5. *Tut, I . . . tragedian*] Ff; *Tut feare not me, I . . . Tragedian* (two lines) Qq. 7. *Tremble . . . straw,*] *Tremble . . . Straw:* Ff; omitted Qq. 8. *deep*] *deere* Q 4.

4. *distraught*] Compare *Romeo and Juliet*, IV. iii. 49. "Distract" is used for "distraught" in *Comedy of Errors*, IV. iii. 42; *King Lear*, IV. vi. 288.

5. *the deep tragedian*] Mr. Craig suggests that this may be an allusion to Burbage, the "deep tragedian" of Shakespeare's company, or to some other well-known actor.

7. *at wagging of a straw*] The proverbial use of this phrase seems to be illustrated by a passage which Mr. Craig points out from Nash, *Lenten Stuffe*, 1599 (McKerrow, iii. 219): "but upon the least *wagging of a straw* to put them in feare where no feare is." Mr. Craig also sends a parallel from North's *Plutarch*, *Life of Fabius* (ed. Rouse, 1898, ii. 195): "To be afeard of the *wagging of every straw*, or to regard every common prating, it is not the part of a worthy man of charge."

8. *Intending*] pretending, as *Timon of Athens*, II. ii. 219. See also III. vii. 45 below. *New Eng. Dict.* quotes *Marriage of Witte and Science*, c. 1570, act iv.: "Friend Wit, are you the man indeed which you *intend?*"

12-21. See Appendix II.

At any time to grace my stratagems.
But what, is Catesby gone?

Glou. He is; and see, he brings the mayor along.

Enter the LORD MAYOR *and* CATESBY.

Buck. Lord mayor,—
Glou. Look to the drawbridge there!
Buck. Hark! a drum.
Glou. Catesby, o'erlook the walls.
Buck. Lord mayor, the reason we have sent—
Glou. Look back, defend thee, here are enemies.
Buck. God and our innocency defend and guard us!
Glou. Be patient, they are friends, Ratcliff and Lovel.

Enter LOVEL *and* RATCLIFF, *with* HASTINGS' *head.*

Lov. Here is the head of that ignoble traitor,
The dangerous and unsuspected Hastings.

Glou. So dear I lov'd the man, that I must weep.
I took him for the plainest harmless creature
That breath'd upon the earth a Christian;
Made him my book, wherein my soul recorded
The history of all her secret thoughts.
So smooth he daub'd his vice with show of virtue,
That, his apparent open guilt omitted—

11. *At any time*] Ff; omitted Qq. 12-14. *But what . . . mayor,—*] Ff; *Enter Maior. Glo. Here comes the Maior. Buc. Let me alone to entertaine him. Lo: Maior.* Qq. 16-18. *Buck. Hark! . . . sent—*] Ff; *Buc. The reason we haue sent for you. Glo. Catesby ouerlooke the wals. Buck. Harke, I heare a drumme.* Qq. 16. *Hark*] *Hark, hark* Capell. 17. *Catesby*] *Some one* Hanmer. 18. *sent—*] *sent for you* Capell. 20. *and guard*] Ff; omitted Qq. 21. *Be . . . Lovel*] Ff; *O, O, be quiet, it is Catesby* Qq. *Enter Lovel and Ratcliffe . . .*] after 20 Ff; *Enter Catesby . . .* Qq. 22. *Lov.*] *Louell.* Ff; *Cat.* Qq. 25. *harmless*] *harmless't* Steevens. *creature*] Ff; *man* Qq. 26. *the earth*] Q 4, Ff; *this earth* Qq 1-3, 5-8. 27. *Made*] *I made,* Qq 5-8. aft. 26. Qq inserts *Look ye my Lo: Maior,* which Capell inserts at end of 34.

25. *plainest harmless*] Steevens altered to "plainest harmless't," citing the latter word as a common contraction in Leicestershire and Warwickshire, and referring to "covert'st" in line 33 immediately below. But "covert'st shelter'd" is exactly parallel to "plainest harmless," and, to be consistent, he should have read the phrase "covert'st shelter'd'st." One superlative is quite sufficient in each case. For "plain," compare I. ii. 237 above.

29. *daub'd . . . virtue*] *New Eng. Dict.* explains "to daub" as "to cover with a specious exterior, to whitewash, cloak, gloss."

30. *open*] evident, as *Twelfth Night,* II. v. 175.

I mean, his conversation with Shore's wife—
He liv'd from all attainder of suspects.
Buck. Well, well, he was the covert'st shelter'd traitor
That ever liv'd.
Would you imagine, or almost believe,
Were 't not that, by great preservation,
We live to tell it, that the subtle traitor
This day had plotted, in the council-house
To murder me and my good Lord of Gloucester?
May. Had he done so?
Glou. What, think you we are Turks or infidels?
Or that we would, against the form of law,
Proceed thus rashly in the villain's death,
But that the extreme peril of the case,
The peace of England, and our persons' safety,
Enforc'd us to this execution?
May. Now, fair befall you! he deserv'd his death;
And your good graces both have well proceeded,
To warn false traitors from the like attempts.

32. *liv'd*] Ff; *laid* Qq. *suspects*] Ff; *suspect* Qq. 34-36. *That ever . . . preservation*] Ff; *That euer liu'd, would you haue imagined, Or almost beleeue, wert not by great preseruation* Qq. 37. *tell it, that*] Ff; *tell it you? the* Qq; *tell it you, the* Camb. 38. *This day had*] Ff; *Had this day* Qq. 40. *Had . . . so*] Ff; *What, had he so* Qq; *Ay, had he so* Capell (conj.). 41. *you*] *ye* Qq 3-8. 42. *form*] *course* Qq 3-8. 43. *in*] Ff; *to* Qq. 44. *extreme*] *very extreame* Q 4. 48. *your good graces*] Ff; *you my good Lords* Qq.

32. *from*] free from, without. Compare *Othello*, I. i. 132. In the passage from More, cited above in the note on III. iv. 24, "he had beene *from* them" = he had been away from them.

attainder of suspects] Compare *Love's Labour's Lost*, I. i. 158.

34. Capell, followed by Steevens, gave an imperfect finish to this imperfect line by transferring the words "Look you, my lord mayor" from after line 26 in Qq, where they obviously are out of place. It is difficult to see where they were intended to stand; and Ff dismiss them altogether.

36. *by great preservation*] "And so had God holpen them, that the mischiefe turned vpon them that would haue doone it" (More).

38, 39. It would have been impossible to disprove this accusation, since the lords who were present at the council were either Gloucester's creatures, or were imprisoned as suspect of complicity with Hastings.

41. *Turks or infidels*] Compare *Merchant of Venice*, IV. i. 32, where the "infidel" Shylock is reminded that Antonio's misfortunes are enough to

"pluck commiseration of his
state . . .
From stubborn Turks and Tartars
never train'd
To offices of tender courtesy."

Compare also the famous phrase in the third Collect for Good Friday: "Have mercy upon all Jews, Turks, Infidels and Hereticks."

47. *fair befall you*] Compare I. iii 282 above; *Taming of the Shrew*, V. ii 111.

Buck. I never look'd for better at his hands,
After he once fell in with Mistress Shore.
Yet had we not determin'd he should die,
Until your lordship came to see his end;
Which now the loving haste of these our friends,
Something against our meanings, have prevented:
Because, my lord, I would have had you heard
The traitor speak, and timorously confess
The manner and the purpose of his treasons,
That you might well have signified the same
Unto the citizens, who haply may
Misconster us in him and wail his death.

May. But, my good lord, your grace's words shall serve,
As well as I had seen and heard him speak:
And do not doubt, right noble princes both,
But I'll acquaint our duteous citizens
With all your just proceedings in this case.

Glou. And to that end we wish'd your lordship here,

50. *Buck.*] Ff; omitted Qq. 52-61. Qq 4, 6-8 give to *Glo.*; *Dut.* Qq 1, 2; *Clo.* Qq 3, 5. 52. *we not*] Ff; *not we* Qq. 53. *end*] Ff; *death* Qq. 54. *loving*] Ff; *longing* Qq. 55. *Something*] Ff, Pope; *Somewhat* Qq. *meanings*] Ff; *meaning* Qq, Pope. *have*] *hath* Pope. 56. *I*] Ff; *we* Qq. *heard*] *hear* Keightley (conj.). 58. *treasons*] Ff; *treason* Qq. 60. *haply*] Ff; *happily* Qq. 61. *Misconster*] Qq 1-5, Ff 1-3; *Misconstrue* Q 6, F 4. 62. *But*] omitted Qq 3-8; *Tut* Hanmer. *words*] Ff; *word* Qq. 63. *and heard*] Ff; *or heard* Qq. 64. *do not doubt*] Ff; *doubt you not* Qq. 65. *our*] Ff; *your* Qq. 66. *case*] Ff, Qq 7, 8; *cause* Qq 1-5; *ease* Q 6. 67. *wish'd*] *wish* Qq 6-8.

50, 51. Qq assign these lines to the Mayor, by whom they might have been spoken. The whole case of Jane Shore was a disgrace in citizenship which would have touched the Londoner deeply. However, the words "I never look'd for better at his hands" seem to point either to Gloucester or Buckingham as the speaker; for the Mayor had nothing to look for at the hands of Hastings. That the words are Buckingham's is most probable: Gloucester already, in line 31, had brought in the mention of Shore's wife to raise the Mayor's prejudice against Hastings. It was now Buckingham's turn to underline the insinuation.

52-61. These words are clearly a continuation of Buckingham's speech. Gloucester adds his further improvement in lines 67, 68. Probably "Dut." before line 52 in Qq 1, 2 is a misprint for "Buc."

55. *have*] The verb apparently has been attracted into the plural after "friends" in the previous line.

61. *Misconster us in him*] misconstrue our behaviour towards him. "Misconster" is the form common to the early Qq and three of the folios. On Mr. Daniel's hypothesis as to the text, the editor of F 1 restored it in place of the new reading "Misconstrue" in Q 6. F 1 has "misconsters" in *As You Like It*, I. ii. 277; "conster," *Twelfth Night*, III. i. 63; but "construe," *Merry Wives of Windsor*, I. iii. 50: *Julius Cæsar*, I. iii. 34, II. i. 307.

To avoid the censures of the carping world.
Buck. But, since you come too late of your intent,
Yet witness what you hear we did intend:
And so, my good lord mayor, we bid farewell.
[*Exit Mayor.*
Glou. Go after, after, cousin Buckingham!
The mayor towards Guildhall hies him in all post:
There, at your meetest vantage of the time,
Infer the bastardy of Edward's children:
Tell them how Edward put to death a citizen,
Only for saying he would make his son
Heir to the crown—meaning indeed his house,
Which, by the sign thereof, was termed so.
Moreover, urge his hateful luxury
And bestial appetite in change of lust,
Which stretcht unto their servants, daughters, wives,
Even where his raging eye or savage heart,
Without control, listed to make a prey.

68. *censures of the carping*] Ff; *carping censures of the* Qq. 69. *But*] Qq; *Which* Ff. *come*] *came* Qq 3-8. *too late of*] *too late for* Capell. *intent*] Ff; *intents* Qq. 70, 71. *Yet . . . farewell*] Ff; *Yet witnesse what we did intend, and so my Lord adue* (one line) Qq. 72. *Go*] Ff; omitted Qq. 74. *meetest*] Qq 6-8, Ff; *meetst* Qq 1-5. *vantage*] Ff; *aduantage* Qq. 82. *stretcht unto*] Ff; *stretched to* Qq. 83. *raging*] Ff; *lustful* Qq; *ranging* Pope. *a prey*] Ff; *his prey* Qq.

68. *censures*] Here, if Ff be adopted, in the usual sense of "adverse judgments," as in *Othello*, v. ii. 368; *Henry VIII.* I. i. 33, III. i. 64. Qq, transferring to it the epithet "carping," give it the simple sense of "judgments," as II. ii. 144 above.

69. *too late of*] For the preposition compare *King Lear*, I. ii. 6.

73. *in all post*] For this phrase compare I. i. 146 above. See also *Richard II.* II. i. 296; and compare "haste-post-haste," *Othello*, I. ii. 37. Mr. Craig notes three instances from *3 Henry VI. viz.* I. ii. 48, III. iii. 222, v. v. 84.

74. *vantage of the time*] Compare *Troilus and Cressida*, III. iii. 2.

75. *Infer*] See III. vii. 12 below, in Buckingham's account of the speech which Gloucester here advises him to make. Compare *Timon of Athens*, III. v. 73, and Mr. Deighton's note. The sense in the present case is "bring in as evidence."

76-79. The story of one Burdet, "a marchaunt dwellyng in Chepesyd at ye signe of ye croune . . . ouer agaynst soper lane," was foisted into More's narrative by Halle, to explain an allusion to Burdet's execution in the text. Halle seems to have confused two separate incidents; for Burdet, punished in 1476, was a squire of Arrow in Worcestershire, and "the word spoken in hast" for which he suffered had nothing to do with the crown. The citizen's name is given otherwise as Walker. See Boswell-Stone, *Shakspere's Holinshed*, p. 375, note 2.

80. *luxury*] lechery, as *Hamlet*, I. v. 83; *Measure for Measure*, v. i. 506; *King Lear*, IV. vi. 119. Compare "luxurious," *Macbeth*, IV. iii. 58. Tourneur, *Revenger's Tragedy*, twice uses the substantive "luxur" as a term of opprobrium.

Nay, for a need, thus far come near my person:
Tell them, when that my mother went with child
Of that insatiate Edward, noble York,
My princely father, then had wars in France,
And, by true computation of the time,
Found that the issue was not his begot;
Which well appeared in his lineaments,
Being nothing like the noble duke my father.
Yet touch this sparingly, as 'twere far off;
Because, my lord, you know my mother lives.

Buck. Doubt not, my lord, I 'll play the orator,
As if the golden fee for which I plead
Were for myself; and so, my lord, adieu.

Glou. If you thrive well, bring them to Baynard's Castle;
Where you shall find me well accompanied
With reverend fathers and well-learned bishops.

Buck. I go; and towards three or four o'clock
Look for the news that the Guildhall affords. [*Exit.*

85. *come*] *comes* Q 4. 87. *insatiate*] Ff; *vnsatiate* Qq. 88. *wars*] *wares* Q 6. 89. *true*] Ff; *iust* Qq. 93. *Yet*] Ff; *But* Qq. *'twere*] Ff; *it were* Qq. *far*] *a farre* Q 4. 94. *my lord, you know*] Ff; *you know, my Lord* Qq. *my mother*] *my brother* Qq 5, 7, 8; *me brother* Q 6. 95. *Doubt*] Ff; *Fear* Qq. 97. *and so . . . adieu*] Ff; omitted Qq. 101, 102. *I go . . . affords.*] Ff; *About three or foure a clocke look to heare What news Guildhall affordeth, and so my Lord farewel.* *Exit.*] *Exx. Buck. and Catesby severally.* Pope.

85. *for a need*] if necessary. So Chapman, *All Fools*, act iv.:—

"If tears, which so abundantly distil
Out of my inward eyes, and *for a need*
Can drown these outward."

87. *insatiate*] Qq have "unsatiate," as they have "unviolable" in II. i. 27 above. Compare Fletcher, *Woman-Hater*, iii. 1: "woman, *unsatiate* woman." The distinction between the prefixes "un-" and "in-" was not thoroughly recognised in Shakespeare's day, although, during his later years, it becomes more marked. Marston's *Insatiate Countess* was printed in 1613. In *Richard II.* II. ii. 126, Ff have "impossible" for Qq "unpossible"; but they have "uncapable" in *Merchant of Venice*, IV. i. 5; *Othello*, IV. ii. 235. See note on III. vii. 7 below.

93. *touch . . . far off*] touch hintingly. Compare *Merry Wives of Windsor*, I. i. 216; III. i. 170 above.

98. *Baynard's Castle*] This castle, which gives its name to a ward of the city of London, was on the Thames, between Blackfriars and London Bridge. It was founded after the Conquest by one Baynard, and eventually passed to the Crown through the hands of the Clares, Fitzwalters, and Humphrey, Duke of Gloucester. From Henry VI. it passed to Richard, Duke of York, and remained in the possession of his family till the death of Richard III. In 1483 it was the residence of the Dowager Duchess of York. In Shakespeare's time it belonged to William Herbert, the Earl of Pembroke whose name is familiar to all Shakespearean students.

99, 100. *accompanied With*] So *Coriolanus*, III. iii. 6, 7.

Glou. Go, Lovel, with all speed to Doctor Shaw;
[*To Cates.*] Go thou to Friar Penker; bid them both
Meet me within this hour at Baynard's Castle.
[*Exeunt all but Gloucester.*
Now will I go to take some privy order
To draw the brats of Clarence out of sight,
And to give order, that no manner person
Have any time recourse unto the princes. [*Exit.*

SCENE VI.—*The same. A street.*

Enter a Scrivener with a paper in his hand.

Scriv. Here is the indictment of the good Lord Hastings;
Which in a set hand fairly is engross'd,
That it may be to-day read o'er in Paul's.
And mark how well the sequel hangs together:

103-105. *Go . . . Castle*] Ff; omitted Qq. 104. *To Cates.*] Capell. 105. *Exeunt . . .*] *Exit* Ff; *Exeunt Lov. and Cates. severally*. Theobald. 106. *go*] Ff; *in* Qq. 108. *order*] Ff; *notice* Qq. *manner*] Qq 3, 4, Ff; *maner of* Qq 1, 2, 5-8. 109. *Have any time*] Ff; *At any time haue* Qq. *Exit.*] *Exeunt.* Ff 1, 2.

Scene VI.

SCENE VI.] omitted Ff; scene continued Pope. *The same. A street.*] Capell. *with . . . hand.*] Qq; omitted Ff. 1. *Here*] Ff; *This* Qq. 3. *to-day*] Ff; *this day* Qq. *o'er*] Ff; *ouer* Qq.

103. *Doctor Shaw*] "John Shaw, clearke, brother to the maior" (More, ap. Holinshed, iii. 725).

104. *Friar Penker*] Among the learned men of Richard's reign enumerated by Bale, Holinshed (iii. 761) mentions "John Penketh an Augustine frier of Warington in Lancashire, a right subtill fellow in disputation." More calls him "prouinciall of the Augustine friers." The name Penketh or Penker is derived, no doubt, from the village of Penketh on the Mersey, about four and a half miles south-west of Warrington. Of Shaw and Penker More says that they were "both doctors of diuinitie, both great preachers, both of more learning than virtue, of more fame than learning."

106. *take . . . order*] make some arrangement. Qq read "take order" at I. iv. 281 above.

108. *no manner person*] It is interesting to find Ff coinciding here with a reading peculiar to Qq 3, 4. Compare Spenser, *Faerie Queene*, IV. x. 7: "all *manner* wights."

Scene VI.

The material for this scene is gathered from a passage in More (ap. Holinshed, iii. 724). "Now was this proclamation made within two houres after that he was beheaded, and it was so curiouslie indicted, & so faire written in parchment, in so well a set hand (line 2), and therewith of it selfe so long a processe, that euerie child might well perceiue that it was prepared before. For all the time, betweene his death and the proclaming, could scant haue sufficed vnto the bare writing alone, all had it bene but in paper, and scribled foorth in hast at aduenture." In the prose narrative the reflections are given to "one that was scholemaister of Powles," and to a merchant that talked with him.

Eleven hours I have spent to write it over,
For yesternight by Catesby was it sent me;
The precedent was full as long a-doing:
And yet within these five hours Hastings liv'd,
Untainted, unexamin'd, free, at liberty.
Here 's a good world the while! Who is so gross,
That cannot see this palpable device?
Yet who so bold, but says he sees it not?
Bad is the world; and all will come to nought,
When such ill dealing must be seen in thought. [*Exit.*

SCENE VII.—*Baynard's Castle.*

Enter GLOUCESTER *and* BUCKINGHAM, *at several doors.*

Glou. How now, how now, what say the citizens?
Buck. Now, by the holy mother of our Lord,
The citizens are mum, say not a word!
Glou. Touch'd you the bastardy of Edward's children?

5. *I have spent*] Ff; *I spent* Qq; *I've spent* Pope. 6. *sent*] Ff; *brought* Qq. 7. *precedent*] Ff; *president* Qq. 8. *Hastings liv'd*] Ff; *liued Lord Hastings* Qq. 10, 11. *Here's . . . device*] *Here's . . . while. Who is . . . deuice* Ff; *Heeres . . . while, Why whoes so grosse That sees not . . . deuice* Qq; *Here's . . . while! Why, who's so gross, That seeth not . . . device* Camb. 12. *who*] Qq 3-7, Ff; *whoes* Q 1; *whose* Q 2; *who's* Q 8. *bold*] Ff; *blinde* Qq. 13. *nought*] *naught* Qq 1, 2. 14. *ill*] Ff; *bad* Qq. *dealing*] *dealings* Q 4.

Scene VII.

SCENE VII. *Baynard's Castle.*] Theobald. *Enter Gloucester . . .*] *Enter Richard . . .* Ff; *Enter Glocester at one doore, Buckingham at another* Qq. 1. *How now, how now*] Ff; *How now my Lord* Qq. 3. *say*] Ff; *and speak* Qq.

7. *precedent*] the rough copy of the document, as *King John*, v. ii. 3. Ff spell the word as we spell it now, in the present instance; but in the passage just referred to, and in *Merchant of Venice*, IV. i. 220, *Richard II.* II. i. 130, *Henry VIII.* I. ii. 91, the form in Ff is "president," as in Qq here. "President" occurs again in all the early editions of Suckling's *Sessions of the Poets*, st. 12, in *Fragmenta Aurea* (1st ed. 1646).

9. *untainted*] without suspicion of guilt. Compare III. v. 32 above. See Griffith's description of Wolsey's fall, *Henry VIII.* iv. ii. 14, "a man sorely *tainted*."

10. *gross*] dull of perception. Compare *Othello*, III. iii. 404.

Scene VII.

3. *mum*] silent. Shakespeare ordinarily uses the word as an interjection, *e.g.* *2 Henry VI.* I. ii. 89; *Measure for Measure*, v. i. 288. Compare Lodge and Greene, *Looking-Glass for London* (Dyce, 133):—

"Strike up the drum,
And say no words but *mum*";

Wilkins, *Miseries of Inforst Marriage*, act ii.: "But *mum*: they have felt thy cheek, Clare, let them hear thy tongue."

Buck. I did; with his contract with Lady Lucy,
And his contract by deputy in France;
The unsatiate greediness of his desire,
And his enforcement of the city wives;
His tyranny for trifles; his own bastardy,
As being got, your father then in France;
And his resemblance, being not like the duke:
Withal I did infer your lineaments,
Being the right idea of your father,
Both in your form and nobleness of mind;
Laid open all your victories in Scotland,
Your discipline in war, wisdom in peace,
Your bounty, virtue, fair humility;
Indeed, left nothing fitting for your purpose
Untouch'd or slightly handled in discourse:
And, when my oratory drew toward end,

5-7. *his contract . . . France*] Ff; omitted Qq (*I did . . . desires* one line). 7. *unsatiate*] Ff; *insatiate* Qq. *desire*] Ff; *desires* Qq. 8. *And his . . . wives*] Ff; omitted Qq. 11. *And his . . . duke*] Ff; omitted Qq. *his resemblance*] *disresemblance* Collier. 14. *your*] *one* Qq 3-6. 15. *open*] *vpon* Qq 6-8. 18. *your*] Ff; *the* Qq. 20. *my*] *mine* Qq 1-2. *drew toward*] Ff; *grew to* Qq. *end*] *an end* Qq 1, 2.

5. *Lady Lucy*] See note on lines 179-82 below.

7. *insatiate*] Compare III. v. 87 and note above. In the present case Qq and Ff reverse their previous readings.

9. *His tyranny for trifles*] Edward IV. "neuer asked little, but euerie thing was hawsed aboue the measure, amercements turned into fines, fines into ransoms, small trespasses into misprison [*sic*], misprison into treason" (More).

11. The construction may be expanded thus: "[I touched] the fact that his resemblance, if it were a resemblance to anybody, was not to the duke." The sentence is one substantival clause; and the comma might be deleted with advantage. More says that, to those who knew the family best, there was some uncertainty as to the parentage of Edward and Clarence: "as those that by their fauours more resembled other knowne men than him."

13. *Being*] The construction is that of III. v. 92 above. Buckingham repeats Gloucester's words in that passage with a slight alteration. More says that Buckingham asserted that Gloucester "as well in all princelie behauiour, as in the lineaments and fauour of his visage, represented the verie face of the noble duke his father."

right idea] exact image. For "idea" = image, form, compare Milton, *Apology for . . . Smectymnuus*: "whether a vehement vein throwing out indignation and scorn upon an object that merits it, were among the aptest *ideas* of speech to be allowed."

15. Gloucester had been entrusted with the command of the Scottish expedition of 1482, in which the English took the part of Alexander, Duke of Albany, against his brother James III. The English army advanced as far as Edinburgh: the substantial advantage of the invasion was the capture of Berwick, which was ceded finally to England by the concluding treaty.

I bid them that did love their country's good
Cry "God save Richard, England's royal king!"
Glou. And did they so?
Buck. No, so God help me! they spake not a word;
But, like dumb statues or breathing stones,
Star'd each on other, and look'd deadly pale.
Which when I saw, I reprehended them,
And ask'd the mayor, what meant this wilful silence?
His answer was, the people were not used
To be spoke to, but by the recorder.
Then he was urg'd to tell my tale again:
"Thus saith the duke, thus hath the duke inferr'd;"
But nothing spoke in warrant from himself.
When he had done, some followers of mine own,
At lower end of the hall, hurl'd up their caps,
And some ten voices cried "God save King Richard!"
And thus I took the vantage of those few;
"Thanks, gentle citizens and friends!" quoth I,
"This general applause and cheerful shout
Argues your wisdom and your love to Richard:"
And even here brake off, and came away.

21. *bid*] *bad* Qq 5-8. *did love*] *loues* Qq 3-8. 23. *And*] Ff; *A and* Qq. 24. *they . . . word*] Ff; omitted Qq. 25. *statues*] illegible misprint Q 1; *statuas* Steevens, Reed, Camb. 26. *Star'd*] Ff; *Gazde* Qq. 28. *meant*] *meanes* Qq 6-8. 29. *used*] Ff; *wont* Qq. 30. *but*] *except* Pope. *by the*] *by their own* Capell. 33. *spoke*] Ff; *spake* Qq 1-5, 7, 8; *speake* Q 6. 35. *At . . . of the*] Ff; *At the . . . of the* Qq; *At . . . o' th'* Pope; *At lower end the* Capell. 37. *And thus . . . few*] Ff; omitted Qq. 38. *gentle*] Ff; *louing* Qq 1-6; *noble* Qq 7, 8. 39. *cheerful*] Ff; *louing* Qq. 40. *wisdom*] *wisedomes* Qq 1, 2. *love*] *loues* Qq 3-6. 41. *even here*] Ff; *so* Qq.

25. *statues*] a trisyllable, as *Julius Cæsar*, II. ii. 76 (see Mr. Macmillan's note), III. ii. 192. In all these cases, later editors, following the advice of Reed, have printed the hybrid forms "statua, statuas." The plural "statuaes" is used by Bacon. In Greene, *Orlando Furioso* (Dyce, 89), "statues" (Q 1 "statutes") is a dissyllable. Similarly in Lodge and Greene, *Looking-Glass for London* (Dyce, 137), "statues" is a dissyllable in the line "The *statues* of our gods are thrown down," where Qq 1-3 print "statutes," and "thrown" must be read as a dissyllable (throwen).

30. *recorder*] The accent is on the first syllable, as in "récord." Such emendations as those of Pope and Capell are therefore unnecessary. The recorder's name was Fitzwilliam, "a sad man, and an honest" (More).

37. *the vantage of those few*] the opportunity offered by those few. Compare III. v. 74 above. Halle gives the name of the ringleader of those who shouted for Gloucester as Nashfield.

Glou. What tongueless blocks were they! would they not speak?
Buck. No, by my troth, my lord.
Glou. Will not the mayor then and his brethren come?
Buck. The mayor is here at hand: intend some fear;
Be not you spoke with, but by mighty suit:
And look you get a prayer-book in your hand,
And stand between two churchmen, good my lord;
For on that ground I 'll make a holy descant:
And be not easily won to our requests;
Play the maid's part, still answer nay, and take it.
Glou. I go; and if you plead as well for them
As I can say nay to thee for myself,
No doubt we 'll bring it to a happy issue.
Buck. Go, go up to the leads! the lord mayor knocks.
[*Exit Gloucester*

Enter the LORD MAYOR *and Citizens.*

Welcome, my lord! I dance attendance here;
I think the duke will not be spoke withal.

42. *What . . . speak*] one line as Qq; *What . . . were they, Would . . . speake* (two lines) Ff. 43. *Buck. No . . . lord*] Qq; omitted Ff. 45. *at hand*] omitted Qq 3-8. *intend*] Ff; *and intend* Qq. 46. *you spoke with*] Ff; *spoken withall* Qq. 48. *between*] Ff; *betwixt* Qq. 49. *make*] Ff; *build* Qq. 50. *And*] Ff; omitted Qq. *easily*] Q 1, Ff; *easie* Qq 2-8. *requests*] Ff, *request* Qq. 51. *still answer nay, and*] Ff; *say no, but* Qq. 52. *I go; and if you*] Ff; *Feare not me, if thou canst* Qq. 53. *can say . . . thee*] *must say . . . them* Johnson conj. 54. *we 'll*] Qq; *we* Ff. 55. *Go, go . . . knocks*] Ff; *You shall see what I can do, get you vp to the leads.* Qq. 55. *Exit Gloucester.*] Camb.; *Exit.* Qq; omitted Ff. aft. 55. *Enter the Lord Mayor . . .*] *Enter the Maior . . .* Ff; omitted Qq. 56. *Welcome, my lord*] Ff; *Now my L. Maior* Qq. 57. *spoke*] *spoken* Qq 3-8.

46. *by mighty suit*] by earnest entreaty.

51. *still . . . take it*] The expression is proverbial. Compare Lodge and Greene, *Looking-Glass for London* (Dyce, 123):—

"Tut, my Remilia, be not thou so coy;
Say nay, and take it."

See *Two Gentlemen of Verona*, I. ii. 55. Mr. Bond, in his note on the above passage (Arden ed. 1906, p. 13), quotes from Steevens the original proverb, "Maids *say nay, and take it.*" Mr. Craig finds in Middleton, *A Trick to Catch the Old One*, 1608, III. i.: "You do so ravish me with kindness, that I am constrained to *play the maid, and take it.*"

53. *to thee*] It is to Buckingham, as introducer and spokesman of the citizens, that Richard will have to play "the maid's part."

Enter CATESBY.

Now, Catesby, what says your lord to my request?
Cates. He doth entreat your grace, my noble lord,
To visit him to-morrow or next day:
He is within with two right reverend fathers,
Divinely bent to meditation;
And in no worldly suits would he be mov'd,
To draw him from his holy exercise.
Buck. Return, good Catesby, to the gracious duke;
Tell him, myself, the mayor and aldermen,
In deep designs, in matter of great moment,
No less importing than our general good,
Are come to have some conference with his grace.
Cates. I'll signify so much unto him straight. [*Exit.*
Buck. Ah, ha, my lord! this prince is not an Edward:
He is not lolling on a lewd love-bed,
But on his knees at meditation;
Not dallying with a brace of courtesans,
But meditating with two deep divines;
Not sleeping, to engross his idle body,

58. *Now Catesby . . . request*] Ff; *Here coms his seruant: how now Catesby what saies he* Qq; *Catesby . . . request* Pope; *Here comes his servant: how now, Catesby, What says he* (two lines) Camb. 59. *He doth . . . lord*] Ff; *My Lord, he doth intreat your grace* Qq. 61. *right*] omitted Qq 3-8. 63. *suits*] Ff; *suite* Qq. 65. *the gracious duke*] Ff; *thy lord again* Qq. 66. *aldermen*] Ff; *Cittizens* Qq. 67. *in matter*] Ff; *and matters* Qq. 68. *than*] *them then* Qq 6-8. 70. *I'll . . . straight*] Ff; *Ile tell him what you say my Lord.* Qq. 72. *lolling*] Pope; *lulling* Qq, Ff. *love-bed*] Ff; *day-bed* Qq.

72. *lolling*] For "lulling," the form common to Qq and Ff, compare the description of Covetyse in *Piers the Plowman*, A-text (Vernon MS.), v. 110: "And like a leþerne pors. lullede his chekes."

love-bed] Qq have "day-bed," *i.e.* a couch or sofa, as in *Twelfth Night*, II. v. 54, 55. *New Eng. Dict.* quotes Overbury's *Characters*, 1613 (An Ordinary Fencer): "Three large bavins set up his trade, with a bench, which, in the vacation of the afternoons, he uses as his day-bed." Compare Fletcher, *Rule a Wife and have a Wife*, 1640, iii. 1 (quoted by Nares), where Margarita asks her servant Altea whether there are "day-beds in all chambers," in preparation for company.

76. *engross*] fatten. *New Eng. Dict.* cites W. Harrison, *Description of England*, 1577: "They (*i.e.* the Scotch) so ingrosse their bodies." Compare Bishop Hall, *Contemplations*, book ix. (*Works*, ed. Pratt, i. 186): "It is a marvel, that neither any noise in his dying, nor the fall of so gross a body, called in some of his attendants." Spenser, *Faerie Queene*, II. vi. 46, uses "engroste" in a kindred sense:—

"The waves thereof so slow and sluggish were,
Engroste with mud which did them fowle agrise."

But praying, to enrich his watchful soul:
Happy were England, would this virtuous prince
Take on his grace the sovereignty thereof!
But, sure, I fear, we shall not win him to it.
May. Marry, God defend his grace should say us nay!
Buck. I fear he will. Here Catesby comes again:

Re-enter CATESBY.

Now, Catesby, what says his grace?
Cates. He wonders to what end you have assembled
Such troops of citizens to come to him,
His grace not being warn'd thereof before:
He fears, my lord, you mean no good to him.
Buck. Sorry I am, my noble cousin should
Suspect me, that I mean no good to him:
By heaven, we come to him in perfect love!
And so once more return and tell his grace.
[*Exit Catesby.*
When holy and devout religious men
Are at their beads, 'tis much to draw them thence,
So sweet is zealous contemplation.

Enter GLOUCESTER *aloft, between two Bishops.* CATESBY *returns.*

May. See, where his grace stands 'tween two clergymen!

78. *virtuous*] Ff; *gracious* Qq. 79. *his grace*] Ff; *himselfe* Qq. *thereof*] Ff; *thereon* Qq. 80. *not*] Ff; *neuer* Qq; *ne'er* Capell, Camb. 81. *defend*] Ff; *forbid* Qq; *shield* Pope. 82. *here . . . again*] Ff; omitted Qq. *Re-enter*] *Enter* Qq, Ff. 83. *Now . . . grace*] Ff; *how now Catesby, What saies your Lord* Qq. 84. *He*] Ff; *My Lo. he* Qq; *My lord, He* Camb. 85. *come to*] Ff; *speake with* Qq. 87. *He fears, my lord*] Ff; *My Lord, he feares* Qq. 90. *we come . . . love*] Ff; *I come in perfect loue to him* Qq. *perfect*] *perfit* Ff. 91. *Exit Catesby.*] Qq 1-6; *Exit.* Ff. 93. *much*] Ff; *hard* Qq. *thence*] *hence* Qq 5-8. 94. *Enter Gloucester . . .*] *Enter Richard . . .* Ff; *Enter Rich. with two Bishops a loste.* Q 1; *Enter Rich. with . . . aloft.* Q 2; *Enter Rich. and . . . aloft.* Qq 3-8. *Catesby returns*] Theobald; *Catesby again, below.* Capell. aft. 94. *SCENE VIII.* Pope. 95. *his grace*] Ff; *he* Qq. *'tween*] *tweene* Ff; *between* Qq.

80. *win*] persuade, as *Richard II.* II. iii. 163.

83-95. This passage is a close following of the chroniclers. Shakespeare introduces Catesby as the messenger employed by Richard, and makes Buckingham, for brevity's sake, take on himself the responsibility of the message, which, in the prose chroniclers, is sent back to the Protector by the mayor and aldermen.

aft. 94. *Enter Gloucester aloft*, etc.] More's words, "with a byshop on euery hand of him," are omitted by

Buck. Two props of virtue for a Christian prince,
To stay him from the fall of vanity:
And see, a book of prayer in his hand!—
True ornaments to know a holy man.
Famous Plantagenet, most gracious prince,
Lend favourable ear to our requests;
And pardon us the interruption
Of thy devotion and right Christian zeal.

Glou. My lord, there needs no such apology:
I do beseech your grace to pardon me,
Who, earnest in the service of my God,
Deferr'd the visitation of my friends.
But, leaving this, what is your grace's pleasure?

Buck. Even that, I hope, which pleaseth God above,
And all good men of this ungovern'd isle.

Glou. I do suspect I have done some offence
That seems disgracious in the city's eye,
And that you come to reprehend my ignorance.

Buck. You have, my lord: would it might please your grace,
On our entreaties, to amend your fault.

Glou. Else wherefore breathe I in a Christian land?

Buck. Know, then, it is your fault that you resign
The supreme seat, the throne majestical,
The sceptred office of your ancestors,
Your state of fortune and your due of birth,

98, 99. *And see . . . man*] Ff; omitted Qq. *ornaments*] *ornament* Dyce. 101. *ear*] Ff; *eares* Qq. *our*] Q 1, Ff; *my* Qq 2-8. *requests* Ff; *request* Qq. 105. *do beseech your grace to*] Ff; *I rather do beseech you* Qq. 106. *my God*] *God* F 2; *th' high God* Ff 3, 4. 107. *Deferr'd*] Ff; *Neglect* Qq. 112. *eye*] Ff; *eyes* Qq. 114. *You . . . grace*] one line as Qq; *You . . . Lord: Would . . . Grace* (two lines) Ff. *might*] Ff; omitted Qq. 115. *On*] Ff; *At* Qq. *your*] Ff; *that* Qq. 117. *Know then*] Ff; *Then know* Qq. 120. *Your . . . birth*] Ff; omitted Qq. *due*] *Deaw* Ff 1, 2.

Holinshed, but adopted by Halle. From this point to the end of the scene, Shakespeare expands his authorities freely.

99. *ornaments*] refers to the bishops as well as the prayer-book. This line is the mayor's criticism of the whole scene in the gallery above.

112. *disgracious*] used again below, IV. iv. 178. *New Eng. Dict.* quotes Speed, *Hist. Great Britaine*, 1611: "As for these causes he was in highest grace with the king, so hee was the more *disgracious* or hated of the people." For "disgrace" used in this sense, compare Puttenham (?), *Arte of English Poesie*, iii. 12 (Arber, 181): "This insertion . . . is no disgrace but rather a bewtie and to very good purpose."

118. *majestical*] Compare *Henry V.* IV. i. 284.

The lineal glory of your royal house,
To the corruption of a blemish'd stock;
Whiles, in the mildness of your sleepy thoughts,
Which here we waken to our country's good,
This noble isle doth want his proper limbs;
His face defac'd with scars of infamy,
His royal stock graff'd with ignoble plants,
And almost should'red in the swallowing gulf
Of dark forgetfulness and deep oblivion.
Which to recure, we heartily solicit
Your gracious self to take on you the charge
And kingly government of this your land—
Not as protector, steward, substitute,
Or lowly factor for another's gain;
But as successively, from blood to blood,

123. *Whiles*] Ff; *Whilst* Q 1; *Whilest* Qq 2-8; *While* Pope. 124. *our*] *vour* Q 6. 125. *This*] Qq; *The* Ff. *his*] *her* Qq 1, 2. 126. *His*] Ff; *Her* Qq. *scars*] *stars* Qq 2-4. 127. *His . . . plants*] Ff; omitted Qq. *His*] *Her* Pope. 128. *in the*] *in this* Qq 3-8; *into th'* Hanmer. 129. *dark*] Ff; *blind* Qq. *deep*] Ff; *darke* Qq. 130. *recure*] *recouer* Qq 6-8. 131, 132. *Your . . . land*] Ff; *Your gratious selfe to take on you the soueraingtie thereof* Qq. 134. *Or*] *Nor* Qq 3-8.

125-127. *his . . . his . . . His*] We naturally should expect "her," which we find in Qq, lines 125, 126. But the repetition of "his" and its occurrence in a line peculiar to Ff (127) suggest that it is deliberate and not merely an error.

127. Malone implies that this line is intended to recall the text of Dr. Shaw's sermon at Paul's Cross, *viz.* Wisdom IV. 3, "Spuria vitilamina non agent radices altas."

128. *should'red in*] The metaphor, as Hanmer and Steevens understood, is that of violent jostling in a crowd. Compare Milton, *Apology for . . . Smectymnuus:* "That just government which pride and ambition . . . hath *shouldered* out of the church." Steevens quotes Drayton, *Barons' Wars*, i. st. 45:—

"Strongly inveigled with delightful hope,
Stoutly t' affront and *shoulder* with debate."

Buckingham says that England, in her adverse circumstances, is almost thrust into the gulf of oblivion. Malone believed that the meaning was "up to the shoulders in," quoting Spenser's *Ruines of Rome*, st. 16, where the sea "in a great mountaine heap't" is "eftsoones of thousand billowes *shouldred* narre." This passage, alleged with much doubt by Malone, is rightly quoted by Aldis Wright in support of the meaning "thrust violently out of place," as implied above. Johnson proposed "smoulder'd," *i.e.* "almost smother'd, covered and lost."

130. *recure*] Compare Beaumont and Fletcher, *Faithful Shepherdess*, v. 5:—

"That may raise thee, and *re-cure*
All thy life that was impure."

134. *factor*] agent, used again below, IV. iv. 72. Compare *1 Henry IV.* III. ii. 147. The word is still used in Scotland of a land-agent.

135. *successively*] by right of succession. So in Chapman (?), *Alphonsus*, act i., the King of Bohemia speaks in the name of

"The seven princes of the German empire,
To whom *successively* it doth belong
To make election of our emperors."

Your right of birth, your empery, your own.
For this, consorted with the citizens,
Your very worshipful and loving friends,
And by their vehement instigation,
In this just cause come I to move your grace.

Glou. I cannot tell, if to depart in silence,
Or bitterly to speak in your reproof,
Best fitteth my degree or your condition :
If not to answer, you might haply think
Tongue-tied ambition, not replying, yielded
To bear the golden yoke of sovereignty,
Which fondly you would here impose on me:
If to reprove you for this suit of yours,
So season'd with your faithful love to me,
Then, on the other side, I check'd my friends.
Therefore, to speak, and to avoid the first,
And then, in speaking, not to incur the last,
Definitively thus I answer you.
Your love deserves my thanks ; but my desert
Unmeritable shuns your high request.
First, if all obstacles were cut away,
And that my path were even to the crown,
As the ripe revenue and due of birth ;

138. *very . . . loving*] *worshipfull and very louing* Qq 3-8. 140. *cause*] Ff; *sute* Qq. 141. *cannot tell, if*] Ff; *know not whether* Qq 1-4; *know not whither* Qq 5-8. 144-53. *If not . . . answer you*] Ff; omitted Qq. 144. *If not*] *For not* Ff 2-4. 152. *not to*] *not* Pope. 158. *As the*] Ff; *As my* Qq. *ripe*] Q 1, Ff; *right* Qq 2-8. *of birth*] Ff; *by birth* Qq.

See also note on III. i. 73 above. Mr. Craig quotes Peele, *Anglorum Ferie* (Bullen, ii. 347) :—

"In her hereditarie royal right
Successively to sit enthronized."

136. *empery*] empire. Compare *Cymbeline*, I. vi. 120 :—

"A lady
So fair, and fasten'd to an *empery*"

(see Prof. Dowden's note); Chapman (?), *Alphonsus*, act ii. :—

"How far is Richard now unlike the man
That cross'd the seas to win an *empery*."

In these passages the word implies territorial sovereignty. In *Titus Andronicus*, I. i. 22, we find "the Roman *empery*"; but, three lines before, the word has the more general sense of sovereign power. Marlowe, in the two parts of *Tamburlaine*, gives it the specific sense of "empire" three times, and the more general sense once.

143. *degree . . . condition*] Compare *2 Henry IV*. IV. iii. 1-6.

150. *I check'd*] *i.e.* I should check.

155. *Unmeritable*] used again in *Julius Cæsar*, IV. i. 12.

158. *revenue*] The accent, until a comparatively recent date, was usually on the second syllable. Compare *Troilus and Cressida*, II. ii. 206. But

Yet so much is my poverty of spirit,
So mighty and so many my defects,
That I would rather hide me from my greatness,
Being a bark to brook no mighty sea,
Than in my greatness covet to be hid,
And in the vapour of my glory smother'd.
But, God be thank'd! there is no need of me;
And much I need to help you, were there need:
The royal tree hath left us royal fruit,
Which, mellow'd by the stealing hours of time,
Will well become the seat of majesty,
And make, no doubt, us happy by his reign.
On him I lay that you would lay on me,
The right and fortune of his happy stars,
Which God defend that I should wring from him!

Buck. My lord, this argues conscience in your grace;
But the respects thereof are nice and trivial,
All circumstances well considered.
You say that Edward is your brother's son:
So say we too, but not by Edward's wife;
For first was he contract to Lady Lucy—

161. *That I would*] Ff; *As I had* Qq. 165. *thank'd! there is*] Ff; *thanked there's* Qq. *of me*] *for me* Qq 3-8. 166. *were there need*] Ff; *if need were* Qq. 170. *no doubt, us*] *us* (*no doubt*) Ff 2-4; *us doubtless* Pope. 171. *that you*] Ff; *what you* Qq. 179. *was he*] Ff; *he was* Qq. *contract*] *contracted* Q 6.

Shakespeare also accentuates the first syllable, as here and in *Richard II.* II. i. 226.

173. *wring*] Compare *3 Henry VI.* II. i. 154.

175. *the respects thereof*] the considerations on which your arguments are founded. Compare *Much Ado About Nothing*, II. iii. 176; *King Lear*, I. i. 251; and "unrespective boys" at IV. ii. 29 below.

nice] scrupulous, fastidious, as *3 Henry VI.* IV. vii. 58; *Taming of the Shrew*, III. i. 80.

179-82. Shakespeare followed More in the details of Edward IV.'s supposed marriage or contract. In the petition ratified by the Parliament of January, 1484, when the crown was settled upon Richard, it was stated that Lady Eleanor Butler, a daughter of the Earl of Shrewsbury, was Edward's trothplight wife at the time of his marriage with Elizabeth. The statement rested on the evidence of only one witness; and, at Henry VII.'s accession, every copy of the scandalous petition was destroyed, and an alternative legend grew up. Holinshed's story is that, just before Edward had fallen in love with Lady Grey, there had been talk of his marriage with Bona of Savoy, sister to the Queen of France; and Warwick had been sent to Louis XI. at Tours, to arrange such a treaty. The Comte de Dammartin was about to come to England and there conclude preliminaries, when Edward pledged his honour to Lady Grey. His mother was so annoyed that, "vnder pretext of hir

Your mother lives a witness to his vow—
And afterward by substitute betroth'd
To Bona, sister to the king of France.
These both put off, a poor petitioner,
A care-craz'd mother to a many sons,
A beauty-waning and distressed widow,
Even in the afternoon of her best days,
Made prize and purchase of his wanton eye,
Seduc'd the pitch and height of his degree
To base declension and loath'd bigamy:
By her, in his unlawful bed, he got
This Edward, whom our manners call the prince.
More bitterly could I expostulate,
Save that, for reverence to some alive,
I give a sparing limit to my tongue.
Then, good my lord, take to your royal self
This proffer'd benefit of dignity;
If not to bless us and the land withal,
Yet to draw forth your noble ancestry
From the corruption of abusing times,
Unto a lineal true-derived course.

180. *his*] Ff; *that* Qq. 183. *put off*] Ff; *put by* Qq. 184. *mother to*] Ff; *mother of* Qq. *a many*] Q 1, Ff; *many* Qq 2-8. *sons*] Ff; *children* Qq. 187. *wanton*] Ff; *lustful* Qq. 188. *his degree*] Ff; *all his thoughts* Qq. 191. *call*] Ff; *term* Qq. 198. *forth . . . ancestry*] Ff; *out your royall stocke* Qq. 199. *abusing times*] Ff; *abusing time* Qq 1-5; *a busing time* Q 6; *a busie time* Qq 7, 8. 200. *true-derived*] Theobald; *true, derived* Pope.

dutie to Godward," she determined to break the engagement by any means, and asserted that Edward already was ensured to Elizabeth Lucy. When called upon for evidence, the lady confessed that Edward had seduced her under a vague promise of marriage, but that no formal contract had passed between them.

184. *care-craz'd*] shattered by care. Compare IV. iv. 17 below; *Midsummer-Night's Dream*, I. i. 92, in which cases "crazed" means "cracked, broken." Mr. Craig refers to the phrase "a *crazy* boat" for a damaged, broken boat. In Lincolnshire "crazy" is still applied to cracked china, etc., *e.g.* "a *crazy* plate".

187. *purchase*] booty, as *1 Henry IV.* II. i. 101. Compare Wilkins, *Miseries of Inforst Marriage*, act iv.: "Down with your dust, our morning's *purchase*."

188. *pitch*] a metaphor from falconry. Compare *Richard II.* I. i. 109; *Julius Cæsar*, I. i. 78.

189. *declension*] Compare *Hamlet*, II. ii. 149, where the word is used of a gradual change to the worse. Here it implies a sudden apostasy from the duties of station.

loath'd bigamy] The use of "bigamy" in connection with a marriage with a widow, as More uses it, is curious. "Loath'd" = loathsome: see note on "unmanner'd," I. ii. 39 above, and compare "effeminate" for "feminine" at line 211 below.

192. *expostulate*] expound, discuss the matter. Compare *Hamlet*, II. ii. 86.

199. *the corruption of abusing times*]

May. Do, good my lord! your citizens entreat you.
Buck. Refuse not, mighty lord, this proffer'd love.
Cates. O! make them joyful, grant their lawful suit.
Glou. Alas! why would you heap this care on me?
I am unfit for state and majesty.
I do beseech you, take it not amiss;
I cannot nor I will not yield to you.
Buck. If you refuse it, as, in love and zeal,
Loath to depose the child, your brother's son—
As well we know your tenderness of heart,
And gentle, kind, effeminate remorse,
Which we have noted in you to your kindred,
And egally, indeed, to all estates—
Yet know, whether you accept our suit or no,
Your brother's son shall never reign our king;
But we will plant some other in the throne,
To the disgrace and downfall of your house;
And in this resolution here we leave you.
Come, citizens: 'zounds! I'll entreat no more.
Glou. O! do not swear, my Lord of Buckingham.
[*Exit Buckingham with the Citizens.*
Cates. Call him again, sweet prince; accept their suit:
If you deny them, all the land will rue it.
Glou. Will you enforce me to a world of cares?

202. *Buck. Refuse . . . love*] Ff; omitted Qq. 204. *this care*] Ff; *these cares* Q 1; *those cares* Qq 2-8. 205. *majesty*] Ff; *dignitie* Qq. 212. *kindred*] Ff; *kin* Qq. 214. *know*] Ff; omitted Qq. *whether*] Qq; *where* Ff; *whe'r* Theobald. *accept*] *except* Q 6. 219. *'zounds! I'll*] Qq; *we will* Ff. 220. *Glou. O . . . Buckingham*] Qq; omitted Ff. *Exit . . . Citizens.*] Capell. 221. *him*] Ff; *them* Qq, Pope. *sweet prince*] Ff, Pope; *my lord* Qq. *accept*] Ff, Pope; *and accept* Qq. 222. *If you . . . rue it*] Ff; *Ano. Doe, good my lord, least all the land do rew it* Qq. 223. *Will*] Ff; *Would* Qq. *cares*] Ff; *care* Qq.

the corruption which it has suffered by periods of abuse. "Abusing time" of the earlier Qq would imply that the abuse came in the natural course of time: the "abusing times" of Ff are the years following Edward's marriage to Elizabeth.

207. *nor I will not*] Compare the double negative below, IV. iv. 496.

211. *remorse*] in the common Shakespearean sense of "pity," as *Macbeth*, I, v. 45.

213. *egally*] Nares notes that in Puttenham (?), *Arte of English Poesie*, i. 20, the forms "egall" and "equall" occur within a few lines of each other. In the same passage "egally" and "unegall" are also employed. Shakespeare uses "egal," *Titus Andronicus*, IV. iv. 4. Mr. Craig, among other references, gives one from Surrey in *Tottel's Miscellany*, 1557 (ed. Arber, p. 27): "The *egall* frend, no grudge, no strife."

Call them again: I am not made of stones,
But penetrable to your kind entreaties,
Albeit against my conscience and my soul.

Re-enter BUCKINGHAM *and the rest.*

Cousin of Buckingham, and sage, grave men,
Since you will buckle fortune on my back,
To bear her burthen, whether I will or no,
I must have patience to endure the load:
But, if black scandal or foul-fac'd reproach
Attend the sequel of your imposition,
Your mere enforcement shall acquittance me
From all the impure blots and stains thereof;
For God doth know, and you may partly see,
How far I am from the desire of this.

May. God bless your grace! we see it, and will say it.

Glou. In saying so, you shall but say the truth.

Buck. Then I salute you with this royal title—
Long live King Richard, England's worthy king!

All. Amen.

Buck. To-morrow may it please you to be crown'd?

Glou. Even when you please, for you will have it so.

224. *Call*] Ff; *Well, call* Qq. after *again*] *Exit Catesby.* Theobald. *stones*] *stone* Pope, Camb. 225. *entreaties*] Ff; *intreates* Qq 1-3, 5-7. aft. 226. *Re-enter . . .*] *Enter . . .* Ff; omitted Qq. 227. *sage*] Ff; *you sage* Qq. 229. *her*] *the* Qq 3-8. *whether*] *where* F 1; *whe'r* Steevens (conj.). 231. *foul-fac'd*] *soule-fac't* Q 2; *so foule-fac't* Qq 3-8; *four-fac'd* F 3. 235. *doth know*] Ff; *he knows* Qq. 236. *of this*] Ff; *thereof* Qq. 239. *royal*] Ff; *kingly* Qq. 240. *King*] omitted Qq 1, 2. *worthy*] Ff; *royall* Qq. 241. *All.*] Ff; *Mai.* Qq; *May. and Cit.* Camb. 242. *may*] Ff; *will* Qq. 243. *please, for*] Ff; *will, since* Qq.

225. *entreaties*] For other substantives of this kind, compare "suspects," for "suspicions," I. iii. 89 above; "exclaims" for "exclamations," IV. iv. 135 below; "relent" for "relentment" in Lodge, *Wounds of Civil War*, act ii.; "repent" for "repentance" in Greene, *Orlando Furioso* (Dyce, 106).

232. *your imposition*] the charge which you lay upon me. Compare *All's Well that Ends Well*, IV. iv. 29.

242. *To-morrow*] The interview with the Mayor and citizens took place on 25th June, 1483, the day following Buckingham's ill-omened speech at the Guildhall. Richard was crowned eleven days later, on 6th July. His accession was dated from 26th June, when he went publicly to Westminster Hall and there took on him the government of the realm.

Buck. To-morrow, then, we will attend your grace ;
And so most joyfully we take our leave.
Glou. Come, let us to our holy work again.
Farewell, my cousin ; farewell, gentle friends.
[*Exeunt.*

245. *And so . . . leave*] Ff; omitted Qq. 246. *Glou.*] Johnson adds *To the Clergymen.* *work*] Ff; *taske* Qq. 247. *my cousin*] Pope; *my Cousins* Ff; *good coosine* Qq.

ACT IV

SCENE I.—*Before the Tower.*

Enter, on one side, QUEEN ELIZABETH, *the* DUCHESS OF YORK, *and the* MARQUESS OF DORSET; *on the other,* ANNE, DUCHESS OF GLOUCESTER, *leading* LADY MARGARET PLANTAGENET, *Clarence's young daughter.*

Duch. Who meets us here? my niece Plantagenet,
Led in the hand of her kind aunt of Gloucester?
Now, for my life! she's wandering to the Tower,
On pure heart's love to greet the tender princes.
Daughter, well met!
Anne. God give your graces both
A happy and a joyful time of day!
Q. Eliz. As much to you, good sister! Whither away?
Anne. No farther than the Tower, and, as I guess,

ACT IV. SCENE I.] ACT III. SCENE VIII. Rann (Johnson conj.). *Before the Tower.*] Theobald. *Enter . . . daughter.*] Malone, Camb. (after Theobald); *Enter Quee. mother, Duchesse of Yorke, Marques Dorset, at one doore, Duchesse of Glocest. at another doore.* Qq; *Enter the Queene, Anne Duchesse of Gloucester, the Duchesse of Yorke, and Marquesse Dorset.* Ff. 1. *Who . . . Plantagenet*] one line as Qq; *Who . . . heere? My Neece Plantagenet* (two lines) Ff. 2-6. *Led . . . time of day.*] Ff; omitted Qq. 4. *princes*] Theobald; *Prince* Ff. 5, 6. *God give . . . time of day*] arranged as Pope, Camb.; *God give . . . a happie And . . . time of day* Ff. 7. *As much . . . away*] Ff; *Sister well met, whether awaie so fast* Qq. 8. *Anne.*] Ff; *Duch.* Q 1; *Du.* Q 2; *Dut. Glo.* Qq 3-8.

1. *niece*] Compare "cousins," II. ii. 8 above; and "niece" in *King John*, II. i. 469.

2. *in the hand*] Compare *Coriolanus*, V. iii. 23; *Titus Andronicus*, V. iii. 138.

4. *On pure heart's love*] Compare *Measure for Measure*, IV. i. 37, "on your knowledge"; *Antony and Cleopatra*, III. vi. 57, "on my free will."

Upon the like devotion as yourselves,
To gratulate the gentle princes there.

Q. Eliz. Kind sister, thanks: we 'll enter all together.

Enter BRAKENBURY.

And, in good time, here the lieutenant comes.
Master lieutenant, pray you, by your leave,
How doth the prince, and my young son of York?

Brak. Right well, dear madam—by your patience,
I may not suffer you to visit them:
The king hath strictly charg'd the contrary.

Q. Eliz. The king? who 's that?

Brak. I mean the lord protector.

Q. Eliz. The Lord protect him from that kingly title!
Hath he set bounds between their love and me?
I am their mother: who shall bar me from them?

Duch. I am their father's mother: I will see them.

Anne. Their aunt I am in law, in love their mother:
Then bring me to their sights; I 'll bear thy blame,
And take thy office from thee, on my peril.

Brak. No, madam, no, I may not leave it so:
I am bound by oath; and theretore pardon me. [*Exit.*

10. *gentle*] Ff; *tender* Qq. aft. 11. *Enter Brakenbury.*] Capell, Camb.; *Enter Lieutenant.* Qq 1, 2; *Enter the Lieutenant of the Tower.* Qq 3-8. 14. *How doth . . . York*] Ff; *How fares the Prince* Qq 1-5; *How feares the Prince* Q 6. 15. *Brak.*] *Lieu.* Qq, Ff (and lines 18, 26). *Right well . . . patience*] Ff; *Wel Madam, and in health, but by your leaue* Qq. 16. *them*] Ff; *him* Qq. 17. *strictly*] Ff; *straightlie* Qq. 18. *who 's that*] Ff; *whie, whose that* Qq 1, 2; *why, who 's that* Qq 3-7; *why who is that* Q 8. *I mean*] Ff; *I crie you mercie, I meane* Qq. 20. *between*] Ff; *betwixt* Qq. 21. *shall bar*] Ff; *should keepe* Qq. 22. *Duch.*] *Du. yor.* Q 1; *Duch. Yorke.* Ff; omitted Qq 2-8. *I am their father's mother: I*] Ff; *I am their Fathers, Mother, I* Q 1; *I am their father, Mother, and* Qq 2-8 (*theirs* Q 4). 24. *Then . . . sights*] Ff; *Then feare not thou* Qq. 26, 27. *No, madam . . . pardon me*] Ff; *I doe beseech your graces all to pardon me: I am bound by oath, I may not doe it.* Qq. *Exit*] *Exit Lieutenant.* Ff; omitted Qq.

9. *Upon the like devotion*] This may mean "from the same impulse of devotion," in which case the use of "upon" is parallel to that of "on," already noticed in line 4. It may also mean "upon the same devout errand"; "with the same devout object."

10. *gratulate*] So *Titus Andronicus*, I. i. 221; Lodge and Greene, *Looking-Glass for London* (Dyce, 117): "See where she comes to *gratulate* my fame."

24. *their sights*] Compare *Timon of Athens*, I. i. 255.

Enter LORD STANLEY.

Stan. Let me but meet you, ladies, one hour hence,
And I 'll salute your grace of York as mother
And reverend looker-on of two fair queens.
[*To Anne.*] Come, madam, you must straight to Westminster,
There to be crowned Richard's royal queen
Q. Eliz. Ah! cut my lace asunder,
That my pent heart may have some scope to beat,
Or else I swoon with this dead-killing news!
Anne. Despiteful tidings! O unpleasing news!
Dor. Be of good cheer: mother, how fares your grace?
Q. Eliz. O Dorset, speak not to me, get thee gone!
Death and destruction dog thee at thy heels;
Thy mother's name is ominous to children.
If thou wilt outstrip death, go, cross the seas,
And live with Richmond, from the reach of hell:
Go, hie thee, hie thee from this slaughter-house,
Lest thou increase the number of the dead,
And make me die the thrall of Margaret's curse,
Nor mother, wife, nor England's counted queen!
Stan. Full of wise care is this your counsel, madam.
Take all the swift advantage of the hours:

28. *one hour*] Ff; *an houre* Qq 1-4; *at an houre* Qq 5-8. 30. *reverend*] Ff, Q 8; *reuerente* Q 1; *reuerent* Qq 2-7. 31. *To Anne*] Capell, Camb. *straight*] Ff; *go with me* Qq. 33-35. *Ah . . . news*] arranged as Ff; *O . . . heart, May . . . else I sound With . . . newes* Qq. 33. *Ah*] Ff; *O* Qq. *asunder*] Ff; *in sunder* Qq. 35. *swoon*] Ff; *sound* Qq. *dead-killing*] Ff; *dead killing* Qq 1-4; *dead liking* Qq 5-8; *dead-striking* Capell conj. 36. *Despiteful . . . news*] Ff; omitted Qq. 37. *Be . . . mother*] Ff; *Madame, haue comfort* Qq. 38. *gone*] Ff; *hence* Qq. 39. *dog*] Qq, Ff 3, 4; *dogges* Ff 1, 2. *thy heels*] Ff; *the heeles* Qq. 41. *outstrip*] *ouerstrip* Qq 6-8. 42. *reach*] *race* Qq 6-8. 48. *hours*] Ff; *time* Qq.

33. *cut my lace*] See Prof. Case's note on *Antony and Cleopatra*, I. iii. 71, and compare *Winter's Tale*, III. ii. 174.

35. *dead-killing*] The first part of the compound is merely intensive. In this play, the ordinary type of compound epithet is that of which the first part qualifies the second, and may be expressed as an adverb, *e.g.*, "childish-foolish," I. iii. 142, "deep-revolving," IV. ii. 42. "Ill-dispersing," in line 52 below, is formed rather exceptionally, for this play. Mr. Craig notes the occurrence of the Irishism "kill her dead" in *Midsummer-Night's Dream*, III. ii. 269, and "kill'd me dead" in *Titus Andronicus*, III. i. 92.

48-50. Stanley, of course, is speaking to Dorset. "My son" is Richmond, whose mother, Lady Margaret Beaufort, Stanley had married about 1482.

You shall have letters from me to my son,
In your behalf, to meet you on the way:
Be not ta'en tardy by unwise delay.

Duch. O ill-dispersing wind of misery!
O my accursed womb, the bed of death!
A cockatrice hast thou hatch'd to the world,
Whose unavoided eye is murderous.

Stan. Come, madam, come; I in all haste was sent.

Anne. And I in all unwillingness will go.
O! would to God that the inclusive verge
Of golden metal, that must round my brow,
Were red-hot steel, to sear me to the brains!
Anointed let me be with deadly venom,
And die ere men can say, God save the queen!

Q. Eliz. Go, go, poor soul, I envy not thy glory;
To feed my humour, wish thyself no harm.

Anne. No! why? When he that is my husband now
Came to me, as I follow'd Henry's corse,
When scarce the blood was well wash'd from his hands,
Which issued from my other angel husband,
And that dear saint which then I weeping follow'd—
O! when, I say, I look'd on Richard's face,
This was my wish: "Be thou," quoth I, "accurs'd,

50. *In your . . . way*] Ff; *To meete you on the way, and welcome you* Qq. 51. *ta'en*] *ta'ne* Ff; *tane* Q 1; *taken* Qq 2-8. 52. *ill-dispersing*] hyphened Theobald. 56. *Come, madam, come*] Ff; *Come Madam* Qq. *sent*] Qq 1, 2, Ff; *sent for* Qq 3-8; *sent for you* Capell (conj.). 57. *Anne*] Ff; *Duch.* Qq. *in all*] Qq; *with all* Ff. 58. *O*] Ff; *I* Qq. 60. *brains*] Ff; *braine* Qq. 61. *venom*] Ff; *poyson* Qq. 63. *Go, go*] Ff; *Alas* Qq. 65. *Anne*] Ff; *Duch. Glo.* Qq. *No! why*] Ff; *No* Qq. 66. *corse*] Ff; *course* Qq. 69. *dear*] Ff; *dead* Qq. *which*] *whom* Capell (conj.).

54. *cockatrice*] See note on "basilisks," I. ii. 150 above. The cockatrice and the basilisk were synonymous in vulgar tradition. Compare Chapman, *All Fools*, act iii.: "Is this the *cockatrice* that kills with sight"; *Romeo and Juliet*, III. ii. 47; *Twelfth Night*, III. iv. 215. Sir Thomas Browne quotes Scaliger on the confusion between the basilisk (a real serpent) and the purely imaginary cockatrice: "Basilisci formam mentiti sunt vulgo gallinaceo similem, et pedibus binis," etc.

55. *unavoided*] unavoidable. Chapman, *All Fools*, act ii. has

"youth and love
Were th' unresisted (*i.e.* irresistible) organs to seduce you";

Eastward Ho, act iv.: "this your unbelieved (*i.e.* incredible) absence." See also note on I. ii. 39 above.

58. *verge*] Used again of the rim of the crown, *Richard II.* II. i. 102; of a magic circle, *2 Henry VI.* I. iv. 25.

For making me, so young, so old a widow!
And, when thou wed'st, let sorrow haunt thy bed;
And be thy wife, if any be so mad,
More miserable by the life of thee
Than thou hast made me by my dear lord's death!"
Lo, ere I can repeat this curse again,
Within so small a time, my woman's heart
Grossly grew captive to his honey words,
And prov'd the subject of mine own soul's curse,
Which hitherto hath held mine eyes from rest;
For never yet one hour in his bed
Did I enjoy the golden dew of sleep,
But with his timorous dreams was still awak'd.

74. *mad*] Qq 1, 2, Ff; *badde* Qq 3-8. 75. *More*] Ff; *As* Qq. *life*] Ff; *death* Qq. 76. *Than*] Ff; *As* Qq. 77. *ere*] Ff; *eare* Q 1; *euen* Qq 2-8. 78. *Within . . . time*] Ff; *Euen in so short a space* Qq. 79. *Grossly*] Q 1, Ff; *Crosselie* Q 2; *Crosly* Qq 3-8. 80. *subject*] Qq 1, 8, Ff; *subiectes* Qq 2-7 (*subsects* Q 3). *mine*] Ff, Qq 7, 8; *my* Qq 1-6. 81. *hitherto*] Ff; *euer since* Qq. *held*] Ff; *kept* Qq. *mine*] Qq 6-8, Ff; *my* Qq 1-5. *rest*] Ff; *sleepe* Qq. 83. *Did I enjoy*] Ff; *Haue I enioyed* Qq. *dew*] *deaw* Qq 3-5, Ff 1, 2. 84. *with his . . . awak'd*] Ff; *haue bene waked by his timorous dreames* Qq.

74-76. Anne's curse in its original form, I. ii. 26-28 above, is delivered before Gloucester comes on the scene. She there wishes that his wife may be made more miserable by his death than she is made by the deaths of those he has murdered. Qq in both passages have "as . . . as" instead of "more . . . than"—a variation which, on its own merits, is merely a matter of taste. Qq also have "death" in both cases, which Ff alter here into "life" (line 75). Ff are clearly right, as the rest of the passage, emphasising the fulfilment of the curse, shows; and probably the editors retained "death" in I. ii. 27 by an oversight. The clause "if any be so mad" (line 74) does not occur in I. ii.; while it is rather curious that two of the later Qq, which here accept the mistaken reading "badde" for "mad," read "mad" for "made" in I. ii. 26.

79. *Grossly*] stupidly, without perception. See note on III. vi. 10 above. "Gross," "grossly," and kindred words, are used by Shakespeare in two derived senses: (1) the subjective sense, "without fineness of perception," as here and in the parallel instance (compare "grossness," III. i. 46 above); (2) the objective sense, implying anything which it needs no fineness of perception to recognise, *i.e.* anything plain and obvious. For the latter use, see *King Lear*, I. i. 295. There is also the third and concrete sense, implying size or extent, as *King Lear*, IV. vi. 14: compare "engross," III. vii. 76 above.

honey] See note on I. iii. 291 above.

83. *golden dew of sleep*] Mr. Craig cites "golden sleep," *Romeo and Juliet*, II. iii. 38; "the honey-heavy dew of slumber," *Julius Cæsar*, II. i. 230, and several passages from other authors. The occurrence of the phrase "golden sleep" in Bacon has been cited on behalf of the Baconian authorship of the plays. Equally improbable traces of Baconian authorship are to be found in Holinshed (ed. 1809, II. iv. 32): "So that he needed now no more for that cause either to wake or to break his *golden sleep*"; Fletcher, *Women Pleased*, 1647: "Sweet rest about thee, sweet and *golden sleep*," etc.

Besides, he hates me for my father Warwick,
And will, no doubt, shortly be rid of me.

Q. Eliz. Poor heart, adieu! I pity thy complaining.

Anne. No more than with my soul I mourn for yours.

Dor. Farewell, thou woful welcomer of glory!

Anne. Adieu, poor soul, that tak'st thy leave of it!

Duch. [*To Dorset.*] Go thou to Richmond, and good fortune guide thee!
[*To Anne.*] Go thou to Richard, and good angels tend thee!
[*To Q. Eliz.*] Go thou to sanctuary, and good thoughts possess thee!
I to my grave, where peace and rest lie with me!
Eighty odd years of sorrow have I seen,
And each hour's joy wrack'd with a week of teen.

Q. Eliz. Stay! yet look back with me unto the Tower.
Pity, you ancient stones, those tender babes,
Whom envy hath immur'd within your walls!
Rough cradle for such little pretty ones,
Rude ragged nurse, old sullen playfellow

86. *no doubt*] Q 1, Ff; omitted Qq 2-8. 87. *Poor heart, adieu*] Ff; *Alas poore soule* Qq. *complaining*] Ff; *complaints* Qq. 88. *with*] Ff; *from* Qq. 89. *Dor.*] Q 1, Ff; *Qu.* Qq 2-8; *Q. Eliz.* Camb. 90. *that*] Ff; *thou* Qq. 91. (*To Dorset.*) *Go . . . guide thee*] F 4; *Go to Richmond, to Dorset, to Anne, to the Queene, and good fortune guide thee* Ff 2, 3. 92. *To Anne*] F 4. *tend*] Ff; *guard* Qq. 93. *To Q. Eliz.*] F 4, (Camb.). *and good*] Ff; *good* Qq. 96. *wrack'd*] F 4; *wrackt* Qq, Ff 1-3; *wreck'd* Camb. 97-103. *Stay . . . farewell*] Ff; omitted Qq.

85. Richard had fled to the Netherlands with Edward IV. when Warwick invaded England in the Lancastrian interest. At Barnet, where Warwick fell, Richard was one of the generals on the winning side.

95. *Eighty odd*] The Duchess of York was born in 1415, and, therefore, was only sixty-eight in 1483. But the tragic pity of the situation is more important than historical accuracy.

96. *teen*] sorrow. Shakespeare uses this old English word again, *Love's Labour's Lost*, IV. iii. 164; *Romeo and Juliet*, I. iii. 13; *The Tempest*, I. ii. 64, etc. It is used several times by Spenser and by poets of his school, *e.g.* William Browne. Mr. Craig says that the word "is frequent in a book which Shakespeare loved, Golding's *Ovid*," and has noted at least six instances there.

101. Johnson, with little sympathy for bold metaphor, thought that "nurse" and "playfellow" were harsh epithets for the Tower, and conjectured that the Queen addressed Brakenbury under these titles. Monck Mason attributed them to the Tower, but explained that the words "foolish sorrow" in line 103 were intended as an excuse for them. Malone justly said that Shakespeare "never could intend to apologize for a practice, of which numerous examples are found in his plays, and in which, assuredly, he perceived no impropriety." The epithet "ragged," applied to a medieval castle like the Tower, is peculiarly appropriate: the raggedness

For tender princes, use my babies well!
So foolish sorrow bids your stones farewell.
[*Exeunt.*

SCENE II.—*London. The Palace.*

Sennet. Enter RICHARD, *in pomp, crowned;* BUCKINGHAM, CATESBY, *a Page, and others.*

K. Rich. Stand all apart! Cousin of Buckingham!
Buck. My gracious sovereign!
K. Rich. Give me thy hand. [*Here he ascendeth the throne.*
Thus high, by thy advice
And thy assistance, is king Richard seated:
But shall we wear these glories for a day?
Or shall they last, and we rejoice in them?
Buck. Still live they, and for ever let them last!
K. Rich. Ah, Buckingham, now do I play the touch,
To try if thou be current gold indeed.
Young Edward lives: think now what I would speak.
Buck. Say on, my loving lord.
K. Rich. Why, Buckingham, I say I would be king.

103. *sorrow bids*] Rowe, Camb.; *Sorrowes bids* Ff 1-3; *sorrows bid* F 4.

Scene II.

London. The Palace.] Camb.; *The same. A Room of State in the Palace.* Capell; *The Court.* Pope. *Sennet.*] Camb.; *Sound a Sennet.* F 1; *Sound a Sonnet.* Ff 2-4; *The Trumpets sound.* Qq. *Enter . . . others.*] Camb.; *Enter Richard crownd, Buckingham, Catesby with other Nobles.* Qq; *Enter Richard in pompe, Buckingham, Catesby, Ratcliffe, Louel.* Ff. 1. *K. Rich.*] Camb.; *Rich.* Qq, Ff. 2. *Buck. . . . sovereign*] Ff; omitted Qq. 3, 4. *K. Rich. Give . . . seated*] arranged as Qq (which print *Give . . . advice* as two short lines); *Giue . . . hand, Thus . . . assistance, Is . . . seated.* (three lines) Ff. 3. *Here . . . throne.*] Qq; *Sound.* Ff. 5. *glories*] Ff; *honours* Qq. 7. *let them*] Ff; *may they* Qq. 8. *Ah*] Ff; *O* Qq. *do I*] Qq 1, 2, Ff; *I do* Qq 3-8. *play*] *ply* Warburton. 10. *speak*] Ff; *say* Qq. 11. *loving lord*] Ff; *gracious soueraigne* Qq.

of the angles of a Norman keep, seen in profile, strikes every observer. Compare *2 Henry IV.* ind. 35, and the metaphor in *King Lear*, III. iv. 31.

Scene II.

8. *play the touch*] play the part of a touch-stone. Timon, *Timon of Athens*, IV. iii. 390, calls gold the "touch of hearts." "Touch" was used for "touch-stone" when employed as building material. Nares quotes Jonson, *The Forest*, 1616, II. ii.:—

"Thou art not, Penshurst, built to envious show
Of *touch* or marble."

Lyly, *Euphues* (Arber, 79), has "the tree is known by his fruit, the gold by his *touch*, the sonne by the fire," and (p. 74) "as the true gold is tryed by the *touch*," etc.

Buck. Why, so you are, my thrice-renowned lord.
K. Rich. Ha! am I king? 'tis so: but Edward lives.
Buck. True, noble prince.
K. Rich. O bitter consequence,
That Edward still should live! "True, noble prince!"
Cousin, thou wast not wont to be so dull:
Shall I be plain? I wish the bastards dead,
And I would have it suddenly perform'd.
What say'st thou now? speak suddenly; be brief.
Buck. Your grace may do your pleasure.
K. Rich. Tut, tut! thou art all ice, thy kindness freezes:
Say, have I thy consent that they shall die?
Buck. Give me some little breath, some pause, dear lord,
Before I positively speak in this:
I will resolve you herein presently. [*Exit.*
Cates. [*Aside to a stander-by.*] The king is angry: see, he gnaws his lip.
K. Rich. I will converse with iron-witted fools
And unrespective boys; none are for me

13. *lord*] Ff; *liege* Qq. 14. *king*] *a king* Pope. 16. *live!* "*True,*] Camb.; *liue true* Qq, Ff; *live, True* Rowe; *live—true* Theobald. 17. *wast*] Ff; *wert* Qq. 20. *say'st thou now*] Ff; *saist thou* Qq 1-5; *saiest thou* Qq 6-8. 22. *freezes*] Ff; *freezeth* Qq. 24. *little breath, some pause*] Ff; *breath, some little pause* Qq 1-6; *breath* Qq 7, 8. *dear lord*] Ff; *my lord* Qq. 25. *in this*] Ff; *herein* Qq. 26. *you herein presently*] Ff; *your grace immediatlie* Qq. *Exit.*] Q 1; *Exit Buck.* Ff; omitted Qq 2-8. 27. *Aside . . .*] Capell, Camb.; *Aside.* Hanmer. *gnaws his*] Ff; *bites the* Qq 1-6; *bites his* Qq 7, 8. 28. *K. Rich.*] Malone adds *Descends from his throne.*

15. *consequence*] Compare *Romeo and Juliet*, I. iv. 107.

26. *resolve you*] give you a definite answer, assure you, as *3 Henry VI.* III. ii. 19.

27. *gnaws his lip*] This personal trait was derived by Holinshed (iii. 760) from Polydore Vergil through Halle: "When he stood musing, he would bite and chaw busilie his nether lip; as who said, that his fierce nature in his cruell bodie alwaies stirred, chafed, and was euer unquiet." More (ap. Holinshed, iii. 722) says that, when Richard returned to the council before Hastings' arrest, he was "all changed, with a woonderfull soure angrie countenance, knitting the brows, frowning, and fretting and *gnawing his lips*."

28. *iron-witted*] Compare *Romeo and Juliet*, IV. v. 126; Nash, *Unfortunate Traveller*, 1594 (Gosse, 103): "onely *iron wits* are not wonne without a long siege of intreatie."

29. *unrespective*] thoughtless, inconsiderate (compare "considerate" in next line). See "respects," III. vii. 175 above. In *Troilus and Cressida*, II. ii. 71, this epithet is applied by metaphor to a sieve. For the antithesis "respective," see *Romeo and Juliet*, III. i. 128; Hooker, *Ecclesiastical Polity*, V. 1: "wary and *respective* men"; Chapman, *All Fools*, act ii.:—

"The bold and careless servant still obtains;
The modest and *respective* nothing gains."

That look into me with considerate eyes:
High-reaching Buckingham grows circumspect.
Boy!

Page. My lord?

K. Rich. Know'st thou not any whom corrupting gold
Will tempt unto a close exploit of death?

Page. I know a discontented gentleman,
Whose humble means match not his haughty spirit:
Gold were as good as twenty orators,
And will, no doubt, tempt him to anything.

K. Rich. What is his name?

Page. His name, my lord, is Tyrrel.

K. Rich. I partly know the man: go, call him hither.

[*Exit Page.*

The deep-revolving witty Buckingham
No more shall be the neighbour to my counsels:

31-33. *High-reaching . . . lord*] Ff; *Boy, high reaching . . . circumspect. Boy. My Lord* Qq 1-7; *Boy. High reaching . . . circumspect. Boy. My Lord* Q 8. 35. *Will*] Ff; *Would* Qq. 36. *I*] Ff; *My lord, I* Qq. 37. *spirit*] Ff; *mind* Qq. 41. *hither* [*Exit Page*] Camb.; *hither* [*Exit Boy*] Pope; *hither, Boy. Exit* Ff; *hither presentlie* Qq. 42. *deep-revolving*] hyphened Pope. 43. *counsels*] Ff; *counsell* Qq.

31. *High-reaching*] For the idea involved compare *Two Gentlemen of Verona*, III. i. 156. Mr. Craig refers to *2 Henry VI.* III. i. 158, and *Pericles*, II. ii. 20.

36. The conversation with the page, in More's account, took place at Warwick, during Richard's journey to Gloucester after his coronation. He had sent his servant John Greene to Brakenbury; and Brakenbury had refused to kill the children. In his impatience, Richard complained to "a secret page of his" that he could trust nobody. "'Sir' (quoth his page) 'there lieth one on your pallet without, that I dare well saie, to doo your grace pleasure, the thing were right hard that he would refuse.' Meaning this by Sir James Tirrell, which was a man of right goodlie personage, and for natures gifts worthie to haue serued a much better prince; if he had well serued God, and by grace obteined as much truth and good will as he had strength and wit. The man had an high heart, & sore longed vpward, not rising yet so fast as he had hoped, being hindered & kept vnder by the meanes of Sir Richard Ratcliffe, and Sir William Catesbie, which . . . kept him by secret drifts out of all secret trust." The page, being Tyrrel's special friend, took this opportunity to advance him. The king obeyed the hint, broke the business immediately to Tyrrel, and "found him nothing strange" in the matter. One weak point in this story is its implications as to Richard's unfamiliarity with Tyrrel. Gairdner shows (pp. 23, 24, 121) that Tyrrel had been used in offices of trust by Richard at a much earlier date.

42. *deep-revolving*] deeply pondering. For "revolving" compare *Cymbeline*, III. iii. 14.

witty] cunning, as *Much Ado About Nothing*, IV. ii. 27; Tourneur, *Revenger's Tragedy*, act v.: "'Twas somewhat *witty* carried, tho' we say it."

Hath he so long held out with me untir'd,
And stops he now for breath? Well, be it so!

Enter STANLEY.

How now, Lord Stanley, what's the news?

Stan. Know, my loving lord,
The Marquess Dorset, as I hear, is fled
To Richmond, in the parts where he abides.
[*Stands apart.*

K. Rich. Come hither, Catesby! rumour it abroad
That Anne my wife is very grievous sick:
I will take order for her keeping close.
Inquire me out some mean poor gentleman,
Whom I will marry straight to Clarence' daughter:
The boy is foolish, and I fear not him.
Look, how thou dream'st! I say again, give out
That Anne, my queen, is sick and like to die.
About it! for it stands me much upon

45. *Well, be it so*] Ff; omitted Qq. aft. 45. *Enter Stanley.*] Ff; *Enter Darby.* Qq. 46. *How now . . . news*] Ff; *How now, what newes with you* Qq. 47-49. *Know . . . abides*] arranged as Craig; *Know . . . Dorset As . . . Richmond, In . . . abides* Ff; *My Lord, I heare the Marques Dorset Is fled to Richmond, in those partes beyond the seas where he abides* Qq; *My lord, I hear . . . fled To Richmond . . . sea Where he abides* Camb. 50. *Come . . . abroad*] Ff; *Catesby. Cat. My lord. King. Rumor it abroad* Qq. 51. *very grievous sick*] Ff; *sicke and like to die* Qq. 53. *poor*] Ff; *borne* Qq. 57. *queen*] Ff; *wife* Qq.

47-50. Spedding suggested the existence of interlinear alterations in the MS., which may have misled the printer of F 1. If Ff represent a return to an original version of the play, Qq reading may be the result of an effort to improve the defective metre of that original. This latter reading, however, was evidently disarranged in printing: the Cambridge reading, perhaps, represents the real intention of the reviser. The call for Catesby and the answer which follows, corresponding in Qq to line 50, are probably stage amplifications of the original text.

51. Halle and Holinshed (iii. 751) say that Richard ordered the queen's death to be reported, "to the intent that she, taking some conceit of this strange fame, should fall into some sudden sicknesse or greeuous maladie: and to prooue, if afterwards she should fortune by that or anie other waies to lease her life, whether the people would impute hir death to the thought or sicknesse, or thereof would laie the blame to him." When this report came to Anne's ears, she sought an interview with Richard, and was answered with fair words. But "howsoeuer that it fortuned, either by inward thought and pensiuenesse of hart, or by infection of poison (which is affirmed to be most likelie), within few daies after the queene departed out of this transitorie life." Anne's death really happened on 16th March, 1485.

58. *it stands me much upon*] it concerns me, depends upon me, greatly. Compare *Antony and Cleopatra*, II. i. 50, 51; Milton, *Of Prelat. Episcopacy*,

To stop all hopes whose growth may damage me.
[*Exit Catesby*.
I must be married to my brother's daughter,
Or else my kingdom stands on brittle glass.
Murder her brothers, and then marry her!
Uncertain way of gain! But I am in
So far in blood that sin will pluck on sin:
Tear-falling pity dwells not in this eye.

Re-enter Page with TYRREL.

Is thy name Tyrrel?
Tyr. James Tyrrel, and your most obedient subject.
K. Rich. Art thou indeed?
Tyr. Prove me, my gracious lord.
K. Rich. Dar'st thou resolve to kill a friend of mine?
Tyr. Please you, but I had rather kill two enemies.
K. Rich. Why, there thou hast it; two deep enemies,
Foes to my rest and my sweet sleep's disturbers
Are they that I would have thee deal upon:
Tyrrel, I mean those bastards in the Tower.
Tyr. Let me have open means to come to them,
And soon I'll rid you from the fear of them.
K. Rich. Thou sing'st sweet music. Hark! come hither, Tyrrel!

59. *Exit Catesby*] Capell. 64. *will pluck*] Q 1, Ff; *plucke* Qq 2-5; *plucks* Qq 6-8. 65. *Tear-falling*] Ff; *Teare falling* Qq 1-5; *Teares falling* Qq 6-8. aft. 65. *Re-enter* . . .] Capell; *Enter Tirrel* Qq; *Enter Tyrrel* Ff. 68. *indeed?*] Pope adds *He takes him aside*. *lord*] Ff; *soueraigne* Qq. 70. *Please you*] Ff; *I my lord* Qq. *two*] Q 1, Ff; *two deepe* Qq 2-8. 71. *there*] Qq; *then* Ff. 72. *disturbers*] Ff; *disturbs* Qq. 77. *Thou sing'st . . . Tyrrel*] one line as Qq; *Thou sing'st sweet Musique: Hearke . . . Tyrrel* (two lines) Ff. *Hark*] Ff; omitted Qq.

1641: "*it stood them much upon* long ere this to uphold their now well tasted hierarchy." See also Lyly, *Euphues*, 1579 (Arber, 94): "if thy reuenge *stand* onely *upon* thy wish, thou shalt neuer liue to see my woe"; and Mr. Craig refers to Golding's *Cæsar*, 1565: "Cæsar thought that *it stood him upon* to beware."

64. *pluck on*] draw on, as *Measure for Measure*, II. iv. 147, etc.

65. *Tear-falling*] that lets fall tears. For the transitive use of "fall," compare Ff stage direction at I. ii. 182 above, "She fals the sword." As to Richard's description of his temperament, see note on I. ii. 157 above.

70. *two enemies*] The reading of Q 2 and its successors is an obvious printer's error. The epithet "deepe" has been taken up from the next line and repeated to the detriment of sense and metre.

72. *disturbers*] Qq "disturbs" is a substantive of the formation noticed at III. vii. 225 above. *New Eng. Dict.* quotes Daniel, *Civil Wars*, 1601-2. vi. st. 47: "From all disturbs to be so long kept free."

77. *Thou sing'st sweet music*] Aldis

Go, by this token: rise, and lend thine ear: [*Whispers.*
There is no more but so: say it is done,
And I will love thee, and prefer thee for it.

Tyr. I will despatch it straight. [*Exit.*

Re-enter BUCKINGHAM.

Buck. My lord, I have considered in my mind
The late request that you did sound me in.

K. Rich. Well, let that rest. Dorset is fled to Richmond.

Buck. I hear the news, my lord.

K. Rich. Stanley, he is your wife's son; well, look to it.

Buck. My lord, I claim the gift, my due by promise,
For which your honour and your faith is pawn'd—
The earldom of Hereford and the moveables,
Which you have promised I shall possess.

K. Rich. Stanley, look to your wife! if she convey
Letters to Richmond, you shall answer it.

Buck. What says your highness to my just request?

K. Rich. I do remember me, Henry the sixth
Did prophesy that Richmond should be king,
When Richmond was a little peevish boy:
A king! perhaps, perhaps,—

78. *this*] Ff; *that* Qq. *Whispers*] Ff; *He whispers in his eare.* Qq. 79. *There is*] Ff; *Tis* Qq. *it is*] Qq 3-5, Ff; *is it* Qq 1, 2, 6-8. 81. *I . . . straight*] Ff; *Tis done my gracious lord. King. Shall we heare from thee Tirrel ere we sleep? Enter Buc. Tir. Ye shall my lord.* Qq (*Yea, my good lord* Qq 6-8). *Exit.*] Ff; omitted Qq. aft. 81. *Re-enter Buckingham.*] Camb.; *Enter Buckingham* Ff; *Enter Buc.* Qq (see preceding note). 83. *request*] Ff; *demand* Qq. 84. *rest*] Ff; *pass* Qq. 85. *the news*] Ff; *that newes* Qq. 86. *son*] *sonnes* Qq 1-3 *to it*] Qq; *unto it* Ff. 87. *the gift*] Ff; *your gift* Qq. 89. *Hereford*] *Herford* Qq 1-3, 5-8; *Herfort* Q 4; *Hertford* Ff. 90. *Which you have promised*] Ff; *The which you promised* Qq. *shall*] Ff; *should* Qq. 93. *request*] Ff; *demand* Qq. 94. *I do remember me*] Ff; *As I remember* Qq. 97. *perhaps, perhaps*—] Camb.; *perhaps perhaps.* Qq 1-3, 5, 6, 8; *perhaps,* Q 4; *perhaps, perhaps,* Q 7; *perhaps.* Ff.

Wright, in a note on I. i. 27, alludes to Richard's well-known love of music. Various allusions scattered through the play, as in this passage, may have a reference to this love; but there is no authority for it in the chief sources from which Shakespeare derived his knowledge.

79. *no more but so*] So Chapman (?), *Alphonsus*, act ii.: "nay, tell her more than so."

89, 90. See III. i. 195 above, and note. The "moveables" are the appurtenances of the earldom not attached to the soil: see *Richard II.* II. i. 161; *Taming of the Shrew*, II. i. 198; Fletcher and Massinger, *Spanish Curate*, iv. 5: "My sheep and oxen, and my *moveables*."

Buck. My lord!
K. Rich. How chance the prophet could not at that time
Have told me, I being by, that I should kill him?
Buck. My lord, your promise for the earldom,—
K. Rich. Richmond! When last I was at Exeter,
The mayor in courtesy show'd me the castle,
And call'd it Rougemont; at which name I started,

98-115. *My lord . . . to-day*] Qq; omitted Ff. 98. *My lord*] *Lord* Qq 3, 4. 104. *Rougemont*] *Ruge-mount* Qq.

98-115. The reason for the omission of these lines from Ff is obscure. That it was deliberate appears probable from the alteration in the Ff version of line 116, which has been retained here. On the other hand, Ff reading may be equally well the original form of line 116, afterwards altered to suit the purpose of Qq. Spedding, while classing this among the alterations in F 1 not intended by Shakespeare, leans noticeably to the conclusion that it may have been due to Shakespeare's feeling that the action was delayed by the intermediate matter. No such feeling, however, seems to have crossed Shakespeare's or his editors' mind, when the long rhetorical speeches in IV. iv., serious impediments to the action, were retained in F 1. Mr. Daniel can account for the omission only on the supposition that the passage was a theatrical insertion, not in the original draught of the play, introduced for the benefit of the chief actor, and so struck out by the editor in the Q from which F 1 was prepared. He further accounts for the omission by Ff of the second "perhaps" in line 97, by suggesting that the word was struck out by accident, when the editor of F 1 drew his line through the succeeding passage. Pickersgill suggests that the metre of lines 107-112 may have proved a bar to the smoothing hand of the editor of F 1. It is also possible that the editor of F 1, for some reason which we can only conjecture, decided to omit the passage, even though it was original: perhaps he felt it to be irrelevant, or thought the double play on words which it contains far-fetched. Even if the passage is a later insertion, at any rate the resort which its author made to Shakespeare's own historical sources, and his selection of this striking anecdote, make it highly probable that the author who inserted it was Shakespeare himself.

102-106. This anecdote, "interlaced" into Holinshed's text by his posthumous editors, came from John Hooker or Vowell, the chamberlain and historian of Exeter. Richard paid a visit to Exeter in November, 1483, after the failure of Buckingham's rebellion and Richmond's first expedition, and was received by the mayor. "He came to the castell; and, when he understood that it was called Rougemont, suddenlie he fell into a dumpe, and (as one astonied) said: 'Well, I see my daies be not long,'" etc. (Holinshed, iii. 746).

104. *Rougemont*] The castle of Exeter, the building of which was ordered by William I. after the taking of the city in 1067, and committed by him to Baldwin of Brionne. The name comes from the natural formation of the site, "rubeus mons extra portam aquilonarem civitatis Exonie." Richmond was the name given to the castle built by Alan of Brittany at the mouth of Swaledale after 1072, and either was derived from a castle of Richemont in Brittany, or was a gallicised form of the English *Rices-munt* (hill of sovereignty). The vast Earldom of Richmond was vested in Henry VII.: his title, derived from his Yorkshire estates, merely lent its name to the Surrey Richmond when Shene Palace became his favourite residence. The popular pronunciation of "Rougemont" and "Richmond" may have been so nearly alike as to make the play on the words tolerable.

Because a bard of Ireland told me once,
I should not live long after I saw Richmond.

Buck. My lord!

K. Rich. Ay, what's o'clock?

Buck. I am thus bold to put your grace in mind
Of what you promis'd me.

K. Rich. Well, but what's o'clock?

Buck. Upon the stroke of ten.

K. Rich. Well, let it strike.

Buck. Why let it strike?

K. Rich. Because that, like a Jack, thou keep'st the stroke
Betwixt thy begging and my meditation.
I am not in the giving vein to-day.

Buck. May it please you to resolve me in my suit?

K. Rich. Thou troublest me; I am not in the vein.

[*Exeunt all but Buckingham.*

Buck. And is it thus? repays he my deep service
With such contempt? made I him king for this?
O, let me think on Hastings, and be gone
To Brecknock, while my fearful head is on!

[*Exit.*

110. *Well*] omitted Pope. 116. *May . . . suit*] Ff; *Whie then resolue me whether you wil or no.* Qq. 117. *Thou*] Ff; *Tut, tut, thou* Qq. *Exeunt . . .*] Camb.; *Exit.* Qq, Ff. *Exeunt Richard and train.* Capell. 118. *And . . . repays*] Ff; *Is it euen so, rewards* (*rewardst* Q 1) Qq. *deep*] Ff; *true* Qq. 119. *such*] Ff; *such deepe* Qq.

105. *a bard of Ireland*] There is no authority for this description in Holinshed.

113. *Jack*] The Jack of the clock was the figure which struck the hours on the bell of an old clock. Compare *Richard II.* v. v. 60. Steevens quotes Decker, *Lanthorne and Candle-Light*: "The *Jacke* of a Clocke-house goes uppon Screws, and his office is to do nothing but strike," and *Guls Horn-Booke*, where the Jacks of the clock in old St. Paul's are mentioned. *New Eng. Dict.* quotes from the accounts of St. Lawrence's Church, Reading, in 1498-9: "It. payed for the settyng of Jak with the hangyng of his bell and mendyng his hond, iiijd." Two wooden Jacks in armour strike the quarters on the clock which is now in the north transept of York Minster. A sitting Jack, locally known as Jack Blandiver, strikes the quarters with his heels on the bell of the clock, once in Glastonbury Abbey, now in the north transept of Wells Cathedral. Other examples are at Southwold and Blythburgh in Suffolk: at Rye in Sussex two gilded cherubs perform the office of Jacks. The expression probably is connected with the rather slighting use of the name, alluded to at I. iii. 53 above. Richard likens Buckingham's hesitation to a Jack suspending his stroke on the clock-bell, and bids him strike at once.

121. *Brecknock*] The lordship of Brecon, and the castle founded by Bernard of Neufmarché about 1092, came through the Braoses to the

SCENE III.—*The same.*

Enter TYRREL.

Tyr. The tyrannous and bloody act is done,
The most arch deed of piteous massacre
That ever yet this land was guilty of.
Dighton and Forrest, whom I did suborn
To do this piece of ruthless butchery,
Albeit they were flesh'd villains, bloody dogs,
Melted with tenderness and mild compassion,
Wept like to children in their deaths' sad story.
"O! thus," quoth Dighton, "lay the gentle babes:"
"Thus, thus," quoth Forrest, "girdling one another
Within their alabaster innocent arms:

SCENE III.] Pope; omitted Ff. *The same*] Capell, Camb. *Enter Tyrrel.*] Ff; *Enter Sir Francis Tirrell* Qq. 1. *act*] Ff; *deed* Qq. 2. *arch deed*] Ff; *arch-act* Qq 1-6; *arch-acts* Q 7; *arch act* Q 8. 4. *whom*] *who* F 1. 5. *piece of ruthless*] Pope; *ruthles peece of* Qq 1, 2; *ruthfull peece of* Qq 3-8; *peece of ruthfull* Ff. 6. *Albeit*] Ff; *Although* Qq. 7. *Melted*] Ff; *Melting* Qq. *mild*] Ff; *kind* Qq 1-5; omitted Qq 6-8. 8. *like to*] Ff; *like two* Qq. *deaths'*] Theobald; *deaths* Qq, Ff. *story*] Ff; *stories* Qq. 9. *O! thus*] Ff; *Lo thus* Qq. *the gentle*] Ff; *those tender* Qq 1-5; *these tender* Qq 6-8. 10. *one*] *on* Qq 1, 2. 11. *alabaster innocent*] F 4; *Alablaster innocent* Ff 1-3; *innocent alablaster* Qq 1-7; *innocent alabaster* Q 8.

Bohuns, Earls of Hereford; from whom it passed by marriage to Thomas of Woodstock, son of Edward III., and so to the house of Stafford. See note on III. i. 195 above.

2. *arch deed*] Compare *Othello*, IV. i. 71, where Ff have the hyphen, apparently rejected in the present case. So "arch-enemy (*3 Henry VI.* II. ii. 2) and "arch-villain" (*Measure for Measure*, v. i. 57) are hyphened in Ff.

4. More tells us that Dighton, "a big, broad, square, and strong knave," was Tyrrel's "horssekeeper." Forrest, "a fellow fleshed (see below) in murder before his time," was one of the warders of the Princes in the Tower.

6. *flesh'd*] Hounds were said to be fleshed when they ate of the first game which they killed. So Fletcher and Massinger, *Elder Brother*, iv. 3, of one using a sword for the first time: "This is my grief, I shall be *flesh'd* on cowards." Compare *King John*, v. i. 71. The word is also applied, at any rate in the eighteenth century, without distinction, to the custom of giving the hounds a portion of the killed game, as in Smollett, *Peregrine Pickle*, 1751, chapter viii. Metaphorically, it is used of one who has tasted slaughter and is become accustomed to it. Compare *Henry V.* III. iii. 11. Fletcher and Massinger, *Spanish Curate*, iv. 2, use the word in the transferred sense of a hardened knave:—

"Tush, he's *flesh'd*,
And knows what vein to strike for his own credit."

11. *alabaster*] The form in most of the early editions, "alablaster," is a very common corruption. For the various spellings current in the fifteenth and sixteenth centuries, see the extracts from the Nottingham Records, etc., in W. H. St. John Hope, *On the Early Working of Alabaster in England* (*Archæol. Journal*, lxi., 1904, 221-40). In Leland's *Itinerary* and Holland's version of Camden's *Britannia*, "ala-

Their lips were four red roses on a stalk,
And in their summer beauty kiss'd each other.
A book of prayers on their pillow lay;
Which once," quoth Forrest, "almost chang'd my mind;
But O! the devil!"—there the villain stopp'd,
Whilst Dighton thus told on: "We smothered
The most replenished sweet work of nature
That from the prime creation e'er she fram'd."
Hence both are gone with conscience and remorse:
They could not speak; and so I left them both,
To bear this tidings to the bloody king.
And here he comes.

Enter KING RICHARD.

All health, my sovereign lord!

K. Rich. Kind Tyrrel, am I happy in thy news?

Tyr. If to have done the thing you gave in charge
Beget your happiness, be happy then;
For it is done.

K. Rich. But didst thou see them dead?

Tyr. I did, my lord.

K. Rich. And buried, gentle Tyrrel?

Tyr. The chaplain of the Tower hath buried them;
But where, to say the truth, I do not know.

12. *were four*] Q 1, Ff; *foure* Q 2; *like foure* Qq 3-8. 13. *And in*] Ff 1, 2; *And* Ff 3, 4; *Which in* Qq 1-5; *When in* Qq 6-8. 15. *once*] Qq; *one* Ff. 16. *devil!"—there*] *devil"—there* Rowe; *diuell their* Q 1; *diuel; their* Q 2; *diuel: there* Qq 3, 4; *divel! there* Qq 5-8; *Diuell, there* Ff. 17. *Whilst*] Qq; *When* Ff. 19. *e'er she*] Ff; *euer he* Qq. 20. *Hence . . . remorse*] Ff; *Thus . . . remorse* Qq 1, 2; omitted Qq 3-8. 22. *bear*] Ff; *bring* Qq. 23. *Enter . . .*] Camb.; after 22 Qq, Ff. *health*] Ff; *hail* Qq. *lord*] Ff; *liege* Qq. 25. *gave*] *give* Qq 1, 2. 27. *done*] Ff; *done my Lord* Qq. 30. *where . . . truth*] Ff; *how or in what place* Qq.

baster" is the form used. Leland, i. fol. 42 (ed. Hearne, 1710-12, i. 40), mentions a popular corruption current in the Isle of Axholme: "The upper part of the Isle hath plentiful Quarres of Alabaster, communely there caullid Plaster." The same form is apparent in the term "plaster of Paris."

18. *replenished sweet*] The first epithet qualifies the second, and the two might be hyphened together. "Replenish'd," in the sense of "complete, fully furnished," occurs in *Winter's Tale*, II. i. 79.

30. *where, to say the truth*] Shakespeare departs from his authority, which expressly says that Tyrrel ordered the murderers "to burie them at the staire foot, meetlie deepe in the ground, vnder a great heape of stones."

K. Rich. Come to me, Tyrrel, soon, at after-supper,
When thou shalt tell the process of their death.
Meantime, but think how I may do thee good,
And be inheritor of thy desire.
Farewell till then.
Tyr. I humbly take my leave.
[*Exit Tyrrel.*
K. Rich. The son of Clarence have I pent up close;
His daughter meanly have I match'd in marriage;
The sons of Edward sleep in Abraham's bosom;
And Anne my wife hath bid this world good night.
Now, for I know the Breton Richmond aims
At young Elizabeth, my brother's daughter,
And, by that knot, looks proudly on the crown,
To her go I, a jolly thriving wooer.

31. *K. Rich.*] *King* Qq 3-8; *Rich.* Ff; *Tir.* Qq 1, 2. *soon, at*] *soone at* Qq 1-6; *soone, and* Ff; *soone* Qq 7, 8; *soon, soon* Rowe. *after-supper*] hyphened Staunton, Craig. 32. *When*] Ff; *And* Qq. *thou shalt*] *thou there shalt* Ff 2-4. 35. *then*] Ff; *soone* Qq. *Tyr. I . . . leave.*] F 1; *Tyr. I humbly take leave* Ff 2-4; omitted Qq. *Exit Tyrrel*] Qq; omitted Ff. 36. *K. Rich.*] *Rich.* Ff; omitted Qq. 39. *this world*] Ff; *the world* Qq. *good night*] *godnight* Qq 1, 2. 40. *Breton*] Capell; *Brittaine* Qq; *Britaine* Ff 1, 2; *Brittain* F 3; *Britain* F 4; *Briton* Rowe. 42. *on*] Ff; *ore* Qq. 43. *go I*] Ff; *I go* Qq.

31. *soon, at after-supper*] Probably Ff reading, which makes no great sense, is founded on a misunderstanding of the phrase. The comma after "soon," which Mr. Craig inserts in his "Little Quarto" edition, makes the meaning clear. For "after-supper," the "rere-supper" or dessert taken after supper and served in another room, see Mr. Cuningham's note on *Midsummer-Night's Dream*, v. i. 34. In that case, where the meaning is unmistakable, the Cambridge editors allow the hyphen: here they read "soon at after supper" within commas. "Soon at night" commonly means "this very night," as *Othello*, III. iv. 198. "Soon at supper-time" occurs in *Comedy of Errors*, III. ii. 179; and "soon at supper" in *Merchant of Venice*, II. iii. 5. This reading presumes either (1) that "at after" is a preposition meaning "after," as in Chaucer, *Canterbury Tales*, B. 1455, etc., or (2) that "soon at" = "soon," which seems improbable.

34. *inheritor*] possessor. Compare "inherit," *Richard II.* I. i. 85; *The Tempest*, IV. i. 154, etc.

40. *Breton*] Richmond was in exile in Brittany, and was welcome, Richard implies, to his place of retreat.

42. *by that knot*] *i.e.* by virtue of that proposed alliance. The marriage of Richmond and Elizabeth had been arranged at Brecon by Buckingham and the Bishop of Ely, during Ely's semi-captivity there. It was communicated to the Countess of Richmond by means of her confidential secretary Reginald Bray, and by her, through her physician Lewis, to the Queen-Dowager. Richmond accepted the proposition, and swore at Rennes on Christmas Day, 1483, to observe this necessary condition of his enterprise. It was not till 1485 that the rumour of Richard III.'s intention to marry Elizabeth was spread abroad (Boswell Stone, *Shakspere's Holinshed*, p 388).

Enter CATESBY.

Cates. My lord!
K. Rich. Good or bad news, that thou com'st in so bluntly?
Cates. Bad news, my lord: Morton is fled to Richmond;
And Buckingham, back'd with the hardy Welshmen,
Is in the field, and still his power increaseth.
K. Rich. Ely with Richmond troubles me more near
Than Buckingham and his rash-levied strength.
Come, I have learn'd that fearful commenting
Is leaden servitor to dull delay;
Delay leads impotent and snail-pac'd beggary:
Then fiery expedition be my wing,
Jove's Mercury, and herald for a king!
Go, muster men! my counsel is my shield;
We must be brief, when traitors brave the field. [*Exeunt.*

SCENE IV.—*Before the Palace.*

Enter QUEEN MARGARET.

Q. Mar. So! now prosperity begins to mellow
And drop into the rotten mouth of death.
Here in these confines slily have I lurk'd,

aft. 43. *Enter Catesby.*] Qq; *Enter Ratcliffe* Ff. 44. *Cates.*] *Cate.* Qq; *Rat.* Ff (and 46). 45. *or bad news*] Ff; *newes or bad* Qq. 46. *Morton*] *Mourton* Ff; *Ely* Qq. 50. *rash-levied*] hyphened Pope. *strength*] Ff; *army* Qq. 51. *learn'd*] Ff; *heard* Qq. 55. *Jove's*] *Ioues* Qq 1, 2, Ff; *Ioue,* Qq 3, 5-8; *Loue,* Q 4. 56. *Go*] Ff; *Come* Qq.

Scene IV.

SCENE IV.] *Scena Tertia.* Ff. *Before the Palace*] Capell. *Enter Queen Margaret.*] *Enter Queene Margaret sola.* Qq; *Enter old Queene Margaret.* Ff.

46. The Bishop of Ely escaped secretly from Brecon, "and came to his see of Elie; where he found monie and friends; and so sailed into Flanders." For Buckingham's expedition and its fate, see the end of the next scene.

50. *rash-levied*] hastily raised. Compare *King John*, II. i. 67.

55. *Jove's Mercury*] "Fiery expedition" is to herald Richard's entry into the field, and be the Mercury to his Jove. The second half of the line explains the allusion. Theobald wished to read "Jove's Mercury 's an herald for a king."

57. *brave the field*] boastfully dispute the field. Compare *King John*, IV. ii. 243; *ibid.* V. i. 70. Schmidt hesitates between this sense and that of "make fine, splendid," which is the sense at V. iii. 280 below.

Scene IV.

1, 2. Steevens quotes what is probably a reminiscence of this passage from Marston, *Antonio and Mellida*, 1602:—

"now is his fate grown mellow,
Instant to fall into the rotten jaws
Of chap-fall'n death."

To watch the waning of mine enemies.
A dire induction am I witness to,
And will to France, hoping the consequence
Will prove as bitter, black, and tragical.
Withdraw thee, wretched Margaret! who comes here?

Enter QUEEN ELIZABETH *and the* DUCHESS OF YORK.

Q. Eliz. Ah! my poor princes! ah! my tender babes!
My unblown flowers, new-appearing sweets!
If yet your gentle souls fly in the air,
And be not fix'd in doom perpetual,
Hover about me with your airy wings,
And hear your mother's lamentation!

Q. Mar. Hover about her! say, that right for right
Hath dimm'd your infant morn to aged night!

Duch. So many miseries have craz'd my voice,
That my woe-wearied tongue is still and mute.
Edward Plantagenet, why art thou dead?

Q. Mar. Plantagenet doth quit Plantagenet;
Edward for Edward pays a dying debt.

Q. Eliz. Wilt thou, O God, fly from such gentle lambs,
And throw them in the entrails of the wolf?
When didst thou sleep, when such a deed was done?

Q. Mar. When holy Harry died, and my sweet son.

4. *enemies*] Ff; *aduersaries* Qq. 9. *poor*] Ff; *young* Qq. 10. *unblown*] *unblowed* F 1. *flowers*] *flower* Qq 6-8. *new-appearing*] hyphened Pope. 13. *about*] *aboue* Qq 6-8. 15. *right for right*] *wrong for wrong* Warburton. 17-19. *Duch. So . . . dead*] as Ff; inserted after 34 in Qq. 18. *still and mute*] Ff; *mute and dumbe* Qq. 20, 21. *Q. Mar. Plantagenet . . . debt*] Ff; omitted Qq. 24. *When*] *Why* Ff 2-4. 25. *Harry*] Qq 1, 2, F 1; *Henry* Ff 2-4; *Mary* Qq 3-8.

6. As a matter of fact, Margaret's departure to France took place in 1476, after which time she never returned to England.

15. *right for right*] Johnson explains, "justice answering to justice." Heaven has given the house of York its just revenge for the atrocities which the house of Lancaster has committed on it; and now the sins of the house of York are to be visited upon its own head.

17. *craz'd*] broken, cracked, as Chaucer, *Canterbury Tales*, G. 934: "I am right siker that the pot was *crazed*"; Milton, *Paradise Lost*, 2nd ed. 1674, xii. 210:—

"God looking forth will trouble all his host
And *craze* their chariot wheels."

Mr. Craig quotes a parallel from *Comedy of Errors*, v. i. 307-10. See note on "care-craz'd," III. vii. 184 above.

Duch. Dead life, blind sight, poor mortal living ghost,
Woe's scene, world's shame, grave's due by life usurp'd,
Brief abstract and record of tedious days,
Rest thy unrest on England's lawful earth, [*Sitting down.*
Unlawfully made drunk with innocent blood!
Q. Eliz. Ah, that thou wouldst as soon afford a grave,
As thou canst yield a melancholy seat!
Then would I hide my bones, not rest them here.
Ah! who hath any cause to mourn but we?
[*Sitting down by her.*
Q. Mar. If ancient sorrow be most reverend,
Give mine the benefit of seniory,
And let my griefs frown on the upper hand.
If sorrow can admit society, [*Sitting down with them.*
Tell o'er your woes again by viewing mine.
I had an Edward, till a Richard kill'd him;
I had a Henry, till a Richard kill'd him:

26. *Dead life, blind sight*] Ff; *Blind sight, dead life* Qq. 28. *Brief . . . days*] Ff; omitted Qq. 29. *thy*] *they* Q 5; *their* Qq 6-8. *Sitting down*] Camb.; *Sitting down on it.* Capell. 30. *Unlawfully*] *Unlawfull* Qq 6, 7. *innocent*] Ff; *innocents* Qq. 31. *Ah*] Ff; *O* Qq. *as soon*] Ff; *as well* Qq. 34. *Ah*] Ff; *O* Qq. *we*] Ff; *I* Qq. *Sitting down by her.*] Camb.; *Throwing herself down upon the earth.* Hanmer (at 31). 35. *If ancient*] *If any ancient* Pope. *reverend*] *reuerent* Qq, Ff. 36. *seniory*] *signorie* Qq 1-5; *signiorie* Qq 6, 7; *signeurie* F 1; *signiory* Q 8; *signeury* Ff 2-4; *seigneurie* Rowe; *seniority* Pope. 37. *griefs*] Ff; *woes* Qq. *hand.*] Warburton; *hand,* Qq; *hand* Ff. 38. *Sitting down with them.*] Camb.; *joining, and taking seat between them.* Capell. 39. *Tell . . . mine*] Qq; omitted Ff. *o'er*] Warburton; *ouer* Qq. 41. *I had a Henry*] Rann (Capell conj.), Craig; *I had a Harry* Camb.; *I had a Richard* Qq; *I had a Husband* Ff.

26-30. Pope put this speech of strained paradoxes into his margin. No doubt, in writing Constance's lamentations in *King John*, III. i., Shakespeare remembered this earlier and more stilted attempt.

28. *Brief abstract*] Compare *Hamlet*, II. ii. 548, 549.

31. *thou*] Elizabeth addresses the earth. The transition is rather abrupt.

36. *seniory*] This is the spelling adopted by most modern editions. The word, in the present passage, implies both superior age (line 35) and superior cause for sorrow (line 37).

40-46. Margaret makes her sorrows common with those of her Yorkist rivals. Richard has murdered, not only Prince Edward and Henry VI., but also his own nephews, Edward V. and Richard of York. The Duchess retorts by reminding Margaret of her responsibility for the deaths of York and Rutland at Wakefield. Margaret answers her by adding the death of Clarence to the list of Richard's crimes, and upbraids her with being the mother of the arch-criminal.

41. *Henry*] Qq are obviously wrong: it is difficult to imagine that the reading in Ff was derived from an original source, as it breaks a sequence of proper names to which the lines owe their point.

Thou hadst an Edward, till a Richard kill'd him;
Thou hadst a Richard, till a Richard kill'd him.
Duch. I had a Richard too, and thou didst kill him;
I had a Rutland too, thou holp'st to kill him.
Q. Mar. Thou hadst a Clarence too, and Richard kill'd him.
From forth the kennel of thy womb hath crept
A hell-hound that doth hunt us all to death:
That dog that had his teeth before his eyes,
To worry lambs and lap their gentle blood,
That foul defacer of God's handiwork,
That excellent grand tyrant of the earth,
That reigns in galled eyes of weeping souls,
Thy womb let loose to chase us to our graves.
O upright, just, and true-disposing God,
How do I thank thee, that this carnal cur
Preys on the issue of his mother's body,
And makes her pue-fellow with other's moan!
Duch. O Harry's wife, triumph not in my woes!
God witness with me! I have wept for thine.
Q. Mar. Bear with me; I am hungry for revenge,
And now I cloy me with beholding it.
Thy Edward he is dead, that kill'd my Edward;
Thy other Edward dead, to quit my Edward;

45. *holp'st*] Ff 2-4; *hop'st* F 1; *hopst* Qq. 46. *Thou . . . him*] one line as Qq; *Thou . . . too, And . . . him* (two lines) Ff. *and*] Q 1, Ff; *till* Qq 2-8. 50. *blood*] Ff, Q 8; *blouds* Qq 1-7. 52, 53. *That excellent . . . souls*] arranged as Capell; transposed Ff; omitted Qq. 55. *true-disposing*] hyphened Ff. 58. *And . . . moan*] omitted Pope. *pue-fellow*] Qq 3-7, Ff; *puefellow* Qq 1, 2. 59. *wife*] *wifes* Q 1. 60. *thine*] Q 1, Ff; *thee* Qq 2-8. 63. *kill'd*] Ff; *stabd* Qq. 64. *Thy*] Qq; *The* Ff.

52, 53. The reversal of these lines in Ff is, no doubt, the result of a crowded interlineation or marginal insertion—probably both combined—in the margin of a printed copy of Q.

52. *excellent*] merely in a superlative sense, like Sir Andrew's "*Excellent* good, i' faith" in *Twelfth Night*, II. iii. 46.

53. *galled eyes*] Compare *Hamlet*, I. ii. 155.

56. *carnal*] used with much the same significance as "flesh'd," IV. iii. 6 above. Richard has tasted flesh, and now hunts after it persistently.

58. *pue-fellow*] companion. Nares quotes, without a reference: "When I was a treuantly scholar in the noble university of Cambridge, though I hope I had as good a conscience as other of my *pew-fellows*." See also Decker, *Bel-Man of London* (Smeaton, 146): "The *Foist* and the *Nip* are *pew-fellowes* together and of one religion." Shakespeare uses the word "pue," *King Lear*, III. iv. 55.

Young York he is but boot, because both they
Match'd not the high perfection of my loss.
Thy Clarence he is dead, that stabb'd my Edward;
And the beholders of this frantic play,
The adulterate Hastings, Rivers, Vaughan, Grey,
Untimely smother'd in their dusky graves.
Richard yet lives, hell's black intelligencer,
Only reserv'd their factor, to buy souls
And send them thither: but at hand, at hand,
Ensues his piteous and unpitied end:
Earth gapes, hell burns, fiends roar, saints pray,
To have him suddenly convey'd from hence.
Cancel his bond of life, dear God, I pray,
That I may live and say, The dog is dead!

Q. Eliz. O! thou didst prophesy the time would come

66. *Match'd*] Ff 3, 4; *Matcht* Ff 1, 2; *Match* Qq. 67. *stabb'd*] Ff; *kild* Qq. 68. *frantic play*] Ff; *tragicke plaie* Qq; *tragick scene* Capell (conj.). 69. *adulterate*] *adulterer* Warburton. 72. *their*] *the* Hanmer. 73. *at hand, at hand*] *at hand at handes* Q 1; *at hand* Qq 7, 8. 75. *Earth gapes*] *Earth gapes, heaven lowers* Seymour (conj.). *hell burns*] *hell burns, heaven weeps* S. Walker. *roar*] *roar for him* Capell. *pray*] *pray for vengeance* Pope. 76. *To have . . . hence*] omitted Pope. *from hence*] Ff; *away* Qq. 78. *and say*] Ff; *to say* Qq.

65. *boot*] the additional item thrown in to equalise a bargain, as *Winter's Tale*, IV. iv. 650. See also *Measure for Measure*, II. iv. 11; *Troilus and Cressida*, IV. v. 40. Margaret reckons that the death of young York is thrown in to equalise the sorrows of herself and her enemies.

69. *adulterate*] Shakespeare uses this form in *Comedy of Errors*, II. ii. 142; *Hamlet*, I. v. 42, and three times in the poems. See also Machin and Markham, *Dumb Knight*, act v. Steevens understands the epithet in a double sense. Hastings was not only an adulterer; he was also adulterate, base metal, to Margaret, who had made experience of his treachery.

71. *intelligencer*] agent, go-between, as *2 Henry IV*. IV. ii. 20. Compare *Winter's Tale*, II. iii. 68. Mr. Craig notes two instances from Nash: one from *The Unfortunate Traveller*, "never anie discredited the trade of *intelligencers* but Judas"; the other from *Pierce Penilesse* (Grosart, ii. 19), "throwing himself abruptly into my company like an *intelligencer*." See also Webster, *Duchess of Malfi*, 1623, i. 1: "flatterers, panders, *intelligencers*, atheists, and a thousand such political monsters."

72. *their factor*] the agent of the powers of hell. Aldis Wright remarks that the "plural of respect" is used by Shakespeare after the mention of heaven and hell alike, and refers to *Othello*, IV. ii. 48, on which see Mr. Hart's note. The term "factor" repeats and emphasises "intelligencer" in the foregoing line. Compare Fletcher and Massinger, *Spanish Curate*, iii. 2:—

"a young *factor*
They call Leandro, that has robb'd his master."

75. In a line of heavily stressed monosyllables, containing four short sentences, nothing is more likely than that a foot should have been missed out by the author. The necessary pauses in the line make the omission almost unnoticeable.

That I should wish for thee to help me curse
That bottled spider, that foul bunch-back'd toad!
Q. Mar. I call'd thee then vain flourish of my fortune:
I call'd thee then poor shadow, painted queen;
The presentation of but what I was;
The flattering index of a direful pageant;
One heav'd a-high, to be hurl'd down below;
A mother only mock'd with two fair babes;
A dream of what thou wast; a garish flag,
To be the aim of every dangerous shot;
A sign of dignity, a breath, a bubble;
A queen in jest, only to fill the scene.
Where is thy husband now? where be thy brothers?
Where be thy two sons? wherein dost thou joy?
Who sues and kneels and says "God save the queen"?
Where be the bending peers that flatter'd thee?
Where be the thronging troops that follow'd thee?
Decline all this, and see what now thou art:
For happy wife, a most distressed widow;
For joyful mother, one that wails the name;
For one being sued to, one that humbly sues;
For queen, a very caitiff crown'd with care;

81. *bunch-back'd*] Q 1, Ff; *hunch-backt* Qq 2-8. 85. *pageant*] *page* Warburton. 86. *a-high*] hyphened Camb.; *on high* Pope. 87. *only mock'd*] Ff, Q 8; *onelie, mockt* Qq 1-7. *fair*] Ff; *sweete* Qq. 88. *what thou wast*] Ff; *which thou wert* Qq. 88-90. *a garish flag . . . bubble*] Ff; *a breath, a bubble, A signe of dignitie, a garish flag, To be . . . shot* Qq. 93. *be*] *are* Qq 1, 2. *two sons*] Ff; *children* Qq. 94. *and kneels and says*] Ff; *to thee* (*me* Q 7), *and cries* Qq. 100, 101. *For one . . . care*] Ff; transposed Qq.

86. *a-high*] on high. So Berners' *Froissart*, (ed. Macaulay), i. 164: "he [Chandos] said to the prince: 'Sir, it were good that you rested here and set your banner *a-high* in this bush, that your people may draw hither'"; *ibid.* i. 160: "the king was on a white courser and said *a-high* to his men." "An hye" occurs in Chaucer, *Hous of Fame*, 215. Compare "on lofte," where we say "aloft" in *Parliament of Foules*, 683. Compare "an end" above, I. iii. 304; and "a-height" in *King Lear*, IV. vi. 58.

88-90. The arrangement of these phrases in Qq may have been derived from a stage misquotation of the original text.

88. *garish*] Mr. Craig quotes several instances. Familiar examples are from Milton, *Il Penseroso*, line 141: "Hide me from Day's *garish* eie," and "I lov'd the *garish* day" from Newman's hymn, "Lead, kindly Light."

97. *Decline all this*] So *Troilus and Cressida*, II. iii. 55.

101. *caitiff*] literally, a "captive." Hence the word comes to mean a "poor wretch," and is used with a compassionate sense by Shakespeare in this

For she that scorn'd at me, now scorn'd of me;
For she being fear'd of all, now fearing one;
For she commanding all, obey'd of none:
Thus hath the course of justice whirl'd about,
And left thee but a very prey to time,
Having no more but thought of what thou wast,
To torture thee the more, being what thou art.
Thou didst usurp my place, and dost thou not
Usurp the just proportion of my sorrow?
Now thy proud neck bears half my burthen'd yoke;
From which even here I slip my wearied head,
And leave the burthen of it all on thee.
Farewell, York's wife, and queen of sad mischance!
These English woes shall make me smile in France.

Q. Eliz. O thou well-skill'd in curses, stay awhile,
And teach me how to curse mine enemies!

Q. Mar. Forbear to sleep the night, and fast the day;
Compare dead happiness with living woe;
Think that thy babes were sweeter than they were,
And he that slew them fouler than he is.
Bettering thy loss makes the bad causer worse:
Revolving this will teach thee how to curse.

Q. Eliz. My words are dull; O! quicken them with thine!

Q. Mar. Thy woes will make them sharp and pierce like
mine. [*Exit.*

102. *For she . . . of me*] Ff; *For one . . . of me* Qq (aft. 104). 103. *For she . . . one*] Ff; *For one . . . one* Pope; omitted Qq. 104. *For she . . . none*] Ff; *For one . . . none* Qq. 105. *whirl'd*] Ff; *wheeld* Qq. 107. *wast*] Ff; *wert* Qq 1, 2; *art* Qq 3-8. 112. *wearied head*] Ff; *wearie necke* Qq 1-5; *wearied necke* Qq 6-8. 115. *woes*] *wars* Q 4. *shall*] Ff; *will* Qq. 118. *night . . . day*] Qq 3-8, Ff; *nights . . . daies* Qq 1, 2. 120. *sweeter*] Ff; *fairer* Qq. 122. *bad causer worse*] *bad causes worse* Q 4; *bad cause worser* Q 8; *bad-causer worse* Steevens. 125. *Thy . . . mine*] one line as Qq; *Thy . . . sharpe, And . . . mine* (two lines) Ff. *Exit*] *Exit Margaret.* Ff; *Exit Mar.* (aft. 126) Qq.

and other passages. Compare *Romeo and Juliet*, V. i. 52; *Othello*, IV. i. 109; and see Mr. Hart's note on the latter passage.

105. Compare *Love's Labour 's Lost*, IV. iii. 384.

111. *burthen'd*] burdensome, as "unmanner'd," I. ii. 39 above. It may be, however, that the epithet may be used in its ordinary sense, and be merely transferred from "neck" to "yoke"; or, again, that it may agree with the possessive case of the personal pronoun implied in "my."

122. *bad causer*] "Causer" has been used above, I. ii. 117. Steevens' reading, "bad-causer," destroys the true force of the epithet.

Duch. Why should calamity be full of words?
Q. Eliz. Windy attornies to their client woes,
Airy succeeders of intestate joys,
Poor breathing orators of miseries!
Let them have scope: though what they will impart
Help nothing else, yet do they ease the heart.
Duch. If so, then be not tongue-tied: go with me,
And in the breath of bitter words let's smother
My damned son, that thy two sweet sons smother'd.
The trumpet sounds: be copious in exclaims.

Enter KING RICHARD, *marching, with drums and trumpets.*

K. Rich. Who intercepts me in my expedition?
Duch. O! she that might have intercepted thee,
By strangling thee in her accursed womb,
From all the slaughters, wretch, that thou hast done!
Q. Eliz. Hid'st thou that forehead with a golden crown,
Where should be branded, if that right were right,
The slaughter of the prince that ow'd that crown,
And the dire death of my poor sons and brothers?
Tell me, thou villain slave, where are my children?
Duch. Thou toad, thou toad, where is thy brother Clarence?
And little Ned Plantagenet, his son?
Q. Eliz. Where is the gentle Rivers, Vaughan, Grey?

127. *their client*] Hanmer, Camb.; *their Clients* Ff; *your Client* Qq 1-3, 5-8; *your clients* Q 4; *your client's* Pope. 128. *intestate*] Qq; *intestine* Ff. 130. *will*] Ff; *do* Qq. 131. *nothing else*] Ff; *not at all* Qq 1-6; *not all* Qq 7, 8. 134. *that*] Ff; *which* Qq. 135. *The trumpet sounds*] Ff; *I heare his drum* Qq. aft. 135. *SCENE V.* Pope. *Enter . . . trumpets.*] Qq; *Enter King Richard, and his Traine.* Ff. 136. *me in*] Ff; omitted Qq. 137. *O! she*] Ff; *A she* Qq. 141. *Where*] Qq; *Where't* Ff. *should*] *would* Q 4. *branded*] Ff; *grauen* Qq. *right,*] Qq; *right?* Ff. 143. *poor*] Ff; *two* Qq. 144. *villain slave*] Qq; hyphened Ff. 145. *Thou . . . Clarence*] one line as Qq; *Thou Toad, thou Toade, Where . . . Clarence* (two lines) Ff. 147. *the gentle*] Ff; *kind Hastings,* Qq.

127. *client*] This is evidently the right reading. Woes are the clients to whom words are but windy attornies. The misreading in the next line seems to point to the F 1 editor's misunderstanding of the text at this point, and to an attempt at altering it on his own account. If "clients" is the right reading, it must be in apposition to "woes," and not in the genitive, qualifying it.

142. *ow'd*] owned. Compare, among many other instances, *Macbeth*, I. iv. 10.

147, 148. Aldis Wright, while retaining Qq reading, points out its inherent improbability. Elizabeth would not be likely to speak of her enemy as "kind

Duch. Where is kind Hastings?
K. Rich. A flourish, trumpets! strike alarum, drums!
Let not the heavens hear these tell-tale women
Rail on the Lord's anointed! strike, I say!
[*Flourish. Alarums.*
Either be patient, and intreat me fair,
Or with the clamorous report of war
Thus will I drown your exclamations.
Duch. Art thou my son?
K. Rich. Ay, I thank God, my father, and yourself.
Duch. Then patiently hear my impatience.
K. Rich. Madam, I have a touch of your condition,
That cannot brook the accent of reproof.
Duch. O! let me speak.
K. Rich. Do, then; but I'll not hear.
Duch. I will be mild and gentle in my words.
K. Rich. And brief, good mother; for I am in haste.
Duch. Art thou so hasty? I have stay'd for thee,
God knows, in torment and in agony.
K. Rich. And came I not at last to comfort you?
Duch. No, by the holy rood! thou know'st it well,
Thou cam'st on earth to make the earth my hell.
A grievous burthen was thy birth to me;

148. *Duch. . . . Hastings*] Ff; omitted Qq. 151. *Flourish. Alarums.*] Ff; *The trumpets* Q 1; *The trumpets sound.* Qq 2, 8; *The trumpets sounds.* Qq 3-7. 159. *That*] Ff; *Which* Qq. 160. *Duch. O . . . hear*] Ff; omitted Qq. 161. *words*] Ff; *speech* Qq. 164. *torment and in*] Ff; *anguish, paine and* Qq.

Hastings." The tragedy of her own family would also be too present in her mind to admit the memory of any kindred crime; and, even if it occurred to her, she hardly would give it the first place in her reproaches. It is natural that the Duchess, on the other hand, recalling the loyalty of Hastings to her eldest son and his family, should add his name to those of the members of the Woodville family and faction.

151. *the Lord's anointed*] The strength, such as it is, of Shakespeare's Richard II., proceeds from his high sense of his dignity as "the deputy elected by the Lord" (*Richard II.* III. ii. 57). Richard III., on the other hand, to whom such a belief is superstition, uses it to awe his adversaries into silence.

152. *intreat me fair*] Compare *Richard II.* III. i. 37.

158. *condition*] temperament, disposition, as *Henry V.* V. ii. 314; *Othello*, II. i. 255.

168. See note on II. iv. 27, 28 above. For Richard's character at the various periods of his life, Shakespeare merely draws inferences from the general description given by More.

Tetchy and wayward was thy infancy;
Thy school-days frightful, desperate, wild, and furious;
Thy prime of manhood daring, bold, and venturous;
Thy age confirm'd, proud, subtle, sly, and bloody,
More mild, but yet more harmful, kind in hatred:
What comfortable hour canst thou name,
That ever grac'd me with thy company?

K. Rich. Faith! none but Humphrey Hour, that call'd your grace

171. *Thy . . . venturous*] omitted Qq 3-8. 172. *sly, and bloody*] Ff; *bloudie, trecherous* Qq. 173. *More . . . hatred*] Ff; omitted Qq. 175. *with*] Ff; *in* Qq. 176. *Faith . . . grace*] one line as Qq; *Faith . . . Hower, That . . . Grace* (two lines) Ff.

169. *Tetchy*] Compare *Romeo and Juliet*, I. iii. 32; *Troilus and Cressida*, I. i. 99. The word has been explained as equivalent to "touchy," *e.g.* by Halliwell, Nares, etc. Skeat, however, defines it as "full of tetches or teches, *i.e.* full of bad habits, freaks, whims, vices." In *Romeo and Juliet* (*u.s.*) it is used perhaps instead of "tettish": compare Fletcher's *Wit without Money*, 1639, v. 2: "He 's the most *tettish* knave!"

172. *age confirm'd*] Aldis Wright explains, "in the full vigour of manhood." More, perhaps, than this is implied in "confirm'd," which means "fixed, resolved," as in *Coriolanus*, I. iii. 65, etc. "Age *confirm'd*" would thus denote the time of life at which early tendencies and character become fixed and settled.

173. *harmful, kind*] Ff have "harmfull; Kinde," and S. Walker suggested "harmful kind," which, if accepted, should be hyphened. However, the meaning of the paradox "kind in hatred" is clear enough. It exactly describes Richard's attitude towards Clarence at the beginning of the play.

176. *Humphrey Hour*] The only satisfactory explanation of this play upon words is that suggested by Steevens, and adopted by Malone. "Shakespeare might indeed by this strange phrase have designed to mark the *hour* at which the good Duchess was as hungry as the followers of Duke Humphrey." Q 8 reads "Humphreys houre," which may be intended to make the phrase clearer. Loiterers who could not buy or beg a dinner, and spent the dinner-interval in lounging about the nave of St. Paul's, were said to "dine with Duke Humphrey." Humphrey, Duke of Gloucester, son of Henry IV., died in 1447, and was buried at St. Albans Abbey; but "a proper chapel and fair monument" on the south side of St. Paul's nave, marking the burial-place of Sir John Beauchamp (d. 1358), were supposed vulgarly to mark that of Duke Humphrey. Decker, *Guls Horn-Booke*, ch. iv., speaks of this part of the nave of St. Paul's as "Duke Humfryes Walke." Gabriel Harvey, *Foure Letters and certain Sonnets*, 1592, has "to seeke his dinner in Poules with Duke Humphrey: to licke dishes, to be a beggar." For other references, see Steevens' note; Nares *s.v.* Duke Humphrey; Brand, *Popular Antiquities*, iii. 384-7. Shakespeare thus may have intended to make Richard answer his mother's question literally with a far-fetched pun: the only hour he can *name* is Duke Humphrey's hour, and that called her away from his company to eat her breakfast. The mention of breakfast instead of dinner is immaterial. Besides this explanation, the only other that seems reasonable is that the "comfortable hour" was a certain Humphrey Hour, for whom there is no historical authority. Shakespeare may have invented the name for a serving-man, merely for the sake of the pun. The idea that Humphrey Hour was a gallant of the Duchess is not warrantable.

To breakfast once forth of my company.
If I be so disgracious in your eye,
Let me march on, and not offend you, madam,
Strike up the drum!

Duch. I prithee, hear me speak.

K. Rich. You speak too bitterly.

Duch. Hear me a word;
For I shall never speak to thee again.

K. Rich. So.

Duch. Either thou wilt die, by God's just ordinance,
Ere from this war thou turn a conqueror;
Or I with grief and extreme age shall perish,
And never more behold thy face again.
Therefore take with thee my most grievous curse,
Which, in the day of battle, tire thee more
Than all the complete armour that thou wear'st!
My prayers on the adverse party fight;
And there the little souls of Edward's children
Whisper the spirits of thine enemies,
And promise them success and victory.
Bloody thou art, bloody will be thy end;
Shame serves thy life, and doth thy death attend. [*Exit.*

Q. Eliz. Though far more cause, yet much less spirit to curse
Abides in me, I say amen to her.

K. Rich. Stay, madam; I must talk a word with you.

Q. Eliz. I have no more sons of the royal blood
For thee to slaughter: for my daughters, Richard,
They shall be praying nuns, not weeping queens;
And therefore level not to hit their lives.

178. *I be*] Q 1, Ff; *it be* Qq 2-8. *disgracious*] *gratious* Qq 3-7; *grieious* Q 8. *eye*] Ff; *sight* Qq. 179. *you, madam*] Ff; *your grace* Qq. 180-83. *Strike up . . . So*] Ff; *Dut. O heare me speake for I shall neuer see thee more. King. Come, come, you are too bitter.* Qq. 184. *thou wilt*] *thou'lt* Pope. 187. *more behold*] Ff; *looke vpon* Qq. 188. *grievous*] Ff; *heauy* Qq. 195. *art*] *art, and* Qq 6-8. 198. *her*] Ff; *all* Qq. aft. 198. Theobald added *Going*. 199. *talk*] Ff; *speake* Qq. 200. *more*] *moe* Q 1. 201. *slaughter*] Ff; *murther* Qq.

196. *serves*] accompanies, is servant to; parallel to "attend" at the close of the line.

203. *level not*] do not aim. Compare Greene, *Orlando Furioso* (Dyce, 92): "Ay, so they guess, but *level* far awry."

K. Rich. You have a daughter call'd Elizabeth,
Virtuous and fair, royal and gracious?
Q. Eliz. And must she die for this? O! let her live,
And I 'll corrupt her manners, stain her beauty,
Slander myself as false to Edward's bed,
Throw over her the veil of infamy:
So she may live unscarr'd of bleeding slaughter,
I will confess she was not Edward's daughter.
K. Rich. Wrong not her birth; she is a royal princess.
Q. Eliz. To save her life, I 'll say she is not so.
K. Rich. Her life is safest only in her birth.
Q. Eliz. And only in that safety died her brothers.
K. Rich. Lo, at their birth good stars were opposite.
Q. Eliz. No, to their lives ill friends were contrary.
K. Rich. All unavoided is the doom of destiny.
Q. Eliz. True; when avoided grace makes destiny:
My babes were destin'd to a fairer death,
If grace had bless'd thee with a fairer life.
K. Rich. You speak as if that I had slain my cousins.
Q. Eliz. Cousins indeed, and by their uncle cozen'd
Of comfort, kingdom, kindred, freedom, life!
Whose hand soever lanch'd their tender hearts,
Thy head, all indirectly, gave direction:
No doubt the murderous knife was dull and blunt
Till it was whetted on thy stone-hard heart,
To revel in the entrails of my lambs.
But that still use of grief makes wild grief tame,

209. *veil*] *vaile* Qq 6-8, Ff; *vale* Qq 1-5. 210. *unscarr'd of*] Ff; *vnskard* (or *unscarde*, etc.) *from* Qq. 212. *a royal princess*] Ff; *of roiall bloud* Qq. 214. *safest only*] Ff; *onlie safest* Qq. 216. *Lo*] *No* Pope. *birth*] Ff; *births* Qq. 217. *ill*] Ff; *bad* Qq. 222-35. *K. Rich. You . . . bosom*] Ff; omitted Qq. 224, 225. *Of comfort . . . hearts*] omitted Pope. 225. *lanch'd*] *lanced* Camb.

218. *unavoided*] unavoidable: see notes on I. ii. 39, I. iv. 27 above.

223. The same pun occurs in Fletcher, *Monsieur Thomas*, i. 3: "cousin, Cozen thyself no more."

225. *lanch'd*] Compare Beaumont and Fletcher, *Faithful Shepherdess*, iv. 3:—

"while he,
Directed by his fury, bloodily
Lanch'd up her breast."

226. Steevens refers to *Hamlet*, II. i. 66. He criticises the jingle as one "in which Shakespeare found more delight than his readers." It is thoroughly in keeping with the elaborate word-splitting of the whole dialogue.

230. *still use*] constant use. Compare "still practice" in *Titus Andronicus*, III. ii. 45, where "still," however may mean "silent."

My tongue should to thy ears not name my boys,
Till that my nails were anchor'd in thine eyes;
And I, in such a desperate bay of death,
Like a poor bark, of sails and tackling reft,
Rush all to pieces on thy rocky bosom.

K. Rich. Madam, so thrive I in my enterprise
And dangerous success of bloody wars,
As I intend more good to you and yours
Than ever you and yours by me were harm'd!

Q. Eliz. What good is cover'd with the face of heaven,
To be discover'd, that can do me good?

K. Rich. The advancement of your children, gentle lady.

Q. Eliz. Up to some scaffold, there to lose their heads?

K. Rich. Unto the dignity and height of fortune,
The high imperial type of this earth's glory.

Q. Eliz. Flatter my sorrow with report of it!
Tell me, what state, what dignity, what honour,
Canst thou demise to any child of mine?

K. Rich. Even all I have; ay, and myself and all,
Will I withal endow a child of thine;
So in the Lethe of thy angry soul

236, 237. *Madam . . . wars*] two lines as Ff; *Madam, so thriue I in my dangerous attempt of hostile armes* (one line) Qq. 239. *and yours*] Qq 6-8, Ff; *or yours* Qq 1-5. *by me were harm'd*] Ff; *were by me wrong'd* Qq. 242. *gentle*] Ff; *mightie* Qq. 244. *Unto*] Ff; *No to* Qq. *fortune*] Ff; *honor* Qq. 245. *high*] Q 1, Ff; *height* Qq 2-8. 246. *sorrow*] Ff; *sorrowes* Qq. 248. *demise*] *deuise* Ff 2-4. 249. *ay*] Ff; *yea* Qq.

237. *success*] sequel, result, as *Othello*, III. iii. 222.

245. *type*] emblem, badge. The phrase is explained by another in Halle's *Chronicle*, p. 414, cited by Aldis Wright, where Richard, in his speech to his soldiers before Bosworth, says: "I haue obteyned the crowne *type* of this famous realm & noble region." See *Henry VIII.* I. iii. 31, where "types of travel" = emblems of travel. In *3 Henry VI.* I. iv. 121, "the *type* of King of Naples" probably means the style or semblance of king, though Schmidt takes it to mean the crown. A more unrestricted use, again, is found in Chapman (?), *Alphonsus*, 1654, i. 2:—

"to unite anew
Unto her former strength and glorious *type*
Our half-declining Roman monarchy."

248. *demise*] Aldis Wright notes this law-term as an ἅπαξ λεγόμενον in Shakespeare, like "pleasing" in I. i. 13 above. A "demise" is a conveyance or transfer of an estate or other real property. Thus, Blackstone defines "the *demise* of the crown" as meaning "that, in consequence of the disunion of the King's natural body from his body politic, the kingdom is transferred or demised to his successor; and so the royal dignity remains perpetual." Perhaps the word was suggested here by the mention, immediately preceding, of "the high imperial type of this earth's glory.

Thou drown the sad remembrance of those wrongs,
Which thou supposest I have done to thee.

Q. Eliz. Be brief, lest that the process of thy kindness
Last longer telling than thy kindness' date.

K. Rich. Then know, that from my soul I love thy daughter.

Q. Eliz. My daughter's mother thinks it with her soul.

K. Rich. What do you think?

Q. Eliz. That thou dost love my daughter from thy soul:
So from thy soul's love didst thou love her brothers;
And from my heart's love I do thank thee for it.

K. Rich. Be not so hasty to confound my meaning:
I mean, that with my soul I love thy daughter,
And do intend to make her queen of England.

Q. Eliz. Well then, who dost thou mean shall be her king?

K. Rich. Even he that makes her queen: who else should be?

Q. Eliz. What, thou?

K. Rich. Even so: how think you of it?

Q. Eliz. How canst thou woo her?

K. Rich. That I would learn of you,
As one being best acquainted with her humour.

Q. Eliz. And wilt thou learn of me?

K. Rich. Madam, with all my heart.

Q. Eliz. Send to her, by the man that slew her brothers,
A pair of bleeding hearts; thereon engrave
Edward and York; then haply will she weep:
Therefore present to her—as sometime Margaret

255. *kindness' date*] Ff; *kindnes doe* Qq. 256. *Then . . . daughter*] one line as Qq; *Then know, That . . . Daughter* (two lines) Ff. 260. *soul's love didst thou love*] Q 1, Ff; *soules loue didst thou* Qq 2-5; *soule didst thou loue* Qq 6-8. 264. *do intend*] Ff; *meane* Qq. 265. *Well then*] Ff; *Saie then* Qq. 266. *Even . . . be*] one line as Qq; *Even . . . Queene: Who . . . bee* (two lines) Ff. *else should be*] Ff; *should be else* Q 1; *should else* Qq 2-8. 268. *Even so*] Ff; *I euen I* Qq; *Even I* Capell; *Ay, even I* Malone. *how*] Ff; *what* Qq. *of it*] Ff; *of it, madam* Qq. 270. *That*] omitted Pope. *I would*] *would I* Qq 1, 2. 271. *being*] Ff; *that are* Qq 1, 2; *that were* Qq 3-8. 273. *Madam*] omitted Pope. 275. *engrave*] *engraven* Collier MS. 276. *will she*] Ff; *she will* Qq. 277. *sometime*] *sometimes* Qq 1, 2, 7, 8.

271. *humour*] disposition, as *Love's Labour's Lost*, v. i. 10; *2 Henry VI*. v. i. 132. Above, IV. i. 64, the word is used in its common sense of "mood": here it implies natural character.

Did to thy father, steep'd in Rutland's blood—
A handkerchief; which, say to her, did drain
The purple sap from her sweet brother's body,
And bid her wipe her weeping eyes withal.
If this inducement move her not to love,
Send her a letter of thy noble deeds;
Tell her thou mad'st away her uncle Clarence,
Her uncle Rivers; ay, and, for her sake,
Mad'st quick conveyance with her good Aunt Anne.

K. Rich. You mock me, madam; this is not the way
To win your daughter.

Q. Eliz. There is no other way;
Unless thou could'st put on some other shape,
And not be Richard that hath done all this.

K. Rich. Say that I did all this for love of her.

Q. Eliz. Nay, then indeed she cannot choose but hate thee,
Having bought love with such a bloody spoil.

K. Rich. Look, what is done, cannot be now amended:
Men shall deal unadvisedly sometimes,
Which after-hours gives leisure to repent.
If I did take the kingdom from your sons;
To make amends, I'll give it to your daughter:

278, 279. *Did . . . handkerchief*] Ff; *Did to thy father, a handkercher* (*handkercheffe* Qq 2-8) *steept in Rutlands bloud* (one line) Qq. 279, 280. *which . . . body*] Ff; omitted Qq. 280. *sap*] *tide* Pope. *brother's body*] *brothers bodies* Rowe; *brothers' bodies* Warburton. 281. *wipe*] Ff; *drie* Qq. *withal*] Ff; *therewith* Qq. 282. *move*] Ff; *force* Qq. 283. *letter*] Ff; *storie* Qq. *deeds*] Ff; *acts* Qq. 285. *ay*] Ff; *yea* Qq. 287. *You mock me, madam*] Ff; *Come, come, you mocke me* Qq 1, 2; *Come, come, ye mocke me* Qq 3-8. *this is*] *this* F 1. 288. *There is*] *There's* Pope. 291-345. *K. Rich. Say . . . years.*] Ff; omitted Qq. 291. *her.*] *her?* Capell. 292. *hate*] *have* Steevens (Mason conj.); *love* Grant White (Tyrwhitt conj.). 293. *bought*] *brought* Pope. 296. *repent*] *repent of* Rowe.

286. *conveyance*] For the sense of dishonest dealing implied here in this word, compare *1 Henry VI.* I. iii. 2, *3 Henry VI.* III. iii. 160.

291. Richard makes use of the argument with which he had tempted Anne, I. ii. 115-24 above. Dr. A. W. Ward (*History of English Dramatic Literature*, new ed. 1899, ii. 99) calls this part of the scene "a weak sort of repetition of the powerful scene between Richard and Anne." Johnson remarked that "part of the dialogue is ridiculous, and the whole improbable." An opposite, but paradoxically expressed opinion is that of Dr. Brandes (*William Shakespeare*, English translation, 1898, ii. 159): "The scene has the air of a repetition. . . . Shakespeare has lavished his whole art on the passage." The last sentence is surely extravagant.

293. *spoil*] waste, havoc (Johnson). Compare *1 Henry IV.* III. iii. 11; *Henry V.* V. ii. 249.

If I have kill'd the issue of your womb;
To quicken your increase, I will beget
Mine issue of your blood upon your daughter:
A grandam's name is little less in love
Than is the doting title of a mother;
They are as children but one step below,
Even of your mettle, of your very blood;
Of all one pain, save for a night of groans
Endur'd of her, for whom you bid like sorrow.
Your children were vexation to your youth;
But mine shall be a comfort to your age.
The loss you have is but a son being king;
And by that loss your daughter is made queen.
I cannot make you what amends I would;
Therefore accept such kindness as I can.
Dorset your son, that with a fearful soul
Leads discontented steps in foreign soil,
This fair alliance quickly shall call home
To high promotions and great dignity:
The king that calls your beauteous daughter wife,
Familiarly shall call thy Dorset brother:

315. *Leads*] *Treads* Collier (Capell conj.).

305. *mettle*] temper, disposition. The same word as "metal." See Mr. Macmillan on *Julius Cæsar*, I. i. 66, and Mr. Hart on *Measure for Measure*, II. iv. 48. Here the spelling in Ff is "mettall," as in *Troilus and Cressida*, I. iii. 22; *1 Henry IV.* II. iv. 383, IV. iii. 22, and V. iv. 24; and in line 385 below. "Metal" occurs in *Measure for Measure*, I. i. 49, where a play is intended on the double meaning of the word. The spelling in *Henry V.* III. v. 15 is "mettell." "Mettle," however, is the form used in the large majority of Shakespearean instances, whether the meaning be that of "metal," "disposition," or, as is very common, be applied in the double sense.

307. *bid*] endured; a past tense formed from "bide." Chaucer, *Canterbury Tales*, E. 1888, uses a past participle "biden" from "bide," with the intransitive sense of "waited." But the past tense used here is uncommon, if not unique. Capell read "'bid."

314-17. *Dorset your son*] On Shakespeare's confusion of historical time in this scene, see note on line 447 below. Dorset, on leaving sanctuary (see IV. i. 38 above), had "gathered together a great band of men in Yorkshire" to help Buckingham. It was after the failure of Buckingham's expedition that he went abroad and joined Richmond. See also IV. ii. 48, 49. According to More (ap. Holinshed, iii. 750), one of the chief inducements by which Richard won over the Queen Dowager was his offer of promotion to Dorset. She actually was so "blinded by auaricious affection, & seduced by flattering words" that she sent letters to her son, "willing him in anie wise to leaue the earle, and without delaie to repaire into England." The whole passage in More is epitomised in this speech.

315. *Leads*] used in the sense of "drags; draws along his steps."

Again shall you be mother to a king;
And all the ruins of distressful times
Repair'd with double riches of content.
What! we have many goodly days to see:
The liquid drops of tears that you have shed
Shall come again, transform'd to orient pearl,
Advantaging their loan with interest
Of ten times double gain of happiness.
Go then, my mother, to thy daughter go;
Make bold her bashful years with your experience;
Prepare her ears to hear a wooer's tale;
Put in her tender heart the aspiring flame
Of golden sovereignty; acquaint the princess
With the sweet silent hours of marriage joys:
And when this arm of mine hath chastised
The petty rebel, dull-brain'd Buckingham,
Bound with triumphant garlands will I come,
And lead thy daughter to a conqueror's bed;
To whom I will retail my conquest won,
And she shall be sole victress, Cæsar's Cæsar.

Q. Eliz. What were I best to say? her father's brother
Would be her lord? or shall I say, her uncle?

326. *loan*] Theobald; *Loue* Ff. 336. *garlands*] *laurels* Capell. 339. *victress*] F 4; *Victoresse* Ff 1-3.

325. *orient pearl*] See Prof. Case's note on *Antony and Cleopatra*, I. v. 41, for the two possible derivations of "orient," *viz.* (1) oriental, eastern; (2) from the resemblance of the colour of a pearl to the clearness of the air before sunrising. A passage in Decker, *Bel-Man of London* (Smeaton, 112), speaks for the second of these: "So are these *Villanies* . . . paynted over with fresh *orient* cullers, because their looks may be more pleasing." For another example of "orient" see the passage from Drayton quoted at v. iii. 251 below.

326. *Advantaging*] "Advantage" is the name given to the favourable terms on which a lender receives back more than the amount of his loan: see *Merchant of Venice*, I. iii. 71; *1 Henry IV.* II. iv. 599.

loan] Theobald conjectured, with every probability, that Ff "Loue" was really "Lone," with the *n* turned upside down. He explains the passage thus: "The tears that you have lent to your afflictions, shall be turned into gems, and requite you by way of interest."

335. *dull-brain'd Buckingham*] Richard, almost secure in the hope of his new marriage, speaks slightingly of Buckingham. However, the "deep-revolving witty Buckingham" (IV. ii. 42), while aiding him, had never been his dupe. In IV. ii. 28-31, Richard reckons "high-reaching" Buckingham as one of those who look into him "with considerate eyes," and contrasts him with "iron-witted fools" like Tyrrel, and "unrespective boys" like Tyrrel's friend, the page.

338. *retail*] "Richard means to say that he will transmit the benefit of his victories to Elizabeth" (Steevens). Probably the real meaning is simply "tell," as at III. i. 77 above.

Or, he that slew her brothers and her uncles?
Under what title shall I woo for thee,
That God, the law, my honour, and her love,
Can make seem pleasing to her tender years?
K. Rich. Infer fair England's peace by this alliance.
Q. Eliz. Which she shall purchase with still lasting war.
K. Rich. Tell her the king, that may command, entreats.
Q. Eliz. That at her hands which the king's King forbids.
K. Rich. Say, she shall be a high and mighty queen.
Q. Eliz. To wail the title, as her mother doth.
K. Rich. Say, I will love her everlastingly.
Q. Eliz. But how long shall that title, ever, last?
K. Rich. Sweetly in force unto her fair life's end.
Q. Eliz. But how long fairly shall her sweet life last?
K. Rich. As long as heaven and nature lengthens it.
Q. Eliz. As long as hell and Richard likes of it.
K. Rich. Say, I, her sovereign, am her subject low.
Q. Eliz. But she, your subject, loathes such sovereignty.
K. Rich. Be eloquent in my behalf to her.
Q. Eliz. An honest tale speeds best, being plainly told.
K. Rich. Then plainly to her tell my loving tale.
Q. Eliz. Plain and not honest is too harsh a style.
K. Rich. Your reasons are too shallow and too quick.
Q. Eliz. O no! my reasons are too deep and dead;
Too deep and dead, poor infants, in their graves.
K. Rich. Harp not on that string, madam; that is past.

348. *Tell her*] Ff; *Say that* Qq. *that*] Ff; *which* Qq. 349. *forbids*] Q 1, Ff; *forbid* Qq 2-8. 351. *wail*] Qq; *vaile* Ff. 353. *ever*] omitted Q 5. 355. *her sweet life*] *that title* Qq 3-8. 356. *As*] Ff; *So* Qq. *lengthens*] *lengthen* Pope. 357. *As*] Ff; *So* Qq. *likes*] *like* Pope. 358. *low*] Ff; *loue* Qq; *now* Pope. 362. *plainly to her tell*] Ff; *in plaine termes tell her* Qq. 364. *Your*] Ff; *Madame your* Qq. 365-67. *Q. Eliz. O no . . . past*] Pope put in margin. 365. *my*] *your* Rann. 366. *graves*] Ff; *graue* Qq. 367, 368. *K. Rich. Harp not . . . break*] Q 1; Qq 2-8 omit 367; *Harpe on it still shall I, till heart-strings break. Rich. Harpe not on that string Madam, that is past* (transposing 367, 368) Ff.

346. *Infer*] in the literal sense, "bring on." See also III. v. 75; III. vii. 12 above.

364. *quick*] Richard means "hasty." Elizabeth, in her answer, plays upon the other meaning, "full of life," to point her taunt.

366. *Too deep*] Pope's reading "Two deep" carries the play on words unnecessarily far.

367. The editor of F 1, reinserting this line in the margin of one of the later Qq, must have misled the printer into transposing it with line 368.

Harp not on that string] Compare *Measure for Measure*, v. i. 64 (and

Q. Eliz. Harp on it still shall I till heart-strings break.
K. Rich. Now, by my George, my garter, and my crown,—
Q. Eliz. Profan'd, dishonour'd, and the third usurp'd.
K. Rich. I swear—
Q. Eliz. By nothing; for this is no oath:
Thy George, profan'd, hath lost his lordly honour;
Thy garter, blemish'd, pawn'd his knightly virtue;
Thy crown, usurp'd, disgrac'd his kingly glory.
If something thou would'st swear to be believ'd,
Swear then by something that thou hast not wrong'd.
K. Rich. Then, by myself—
Q. Eliz. Thyself is self-misus'd.
K. Rich. Now, by the world—
Q. Eliz. 'Tis full of thy foul wrongs.
K. Rich. My father's death—
Q. Eliz. Thy life hath it dishonour'd.
K. Rich. Why then, by God—
Q. Eliz. God's wrong is most of all.
If thou didst fear to break an oath with Him,
The unity the king my husband made

369. *K. Rich.*] omitted Ff. 372. *Thy*] Ff; *The* Qq (and so 373, 374). *lordly*] Ff; *holie* Qq. 373. *knightly*] *kingly* Ff 2-4. 374. *glory*] Ff; *dignitie* Qq. 375. *something thou would'st*] Ff; *something thou wilt* Qq 1-6; *nothing thou wilt* Qq 7, 8. 377. *Then . . . self-misus'd*] Qq place between lines 379, 380. *is self-misus'd*] Ff; *thy selfe misusest* Qq 1-7; *thy selfe misused* Q 8. 379. *it*] Ff; *that* Qq. 380. *God . . . God's*] Qq; *Heauen . . . Heauens* Ff. 381. *didst fear*] Ff; *hadst feard* Qq. *with Him*] Ff; *by him* Qq; *with heav'n* Pope. 382. *my husband*] Ff; *thy brother* Qq 1-6; *my brother* Qq 7, 8.

see Mr. Hart's note); *Coriolanus*, II. iii. 260, etc. A similar metaphor is used by Fletcher, *Monsieur Thomas*, i. 1: "Touch no more *that string*, 'tis too harsh and jarring"; *Span. Curate*, i. 2:—

"Touch not *that string*,
'Twill but increase your sorrow."

Among instances supplied by Mr. Craig may be noted one from Speed's *Chronicle*, p. 909: "The Cardinall made a countenance to the other lord that he should *harpe no more on that string*."

368. *heart-strings*] Mr. Craig notes that Cotgrave has "Precordiaux: the *heart-strings* or filme of the heart," and that in the old anatomy the heart-strings are nerves supposed to brace and sustain the heart: compare W. Horman, *Vulgaria*, 1517: "The *hert strynges* do minister the pulse." So Heywood, *Faire Maide of the West*, 1631, iii. 4:—

"if she still love him,
I 'll break her *heart-strings* with some false report
Of his unkindness."

369. *George*] The figure of St. George and the dragon, which is the pendent of the collar of the Garter. The George, as Aldis Wright notes, was not added till the reign of Henry VII.

377. The re-arrangement of lines in Ff makes no great difference, but the order in which Richard's oaths come is perhaps more natural.

380. *God*] For Ff reading, compare I. iv. 21, 117, 188, 189, etc., and notes on those passages.

Thou hadst not broken, nor my brothers died:
If thou hadst fear'd to break an oath by Him,
The imperial metal, circling now thy head,
Had grac'd the tender temples of my child,
And both the princes had been breathing here,
Which now, two tender bedfellows for dust,
Thy broken faith hath made the prey for worms.
What canst thou swear by now?

K. Rich. The time to come.

Q. Eliz. That thou hast wronged in the time o'erpast;
For I myself have many tears to wash
Hereafter time, for time past wrong'd by thee.
The children live, whose fathers thou hast slaughter'd,
Ungovern'd youth, to wail it with their age;
The parents live, whose children thou hast butcher'd,
Old barren plants, to wail it with their age.
Swear not by time to come; for that thou hast
Misus'd ere us'd, by times ill-us'd o'erpast.

K. Rich. As I intend to prosper and repent,
So thrive I in my dangerous affairs
Of hostile arms! myself myself confound!
Heaven and fortune bar me happy hours!
Day, yield me not thy light; nor, night, thy rest!
Be opposite, all planets of good luck,
To my proceeding, if with dear heart's love,
Immaculate devotion, holy thoughts,
I tender not thy beauteous princely daughter!

383. *Thou hadst not*] Ff; *Had not bene* Qq. *brothers died*] Ff; *brother slaine* Qq. 385. *head*] Ff; *brow* Qq. 386. *grac'd*] Ff; *grast* Qq 1-5; *grac't* Qq 6-8. 388. *two*] *too* Capell. *bedfellows*] Ff; *plaie fellowes* Qq. 389. *the prey for*] Ff; *a praie for* Qq; *a prey to* Pope. 390. *What . . . now*] Ff; omitted Qq, Pope. *The time*] Ff; *By the time* Qq; *By time* Pope. 391. *wronged in the time*] Ff; *wrongd in time* Qq. 393. *past wrong'd by thee*] Ff; *by the past wrongd* Qq. 394. *fathers*] Ff; *parents* Qq. 395. *with their*] Q 5, Ff; *in their* Qq 1-4; *with her* Qq 6-8. 397. *barren*] Ff; *withered* Qq. *with*] *in* Pope. 398, 399. *Swear . . . o'erpast*] Pope put in margin. 399. *ere*] *eare* Qq 1-3, 5; *nere* Q 4. *times ill-us'd*] Ff; *time misused* Qq. *o'erpast*] *orepast* Qq; *repast* Ff. 401. *affairs*] Ff; *attempt* Qq. 403. *Heaven . . . hours*] Ff; omitted Qq; *So Heaven . . . hours* Keightley (conj.). 406. *proceeding*] Ff; *proceedings* Qq. *dear*] Ff; *pure* Qq. 407. *Immaculate*] Q 1, Ff; *Immaculatd* Q 2; *Immaculated* Qq 3-8. 408. *tender*] *render* Qq 3-7.

393. *Hereafter time*] after this. The two words should perhaps be hyphened.

408. *tender*] The word is used exactly in the present sense by Horace Walpole,

In her consists my happiness and thine;
Without her, follows to myself and thee,
Herself, the land, and many a Christian soul,
Death, desolation, ruin, and decay:
It cannot be avoided but by this;
It will not be avoided but by this.
Therefore, dear mother,—I must call you so—
Be the attorney of my love to her:
Plead what I will be, not what I have been;
Not my deserts, but what I will deserve:
Urge the necessity and state of times,
And be not peevish found in great designs.

Q. Eliz. Shall I be tempted of the devil thus?

K. Rich. Ay, if the devil tempt you to do good.

Q. Eliz. Shall I forget myself to be myself?

K. Rich. Ay, if yourself's remembrance wrong yourself.

Q. Eliz. Yet thou didst kill my children.

K. Rich. But in your daughter's womb I bury them;
Where, in that nest of spicery, they will breed
Selves of themselves, to your recomforture.

Q. Eliz. Shall I go win my daughter to your will?

K. Rich. And be a happy mother by the deed.

410. *myself and thee*] Ff; *this land and me* Qq. 411. *Herself, the land*] Ff; *To thee her selfe* Qq. 412. *Death, desolation*] Ff; *Sad desolation* Qq 1-6; *Sad desolate* Qq 7, 8. 414. *by this*] *this* Q 1. 415. *dear*] Ff; *good* Qq. 418. *my*] Ff; *by* Qq. *deserts*] *desires* F 4. 419. *and state of*] *of state and* Collier MS. 420. *peevish found*] Ff; *pieuish, fond* Q 1; *peeuish, fond* Q 2; *peeuish fond* Qq 3-8; *peevish-fond* Staunton (Malone conj.), Camb. 422. *you*] Ff; *thee* Qq. 425. *Yet*] Ff; *But* Qq. 426. *I bury*] Q 3, Ff; *I buried* Qq 1, 2; *Ile burie* Qq 4-8. 427. *they*] *there* Qq 3-8. *will*] Ff; *shall* Qq. 428. *recomforture*] Ff; *recomfiture* Qq.

writing to Sir Horace Mann, 15th December, 1748: "Somerset *tendered* his pride even beyond his hate."

416. *Be the attorney*] The metaphor is common in Shakespeare. See line 127 above, v. iii. 83 below.

420. *peevish found*] For "peevish" see I. iii. 194, III. i. 31 above. The plausible reading "peevish-fond" is probably the result of the omission of a letter in Qq. "Peevish-fond" is equivalent to "childish-foolish"; not in the sense of childish simplicity, as in I. iii. 142 above, but of childish waywardness. Steevens defended Ff, quoting *Henry VIII.* II. ii. 79.

423, 424. Elizabeth asks "Shall I forget myself, the wronged mother, to be myself, the royal queen-mother?" Richard's answer, as usual, is double-edged, and is delivered with an appearance of sincerity, as though Elizabeth's words had only their surface-meaning.

427, 428. Richard, as Steevens notes, refers to the fable of the phœnix.

428. *to your recomforture*] to the recovery of your comfort. For the form "recomforture" compare "recure" in III. vii. 130 above.

Q. Eliz. I go. Write to me very shortly,
And you shall understand from me her mind.
K. Rich. Bear her my true love's kiss; and so, farewell.
[*Exit Queen Elizabeth.*
Relenting fool, and shallow-changing woman!

Enter RATCLIFF; CATESBY *following.*

How now, what news?
Rat. Most mighty sovereign, on the western coast
Rideth a puissant navy; to our shores
Throng many doubtful hollow-hearted friends,
Unarm'd and unresolv'd to beat them back:
'Tis thought that Richmond is their admiral;
And there they hull, expecting but the aid
Of Buckingham to welcome them ashore.
K. Rich. Some light-foot friend post to the Duke of Norfolk:
Ratcliff, thyself, or Catesby; where is he?

431. *to me*] *to me, Richard* Collier MS. *very*] omitted Pope. 432. *And . . . mind*] Ff; omitted Qq. 433. *and so*] Ff; omitted Qq.; Johnson adds *Kissing her.* *Exit Queen Elizabeth.*] *Exit.* Qq 1, 2; *Exit Qu.* Qq 3-8; *Exit Q.* Ff (aft. 432). 434. *shallow-changing woman*] Ff; *shallow changing woman* Qq; *shallow, changing—woman* Capell. aft. 434. *Enter . . . following*] Capell, Camb.; *Enter Rat.* Qq; *Enter Ratcliffe.* Ff (aft. 435.) 435. *How . . . news*] Ff; omitted Qq. aft. 435. *SCENE VI.* Pope. 436. *Most mighty*] Ff; *My gracious* Qq. 437. *our shores*] Ff; *the shore* Qq. 443. *Norfolk*] *Norff.* Qq 1-5.

431. Steevens reads "shortly" as a trisyllable, which removes the metrical irregularity. Possibly, however, there is an intentional break in the line after "I go."

434. More's account of Elizabeth's behaviour is most unfavourable to her strength of character. Her conduct in the present scene is the result of Shakespeare's imagination; but it is highly probable that she succumbed to personal overtures by Richard, after her departure from sanctuary.

shallow-changing woman] Whatever knowledge Shakespeare had of the Latin classics, he hardly can have forgotten Virgil, *Æneid*, iv. 569, 570.

441. *hull*] drift; float at the mercy of the wind, which drives the hull of the boat along without the aid of sails. For examples, see Nares *s.v.*, and Mr. Luce's note on *Twelfth Night*, I. v. 217. *New Eng. Dict.* quotes Smith, *Seaman's Grammar*, "*hull*, which is to beare no saile. . . . They call it hulling also in a calme swelling sea, which is commonly before a storme, when they strike their sailes lest she should beat them against the mast by rolling." Mr. Craig notes from Frobisher, *Voyage*, 1578, p. 121: "being then becalmed, and lying a-*hull* openly upon the great bay."

443. *light-foot*] light-footed, as "venom" for "venomed," I. iii. 291 above. *New Eng. Dict.* quotes Spenser, *Shepheards Calendar*, June, line 26:—

"And *light-foote* Nymphes, can
chace the lingring night."

Cates. Here, my good lord.
K. Rich. Catesby, fly to the duke!
Cates. I will, my lord, with all convenient haste.
K. Rich. Ratcliff, come hither! post to Salisbury:
When thou com'st thither,—[*To Catesby*] Dull, unmindful villain!
Why stay'st thou here, and go'st not to the duke?
Cates. First, mighty liege, tell me your highness' pleasure,
What from your grace I shall deliver to him.
K. Rich. O, true, good Catesby: bid him levy straight
The greatest strength and power that he can make,
And meet me suddenly at Salisbury.
Cates. I go. [*Exit.*
Rat. What, may it please you, shall I do at Salisbury?
K. Rich. Why, what wouldst thou do there before I go?
Rat. Your highness told me I should post before.
K. Rich. My mind is chang'd.

445. *good*] Ff; omitted Qq. *Catesby, fly*] Ff; *Flie* (new line) Qq. 446, 447. *Cates. I will . . . hither*] Ff; omitted Qq. 447. *Ratcliff*] *Catesby* Ff. *post*] Ff; *post thou* Qq (continuing 445); [*To Ratcliff*] *Post thou* Camb. 448. *thither*] Ff; *there* Qq. [*To Catesby.*] Rowe, Camb. 449. *stay'st*] Ff; *standst* Qq 1-3, 5, 6, 8; *stands* Qq 4, 7. *here*] Ff; *still* Qq. 450. *liege . . . pleasure*] Ff; *Soueraigne, let me know your minde* Qq. 451. *to him*] Ff; *them* Qq 1, 2; *him* Qq 3-8. 453. *that*] Ff; omitted Qq. 454. *suddenly*] Ff; *presentlie* Qq. 455. *Cates. I go. Exit.*] Ff; omitted Qq. 456. *What . . . shall I*] Ff; *What is it your highnes pleasure, I shall* Qq 1-4; *What it is your . . . shall* Q 5; *What is your . . . shall* Qq 6-8. *at Salisbury*] new line Camb. (adopting Qq in 456). 459. *My . . . chang'd*] Ff; *My mind is changd, sir, my minde is changd* Qq; *My mind is changed, sir, my mind is changed* Camb.

445-49. The omissions in Qq, although, without stage-directions involving the presence of Ratcliff, they make imperfect sense, may have been due to the possible fact that, in this scene, at any rate, the parts of Ratcliff and Catesby were doubled by one player. Qq direction at line 435 seems to point to this. When Catesby went out at line 455, the same player might enter again as Ratcliff, or even go on with Ratcliff's part without retiring. Ff make Richard call for Catesby in line 447: this is probably an oversight, or a too faithful following of an oversight in the original MS.

447. *Salisbury*] Richmond was off the south-western coast, close to Dorset. Richard hastened to Salisbury to prevent his junction with Buckingham's forces from the Welsh borders. Shakespeare makes nothing of the interval which elapsed between the failure of Buckingham and the ultimate success of Richmond. Buckingham's rebellion and Richmond's first attempt failed in October, 1483: it was not until August, 1485, that Richmond set out on his successful voyage.

Enter LORD STANLEY.

Stanley, what news with you?
Stan. None good, my liege, to please you with the hearing;
Nor none so bad, but well may be reported.
K. Rich. Hoyday! a riddle! neither good nor bad!
What need'st thou run so many miles about,
When thou may'st tell thy tale the nearest way?
Once more, what news?
Stan. Richmond is on the seas.
K. Rich. There let him sink, and be the seas on him!
White-liver'd runagate, what doth he there?
Stan. I know not, mighty sovereign, but by guess.
K. Rich. Well, as you guess?
Stan. Stirr'd up by Dorset, Buckingham, and Morton,
He makes for England, here to claim the crown.

Enter Lord Stanley] Ff; *Enter Darbie* (aft. 459) Qq. *Stanley*] Ff; *How now* Qq. 460. *None . . . liege*] Theobald; *None, good my liege* Ff; *None good my Lord* Qq; *None good, my lord* Camb. 461. *well . . . reported*] Ff; *may well be told* Qq. 462. *Hoyday*] *Heyday* Pope. 463. *What need'st*] Ff; *Why doest* Qq. *miles*] Ff, Qq 7, 8; *mile* Qq 1-6. 464. *the nearest*] Ff; *a neerer* Qq. 469. *Well, as you guess*] Ff; *Well sir, as you guesse, as you guesse* Qq 1-6; *Well, sir, as you guesse* Qq 7, 8. 470. *Morton*] Ff; *Elie* Qq. 471. *here*] Ff; *there* Qq.

460. *None good, my liege*] Theobald's punctuation is probably right. An antithesis is needed to "bad" in the next line.

462. *Hoyday*] Aldis Wright refers to *Troilus and Cressida*, v. i. 73. See also *Timon of Athens*, I. ii. 137. Mr. Craig furnishes an example from R. Brome, *Covent Garden Weeded*, 1639 (ed. Pearson, 1873, p. 33): "*Hoyday*, here 's a din."

467. *White-liver'd*] cowardly. Compare *Merchant of Venice*, III. ii. 86, and see Mr. Pooler's note.

runagate] A corruption of "renegade," from *renegatus*: not a variant on "runaway." See *Cymbeline*, I. vi. 137. Aldis Wright explains it here as "vagabond"; and it looks very much as if Shakespeare had used it here in the sense which does not belong to it etymologically. But Richmond would be also, in Richard's mind, a renegade to his true sovereign.

469. *as you guess*] The impatient repetition in Qq probably originated on the stage.

470, 471. The Bishop of Ely, after the fatal Council at the Tower (III. iv.), was sent to Buckingham's castle at Brecon (see note on IV. ii. 121). There Buckingham found him, on his return from court. Buckingham was already disposed to rebellion by Richard's cavalier treatment of his deserts. The historians tell us the story of his journey. At Tewkesbury he came to the conclusion that he was "indubitate heire of the house of Lancaster." But, between Worcester and Bridgenorth, he met the Countess of Richmond herself, on her way to the shrine of Our Lady at Worcester. He then remembered, that she and his mother were first cousins, and that the Countess was a daughter of the elder branch of the house of Beaufort. Thus his "earnest title" was "turned to a tittell not so good as *Est Amen*"; and he was prepared, under the influence of his prisoner at Brecon, to support the claim of Richmond to the throne. Morton heard his complaints with sympathy, and threw out plausible suggestions on his

K. Rich. Is the chair empty? is the sword unsway'd?
Is the king dead? the empire unpossess'd?
What heir of York is there alive but we?
And who is England's king but great York's heir?
Then tell me, what makes he upon the seas?
Stan. Unless for that, my liege, I cannot guess.
K. Rich. Unless for that he comes to be your liege,
You cannot guess wherefore the Welshman comes.
Thou wilt revolt and fly to him, I fear.
Stan. No, my good lord; therefore mistrust me not.
K. Rich. Where is thy power, then, to beat him back?
Where be thy tenants and thy followers?
Are they not now upon the western shore,
Safe-conducting the rebels from their ships?
Stan. No, my good lord, my friends are in the north.
K. Rich. Cold friends to me! what do they in the north,
When they should serve their sovereign in the west?
Stan. They have not been commanded, mighty king:
Pleaseth your majesty to give me leave,
I'll muster up my friends and meet your grace,
Where and what time your majesty shall please.
K. Rich. Ay, ay, thou would'st be gone to join with Richmond;
But I'll not trust thee.
Stan. Most mighty sovereign,

476. *makes he*] Ff; *doeth he* Qq; *makes him* Hanmer. *seas*] Ff, Q 8; *sea* Qq 1-7. 479. *Welshman*] *Welchmen* Qq 4, 7, 8. 481. *my good lord*] Ff; *mightie liege* Qq. 483. *be*] Ff; *are* Qq. 485. *Safe-conducting*] hyphened Ff; *Conducting safe* Pope. 487. *me*] Ff; *Richard* Qq. 489. *king*] Ff; *soueraigne* Qq. 490. *Pleaseth*] Ff; *Please it* Qq. 493. *Ay, ay, thou would'st*] Qq; *I, thou would'st* Ff; *Ay, thou would'st fain* Pope. 494. *But . . . thee*] Ff; *I will not trust you Sir* Qq. *Most*] omitted Pope.

own side, so that "he rather seemed to follow him, than to lead him." The end of their conference was an agreement to further the marriage of Richmond with Elizabeth of York.

479. *Welshman*] On his father's side. Edmund of Hadham, Earl of Richmond, was the eldest son of Owen Tudor and Katharine, widow of Henry V.

494-96. In spite of Stanley's asseverations, Richard's suspicions were fully justified. "When the said lord Stanleie would haue departed into his countrie to visit his familie, and to recreate and refresh his spirits (as he openlie said, but the truth was, to the intent to be in a perfect readinesse to receiue the earle of Richmond at his first arriuall in England), the king in no wise would suffer him to depart, before he had left as an hostage in the court George Stanleie, lord Strange, his first begotten sonne and heire."

You have no cause to hold my friendship doubtful:
I never was, nor never will be false.
K. Rich. Go then, and muster men; but leave behind
Your son George Stanley: look your heart be firm,
Or else his head's assurance is but frail.
Stan. So deal with him, as I prove true to you! [*Exit.*

Enter a Messenger.

Mess. My gracious sovereign, now in Devonshire,
As I by friends am well advertised,
Sir Edward Courtney, and the haughty prelate,
Bishop of Exeter, his elder brother,
With many moe confederates, are in arms.

496. *nor never*] *nor ever* Pope. 497. *Go then, and*] Ff; *Well, go* Qq; Camb. puts *Well* in separate line. *but*] Ff; *but heare you* Qq. 498. *heart*] Ff; *faith*] Qq. 500. *Exit*] Qq 6-8; omitted Qq 1, 2; *Exit Dar.* Qq 3-5; *Exit Stanley* Ff. 503. *Edward*] Ff; *William* Qq; *Edmond* Pope. 504. *elder brother*] Ff; *brother there* Qq. 505. *moe*] *more* Qq 7, 8, Ff 2-4.

498. *George Stanley*] Ferdinando, Lord Strange, was patron of the company by whom this play was produced, from 1588 to his death in 1594, two years after he had succeeded, as fifth earl, to the earldom of Derby. The repeated mention of his ancestor (see IV. v. 3; V. iii. 62, 96, 345-47; V. v. 9, 10 below), by whose preservation after Bosworth the unbroken succession of the house of Stanley was secured, was probably intended as a compliment to Lord Derby. "Young George Stanley" married the heiress of Lord Strange of Knocking, and thus brought the title of Strange into the family. He predeceased his father; and his son, the second Earl of Derby, was great-grandfather of the fifth earl, who left no male issue, and was succeeded by his brother William in 1594. After the death of the fifth earl, his company of players attached themselves to the service of the Lord Chamberlain, Henry Carey, Lord Hunsdon.

503, 504. Sir Edward Courtenay of Haccombe, descended from a younger son of the second Earl of Devon, was the head of the house of Courtenay. The direct line had failed in the three brothers, Thomas, sixth Earl of Devon, Hugh, and John, who all fell victims to the house of York. Thomas was beheaded at York after Towton (1461); Hugh was beheaded at Salisbury (1466); and John fell at Tewkesbury (1471). Their kinsman Edward was created Earl of Devon on Henry VII.'s accession; and his son William married Katharine, daughter of Edward IV. Shakespeare followed More in the error of calling Peter Courtenay, Bishop of Exeter 1478-87, brother of Sir Edward: that he was not his elder brother is obvious, as the Bishop did not die till 1492, when Edward was already earl. Peter Courtenay was son of Sir Philip Courtenay of Powderham, whose grandfather was sixth son of the second Earl. He was attainted by Richard III. and fled to Brittany. Henry VII. created him Lord Keeper; and, from 1487 to his death, he was Bishop of Winchester.

505. *moe*] Compare Q 1, line 200 above. "Moe" is usually taken as a comparative of number, "more" as a comparative of size. Here and in other passages, *e.g. Richard II.* II. i. 239, *Merchant of Venice*, I. i. 108, etc., it implies number. But Nares remarks that, in the sixteenth century, "*mo*, and *more*, were both used, and it does

Upon his party: he, mistrusting them,
Hois'd sail, and made his course again for Bretagne.

K. Rich. March on, march on, since we are up in arms!
If not to fight with foreign enemies,
Yet to beat down these rebels here at home.

Re-enter CATESBY.

Cates. My liege, the Duke of Buckingham is taken;
That is the best news: that the Earl of Richmond
Is with a mighty power landed at Milford,
Is colder news; but yet they must be told.

K. Rich. Away towards Salisbury! while we reason here,
A royal battle might be won and lost:
Some one take order Buckingham be brought
To Salisbury; the rest march on with me.
[*Flourish. Exeunt.*

530. *his course . . . Bretagne*] *his course . . . Brittaine* Ff; *away for Brittaine* Qq; *away for Britanny* Camb. 535. *That is*] Ff; *Thats* Qq. 537. *news*] Qq 6-8, Ff; *tidings* Qq 1-5. *but yet*] Ff; *yet* Qq. *they must*] *it must* Rowe. 541. *Flourish.*] F 1; omitted Qq, Ff 2-4. *Exeunt.*] Q 1, Ff; omitted Qq 2-8.

530. *Hois'd*] "Halsed" is the word employed by the chroniclers. "To hoise" = to lift, hoist, heave away. Compare *The Tempest*, I. ii. 148; Greene, *Menaphon*, 1589 (Arber, 58): "Eurilochus . . . awaited no farther parley, but willed his men perforce to *hoyse* him a shipboord"; Hall, *Virgidemiarum*, 1598, IV. iv. 58:—

"Or *hoyseth* sail up to a forraine shore,
That he may live a lawlesse conqueror."

534-37. See notes on lines 447, 471 above. Buckingham was taken at Shrewsbury in October, 1483. Richmond set sail from Harfleur early in August, 1485, and landed at Milford Haven about a week later. His "mighty power" this time consisted of only two thousand men.

536. *Milford*] See *Cymbeline*, III. ii. 61.

SCENE V.—*Lord Derby's house.*

Enter DERBY *and* SIR CHRISTOPHER URSWICK.

Der. Sir Christopher, tell Richmond this from me;
That in the sty of the most deadly boar
My son George Stanley is frank'd up in hold:
If I revolt, off goes young George's head;
The fear of that holds off my present aid.
So, get thee gone: commend me to thy lord.
Withal say that the queen hath heartily consented
He should espouse Elizabeth her daughter.
But tell me, where is princely Richmond now?
Chris. At Pembroke, or at Ha'rford-west, in Wales.

SCENE V.] Capell; *Scena Quarta.* Ff; *SCENE VII.* Pope. *Lord Derby's house.*] *Lord Stanley's House.* Hanmer. *Enter Derby*] *Enter Lord Stanley.* Pope, Theobald. *Urswick.*] Theobald. 2. *the most deadly*] Ff; *this most bloudie* Qq; *the most bloody* Collier. 5. *holds off*] Ff; *with holdes* Qq. 6-8. *So, get . . . daughter*] Ff; substantially in Qq aft. 18. 6. *So, get . . . lord*] Ff; *Retourne vnto thy Lord, commend me to him* Qq; *Well, hie thee to thy lord, commend me to him* Capell. 7. *Withal say that*] Ff; *Tell him* Qq; *Say, too,* Pope. 8. *should*] Ff; *shall* Qq. 10. *Pembroke*] *Penbroke* Ff 1, 2; *Penbrook* F 3. *Ha'rford-west*] Capell; *Harford-west* Q 1; *Herford-west* Qq 2, 5; *Hertford-west* Qq 3, 4; *Hertford west* Qq 6, 7; *Hertford West* Ff; *Hertford, west* Q 8.

1. *Sir Christopher*] For "Sir" applied to a priest, compare III. ii. 109 above. Urswick was sent into Brittany by the Countess of Richmond in 1483. He seems to have been recalled at the last moment; and Hugh Conway sent instead, as a "personage of more estimation than her chapleine." Richard Guildford sent an envoy from Kent with the same instructions, in case Conway were taken captive at Plymouth. Here Shakespeare continues to weld together the events of 1483 and 1485. George Stanley's detention belongs also to 1483.

2, 3. For the metaphor, see notes on "rooting hog," I. iii. 228, and "frank'd up," I. iii. 314.

6-8. These lines are misplaced in Qq, probably owing to the care of an editor, who thought that the words of farewell came prematurely, before the bulk of the conversation.

10-18. Richmond landed at Dale, at the north-west corner of Milford Haven; and, at sunrise the next day, marched to Haverfordwest, where he was received with joy. Here he heard that the men of Pembroke were ready to follow his uncle, Jasper of Hatfield, "their naturall and immediate lord"; but also that his expected ally, Rhys ap Thomas, was going to join Richard's party. With increased forces, he went on to Cardigan, not without fear of Sir Walter Herbert, who was said to be at Carmarthen "with a great crue of men," and with doubtful intentions. As he advanced through Wales to the passage of the Severn at Shrewsbury, these fears proved groundless. Welsh gentlemen joined him; and Rhys ap Thomas, who probably had dallied between the two parties, swore fealty to him, if he had not sworn it before, in return for a promise of the governorship of Wales. At Newport in Shropshire, he was joined by Sir Gilbert Talbot; at Stafford, by Sir William Stanley, his step-father's brother; and so, "his power increasing," he marched forward to Lichfield. Stanley, with

False to his children and his wife's allies:
This is the day wherein I wish'd to fall
By the false faith of him whom most I trusted.
This, this All-Souls' day to my fearful soul
Is the determin'd respite of my wrongs:
That high All-seer, which I dallied with,
Hath turn'd my feigned prayer on my head,
And giv'n in earnest what I begg'd in jest.
Thus doth he force the swords of wicked men
To turn their own points in their masters' bosoms.
Thus Margaret's curse falls heavy on my neck:
"When he," quoth she, "shall split thy heart with sorrow,
Remember Margaret was a prophetess."
Come, lead me, officers, to the block of shame;
Wrong hath but wrong, and blame the due of blame.
[*Exeunt.*

SCENE II.—*The camp near Tamworth.*

Enter RICHMOND, OXFORD, BLUNT, HERBERT, *and others, with drum and colours.*

Richm. Fellows in arms, and my most loving friends,
Bruis'd underneath the yoke of tyranny,

15. *and*] Ff, Q 8; *or* Qq 1-7. 17, *whom . . . trusted*] Ff; *I trusted most* Qq. 18. *This . . . soul*] omitted Pope. 19. *respite*] *despite* Qq 7, 8; *respect* Warburton. 20. *which*] Ff; *that* Qq; *whom* Capell. 23. *swords*] *sword*] Qq 3-8. 24. *own*] omitted Qq 3-8. *in*] Ff; *on* Qq. *bosoms*] Ff; *bosome* Qq. 25. *Thus*] Ff; *Now* Qq. *falls . . . neck*] Ff; *is fallen vpon my head* Qq; *falls . . . head* Pope. 28. *lead me, officers*] Ff; *sirs, conuey me* Qq. 29. *Exeunt*] *Exeunt Buckingham with Officers.* Ff; omitted Qq.

Scene II.

The camp near Tamworth] Hanmer, Camb. *Enter . . . colours.*] Ff; *Enter Richmond with drums and trumpets.* Qq.

19. *the determin'd respite of my wrongs*] the time to which the punishment of my evil practices was respited (Johnson, following Hanmer). For "wrongs" in this sense, compare *Midsummer-Night's Dream*, II. i. 240.

24. *in*] into. Compare III. vii. 128 above.

29. Johnson wished to add this scene to the foregoing act, abandoning a division due "to the judgment or caprice of the first editors." The fourth act would have thus "a more full and striking conclusion; and the fifth act will comprise the business of the important day, which put an end to the competition of York and Lancaster."

Scene II.

1. *The camp near Tamworth*] Richmond's army moved up a line parallel to Watling Street from Lichfield to Tamworth, while Stanley, pretending

Thus far into the bowels of the land
Have we march'd on without impediment;
And here receive we from our father Stanley
Lines of fair comfort and encouragement.
The wretched, bloody, and usurping boar,
That spoil'd your summer fields and fruitful vines,
Swills your warm blood like wash, and makes his trough
In your embowell'd bosoms—this foul swine
Is now even in the centre of this isle,
Near to the town of Leicester, as we learn:

8. *summer fields*] Ff; *somer-fieldes* Q 1; *summer-fields* Q 2; *sommer-field* Qq 3-8. 10. *embowell'd*] Ff; *inboweld* or *imboweld* Qq. 11. *Is*] Ff; *Lies* Qq. *centre*] *Centry* F 1. 12. *Near*] *Ne're* F 1.

flight, lay in front of them at Atherstone. Richard was at this time in Nottingham or at the royal park of Bestwood, close by. Between Lichfield and Tamworth, Richmond was joined by Sir Walter Hungerford and Sir Thomas Bourchier, who had deserted from Brakenbury's forces at Stony Stratford. The army arrived at Tamworth without Richmond, who had lingered behind them, distressed by moody doubts; and, losing his way as evening fell, had spent the night in nervous anxiety at a small village. He rejoined his troops next morning, characteristically explaining his absence as designed "to receiue some glad message from certeine of his priuie friends and secret allies." The next day he made another lonely journey to Atherstone, where he met his step-father (see note on IV. v. 10-18 above).

3. *bowels*] centre. Mr. Craig notes Gilbert, *Voyage*, 1583 (Payn, *English Voyagers*, p. 175): "Many voyages have been pretended, yet hitherto never any throughout accomplished by our nation of exact discovery into the *bowels* of those ample and vast nations."

5, 6. Probably an allusion to the "glad message," which (see note on line 1) Richmond had made the excuse for his separation from his army near Tamworth. The chroniclers make no mention of a definite communication from Stanley; but Sir William Stanley, on joining Richmond at Stafford, must have made his brother's plans clear.

6, 7. Shakespeare may have remembered the figure of the vine in Psalm lxxx.: "The wild boar out of the field doth root it up: and the wild beasts of the field devour it."

9. *Swills*] Malone and Aldis Wright remark on the change of tense from past to present, "not uncommon in animated description." But the sense of the passage requires the change. What Richmond says is: the boar, who in time past destroyed your summer fields and fruitful vines (*i.e.* the young princes and the whole royal stock), is now turning against you yourselves, and is swilling your own blood in the very bowels of the land. Lines 10, 11 further explain the metaphor. The past tense of "spoil'd" in line 8 requires that "summer fields and fruitful vines" should refer to that royal "harvest" (II. ii. 116) which Richard had laid waste, and not to the material crops which his march from Nottingham was endangering. See another metaphor drawn from the harvest in line 15 below.

wash] Mr. Craig notes from Cotgrave, "Lavailles: swillings, hog's *wash*, washings for swine."

10. *embowell'd*] The same as "disembowell'd," or, in legal language, "drawn." Compare *1 Henry IV.* v. iv. 109.

12. *Leicester*] Richard arrived in Leicester from Nottingham, where he had resided much during 1484 and 1485. On 20th August "he (inuironed with his gard), with a frowning countenance and cruell visage, mounted on a great white courser, and followed with his

Enter, on the other side of the field, RICHMOND, SIR WILLIAM BRANDON, OXFORD, *and others. Some of the soldiers pitch Richmond's tent.*

Richm. The weary sun hath made a golden set,
And by the bright tract of his fiery car
Gives token of a goodly day to-morrow.
Sir William Brandon, you shall bear my standard.
Give me some ink and paper in my tent:
I'll draw the form and model of our battle,
Limit each leader to his several charge,
And part in just proportion our small power.
My Lord of Oxford, you, Sir William Brandon,
And you, Sir Walter Herbert, stay with me.
The Earl of Pembroke keeps his regiment:
Good Captain Blunt, bear my good-night to him,

aft. 18. *Scene changes to another part of Bosworth field.* Theobald. *Enter . . . tent.*] Camb. (fr. Capell); *Enter Richmond with the Lordes &c.* Qq; *Enter Richmond, Sir William Brandon, Oxford, and Dorset.* Ff. 19. *set*] Ff; *sete* Q 1; *seate* Qq 2-5; *seat* Qq 6-8. 20. *tract*] Ff; *tracke* Qq. 21. *token*] Ff; *signall* Qq. 22. *Sir . . . you*] Ff; *Where is Sir . . ., he* Qq. 23-26. *Give . . . power*] as Ff; see aft. 44 for Qq. 26. *power*] Ff; *strength* Qq. 27, 28. *My Lord . . . me*] Ff; omitted Qq. 28. *you*] *your* F 1. 29. *keeps*] Ff; *keepe* Qq.

20. *tract*] trace. Compare *Timon of Athens*, I. i. 50, on which Mr. Deighton remarks that there is no etymological connection between "tract" and "track." The verb "to tract" is not uncommon. See Greene, *Orlando Furioso* (Dyce, 90):—

"when bright Phœbus mounteth up his coach,
And *tracts* Aurora in her silver steps";

Spenser, *Faerie Queene*, II. vi. 39:—

"As Shepheards curre, that in darke evenings shade
Hath *tracted* forth some salvage beastes trade."

Spenser also uses the substantive, *ibid.* VI. xii. 22.

fiery car] Shakespeare's references to the car of Phœbus were doubtless derived from the description in Golding's *Ovid*, book 2. See *Cymbeline*, V. v. 190; *Antony and Cleopatra*, IV. viii. 29.

29. *The Earl of Pembroke*] Richmond's uncle, Jasper of Hatfield, second son of Owen Tudor and Queen Katherine. He was created Earl of Pembroke in 1453, and, on Henry VII.'s accession, Duke of Bedford. Always faithful to the house of Lancaster, he had presented his nephew Richmond, when a boy of ten, to Henry VI., and, after Tewkesbury, had taken him to Britanny. He aided his nephew in his earlier attempt on England; and it was in his country that Henry made his successful landing at Milford. There seems to be no account of his conduct at Bosworth in any of the primary authorities for the story of the battle.

keeps] Compare Beaumont and Fletcher, *Woman-Hater*, iv. 2: "I will retire henceforth, and *keep* my chamber, live privately, and die forgotten"; Fletcher, *Wit without Money*, i. 1: "And tho' I have no state, I *keep* the streets still." Shakespeare several times uses the verb intransitively, *e.g. Troilus and Cressida*, IV. v. 278.

And by the second hour in the morning
Desire the earl to see me in my tent:
Yet one thing more, good captain, do for me—
Where is Lord Stanley quarter'd, do you know?

Blunt. Unless I have mista'en his colours much,
Which well I am assur'd I have not done,
His regiment lies half a mile at least
South from the mighty power of the king.

Richm. If without peril it be possible,
Sweet Blunt, make some good means to speak with him,
And give him from me this most needful note.

Blunt. Upon my life, my lord, I'll undertake it;
And so God give you quiet rest to-night!

Richm. Good night, good Captain Blunt. Come, gentlemen,
Let us consult upon to-morrow's business:
Into my tent! the dew is raw and cold.

[*They withdraw into the tent.*

Enter to his tent, KING RICHARD, NORFOLK, RATCLIFF, CATESBY, *and others.*

K. Rich. What is't o'clock?

Cat. It's supper-time, my lord; it's nine o'clock.

33. *captain . . . me*] Ff; *Blunt before thou goest* Qq. 34. *do you*] Ff; *doest thou* Qq. 35. *colours*] *quarters* Warburton. 37. *lies*] *liet* Qq 3, 5; *lieth* Qq 4, 6-8. 40. *Sweet . . . him*] Ff; *Good captaine Blunt beare my good night to him* Qq. 41. *note*] Ff; *scrowle* Qq. 42. *life*] *selfe* Ff 2-4. 43. *And . . . to-night!*] Ff; omitted Qq. 44. *Good . . . gentlemen*] *Good . . . Blunt: Come Gentlemen* (two lines) Ff; *Farewell good Blunt.* Qq. aft. 44. Qq insert 23-26, omitted above. 45. *Let us*] Ff; *Come, let vs* Qq. 46. *my*] Ff; *our* Qq. *They withdraw . . .*] Ff; omitted Qq. aft. 46. *Scene changes back to King Richard's tent.* Theobald. *to his tent.*] Capell, Camb. *and others*] *&c.* Qq 1, 2; omitted Qq 3-8, Ff. 47. *is't o'clock*] *is't a Clocke* Ff; *is a clocke* Qq. 48. *It's . . . o'clock*] Ff; *It is sixe of* [*of the* Qq 3-8] *clocke, full supper time* Qq; *It's . . . lord; It's . . . o'clock* Pope (continuing 47).

40. *make some good means*] contrive some good opportunity. So *All's Well that Ends Well*, v. i. 35; and see *Two Gentlemen of Verona*, II. vii. 5; *Merry Wives of Windsor*, II. ii. 189.

48. *nine o'clock*] Steevens preferred Qq reading with the just criticism that "a supper at so late an hour as nine o'clock, in the year 1485, would have been a prodigy." Aldis Wright recognises, however, that the time is after sunset on 21st August, and adopts Ff reading. Nares quotes Harrison, *Description of England*, 1577: "With us, the nobilitie, gentrie, and students doo ordinarilie go to dinner at eleven before noone, and to supper at five, or between five and sixe at afternoone." It is, perhaps, unnecessary to add that, after a day's march and the subsequent encampment, supper would probably be deferred considerably.

K. Rich. I will not sup to-night.
Give me some ink and paper.
What, is my beaver easier than it was?
And all my armour laid into my tent?
Cat. It is, my liege; and all things are in readiness.
K. Rich. Good Norfolk, hie thee to thy charge;
Use careful watch, choose trusty sentinels.
Nor. I go, my lord.
K. Rich. Stir with the lark to-morrow, gentle Norfolk.
Nor. I warrant you, my lord. [*Exit.*
K. Rich. Catesby!
Cates. My lord?
K. Rich. Send out a pursuivant at arms
To Stanley's regiment: bid him bring his power
Before sun-rising, lest his son George fall
Into the blind cave of eternal night. [*Exit Catesby.*
Fill me a bowl of wine. Give me a watch.

49, 50. *I . . . to-night. Give . . . paper*] two lines as Ff; one line in Qq. 54. *charge*] *charge, away* Capell. 55. *sentinels*] *Centinels* Ff; *centinell* Qq. 58. *Exit.*] Ff; omitted Qq. 59. *Catesby*] Qq; *Ratcliffe* Ff. 60. *Cates.*] Pope; *Rat.* Qq, Ff. 63. *Exit Catesby.*] Camb.; omitted Qq, Ff. 64. *To Ratcliffe.* Pope; *To Catesby.* Capell. *watch*] *watch-light* Keightley conj.

51. *beaver*] properly the face-guard of the helmet, as *Hamlet*, I. ii. 230; *2 Henry IV.* IV. i. 120. Knight, and, after him, Fairholt, *Costume in England*, (ed Dillon, ii. 45), figure an armet, or helmet with removable beaver, of the time of Philip and Mary. "In ordinary helmets, the beaver, when up, displays the face; but to do that, it falls down to the chin" (Fairholt). The earliest example in England is said to be the beaver in the effigy of Thomas, Duke of Clarence (d. 1421), in St. Michael's Chapel of Canterbury Cathedral. In this passage the beaver is probably used for the whole helmet. Compare *1 Henry IV.* IV. i. 104.

63. Compare the phrase used by Queen Elizabeth, II. ii. 46 above. The occurrence of this Marlowe-like and grandiloquent image in the midst of so much action and plainness of speech is rather noticeable. Both passages recall similar phrases in the Senecan plays—*e.g. Medea*, 740: Et Chaos cæcum, atque opacam Ditis umbrosi domum [precor]; *ibid.* 9: Noctis æternæ chaos Adversa superis regna; *Herc. Fur.* 610: noctis æternæ chaos.

64. *watch*] a watch-light or candle. Steevens says, in answer to a doubt of Johnson's as to whether line 77 does not contain a repetition of this order: "A watch, *i.e.* guard, would certainly be placed about the royal tent, without any request of the king concerning it. I believe, therefore, that particular kind of candle is here meant, which was anciently called a *watch*, because, being marked out into sections, each of which was a certain portion of time in burning, it supplied the place of the more modern instrument by which we measure the hours." Mr. Craig gives a reference ("Little Quarto" ed. p. 268) to an example from Decker, *Bel-Man of London* (Smeaton, 90): "I that all this while had stood in a corner (like a watching candle) to see all their villanies."

Saddle white Surrey for the field to-morrow.
Look that my staves be sound, and not too heavy.
Ratcliff!

Rat. My lord?

K. Rich. Saw'st thou the melancholy Lord Northumberland?

Rat. Thomas the Earl of Surrey, and himself,
Much about cock-shut time, from troop to troop
Went through the army, cheering up the soldiers.

K. Rich. So, I am satisfied. Give me a bowl of wine:
I have not that alacrity of spirit

66, 67. *heavy. Ratcliff!*] Rowe, Camb.; *heauy Ratliffe* Qq; *heauy. Ratcliff* (all one line) Ff. 69. *Saw'st thou*] Qq; *Saw'st* Ff. 71. *about*] *like* Qq 6-8. 73. *I am*] *I 'm* Capell, Pope.

65. *white Surrey*] The name is Shakespeare's invention. He took the hint, no doubt, from the "great white courser" on which, according to the chroniclers, Richard had entered Leicester.

66. *staves*] *i.e.* the staves, or wooden shafts of the lances. See below, line 342; and compare the metaphor in *Much Ado About Nothing*, v. i. 138.

69. *melancholy*] Malone explains this epithet by the inactivity of Northumberland, "which . . . stood still with a great companie, and intermitted not in the battell." Henry Percy, fourth Earl of Northumberland, had been an adherent of Richard. It is probable, however, that he came to an understanding with Richmond not long before Bosworth: his wife was a sister of Richmond's supporter, Sir Walter Herbert. At any rate, he submitted himself to the conqueror after the battle, and "was incontinentlie receiued into fauour and made of the councell." There are indications that, after his death near Thirsk in 1489, Northumberland's conduct at Bosworth was regarded in the North with scant respect. Richard, noticing his follower's moodiness and thoughtfulness before the critical moment of treachery, might well apply to him the epithet "melancholy."

71. *cock-shut time*] twilight. The old explanation was that a cock-shut was a large net, used to snare woodcocks. Nares says that it was "stretched across a glade, and so suspended upon poles as to be easily drawn together" by a cord, called by Dame Juliana Berners, *Treatyse on Fysshynge*, 1496, a "cockeshote corde." It was generally spread in the evening twilight, when woodcocks came out to feed; and thus "cock-shut time" became a synonym for twilight. *New Eng. Dict.*, however, rejects this derivation, and explains the word as "perhaps the time when poultry go to rest and are shut up." Schmidt also suggests this sense. *New Eng. Dict.* quotes Florio, 1598: "*Cane e lupo Cock-shut*, or twilight, as when a man cannot discerne a dog from a wolfe." Steevens quotes several examples, *e.g.*, Jonson, *The Satyr*;—

"Mistress, this is only spite:
For you would not yesternight
Kiss him in the *cock-shut* light";

Middleton, *The Widow*, iii. 1: "Come, come away then: a fine *cock shoot* evening." Tollet, while recognising that there was a net known as a "cock-shut," regarded "cock-shoot" as implying the flight of the woodcock, and "cock-shoot time" as the time of evening at which that flight took place. *New Eng. Dict.* defines "cock shoot" as "a broad way or glade in a wood, through which woodcocks, etc., might dart or shoot so as to be caught by nets stretched across the opening," and admits this as an alternative derivation of the phrase. Probably the older dictionary makers applied the term for the glade to the net stretched across it.

Nor cheer of mind that I was wont to have.
Set it down. Is ink and paper ready?

Rat. It is, my lord.

K. Rich. Bid my guard watch. Leave me.
Ratcliff, about the mid of night come to my tent
And help to arm me. Leave me, I say.

[*Exeunt Ratcliff and the other attendants.*

Enter DERBY *to* RICHMOND *in his tent, Lords and others attending.*

Der. Fortune and victory sit on thy helm!

Richm. All comfort that the dark night can afford
Be to thy person, noble father-in-law!
Tell me, how fares our loving mother?

Der. I, by attorney, bless thee from thy mother,
Who prays continually for Richmond's good:
So much for that. The silent hours steal on,
And flaky darkness breaks within the east.
In brief, for so the season bids us be,
Prepare thy battle early in the morning,
And put thy fortune to the arbitrament
Of bloody strokes and mortal-staring war.

76. *Set*] *So, set* Capell; *There, set* Pope. 77, 78. *Leave me. Ratcliff*] *and leave me* Pope. 78. *mid*] *midst* Qq 6-8. 79. *arme me*] *arm me, Ratcliffe* Capell. *me*] omitted Ff 3, 4. *Leave me*] *Leave me now* Pope. *Exeunt . . .*] Camb.; *King Richard retires into his tent. Exeunt Ratcliffe and Catesby.* Malone; *Exit Ratliffe.* Qq; *Exit Ratclif.* Ff. aft. 79. *SCENE IV.* Pope (ed. 2). *Lords . . . attending.*] Camb. 80. *sit*] *set* Q 1. 83. *Tell me*] *Tell me, I pray* Collier. *fares*] *fares it with* Hanmer. *loving*] Qq 1, 2; *noble* Qq 3-8, Ff. *mother*] *mother now* Keightley conj. 86. *that. The*] Ff; *that the* Qq 1, 2. 91. *mortal-staring*] hyphened Steevens; *mortal-fearing* Capell; *mortal-scaring* Malone conj.; *mortal-stabbing* Staunton conj.

80. Pope's subdivision of this scene into separate little scenes is noted above, here and at the other dividing-points. In his first edition his scenes are numbered wrong. Scene iii. occurs twice, at v. iii. 1 and here; and the subsequent scenes are numbered accordingly (Scene iv. line 119; Scene v. line 224; Scene vi. line 272; Scene vii. v. iv. 1 and v. 5). The scene, however, in spite of its double character, is indivisible. The tents of the rivals are on either side of the stage; and the interest shifts from one to the other. When the ghosts appear, they obviously take their position between the two tents, which are thrown open in front to display the sleeping generals, and they address their remarks to each in turn.

87. *flaky darkness breaks*] *i.e.* darkness breaks into flakes of cloud, as the dawn rises. *New Eng. Dict.* quotes Sidney, Psalm cxxxv. 3: "In *flaky* mists, the reaking vapors rise." Mr. Craig thinks that Shakespeare may have derived the epithet from Golding's *Ovid*, iii. fol. 34 (*b*): "The *flakie* clouds all grieslie black."

91. *mortal-staring war*] Steevens

I, as I may—that which I would I cannot—
With best advantage will deceive the time,
And aid thee in this doubtful shock of arms:
But on thy side I may not be too forward,
Lest, being seen, thy brother, tender George,
Be executed in his father's sight.
Farewell: the leisure and the fearful time
Cuts off the ceremonious vows of love
And ample interchange of sweet discourse,
Which so long sund'red friends should dwell upon:
God give us leisure for these rites of love!
Once more, adieu: be valiant, and speed well!

Richm. Good lords, conduct him to his regiment:
I'll strive with troubled noise to take a nap,
Lest leaden slumber peise me down to-morrow,

96. *brother, tender*] *tender brother* Q 6. 97. *his*] *thy* Q 4. 98. *leisure*] *lack of leisure* Anon ap. Camb. 101. *sund'red*] *sundried* Qq 1, 2; *sundired* Qq 3, 4; *sundered* Qq 5, 6. 102. *rites*] Ff; *rights* Qq. 105. *with troubled noise*] Ff; *with troubled thoughts* Qq; *troubled with noise* Grant White.

explains "war that looks big, or stares fatally on its victim." Compare "grim-visag'd war," I. i. 9. The present epithet is rather harsh; but none of the many alternative readings is as simple and effective. Schmidt takes "mortal living" at IV. iv. 26 above as a similar epithet, and hyphens the two words. Mr. Craig ("Little Quarto" ed. p. 271) says "the idea is of War personified with a fierce, savage look in his eye," and gives several instances of the Elizabethan use of "stare." He parallels from Shakespeare "wall-ey'd wrath" (*King John*, IV. iii. 49) and *Othello*, V. ii. 37, 38.

93. More (ap. Holinshed, iii. 753) calls Stanley "this wilie fox." The reason which he here gives to Richmond is recognised by the chroniclers as the true motive of his actions.

96. *tender George*] Aldis Wright notes that George Stanley was a grown man. The epithet "tender" seems to be derived from the chroniclers' account of the end of the battle. Richard had given over Lord Strange in custody to the keepers of his tents, "which, when the field was doone, and their maister slaine, and proclamation made to know where *the child* was, they submitted themselves as prisoners to the lord Strange, and he gentlie received them, and brought them to the new proclaimed king." But the passage seems to indicate that "child" here is equivalent to "young nobleman," as in Spenser and the ballad quoted in *King Lear*, III. iv. 187, and that Shakespeare did not catch this meaning.

98. *leisure*] Compare line 239 below. The word means, here and in many other passages of Shakespeare, not "time to spare," but "the time at a man's disposal." Johnson's explanation, "want of leisure," is hardly necessary. For "leisure" in the special sense, see line 102 below.

105. *with troubled noise*] This seems to be the right reading. "Thoughts" may have arisen through an error in a stage MS. or on the stage itself. "Troubled" is for "troublesome." Compare I. ii. 39, III. vii. 189.

106. *leaden slumber*] Malone quotes *Lucrece*, 124. Compare *Julius Cæsar*, IV. iii. 268.

peise] weigh. The same word as "poise." Compare French *peser*, and see *King John*, II. i. 575. Compare

When I should mount with wings of victory.
Once more, good night, kind lords and gentlemen.
[*Exeunt all but Richmond.*
O Thou, whose captain I account myself,
Look on my forces with a gracious eye:
Put in their hands thy bruising irons of wrath,
That they may crush down with a heavy fall
The usurping helmets of our adversaries:
Make us thy ministers of chastisement,
That we may praise thee in thy victory!
To thee I do commend my watchful soul,
Ere I let fall the windows of mine eyes:
Sleeping and waking, O, defend me still! [*Sleeps.*

Enter the Ghost of PRINCE EDWARD, *son to Henry the Sixth.*

Ghost. [*To K. Rich.*] Let me sit heavy on thy soul to-morrow!
Think how thou stab'dst me in my prime of youth
At Tewkesbury: despair therefore, and die!
[*To Richm.*] Be cheerful, Richmond; for the wronged souls
Of butcher'd princes fight in thy behalf:
King Henry's issue, Richmond, comforts thee.

108. *Exeunt . . .*] *Exeunt. Manet Richmond* Ff; *Exunt* or *Exeunt.* Qq. 113. *helmets*] *helmet* Qq 6-8. 115. *thy*] Qq 3-5, Ff; *the* Qq 1, 2, 6-8. 118. *Sleeps.*] Ff; omitted Qq. aft. 118. *SCENE V. Between the Tents of Richard and Richmond: They sleeping.* Pope. *Prince*] Ff; *young Prince* Qq. *Henry*] *Harry* Q 1. *Sixth*] *sixt, to Ri.* Qq 1, 2. 120. *stab'dst*] Camb.; *stabst* Qq; *stab'st* Ff 1, 2; *stabb'st* Ff 3, 4; *stabb'dst* Rowe. 121. *despair therefore*] *therefore despair* Pope. 122. *Be . . . souls*] one line as Qq; *Be . . . Richmond, For . . . Soules* (two lines) Ff.

Merchant of Venice, III. ii. 22, and Mr. Pooler's note. Steevens quotes parallels from late sixteenth century authors; among them Christopher Middleton, *Legend of Humphrey, Duke of Gloucester*, 1600: "Nor was her schooles *peis'd* down with golden waights." The substantive "peise" is used to mean a weight. Compare Pecock, *Repressor*, 1455, i. 19: "certis neuere saue in late daies was eny clok telling þe houris of þe dai & nyȝt bi *peise* & bi stroke"; and see Nares, *s.v.*

111. *bruising irons*] *i.e.* maces, which were usually made of iron.

115. *thy victory*] the victory which is in truth thine. This seems the preferable reading.

118. The forms which Richard's visions took are not specified by the chroniclers. According to them, "it seemed to him being asleepe, that he did see diuerse images like terrible diuels, which pulled and haled him, not suffering him to take anie quiet or rest."

Enter the Ghost of HENRY THE SIXTH.

Ghost. [*To K. Rich.*] When I was mortal, my anointed body
By thee was punched full of deadly holes:
Think on the Tower, and me: despair, and die!
Harry the Sixth bids thee despair and die!
[*To Richm.*] Virtuous and holy, be thou conqueror!
Harry, that prophesied thou shouldst be king,
Doth comfort thee in thy sleep: live and flourish!

Enter the Ghost of CLARENCE.

Ghost. [*To K. Rich.*] Let me sit heavy in thy soul to-morrow!
I, that was wash'd to death with fulsome wine,
Poor Clarence, by thy guile betray'd to death—
To-morrow in the battle think on me,
And fall thy edgeless sword: despair, and die!
[*To Richm.*] Thou offspring of the house of Lancaster,
The wronged heirs of York do pray for thee:
Good angels guard thy battle! live, and flourish!

Enter the Ghosts of RIVERS, GREY, *and* VAUGHAN.

Ghost of Riv. [*To K. Rich.*] Let me sit heavy in thy soul to-morrow—
Rivers, that died at Pomfret! despair, and die!

Ghost of Grey. [*To K. Rich.*] Think upon Grey, and let thy soul despair!

Ghost of Vaughan. [*To K. Rich.*] Think upon Vaughan, and, with guilty fear,
Let fall thy lance: despair, and die!

126. *deadly*] Q 1; omitted Qq 2-8, Ff. 128. *Harry*] *Henry* Ff 2-4. 131. *in thy sleep: live*] *in sleep: live thou* Rowe. 132. *sit*] *set* Q 1. *in*] Qq 1-4, Ff; *on* Qq 5, 6, 8; *one* Q 7 (and so 140). 133. *with*] *in* Qq 3, 4. 140. *Ghost of Riv.* [*To K. Rich.*] *Riu.* Qq 3-8, Ff; *King.* Qq 1, 2. 144. *lance*] *hurtless lance* Capell; *pointless lance* Collier MS. *despair*] *Richard, despair* Pope.

132. *in thy soul*] Compare *Richard II.* I. ii. 50.

133. *fulsome*] cloying, especially applicable to the thick, sweet wine in which Clarence's body was thrown. *New Eng. Dict.* cites Harrison, *Description of England*, ii. 6: "Our ale is more thicke, *fulsome*, and of no continuance." Steevens objected that Clarence was dead before he was thrown into the wine, so that he could hardly be said to find the wine "fulsome," or to be "washed to death."

136. *fall*] let fall, drop. See note on I. iii. 353 above. The line is repeated at line 164.

144. *lance*] Perhaps some epithet has dropped out, like those suggested by Capell and Collier.

All. [*To Richmond.*] Awake, and think our wrongs in Richard's bosom
Will conquer him! Awake, and win the day!

Enter the Ghost of HASTINGS.

Ghost. [*To K. Rich.*] Bloody and guilty, guiltily awake,
And in a bloody battle end thy days!
Think on Lord Hastings: despair, and die!
[*To Richm.*] Quiet untroubled soul, awake, awake!
Arm, fight, and conquer, for fair England's sake!

Enter the Ghosts of the two young PRINCES.

Ghosts. [*To K. Rich.*] Dream on thy cousins smothered in the Tower:
Let us be lead within thy bosom, Richard,
And weigh thee down to ruin, shame, and death!
Thy nephews' souls bid thee despair and die!
[*To Richm.*] Sleep, Richmond, sleep in peace, and wake in joy:
Good angels guard thee from the boar's annoy!
Live, and beget a happy race of kings!
Edward's unhappy sons do bid thee flourish.

Enter the Ghost of LADY ANNE.

Ghost. [*To K. Rich.*] Richard, thy wife, that wretched Anne thy wife,
That never slept a quiet hour with thee,
Now fills thy sleep with perturbations:
To-morrow in the battle think on me,
And fall thy edgeless sword: despair, and die!

145. *Awake . . . bosom*] one line as Qq; *Awake, And . . . Bosome* (two lines) Ff. aft. 146-151. *Enter . . . sake!*] arranged as Qq 3-8, Ff; Qq 1, 2 transpose with 152-59. 149. *despair*] *and despair* Pope; *so despair* Collier MS. 150. *Quiet . . . awake*] one line as Qq; *Quiet . . . soule, Awake, awake* Ff. 152. *Dream . . . Tower*] one line as Qq; *Dreame . . . Cousins Smothered . . . Tower* (two lines) Ff. 153. *lead*] Q 1; *laid* or *layd* Qq 2-8, Ff. 155. *souls bid*] Qq, F 4; *soule bids* Ff 1-3. 156. *Sleep . . . joy*] one line as Qq; *Sleepe Richmond Sleepe . . . Ioy* (two lines) Ff. aft 159. *Lady Anne*] Camb.; *Ladie Anne his wife* Qq 1, 2; *Queene Anne his wife.* Qq 3-8; *Anne his wife.* Ff. 160. *Richard . . . Anne thy wife*] one line as Qq; *Richard, thy Wife, That . . . Anne thy Wife* (two lines) Ff. 162. *perturbations*] *preturbations* Q 1.

[*To Richm.*] Thou quiet soul, sleep thou a quiet sleep:
Dream of success and happy victory!
Thy adversary's wife doth pray for thee.

Enter the Ghost of BUCKINGHAM.

Ghost. [*To K. Rich.*] The first was I that help'd thee to the crown;
The last was I that felt thy tyranny:
O! in the battle think on Buckingham,
And die in terror of thy guiltiness!
Dream on, dream on, of bloody deeds and death:
Fainting, despair: despairing, yield thy breath!
[*To Richm.*] I died for hope ere I could lend thee aid:
But cheer thy heart, and be not thou dismay'd!
God and good angels fight on Richmond's side;
And Richard fall in height of all his pride!

The Ghosts vanish. King Richard starts out of his dream.

K. Rich. Give me another horse! bind up my wounds!
Have mercy, Jesu!—Soft! I did but dream.
O coward conscience, how dost thou afflict me!

165. *Thou . . . sleep*] one line as Qq; *Thou . . . soule, Sleepe . . . sleepe* (two lines) Ff. 168. *The first . . . crown*] one line as Qq; *The first was I That . . . Crowne* (two lines) Ff. 174. *I died . . . aid*] one line as Qq; *I dyed . . . hope Ere . . . Ayde* (two lines) Ff. *for hope*] *for holpe* Theobald conj.; *forsoke* Hanmer; *forholpe* Steevens conj.; *fore-done* Tyrwhitt conj. 177. *fall*] Ff; *fals* Qq. aft. 177. *The Ghosts vanish.*] Rowe, Camb.

174. *for hope*] The meaning may be, "I died *for hoping* to give you aid, before I could actually give it." This is the interpretation suggested by Steevens. Aldis Wright's explanation, "I died as regards hope," is equally good, if not better. In that case the passage means, "Before I could give thee aid, I was dead so far as hope was concerned; but be not *thou* without hope." There is also much to be said for Steevens' conjecture "forholpe," and for the whole idea that "for —" is here a privative prefix. The passage cited by Dyce from Greene, *James IV.* 1598, v. 6. (Dyce, 217): "Some then will yield when I am dead *for hope*," is, however, in favour of the received text and of Wright's explanation.

178. The speech, full of self-questioning argument, which follows, is perhaps the weakest passage in the play. It seems to mark a stage in Shakespeare's development at which he was unequal to the psychological skill which such a speech required; and it may stand out as a conspicuous failure, because it demanded more from him than any other speech in the play. The attempt to portray the king's mingled emotions is thoroughly in keeping with the statement of the chronicles, that the "strange vision not so suddenlie strake his heart with a sudden feare, but it stuffed his head and troubled his mind with manie busie and dreadfull imaginations." The phrase "coward conscience" (line 180) recalls *Hamlet*, III. i. 83, part of a speech which is a triumph in the very field in which this is a first effort.

The lights burn blue. It is now dead midnight.
Cold fearful drops stand on my trembling flesh.
What do I fear? myself? there 's none else by:
Richard loves Richard; that is, I am I.
Is there a murderer here? No. Yes, I am.
Then fly. What, from myself? Great reason: why?
Lest I revenge. What, myself upon myself?
Alack, I love myself. Wherefore? for any good
That I myself have done unto myself?
O, no! alas, I rather hate myself
For hateful deeds committed by myself.
I am a villain: yet I lie, I am not.
Fool, of thyself speak well: fool, do not flatter.
My conscience hath a thousand several tongues,
And every tongue brings in a several tale,
And every tale condemns me for a villain.
Perjury, perjury, in the high'st degree;
Murder, stern murder, in the dir'st degree;
All several sins, all us'd in each degree,

181. *It is now*] Q 1; *It is not* Qq 2-8, Ff; *Is it not* Rowe. 183-204. *What . . . to myself?*] Ritson proposed to put in margin. 183. *What do I fear? myself?*] *What doe I feare my selfe?* Qq 2-8; *What? do I feare my selfe?* Ff. 184. *Richard . . . I am I*] omitted Pope. *am*] *and* Q 1. 186. *fly.*] *flye?* Ff 2-4. *reason: why?*] Ff; *reason whie?* Q 1; *reason why?* Q 2; *reason why*, Qq 3-8. 186-93. *Then fly . . . flatter*] Pope put in margin. 187. *What*] omitted Capell. 188. *Alack*] omitted Pope. 189. *I*] omitted Qq 6-8. 197. *Perjury, perjury*] Qq 1, 2; *Periurie* Qq 3-8, Ff; *Perjury, foul perjury* Collier MS. *the*] omitted Pope.

181. *The lights burn blue*] Brand, *Popular Antiquities*, iii. 69, quotes Grose: "If, during the time of an apparition, there is a lighted candle in the room, it will burn extremely blue: this is so universally acknowledged, that many eminent philosophers have busied themselves in accounting for it, without once doubting the truth of the fact." Steevens quotes Lyly, *Galathea*, 1592: "I thought there was some spirit in it because it burnt so blue; for my mother would often tell me when the candle *burnt blue*, there was some ill spirit in the house." Compare *Julius Cæsar*, IV. iii. 275.

now] This is one of several cases where the editor of F 1 seems, at this point in the play, to have been without MS. guidance, and to have relied on the later Qq alone. Another example follows at line 183. In these cases Q 1 supplies us with the right reading.

184. Pope was perhaps justified in rejecting this feeble line to the margin. But the words "I am I" bring out, in Richard's extremity, his unfailing belief in the doctrine "I am myself alone," already enunciated at *3 Henry VI*. v. vi. 83.

186. *Great reason: why?*] Ff, whose emendation at line 183 was less successful, seem here to have hit upon the right reading. For another emendation of Ff, in default of MS. authority, see line 200 below.

Throng to the bar, crying all, "Guilty! guilty!"
I shall despair. There is no creature loves me;
And, if I die, no soul will pity me:
Nay, wherefore should they, since that I myself
Find in myself no pity to myself?
Methought the souls of all that I had murder'd
Came to my tent, and every one did threat
To-morrow's vengeance on the head of Richard.

Enter RATCLIFF.

Rat. My lord!
K. Rich. 'Zounds! who is there?
Rat. My lord, 'tis I. The early village-cock
Hath twice done salutation to the morn;
Your friends are up, and buckle on their armour.
K. Rich. O Ratcliff, I have dream'd a fearful dream.
What thinkest thou? will our friends prove all true?
Rat. No doubt, my lord.
K. Rich. O Ratcliff, I fear, I fear!
Rat. Nay, good my lord, be not afraid of shadows.
K. Rich. By the apostle Paul, shadows to-night
Have struck more terror to the soul of Richard
Than can the substance of ten thousand soldiers
Armed in proof, and led by shallow Richmond!

200. *Throng*] Qq 1, 2; *Throng all* Qq 3-8, Ff. *to the*] *to th'* Ff. *crying all*] *all crying* Pope. 201. *shall*] *will* Pope. 202. *will*] Qq 1, 2; *shall* Qq 3-8, Ff. 203, 204. *Nay . . . to myself?*] Pope put in margin. 205. *had*] Q 1, Ff; omitted Qq 2-6; *have* Qq 7, 8. 206. *Came*] *Came all* Qq 3-6. 209. *'Zounds! who is*] Qq; *Who's* Ff. 210. *My lord*] Qq 7, 8; *Ratcliffe, my Lord* Qq 1-6, Ff. 213-15. *O Ratcliff . . . my lord*] Qq; omitted Ff. 214. *thinkest*] Capell, Camb.; *thinkst* Qq. 215. *O*] omitted Pope. *O . . . fear.*] Collier replaces by 213.

209. *'Zounds*] For Ff reading compare note on I. iv. 117 above.

210. *My lord*] I have ventured to leave out the unnecessary "Ratcliff" at the beginning of the line, which was most likely a printer's error, originating in Q 1 and emended in no following edition until Q 7. Had any MS. been to hand at this point, the editor of F 1 would probably have made this correction.

213. The chroniclers say that, to avoid any appearance of fear of his enemies (see lines 217-220), the king "recited and declared to his familiar freends in the morning his wonderfull vision and fearefull dream." The omission of lines 213, 214 in Ff is obviously due to the printer, who mistook the "O Ratcliff" in the latter half of line 215 for that at the beginning of line 213, and proceeded accordingly. As the passage stands in Ff, Ratcliff has not sufficient information to justify his words in line 216.

'Tis not yet near day. Come, go with me;
Under our tents I'll play the eaves-dropper,
To hear if any mean to shrink from me. [*Exeunt.*

Enter the Lords to RICHMOND, *sitting in his tent.*

Lords. Good morrow, Richmond!
Richm. Cry mercy, lords and watchful gentlemen,
That you have ta'en a tardy sluggard here.
Lords. How have you slept, my lord?
Richm. The sweetest sleep and fairest-boding dreams
That ever enter'd in a drowsy head,
Have I since your departure had, my lords.
Methought their souls, whose bodies Richard murder'd,
Came to my tent and cried on victory:
I promise you, my heart is very jocund
In the remembrance of so fair a dream.
How far into the morning is it, lords?
Lords. Upon the stroke of four.
Richm. Why, then 'tis time to arm and give direction.

His Oration to his Soldiers.

More than I have said, loving countrymen,
The leisure and enforcement of the time

221. *'Tis*] Qq, Ff; *It is* Pope. 222. *eaves-dropper*] F 4; *ease dropper* Q 1; *ewse dropper* Q 2; *ewse-dropper* Q 3; *eawse-dropper* Q 4; *ewese-dropper* Qq 5-8; *Ease-dropper* Ff 1-3. 223. *hear*] Qq 3-8, Ff; *see* Qq 1, 2. *mean to shrink*] *means to shrinke* Q 4; *man shrinks* Ff 3, 4. aft. 223. SCENE VI. Warburton. Pope (ed. 1) misprinted SCENE V.; (ed. 2) misprinted SCENE IV. *sitting . . . tent*] Ff; omitted Qq. 224. *Lords.*] Qq; *Richm.* Ff. 225. *Cry mercy*] *Cry you mercy* Ff 2-4; *I cry you mercy* Pope. 228. *The . . . dreams*] one line as Qq; *The . . . sleepe, And . . . Dreames* (two lines) Ff. *fairest-boding*] hyphened Theobald. 232. *cried on victory*] *cried out, Victory* Pope; *cried On! Victory* Warburton. 233. *heart*] Ff; *soule* Qq. 237. *Arms and comes forth.* Capell. aft. 237. *His . . . Soldiers.*] *To his Troops; who now gather about the Tent.* Capell.

226. *Cry mercy*] The full form is "I cry you mercy": see I. iii. 235 above. The pronoun is omitted, as when we say "Thank you."

231, 232. Richmond's dreams are a dramatic interpolation which find no warrant in the chroniclers' accounts.

238. "When the earle of Richmond knew by his foreriders that the king was so neere imbatelled, he rode about his armie from ranke to ranke, & from wing to wing, giuing comfortable words to all men, and that finished (being armed at all peeces, sauing his helmet) mounted on a little hill, so that all his people might see and behold him perfectlie, to their great reioicing" (Holinshed, iii. 757).

Forbids to dwell upon: yet remember this.
God and our good cause fight upon our side;
The prayers of holy saints and wronged souls,
Like high-rear'd bulwarks, stand before our faces.
Richard except, those whom we fight against
Had rather have us win than him they follow:
For what is he they follow? truly, gentlemen,
A bloody tyrant and a homicide;
One rais'd in blood, and one in blood establish'd;
One that made means to come by what he hath,
And slaughter'd those that were the means to help him;
A base foul stone, made precious by the foil
Of England's chair, where he is falsely set;
One that hath ever been God's enemy.
Then, if you fight against God's enemy,
God will in justice ward you as his soldiers;
If you do sweat to put a tyrant down,
You sleep in peace, the tyrant being slain;
If you do fight against your country's foes,
Your country's fat shall pay your pains the hire;
If you do fight in safeguard of your wives,
Your wives shall welcome home the conquerors;
If you do free your children from the sword,

240. *upon*] *on* Pope. 244. *Richard except*,] Qq 3-8, Ff; *Richard, except* Qq 1, 2. 250. *slaughter'd*] *slandered* Q 4. 251. *foil*] Qq 1, 2; *soile* Qq 3-5; *soyle* Qq 6-8, Ff 1-3; *soyl* F 4. 256. *sweat*] Qq 1, 2; *sweare* Qq 3-8, Ff.

247. *homicide*] The word is taken from Holinshed: "an *homicide* and murtherer of his owne bloud or progenie."

249. *made means*] Compare line 40 above. Here a sinister meaning is given to the phrase.

251. *foil*] A thin leaf of metal placed under a precious stone to relieve its brilliancy. See Drayton, *Eng. Her. Epp.*, Mary to Brandon:—

"Which [a precious stone] then appears more orient and more bright,
Having a *foil* whereon to show its light."

Metaphors from the jewel and its foil are common. Compare *Richard II*. I. iii. 265-67; Beaumont and Fletcher, *Faithful Shepherdess*, i. 3:—

"Yet, if I may believe what others say,
My face has *foile* enough";

Chapman, etc., *Eastward Ho*, act iv.: "I will charge 'hem and recharge 'hem, rather than authority should want *foil* to set it off." The history of the reading here is obvious. See note on "now," line 181 above.

255. *ward*] protect. Q 8 mistakenly printed "reward."

256. *sweat*] Holinshed has "Therefore labour for your gaine, & *sweat* for your right," which is fairly conclusive as to the right reading.

Your children's children quits it in your age.
Then, in the name of God and all these rights,
Advance your standards, draw your willing swords!
For me, the ransom of my bold attempt
Shall be this cold corpse on the earth's cold face;
But, if I thrive, the gain of my attempt
The least of you shall share his part thereof.
Sound drums and trumpets boldly and cheerfully;
God and Saint George! Richmond and victory!

[*Exeunt.*

Re-enter KING RICHARD, RATCLIFF, *Attendants and Forces.*

K. Rich. What said Northumberland as touching Richmond?
Rat. That he was never trained up in arms.
K. Rich. He said the truth. And what said Surrey then?
Rat. He smil'd and said "The better for our purpose."
K. Rich. He was in the right; and so indeed it is.

[*The clock striketh.*

Tell the clock there. Give me a calendar.
Who saw the sun to-day?
Rat. Not I, my lord.
K. Rich. Then he disdains to shine; for, by the book,
He should have brav'd the east an hour ago:

263. *quits*] Qq, Ff; *quit* Pope. 270. *boldly*] *bold* Staunton. *and*] omitted Pope. 271. *Exeunt.*] *Shouts &c., and Exeunt.* Capell; omitted Qq, Ff. aft. 271. *SCENE VII.* Pope. *Re-enter* . . .] Camb.; *Enter King Richard, Rat. &c.* Qq; *Enter King Richard, Ratcliffe, and Catesby.* Ff. 276. *in the*] *i' th'* Pope. *The clock striketh.*] after *there* in 277 Qq, Ff. 277, 278. *Tell . . . my lord*] arranged as Pope, Camb.; *Tell . . . there. Give . . . to day? Rat. Not I my lord.* (3 lines) Qq, Ff.

263. *quits*] There is no reason for altering the old plural, which occurs in all the printed copies.

265. *Advance*] raise. Compare I. ii. 40 above. Holinshed has, "And therefore, in the name of God and St. George, let euerie man couragiouslie *aduance* foorth his standard!" Compare Milton, *Paradise Lost*, v. 588: "Ten thousand thousand Ensignes high *advanc'd*."

267. Richmond's words in Holinshed are: "You shall find me this daie rather a dead carrion vpon the cold ground, than a free prisoner on a carpet in a ladies chamber."

277. *Tell the clock*] Count the strokes of the clock. Compare "as one tells twenty," I. iv. 118 above, and see *The Tempest*, II. i. 289.

279. *the book*] the calendar which he has just consulted.

A black day will it be to somebody.
Ratcliff!
Rat. My lord?
K. Rich. The sun will not be seen to-day;
The sky doth frown and lour upon our army.
I would these dewy tears were from the ground.
Not shine to-day? Why, what is that to me
More than to Richmond? for the self-same heaven
That frowns on me looks sadly upon him.

Enter NORFOLK.

Nor. Arm, arm, my lord! the foe vaunts in the field.
K. Rich. Come, bustle, bustle! Caparison my horse.
Call up Lord Stanley, bid him bring his power.
I will lead forth my soldiers to the plain,
And thus my battle shall be ordered:
My foreward shall be drawn out all in length,
Consisting equally of horse and foot;
Our archers shall be placed in the midst:
John Duke of Norfolk, Thomas Earl of Surrey,
Shall have the leading of this foot and horse.
They thus directed, we will follow

281, 282. *A black . . . somebody. Ratcliff*] arranged as Johnson, etc.; *A blacke . . . some bodie Rat.* (one line) Qq 1-6; *A blacke . . . somebody. Ratcliffe.* (one line) Ff; *A black . . . somebody—Ratcliff,—* (one line) Capell. 288. *looks*] *looke* Q 6. aft. 288. *Enter Norfolk.*] *Re-enter Norfolk.* Camb. 294. *shall be drawn out all*] Q 1; *shall be drawne* Qq 2-8, Ff; *battel shall be drawn* Hanmer. 298. *this*] Qq 1, 2; *the* Qq 3-8, Ff. 299. *we*] *we ourself* Pope. *follow*] *follow them* Collier MS.

281. *A black day . . . somebody*] Mr. Craig points out that this seems to be a proverbial expression, and compares *2 Henry IV.* v. iv. 14. See also *3 Henry VI.* v. vi. 85: "I will sort a pitchy *day* for thee."

285. *from*] away from, off. Compare *Antony and Cleopatra*, II. vi. 30, and see note on III. v. 32 above.

290. *Caparison*] The caparison of a horse was, strictly speaking, the rich covering or housing which was worn by the spare horse at a battle or tournament (Demmin, *Arms and Armour*, English translation, 1894, p. 349). The armed horse was often covered with a caparison of cloth.

292-301. Shakespeare follows Holinshed closely. Richard, "bringing all his men out of their campe into the plaine, ordered his fore-ward in a maruellous length, in which he appointed both horsmen and footmen . . . and in the fore-front he placed the archers like a strong fortified trench or bulworke. Ouer this battell was capteine, Iohn, duke of Norffolke, with whome was Thomas earle of Surrie, his sonne. After this long vant-gard, followed king Richard himselfe with a strong companie of chosen and approued men of warre, hauing horssemen for wings on both sides of his battell."

In the main battle, whose puissance on either side
Shall be well winged with our chiefest horse.
This, and Saint George to boot! What think'st thou,
Norfolk?

Nor. A good direction, warlike sovereign.
This found I on my tent this morning.
[*He showeth him a paper.*

K. Rich. [*Reads.*] "*Jockey of Norfolk, be not so bold,*
For Dickon thy master is bought and sold."
A thing devised by the enemy!
Go, gentlemen, every man unto his charge.
Let not our babbling dreams affright our souls:
Conscience is but a word that cowards use,
Devis'd at first to keep the strong in awe;
Our strong arms be our conscience, swords our law!
March on, join bravely, let us to 't pell-mell,
If not to heaven, then hand in hand to hell!

His Oration to his Army.

What shall I say more than I have inferr'd?
Remember whom you are to cope withal;
A sort of vagabonds, rascals, and runaways,

300. *whose puissance*] *which* Pope. 301. *well winged*] hyphened Ff. 302. *This . . . Norfolk*] one line as Qq; *This . . . boote. What . . . Norfolke* (two lines) Ff. *boot*] *bootes* Qq 1, 2. *think'st thou, Norfolk*] Ff; *thinkst thou Norffolke* Q 1; *thinkest thou Nor.* Qq 2-5; *thinkest thou not* Qq 6-8. 304. *This*] *This paper* Pope. *He . . . paper*] Qq; omitted Ff; *Giving a Scrowl.* Rowe. 305. *K. Rich.* [*Reads.*] Capell, Camb. *so*] *too* Capell. 307. *A thing*] *King. A thing* Qq, Ff. 308. *every man unto*] Qq; *euery man to* Ff; *go each man to* Pope. 310. *Conscience is but*] Qq 1, 2; *Conscience is* Qq 3-8; *For Conscience is* Ff. aft. 313. *His . . . Army*] Qq; omitted Ff; *turning to his Troops.* Capell. 317. *rascals, and*] *rascals* Ff 2-4; *of rascals* Pope.

302. *Saint George to boot!*] Saint George to aid us as well. On "boot" see note at IV. iv. 65 above.

303. *direction*] order of battle. Compare line 16 above.

304. *morning*] probably a trisyllable, like the older form "morweninge."

305. *so bold*] The line in the chroniclers runs: "Iacke of Norffolke be not too bold"; and Q 6, perhaps in accordance with this version (which is certainly the better), or, which is quite as likely, by a press error, altered from "so" to "to."

313. *pell-mell*] So *King Lear*, IV. vi. 119, and see Mr. Craig's note (Arden ed. 1901, p. 198).

315. *I have inferr'd*] *i.e.* the arguments I have stated already.

317. *sort*] number, company. "Ye see further how a companie of traitors, theeues, outlawes, and runnagates of our owne nation, be aiders and partakers of his feat and enterprise." See

A scum of Bretons, and base lackey peasants,
Whom their o'er-cloyed country vomits forth
To desperate adventures and assur'd destruction.
You sleeping safe, they bring to you unrest;
You having lands and blest with beauteous wives,
They would restrain the one, distain the other.
And who doth lead them but a paltry fellow,
Long kept in Bretagne at our mother's cost?
A milk-sop, one that never in his life
Felt so much cold as over shoes in snow!
Let's whip these stragglers o'er the seas again,
Lash hence these overweening rags of France,
These famish'd beggars, weary of their lives,
Who, but for dreaming on this fond exploit,
For want of means, poor rats, had hang'd themselves!
If we be conquer'd, let men conquer us,
And not these bastard Bretons, whom our fathers

318. *Bretons*] Capell, Camb.; *Brittains* or *Brittaines* Qq, Ff. 320. *adventures*] *ventures* Capell. *assur'd*] omitted Pope. 321. *to you*] Q 1; *you to* Qq 2-8, Ff. 323. *restrain*] *distrain* Hanmer (fr. Warburton). 325. *Bretagne*] Hanmer, Camb.; *Brittaine* Qq; *Britaine* Ff 1, 2; *Britain* Ff 3, 4. *our mother's*] *his mother's* Theobald conj., Pope; *our brother's* Capell. 326. *milk-sop*] Ff 3, 4; *milkesopt* Qq 1-5; *milkesope* Q 6; *milke-sop* Ff 1, 2, Qq 7, 8. 334. *these*] *those* Rowe. *bastard Bretons*] Capell; *bastard Brittains* (or *Brittaines*, etc.) Qq, Ff 1, 2; *bastard-Britains* Ff 3, 4; *bastard-Britons* Pope.

Richard II. IV. i. 246. Compare Berners' *Froissart*, i. 146: "We are here within, a small *sort* of knights and squires"; A. M., *Captivity of John Fox*, ap. Hakluyt (Arber, *Eng. Garner*, i. 206): "Which the same John Fox seeing, delivered unto them a *sort* of files, which he had gathered together for this purpose."

318. Holinshed has "What a number of beggerlie Britans and faint-hearted Frenchmen be with him arriued to destroie us, our wiues and children." The epithet "lackey" may be intended to convey an Englishman's contempt for Frenchmen.

323. *restrain*] *i.e.* hold back from us.

distain] stain, defile. So *Troilus and Cressida*, I. iii. 241.

325. *our mother's*] Holinshed (ed. 2) has: "brought up by my *moothers* meanes, and mine, like a captiue in a close cage, in the court of Francis duke of Britaine." Halle and Holinshed (ed. 1) have "my brothers meanes," which is nearer the truth. Malone explains "our brother" as Charles the Bold of Burgundy, who was Richard's brother-in-law. Here Shakespeare has copied his original too closely. The phrase which follows, "and neuer saw armie, nor was exercised in martiall affaires: by reason whereof he neither can, nor is able by his owne will or experience to guide or rule an hoast," was probably the origin of the statement (line 273) which Shakespeare quotes as coming from Northumberland. "Milk-sop" in line 326 is the term of contempt in Holinshed: compare "homicide," line 247. Aldis Wright compares Iago's contempt for Cassio, *Othello*, I. i. 20-27.

326. *milk-sop*] Compare *1 Henry IV*. II. iii. 35, 36.

Have in their own land beaten, bobb'd, and thump'd,
And in record left them the heirs of shame.
Shall these enjoy our lands? lie with our wives?
Ravish our daughters? [*Drum afar off.*] Hark! I hear
their drum.
Fight, gentlemen of England! fight, bold yeomen!
Draw, archers, draw your arrows to the head!
Spur your proud horses hard, and ride in blood!
Amaze the welkin with your broken staves!

Enter a Messenger.

What says Lord Stanley? will he bring his power?

Mess. My lord, he doth deny to come.

K. Rich. Off with his son George's head!

336. *in*] Qq 1, 2; *on* Qq 3-8, Ff. 338. *Ravish . . . drum*] one line as Qq: *Rauish . . . daughters? Hearke, . . . Drumme* (two lines) Ff. 339. *Fight*] Qq 1, 2, 8; *Right* Qq 3-7. *bold*] Q 1; *boldly* Qq 2-8, Ff. aft. 343. *Enter a Messenger.*] Ff; omitted Qq. 344. *come*] *come to you* Capell. 345. *Off*] *Off instantly* Hanmer.

335. *bobb'd*] As Aldis Wright points out, to "bob" is much the same as to beat or thump, with an additional spice of contempt in the word. See Mr. Deighton's note on *Troilus and Cressida*, II. i. 76, and Mr. Craig's note in "Little Quarto" ed. of this play, pp. 289, 290. A very common meaning of the word is "to cheat or fool": compare *Othello*, V. i. 16; *Troilus and Cressida*, III. i. 75; Fletcher and Massinger, *Spanish Curate*, 1622, V. 2:—

"Though I were angry yesterday
with you all,
And very angry, for methought ye
bobb'd me";

and "Ye shall be *bobb'd*, gentlemen." For the substantive "bob" and the phrase "to give the *bob*" see *As You Like It*, II. vii. 55; Greene, *Menaphon* (Arber, 85): "He smiled in his sleeue to see howe kindely hee had giuen her the *bobbe*"; Fletcher, *Wit without Money*, V. 1: "These are fine *bobs*, i' faith!"

342. *Amaze the welkin*] Frighten the sky, *i.e.* lest it be hit by the broken splinters of the lance-shafts. The conceit is explained by Malone's quotation from W. Smith, *The Hector of Germany, or The Palsgrave*, 1615: "Spears flew in splinters half the way to heaven," and by *Coriolanus*, IV. v. 115. Compare *King John*, V. ii. 172.

343-47. Richard had sent a pursuivant to Stanley, bidding him bring his company forward, "which thing if he refused to doo, he sware, by Christes passion, that he would strike off his sonnes head before he dined. The lord Stanleie answered the purseuant that, if the king did so, he had more sonnes alive; and, as to come to him, he was not then so determined. When king Richard heard this answer, he commanded the lord Strange incontinent to be beheaded: which was at that verie same season, when both the armies had sight ech of other." Richard's councillors, however, advised him to spare Lord Strange till after the battle. "So (as God would) king Richard brake his holie oth, and the lord was delivered to the keepers of the kings tents, to be kept as prisoner." The abrupt order in line 345 may have suggested Cibber's famous addition after IV. iv. 534 above, "Off with his head. So much for Buckingham."

Nor. My lord, the enemy is past the marsh:
After the battle let George Stanley die.

K. Rich. A thousand hearts are great within my bosom.
Advance our standards, set upon our foes;
Our ancient word of courage, fair Saint George,
Inspire us with the spleen of fiery dragons!
Upon them! Victory sits on our helms.

[*Exeunt.*

SCENE IV.—*Another part of the field.*

Alarum: excursions. Enter NORFOLK *and forces fighting; to him* CATESBY.

Cates. Rescue, my lord of Norfolk, rescue, rescue!
The king enacts more wonders than a man,
Daring an opposite to every danger:
His horse is slain, and all on foot he fights,
Seeking for Richmond in the throat of death.
Rescue, fair lord, or else the day is lost!

350. *fair*] *fare* Q 2. 352. *helms*] Qq 1, 2, 4, 8; *helpes* Qq 3, 5, 6, 7, Ff. *Exeunt*] Rowe; *Drums, and Exeunt.* Capell; omitted Qq, Ff.

Scene IV.

SCENE IV.] Capell; *SCENE VIII.* Pope; scene continued Ff. *Another . . . field.*] Capell, Camb. *Enter Norfolk . . .*] Capell, Camb.; *Enter Catesbie.* Qq, Ff. 1. *Rescue . . . rescue*] one line as Qq; *Rescue . . . Norfolke, Rescue, rescue* (two lines) Ff.

346. A "great marish" separated both armies. Richmond, in his advance, left this on his right; and thus put the sun at his back, and in the faces of his enemies. This statement of the chroniclers seems to imply that the subject of lines 278-88 above is due to the invention of the dramatist. "When king Richard saw the earles companie was passed the marish, he did command with all hast to set vpon them."

351. *spleen of fiery dragons*] Compare *King John*, II. I. 68. Mr. Craig remarks that the expression "to fight like a dragon" seems to have been proverbial, and refers to *Coriolanus*, IV. vii. 23.

352. *helms*] The variation in Ff is worth noticing. Apart from the fact that first-hand MS. authority was evidently wanting, and that copies of neither of the earliest quartos were available, it is clear that Q 4 was not referred to by the editor. Q 3 or Q 5 was thus the alternative copy of the play which he must have used in seeking earlier authority for the readings of Q 6.

Scene IV.

3. *Daring an opposite*] Malone quotes Marston, *Antonio and Mellida*: "Myself, myself, will dare all *opposites*." An "opposite" is an enemy, adversary, as *Twelfth Night*, III. iv. 293; *King Lear*, V. iii. 42. Tyrwhitt, who proposed to read "Daring and opposite," probably regarded the phrase as meaning "daring in his opposition to every danger." Wherever Richard meets an opposite on the field, he dares him *à l'outrance*.

Alarums. Enter KING RICHARD.

K. Rich. A horse! a horse! my kingdom for a horse!
Cates. Withdraw, my lord; I'll help you to a horse.
K. Rich. Slave, I have set my life upon a cast,
And I will stand the hazard of the die!
I think there be six Richmonds in the field;
Five have I slain to-day instead of him.
A horse! a horse! my kingdom for a horse!

[*Exeunt.*

SCENE V.—*Another part of the field.*

Alarum. Enter KING RICHARD *and* RICHMOND; *they fight.* KING RICHARD *is slain. Retreat and flourish. Re-enter* RICHMOND, DERBY *bearing the crown, with divers other lords.*

Richm. God and your arms be prais'd, victorious friends!
The day is ours; the bloody dog is dead.
Der. Courageous Richmond, well hast thou acquit thee.

7. *Alarums.*] Ff; omitted Qq. 13. *Exeunt.*] Theobald; omitted Qq, Ff.

Scene V.

SCENE V.] Dyce; Ff, Pope, Capell, etc., continue scene. *Another . . . field.*] Dyce, Camb. *Retreat and flourish.*] Ff; *then retrait being sounded* Qq. *Re-enter Richmond*] Camb.; *Enter Richmond* Qq, Ff. 1. *God . . . friends*] one line as Qq; *God . . . Armes Be . . . Friends* (two lines) Ff. 3. *Der.*] *Stan.* Pope. 3, 4. *Courageous . . . royalty*] two lines as Qq; *Couragious Richmond, Well . . . Loe Heere . . . Royalties* (three lines) Ff.

13. The chronicles contain no mention of the loss of Richard's horse. This famous line was possibly suggested by the statement that "when the losse of the battell was imminent and apparant, they brought to him a swift and a light horsse, to conueie him awaie." The "six Richmonds in the field" are also without authority. Richard knew the earl at once "by certeine demonstrations and tokens, which he had learned and knowen of others that were able to giue him full information." He put spurs to his horse, and, riding out of his part of the host, "like a hungrie lion ran with speare in rest toward him." To make his way to his enemy, he killed Sir William Brandon and overthrew Sir John Cheney. The single combat which followed was stopped by the arrival of Sir William Stanley's reinforcements. These surrounded and overpowered Richard, isolating him from his army; and "he himself, manfullie fighting in the middle of his enimies, was slaine." Steevens mentions various imitations of Richard's cry for a horse, and quotes Heywood, *Iron Age*:—

"a horse, a horse!
Ten kingdoms for a horse to enter Troy!"

The line is reproduced by Marston, *What you Will*, act ii. (quoted by Reed).

Lo, here this long usurped royalty
From the dead temples of this bloody wretch
Have I pluck'd off, to grace thy brows withal:
Wear it, enjoy it, and make much of it.

Richm. Great God of Heaven, say amen to all!
But, tell me, is young George Stanley living?

Der. He is, my lord, and safe in Leicester town;
Whither, if it please you, we may now withdraw us.

Richm. What men of name are slain on either side?

Der. John Duke of Norfolk, Walter Lord Ferrers,
Sir Robert Brakenbury, and Sir William Brandon.

Richm. Inter their bodies as become their births:
Proclaim a pardon to the soldiers fled,
That in submission will return to us;
And then, as we have ta'en the sacrament,
We will unite the white rose and the red.
Smile Heaven upon this fair conjunction,
That long have frown'd upon their enmity!
What traitor hears me, and says not amen?
England hath long been mad, and scarr'd herself;
The brother blindly shed the brother's blood;
The father rashly slaughter'd his own son;
The son, compell'd, been butcher to the sire:

4. *royalty*] Q 1; *roialties* Qq 2-8, Ff. 7. *enjoy it*] Qq 1, 2; omitted Qq 3-8, Ff. 11. *if it please you*] Qq 2-8; *it is please you* Q 1; (*if you please*) Ff; *if you so please* Pope. *if . . . withdraw us*] *if you please, we will withdraw us now* Keightley conj. 13, 14. *John . . . Brandon.*] Qq print in italics. 13. *Der.*] Ff; omitted Qq. *Lord*] *the Lord* Pope. *Ferrers*] Capell; *Ferris* Qq, Ff. 14. *Brakenbury*] *Brookenbury* Qq 1, 2; *Brokenbury* Qq 3-8, Ff. *and*] omitted Pope. 15. *become*] Qq, Ff; *becomes* Rowe, Camb. 25. *rashly*] *madly* Capell.

4. *royalty*] So *1 Henry IV*. IV. iii. 55. Holinshed has: "When the lord Stanleie saw the good will and gladnesse of the people, he tooke the crowne of king Richard (which was found amongst the spoile in the field), and set it on the earles head; as though he had beene elected king by the voice of the people."

10, 11. Lord Strange was on the field, with the keepers of the king's tents. "The same night, in the euening, king Henrie with great pompe came to the town of Leicester."

12. *men of name*] Compare *Much Ado About Nothing*, I. i. 7.

13, 14. Qq print these lines in italics and assign them to no speaker. In addition to those slain Holinshed gives the name of "Sir Richard Radcliffe." Sir William Brandon was Richmond's standard-bearer. See note on V. iv. 13 above.

15. *become*] If this is not a misprint of the early editions, it is a case of an impersonal verb being attracted into the number of its object.

All this divided York and Lancaster,
Divided in their dire division,
O, now let Richmond and Elizabeth,
The true succeeders of each royal house,
By God's fair ordinance conjoin together!
And let their heirs, God, if Thy will be so,
Enrich the time to come with smooth-fac'd peace,
With smiling plenty and fair prosperous days!
Abate the edge of traitors, gracious Lord,
That would reduce these bloody days again
And make poor England weep in streams of blood!
Let them not live to taste this land's increase,
That would with treason wound this fair land's peace!
Now civil wounds are stopp'd, peace lives again:
That she may live long here, God say amen!

[*Exeunt.*

32. *their*] Qq 1, 2, 8; *thy* Qq 3-7, Ff. 33. *smooth-fac'd*] Ff; *smooth-faste* Qq 1-3, 5; *smooth fast* Q 4; *smooth-fac't* Qq 6-8. 41. *here*] *heare* Qq 1-3, 5-7. *Exeunt.*] Ff; omitted Qq.

27. *this*] Johnson wished to change to the relative "that." But it is the objects divided, and not the causes of division, which can be conjoined together.

35. *Abate*] blunt, depress, lower. Aldis Wright quotes *2 Henry IV.* I. i. 117, where the metaphor is very complete. The more usual word is "rebate." See *Measure for Measure*, I. iv. 60; Lodge and Greene, *Looking-Glass for London* (Dyce, 117): "Could not rebate the strength that Rasni brought."

APPENDIX I

I. iv. 257-68. Ff admit six lines which are not in Qq, five of which (or, rather, four and a half) are inserted between Clarence's appeal in line 256, "Relent, and save your souls," and the first murderer's repetition of the word "Relent." (1) It is quite obvious that the force of the repetition, and of Clarence's subsequent comments upon it, is thus destroyed. (2) The reading

> Would not intreat for life, as you would begge
> Were you in my distresse.

is awkward, as it makes Clarence say over again what he already has said. In his extremity, however, he might be excused for repeating himself, as Queen Elizabeth already has been excused for her grammar, I. iii. 62-9 above. The advantage of Ff reading is that Clarence, attempting to work on the feelings of both murderers, is repulsed by the first, and then turns to the second for compassion, with such effect that, when the fatal blow is about to descend, the second murderer warns the victim. The reading adopted in the text has these drawbacks: (1) it places Clarence's appeal to both murderers after the first murderer's refusal to relent; (2) it pieces together the two appeals; and (3) separates the words "as you would beg . . distress" in a way for which there is no warrant in the origina text. On the other hand, (1) the refusal of the first murderer is not absolute, and Clarence might still attempt to soften him; (2) the appeal, producing no effect upon him, might be broken off, and a special appeal be begun to the second murderer. (3) brings us to the root of the whole matter. We assume that the editor of F 1 used a copy of Q, probably Q 6; that he checked it by comparison with a MS. of the play; that he noted down in the margin or between the lines of the printed book the variations which he preferred from the MS.; and that, having done so, he sent his corrected copy of Q to the printer. In the present case, he would have crowded his margin with a number of lines which are not in Qq; and it is easy to see that the printer would have found some difficulty in gathering the method of their arrangement and insertion. He would have taken the course which seemed to him most probable; and, as the editor probably never saw a printer's proof of the text, the arrangement retained in Ff is, on this hypothesis, that of the printer. If this does not actually vindicate Tyrwhitt's conjecture, it at any rate vindicates his right to make it; and the sense, as it stands, is excellent. In addition to the arrangements mentioned in the collation, we may notice that Theobald followed Ff, proposing the emendation "Ah! you would beg," which was accepted by Warburton and Johnson. Johnson, however, wished to transfer "Which of you . . . distress" to the end of the passage. After the words "what beggar pities not?" one of the murderers should repeat "A begging prince!"; and then Clarence should amplify his illustration with the new lines. "Upon which provocation," adds Johnson, "the villain naturally strikes him." The provocation seems very slight. Spedding agrees with Johnson as to the place of the lines, but observes that the murderer's cry, "A begging prince!" is not wanted, and would read the end of the new lines thus: "Would not entreat for life? As you would beg Were you in my distress—— 2. Look behind," etc. Collier eked out the imperfect line from his MS. thus: "Would not entreat for life? As you would beg, Were you in my distress, so pity me."

APPENDIX II

II. i. 66-68. Two difficulties are involved: (1) The word "all" in line 67, apparently referring to two people only, so that we should expect "both"; (2) the omission of the extra line inserted in Ff. With regard to (1), a judicious re-arrangement of stops surmounts the difficulty thus:

> Of you, Lord Rivers and Lord Grey; of you
> That all without desert have frown'd on me,
> Dukes, earls, lords, gentlemen; indeed of all.

Spedding proposed to read line 66 in Ff thus: "Of you [*to Grey*] and you, Lord Rivers,—and of Dorset, That all," etc. Pickersgill took "all" as an adverb, and "all without desert" as meaning "altogether without desert": *cf.* II. iv. 48. If "all" be taken in this sense, the flatness of its repetition at the end of line 68 is somewhat lessened. (2) Spedding was ready to accept the line, "Of you Lord Wooduill, and Lord Scales of you" as Shakespeare's, but without any cogent reason apart from its appearance in Ff. Pickersgill thought that it was original, but was omitted in Qq, because it repeated the form of line 66, so that the editor of F 1 in restoring it, felt it necessary to change the form in the latter case. Malone, however, long ago pointed out that there was no such person as Lord Woodville: if the title refers to anybody, it can refer only to Rivers. Rivers also, as Malone might have added, was the only person who could have been addressed as Lord Scales; since this actually was his style, from the time of his marriage with Elizabeth, daughter and heiress of the seventh Lord Scales, and Baroness Scales and Neucelles in her own right, until he succeeded to his father's earldom in 1469. If we accept the line, then, we have to imagine Gloucester begging the pardon of a man whom he already has addressed by his proper title, not only under a second style, but also under a third which does not belong to him. This may be in keeping with Richard's usual irony; but, on this occasion, if he had used his opportunity to taunt his enemy so obviously with his many great preferments, he could hardly have achieved his object of lulling his suspicions and effecting, as he did, an apparent reconciliation. This Shakespeare must have seen. It is not impossible that he made a mistake about the titles: "Lord Grey" in Qq is, of course, an inaccuracy. But it is difficult to think that the line, whose point, if it has any, must defeat the intention of Gloucester's speech, can have appeared in Shakespeare's original MS.—at any rate, in such a form that the editor of F 1, if he had access to that MS., would have been able to reproduce it correctly. The position of the line is awkward, whether we take it as it stands, or assume that the printer has transposed it with the line before. Its meaning and point are doubtful and unsatisfactory. My own conclusion is that the editor of F 1 found, in the margin of the MS. which he used, some notes intended as the beginning of an alteration of line 66; that the words "Woodville" and "Scales" were among them; and that, wishing to preserve as much of Shakespeare's text as could be recovered, he assumed that a line had been dropped and so worked in a new line composed of these fragments. The difficulty of "all" was thus settled; but the printer, working with the interlined copy of Q, made a mistake as to the order of the lines, and so perpetuated the state of things which the new line was intended to remove.

APPENDIX III

READINGS OF THE FOLIO IN ACT II. SCENE IV

THE stage-direction at the opening of II. iv. and the first three lines of the scene are of high importance with respect to the methods adopted by the editor of F 1.

(*a*) Ff read "Enter Arch-bishop." Qq read "Enter Cardinall." In III. i. Qq again read "Enter Cardinall." Ff read "Enter . . . Lord Cardinall." The impression which these passages leave is that the archbishop, introduced by Ff in II. iv. was not a cardinal, but a distinct person from the Cardinal of III. i. and Qq. In III. i. it is unquestionable that the prelate employed to persuade Elizabeth to give up the Duke of York was Thomas Bourchier, Cardinal of San Ciriaco and Archbishop of Canterbury. But the prelate who, as in this scene, delivered up the great seal to the queen-dowager, was Thomas Rotherham, Archbishop of York, and not a cardinal. He fell into disgrace with Richard on account of his conduct about the seal. The fact that he and Bourchier bore the same Christian name caused some confusion among the historians. More, by an oversight, made "the archbishop of Yorke" the prelate who advised Elizabeth, as in III. i., to give up the Duke of York, and speaks of him as "our reuerend father here present, the lord cardinall." Halle saw the error, and substituted "Cauntorburye" and "the reuerend father my lord Cardinall archebishop of Cauntorbury," in the places mentioned above. However, Holinshed followed More's account. It is clear that, in the present passage, either Shakespeare himself, or the editor of F 1, intended the Archbishop and the Cardinal to be, as they were, different persons. Probably Shakespeare is responsible for this. Scarcity of actors may have led to the union of the two parts, which thus may have passed into Qq as one. The editor of F 1 probably restored them from his MS. copy of the play.

(*b*) The opposed readings are:—

Qq. *Car.* Last night I heare they lay at Northampton.
At Stonistratford will they be to night,
To morrow or next day, they will be here.

Ff. *Arch.* Last night I heard they lay at Stony Stratford,
And at Northampton they do rest to night:
To morrow, or next day they will be heere.

Ff reading, while improving the defective metre, is generally supposed to be in harmony with history. Edward V., after sleeping a night at Stony Stratford, was actually taken back by Gloucester to Northampton. If we can satisfy ourselves that Ff reading is (1) a distinct metrical improvement; (2) intentionally consonant with the true details of time and place in the historical account of the affair; and (3) the original reading of the passage, it should no doubt be adopted in preference to Qq.

(1) The metrical improvement is obvious. If we lay stress on the first syllable of "Northampton," it is just possible to make Qq reading scan. We still speak of Bérkhamstead, Wénhaston, where the second syllable might seem to demand the chief accent. But I can find no instance in Shakespeare's time in which the accent of Northampton is thrown so far back. Pope read the passage, "I heard they lay the last night at Northampton"; Capell, "Last night, I hear, they rested at Northampton." Reed followed Ff; and Steevens, recognising the historical difficulty, wrote, "Where sense cannot claim a preference, a casting vote may be safely given in favour of sound."

(2) The historical facts of Edward V.'s journey to London are as follows: On his way from Ludlow, he passed through Northampton, and went on with his train to Stony Stratford. Gairdner (p. 49) says that Rivers and Lord Richard Grey rode back to Northampton to salute Gloucester, who was expected there the same day (April 29). More's statement is that Rivers stayed behind, perhaps for the above reason, and probably because the whole train could not have been accommodated at Stony Stratford. Gloucester, having joined forces with Buckingham, as he came south from York, arrived at Northampton soon after the king had left. More's account is that they were very friendly with Rivers; but, after he was gone to bed, they held a long council with some of their most privy friends. They got hold of the keys of the inn, picketed the road to Stony Stratford, and anticipated Rivers' household in getting to horse, explaining that they were anxious to be the first to greet the king that day. When Rivers in person asked for an explanation of their movements, they accused him of

wishing to estrange them from the king and compass their downfall, and, without more ado, put him in ward. When they reached Stony Stratford, the king was about to depart. He received them graciously and without suspicion; but, in his presence, they picked a quarrel with Grey and cast reflections on his absent brother Dorset, accusing them of conspiracy with Rivers to rule the king and realm. In spite of Edward's readiness to uphold the honesty of his relations, the dukes there and then arrested Grey, Sir Thomas Vaughan, and Sir Richard Hawte, and took the whole party back to Northampton, in order to bring the prisoners together and take further counsel. They dined at Northampton, where Gloucester behaved encouragingly. But, before he set out again for London, he either directed or provided for the despatch of the prisoners to various strongholds in the north of England.

It does not appear that the king, with his new guardian, stopped another night at Northampton. The arrest of the lords took place on 30th April. It was on 4th May that Gloucester and the king arrived in London, which is sixty-six miles from Northampton.

In London the news became common property about midnight of 30th April. The tidings were announced to Archbishop Rotherham by a messenger from the Lord Chamberlain Hastings. He immediately went to the queen, whom he found preparing to go into sanctuary, and committed the great seal to her charge. When he returned to York House in the dawn of 1st May, he "might in his chamber window see all the Thames full of boates of the Duke of Glocester's servants, watching that no man should go to sanctuarie, nor none could pass unsearched." In the course of the day, the Archbishop, fearing that he had acted precipitately, sent to the sanctuary at Westminster for the great seal, and so recovered it. The day was one of disquiet. Hastings did his best to quiet the rising tumult; and the common people were satisfied by the arrival of some of Gloucester's servants with the baggage of the arrested lords, in which arms and armour were included. The duke's men explained, "Lo, here be the barrels of harnesse that these traitors had priuilie conueied in their carriage to destroie the noble lordes withall." The intelligence of the mob could draw no other inference from this palpable testimony.

(3) We must not expect Shakespeare, of course, to be in complete accordance with the details of history. The interview in II. iv. clearly is derived from that which took place early on 1st May between Rotherham and the queen. If the chroniclers' accounts are correct, (1) Rotherham knew all before he

went to the queen; (2) a messenger from Hastings had reached him at York House; (3) the queen had received the news at least as soon, and was preparing to go to Westminster when Rotherham arrived. But in Shakespeare, (1) Rotherham knows nothing: all he can do is to calculate the point on the road which the party has reached; (2) the news arrives during the interview; and (3) the queen thereupon decides to go to sanctuary, and takes the great seal with her.

Shakespeare, therefore, makes it impossible for Rotherham to know of any change of route on the king's journey. Qq reading represents exactly the natural calculations of a man who knew the ordinary halting-places on the road from the north, and had no reason to suppose that they had been changed in this case. So far as Rotherham knew, the coronation was to take place on 4th May. The king would therefore arrive in London on 2nd May or 3rd May. On 29th April he would naturally spend the night at Northampton. What actually had happened was that he had passed through Northampton without stopping, probably because Rivers wished to keep ahead of Gloucester. Of this movement, as of its sequel, Rotherham was unaware. Ff, on the other hand, assume that Rotherham knew of the unusual change of route, but without feeling any curiosity about it, or awaking any interest in his hearers. They assume that, while aware of the fact, he had no idea of the division of the party which made Rivers' arrest an easy matter, or of the junction of the dukes with the king. In short, he says, as if it were the most natural thing in the world, that the party has stopped a night at one place, and then has gone thirteen miles back to spend a night at another, which it had passed through the day before. Ff reading is thus dramatically inaccurate, even if its accuracy as to the king's real movements be allowed.

We need not suppose, of course, that Shakespeare troubled himself about the actual hour of the scene as it took place in history. He simply compressed into one scene a sequence of necessary events, giving them their true dramatic relief. An imaginary meeting between the queen and Rotherham is made the occasion for the discovery of Gloucester's action. Before the messenger arrives with his startling news, Rotherham is ignorant that anything has happened. It is utterly impossible, therefore, unless we assume a slip of the tongue, that he can put Stony Stratford before Northampton.

Shakespeare may have written the passage in Ff. That, in this instance, he made a careless comparison of his authorities with the dramatic exigencies of the passage, is not unlikely.

That the editor of F 1 found the more metrical reading in the MS. which he used is highly probable. But Qq already had altered it, at the expense of regular metre, it is true, but with advantage to the truth of drama. The variation in Qq was probably used on the stage; and, whether it was made by Shakespeare himself or by the actors, it is the only reading which has any consistency with the facts of the scene.

My conclusion, then, is that, while Ff have a metrical advantage over Qq, and their reading may have been originally written by Shakespeare, it does not represent a reading to which Shakespeare could or would have adhered consistently. And this because it is at variance with the probabilities of the drama, and is not quite free in itself from historical error.

I may add a summary of previous editors' conclusions. Malone very justly says, "By neither reading can the truth of history be preserved, and therefore we may be sure that Shakespeare did not mean in this instance to adhere to it." At the opposite pole is Grant White's unqualified praise of Ff reading: it has, he says, "on its side authority, rhythm, and—according to the chronicles which Shakespeare followed—historical truth." Equally short-sighted is Delius' defence of Ff as the result of Shakespeare's work with "the authorities open before him": on his theory, Qq would introduce a piratical emendation. The Cambridge editors adopt Qq reading, assuming the supposed coincidence between Ff and history to be accidental, but discovering an inconsistency between lines 1, 2 and line 3. Spedding refuted the latter notion; but upheld Ff on the usual historical assumption, estimating Qq reading as a correction "by some one whose topographical knowledge was superior to his historical." Pickersgill's view is closely allied, though with a slight difference in detail, to the view which I have taken.

APPENDIX IV

ON THE READINGS AT III. IV. 80 AND III. V. 12-21

(1) At III. iv. 80 Qq read "some see it done" at the end of a line. Ff introduce a new line: "*Louell* and *Ratcliffe*, looke that it be done."

(2) In III. v. 12-21 I have adopted Ff reading substantially. For the variations in Qq, see collation *ad loc.* The difficulty which Qq introduce is in their stage-directions, corresponding to that after line 21, "Enter Catesby with Hastings' head." The conspirators, according to Theobald, are standing on the walls of the Tower; and Catesby is told to "overlook" the walls, *i.e.* to look down and see whether any one is coming. Only four lines later, Gloucester calms Buckingham's pretended agitation at the sound of a drum, with the words "O, O, be quiet, it is Catesby"; and Catesby thereupon enters with Hastings' head. The supposition on which this entry of Catesby, inconsistent even with dramatic probability, can be defended, is that Catesby, overlooking the walls and seeing Hastings' executioners approaching, hastens from the scene, receives the head from them, and reappears bearing it. Even so, the interval is very short indeed between his disappearance and return.

Ff make Catesby introduce the mayor, and remain on the scene. Buckingham hears the drum; Gloucester tells Catesby to overlook the walls, and Ratcliff and Lovel, the executioners deputed in III. iv. 80, enter with the head of Hastings.

The probable explanation of the difference lies in the circumstance that Qq require only one actor on the stage to fill the parts which Ff allot to three. A scarcity of actors very conceivably may have led to a grouping of the parts in the stage version. And here is one of many signs that the original of the Qq text of the play is to be found in such a version and re-arrangement for stage purposes of Shakespeare's text.

However, by the introduction of Ratcliff, Ff reading involves a fresh difficulty. Following the chroniclers, it puts Ratcliff (III. iii.) in charge of the execution of the lords at

Pontefract, on the same day that Hastings suffers in London (III. iv. 49, 50, etc.) Ratcliff is thus in two widely distant places at once, Pontefract being 179 miles by road from London. The discrepancy would not be noticed by a casual spectator of the play, who would see each scene complete in itself, and would not remember details of place and time. But we cannot imagine Shakespeare making the mistake wilfully. If he did it involuntarily, he would have found it out on revising the play.

Theobald retained Catesby, as Qq had laid down the part, in III. v. In III. iv. he read "Lovel and Catesby, look that it be done." This is in accordance with the stage-directions of Qq, which assign III. iv. 96, 97 to Catesby and III. iv. 104 to Lovel. But in Ff, III. iv. 96, 97 are given to Ratcliff.

To alter Ff reading substantially would be, as the Cambridge editors point out, to take liberties with the text. It is a great improvement on Qq in the point of metre and rhythm. Thus, in the absence of any indication of a satisfactory alternative, Ratcliff must be kept in both passages. It is noticeable that, in III. iv., he speaks only two lines, which might well be given to Lovel; while, in III. v., he says nothing, and is not included in Gloucester's instructions at the end of the scene. Both in Qq and Ff, Lovel alone is necessary to Hastings' execution. The chroniclers make no specific mention of the ministers employed to carry out this sentence. It is not likely that Catesby would have taken an active part in it. He had been Hastings' trusted servant; and, in a play so rhetorical as this, he hardly would have been allowed to die without some word of reproach to the traitor who bids him make haste that the duke may have his dinner.

The only possible conclusion seems to be that, at III. iv. 80, Shakespeare wrote "Ratcliffe" in a moment of forgetfulness, and continued the error in III. v.; that, on the stage, the mistake in III. iv. was recognised, and, in III. v., the parts were cut down from motives of economy; that Qq reproduced his alteration; and that Ff, correcting the misplacement of the lines and the rough prose of Qq, returned, in this case also, to the earlier reading, in spite of its drawbacks.

PRINTED IN GREAT BRITAIN AT THE UNIVERSITY PRESS, ABERDEEN